Readings in the Theory of Growth

Readings in the Theory of Growth

a selection of papers from the *Review of Economic Studies*

edited by

F. H. HAHN

Macmillan

St Martin's Press

First published 1971 by
MACMILLAN AND CO LTD
London and Basingstoke
Associated companies in New York Toronto Dublin Melbourne Johannesburg and Madras

SBN 333 10303 3 (hard cover)
333 10299 1 (paper cover)

Library of Congress catalog card no. 70-140572

Printed in Great Britain by
LOWE AND BRYDONE (PRINTERS) LTD
London

Contents

Introduction

Many of the most important contributions to the modern theory of economic growth were first published in the *Review of Economic Studies*. This volume presents a selection of these.

It will be clear that there are notable omissions. In particular none of the important papers dealing with capital-theoretic problems are here reprinted. This is entirely due to considerations of space. To make a useful and representative selection on this topic would have added at least a hundred pages. For exactly the same reason none of the important papers which relate the theories of planning and growth have been included. The reader, and especially the student reader, should, however, bear it in mind that a number of "deep" matters, directly relevant to growth theory, are not treated here.

Authors were given the opportunity to comment on their own papers in the light of their subsequent intellectual development. These comments appear at the end of the papers in question.

This introduction offers some general comments on the state of the theory as represented by the papers here printed.

I

The theory of growth is not a theory of economic history. It is of no help in answering Max Weber's famous question and only of marginal use in understanding, say, the Industrial Revolution. Where the theory is to be taken descriptively, it takes the institutional setting for granted and highly idealises it. The parts of the theory which are to be understood as prescriptive have hardly anything to say on either the actual problems of "control" or on the society to be controlled. The theories of technical change, while suggestive (Arrow, Kaldor–Mirrlees, Weizsäcker), are plainly of a rudimentary kind; theories of population growth are rarely formulated or used. In almost all of the work the economy is always in equilibrium, and in much of it always in steady state. There is no class conflict, no "rising middle class", no actual government, no labour unions, no war, no financial panic, no history. If a historical theory ever comes to be formulated, the growth literature may be of some use; the bulk of the work will remain to be done.

While all this certainly means that it would be singularly unwise to use the present theory alone in analysing some past episode, or perhaps even in formulating present policies, it certainly does not mean that it has all been a waste of time. To formulate, say, conditions for an economy to be in steady state is not to engage in the activity of describing a particular society, but it is a worth-while activity none the less. For evidently it may greatly help in an eventual understanding of why in this or that instance such steady states proved impossible. To examine, to take another example, the equilibrium paths of an economy when there are fixed proportions and embodied technical change may be a necessary first step to understanding actual paths when the concrete remains of past decisions and mistakes are preserved in the existing stock of machines. It was right for economists to investigate these simpler and more abstract questions first and, as the following papers testify, this was by no means always an easy task. If the answers we have are not made to bear a weight much larger than that intended by the original questions, they will be found useful in disposing of certain claims and of silly theories. Whether they can be used as part of the foundations for much more complex (and realistic) undertakings, remains to be seen; certainly there is no evidence to date to suggest that they cannot.

II

Steady states are quasi-stationary equilibria. By this I mean that it is possble to find a simple transformation of those variables which in steady-state equilibrium vary with time into variables which do not. Thus if $x^*(t)$ is the steady-state vector of variables depending on time, then there is a transformation $e^{-gt}x^*(t)=y^*$, so that y^* is stationary. The idea is sufficiently general to allow capital accumulation and certain kinds of technical progress as consistent with a stationary state in the new variables. Thus the class of cases considered by older economists as stationary is considerably enlarged. However, they remain pretty abstract. In particular the essential " stationariness " of steady state at once suggests that such constructions may be quite unable to capture the rich process of actual economic growth.

The von Neumann paper is the fundamental contribution to steady-state theory. This is not only due to the elegance, economy and considerable generality of this work, but also to the fact that the model is highly adaptable. That this was realised early on to be the case can be seen from Mr. Champernowne's splendid comments on von Neumann. He saw at once that the construction was sufficiently rich to lead one to hope that its most important features would survive such modifications as consumption out of profits and the " non-production" of labour. He also recognised the striking feature of the model which allowed one to determine steady-state prices and the rate of interest without reference to the conditions of demand. The work of Morishima [5] in particular has amply confirmed what Champernowne had to say on this occasion. On one point only was he insufficiently prescient, namely in not spotting, as did Kemeny, Morgenstern and Thompson [4] a good deal later, that condition (9) on p. 3 of von Neumann could be considerably relaxed.

The von Neumann construction is one where there are no scarce inputs and no technological progress. Recent empirical work, e.g. by Jorgenson and Griliches [2], suggests that these assumptions may not be as damaging as they appear to be at first sight. For instance, while it is no doubt fanciful to have rigid production processes for human beings, the same is not true of human skills. Technical progress, too, may perhaps be thought of as dependent on the intensities with which various processes, e.g. research processes, are used. This is not to say that these features, if they are to be incorporated into the construction, may not lead to technical modifications; for instance, the linear technology may have to be abandoned. But one has the strong impression that when a proper steady-state model comes to be formulated which treats neither the supplies of various skills nor the improvements in the capital equipment as exogenous, the von Neumann apparatus will again be a fruitful point of departure.

If growth, however, is taken as exogenous, the von Neumann model in no way becomes less useful. It can certainly accommodate Harrod-neutral technical progress and it is not destroyed by any savings assumption so far proposed. Of course, the interpretation is changed by these modifications. In particular if a (feasible) growth rate is specified, the model, together with the condition that the value of investment should equal that of savings at all time, will determine all steady-state relative prices (including the real wage), interest rate,[1] composition of output and choice of techniques of production. Of course, the existence of such steady states must be proved, and this has been done by Morishima [5].

All sorts of other, fairly recent, results are fully implicit in the von Neumann paper. To take just one more example, consider the proposition that steady-state consumption is maximised when the rate of interest is equal to the rate of growth (the " golden rule "). Suppose that the coefficients of the " labour-producing process " always bear the same

[1] No distinction is here made between the interest rate and the rate of profit on capital. Since the models contain ho financial sector, it is obvious why no distinction is required.

ratio to each other. Multiplying this process by k, then, changes the " real wage " by k. Consumption is equal to the real wage in von Neumann. Now let the growth rate be given exogenously. Suppose there is one k^* such that multiplying the labour-producing process by k^* makes the von Neumann maximal rate equal to the exogenously given one (and, of course, equal to the rate of interest). Then for any $k<k^*$ the economy is capable of producing goods in excess of its consumption and investment requirements. Certainly $k>k^*$ is not possible by construction. Therefore steady-state consumption is at a maximum when the exogenous rate of growth is the maximal rate for some real wage, and so when the rate of growth and rate of interest are the same

The von Neumann model is quite explicit as to what it is about. In particular it is clear from its formulation that in all steady states the relative outputs of all goods are constant. Since it is a matter of common observation that this is not in fact, the case the von Neumann steady states, and all others resulting from simple modifications of the model, are not likely to be of great descriptive power. In particular it seems doubtful that a macro-economic analysis of the Harrod–Domar variety requires assumptions as to the composition of output less stringent than those of von Neumann.

It is indeed one's impression that the macro-models may have shed more darkness than light, for if they are taken as representing a single-good economy they are not worthy of attention, while if they are taken as aggregations of many goods they cannot, except in quite exceptional circumstances, be given a precise formulation and meaning. In the latter—" parable "—guise they have generated much controversy. The most prolonged concerned the specification of suitable technological conditions in terms of satisfactory aggregates. It is now agreed that it will not in general be possible to justify rigorously a " well-behaved " technological relationship between the aggregated inputs and outputs, such as is required by the macro-models which have been proposed.

To the theorist this controversy has been of some use. Consider two economies with the same technological possibilities, in steady state. Allow consumption out of profits but no savings out of wages. Then if both economies have the same rate of growth, but different interest rates, the von Neumann theorist will say that this is due to the fact that the economy with the higher interest rate has a less thrifty capitalist class. Compare this with the alternative view that the higher interest rate is to be ascribed to a lower " capital intensity of production ". We now know that there may be no choice of an index of capital which makes this statement true. On the other hand, let savings be a constant fraction of income. Then the economy with the lower saving propensity will have the lower steady-state value of capital to value of income ratio, since they both grow at the same rate.[1] But we cannot, without solving the particular case, say which economy will have the higher steady-state rate of interest. It is good to know that even in so abstract a matter of steady-state theory one may actually have to look at the world before being able to pronounce on it.

It seems a rather doubtful claim that a variety of goods, while introducing complications, in no way invalidates the "essential insights " gained from a macro-model. For instance, in a recent paper Hugh Rose [9] offers as an " apology " for doing macro-economics the " usual one—that the consequences of changes in the relative prices of goods have no essential part to play in the drama on which our main interest is focused " (p. 155, fn. 1). Since, however, the model is in terms of " representative " agents and totally " macro ", there is no way of falsifying his statement. If one can get a macro-model to behave in a certain way, the question of what modifications changing relative prices would induce is wide open and cannot be answered by the model. In the context of growth all that needs to be said is that the macro-models do not generalise in their essential conclusions to more disaggregated constructions. They also make it impossible to study the rather important structural changes which economic history teaches us as accompanying growth. But, of course, even steady-state theory becomes very complicated

[1] Since the value-capital-output ratio need not be monotone in the rate of profit, a variety of techniques and profit rates may be consistent with a steady state. The "non-uniqueness " of steady-state profit rate of course does not mean that we have no theory of what it can be.

when one seeks to make it more " realistic; this is specially true when technical progress is introduced. Macro-models then become a legitimate first step on a complicated journey.

Professor Robinson's famous article introduced one way of organising one's thoughts about technical progress. It is plain that the classification she introduces depends heavily on the single-output, " capital "-labour construction. As Diamond's paper shows, matters become a good deal more complicated even in a two-sector model. In particular the classification of inventions is not now independent of market forces; it is no longer a technological datum. In a many-goods world the matter becomes more difficult still. Considering technical progress in the way it is done in these papers shows that only very special types are consistent with steady state. Since no theory of innovation is offered, there is no reason to suppose that they will be just of that type.

Johansen was one of the first to attempt to take formal account of the argument that technical progress is " embodied " and that the choice of technique once made may be impossible to undo. The paper by Solow, Tobin, Weizsäcker and Yaari (for the fixed proportions *ex post* and *ex ante* case) and Bliss's paper (for fixed proportions *ex post* but not *ex ante*) are important contributions to the problems which now arise.

Technical progress, in these models, leads to the obsolescence of old machines which do not share in the technical improvement and have to continue to be used in a given way. It follows that if there is a choice of techniques when the investment is first made, or even if not, if one wants to calculate steady-state prices one must postulate that the scrapping date of a machine is correctly foreseen. In earlier models the future had no influence on the present because no choice ever committed one beyond the present. This is now no longer the case, and to the already stringent requirements of steady state there is now added the further one of correct foresight.

The new margin—the scrapping date—makes the technology more complicated to analyse but also helps to make it less rigidly corseted in engineering specifications. For instance Solow *et al.*, working as they do with a model of fixed technical coefficients, have none the less no difficulty in showing that the steady-state real wage rate measures the increase in steady-state output another labourer would make possible. This is because if the economy had one more man, everything else constant, he could work on a machine just on the margin of being scrapped (i.e. where product per man on the machine equals the wage). It should not need saying that this result has nothing to do with the proposition that the marginal product of labour " determines " the real wage, whatever that proposition may mean. The steady-state value of variables is what it is because that is what makes them consistent with steady state.[1]

Complications, even in steady-state analysis, are well brought out by Bliss. If one wants to compare steady state, say with different thrift conditions, one cannot make general predictions on the important matter of comparative scrapping dates. This is so even if it is true that thriftiness and steady-state interest rate are inversely related. There is also the further difficulty that owing to the need for telescopic faculties, i.e. the need to consider the present value of gains from particular choices, the optimum choice of technique for the latest investment need not be uniquely determined by input prices. Thus even, in what is, after all, still a highly simplified construction, no simple generalisation seems possible

Both the papers just discussed take technical progress as given from " outside ". As is well known, Kaldor first introduced the notion that technical progress was to be explained by the process of investment itself. In the Kaldor–Mirrlees paper this idea has taken on a " vintage " formulation. One of the advantages of this idea is that it leads to the " Harrod-neutrality " of steady-state technical progress not by an appeal to the Harrod-impartiality of the inventor's muse, but through the choice of economic agents. The pace at which investment grows, if not consistent with a constant investment output ratio, will also thereby change the profitability of investment by changing the rate of growth in output

[1] Professor Joan Robinson has drawn my attention to certain difficulties which arise when net saving's are taken as proportional to net income or net profit.

per man. Hence steady state is only possible when investors have chosen just that pace of investment the consequences of which are Harrod-neutral.

The other main modification introduced by Kaldor–Mirrlees into putty-clay models is the assumption that the choice of technique on new investment is governed by a " pay-off period ". Certainly this does make for some recognition of the uncertainties facing real investors in the world. It is this assumption which gives the construction its " non-neoclassical " flavour.

It is useful to have a proper understanding of this and that can be conveniently done by means of comparison with Bliss. The Kaldor–Mirrlees equation (4) takes the place of Bliss's equation (16). Equation (3′) of Kaldor–Mirrlees corresponds to (15) of Bliss. The savings function is different in the two papers, but this function has in any case nothing to do with " marginal productivity " doctrines. By differentiation of (6) and (7) of Kaldor–Mirrlees one has $\delta Y_t/\delta N_t = p_{t-T} = w_t$ (by equation 9), and that is the same as in Bliss. That is, as far as the economy is concerned, having an extra man increases total output by the amount that could be produced on the machine which would otherwise have been retired and that is also the real wage of labour. On the other hand, it is not the case that the rate of profit in Kaldor–Mirrlees has a social marginal product interpretation. This can be rather clearly seen from Bliss's Theorem 7. The pay-off period convention will in general imply that the economy is not in what Bliss calls first-order competitive equilibrium and hence not efficient. As Solow *et al.* note (p. 94), it is only for efficient economies that the marginal social product of investment can be given any meaning.

The "pay-off" notion is certainly attractive, since many investigators have reported this kind of behaviour. But there are difficulties. One must remind oneself that one is dealing with steady state. Should an economy be in steady state (so that it has been in approximate steady state for " most of its history "), one would imagine uncertainty considerations to be rather unimportant—after all, everything is essentially being repeated over and over again. If the model is meant to be consistent with all sorts of structural changes and variations in relative prices, this would require demonstration. Apart from this it seems that the assumption perhaps overstates the absence of competitive forces. If all agents act on conventions rather than on calculations of gains, then no Marshallian competitive selective forces can operate. But it is not clear that if profits are to be made by being a little less cautious, no one will be found to make them. On the other hand, it would be hard to maintain that the pay-off period criterion is less " realistic " than the thorough-going maximisation assumption of Bliss.

Arrow's " learning by doing " function is certainly closely related to Kaldor's " technical progress function ", although the mechanism is different. He combines it with a putty-clay model which is otherwise neoclassical. His rather special assumptions are removed by Levhari. The social and private returns on investment (in steady state) differ because the learning mechanism acts like an external economy.

Weizsäcker takes a first step in analysing a model where technical progress is the outcome of the allocation of resources (in his case labour) to the task of producing productivity changes. He combines this with some ideas suggested by Kennedy. This is an important line of thought which no doubt will be further explored. That the amount of technical progress one can expect is not totally unrelated to our choice as to resources devoted to research, education, etc., seems reasonable.

The point we have now reached is this: it is possible in a macro-model to introduce a number of features which strike one as " realistic " but which are absent from von Neumann. By " possible " I mean that a steady state can be shown to exist and that it can be described. No one has yet attempted to introduce any of the complications we have been discussing into a less aggregated construction. It seems likely that such an attempt would only succeed on the basis of some very heroic assumptions; for instance, the rate of technical progress will have to be taken as similar in all sectors, and both the " learning by doing " and the technical progress function would in some way have to be modified without destroying the possibility of balanced growth. There may also be difficulties connected with differences in the lifetime of equipment in different sectors. One may argue that these matters ought not to be explored since one may also conjecture that the resulting construction will only confirm what we already suspect, namely that steady states are not to be found in the world. On the other hand, it may be useful to know precisely what requirements of such a more ambitious construction offend our sense of reality.

As is well known, the study of steady states involved a number of related matters. Of these, this volume only reproduces the discussion of the relation between the rate of profit, thriftiness and the rate of growth.

Pasinetti was able to show that on certain assumptions the equality between the rate of profit and the rate of growth, divided by a certain saving propensity, would continue to be true for steady state even if wage-earners saved. In this work he postulated that the saving propensities differed by class rather than by type of income (a sociologically appealing idea) and that the classes were intergenerationally stable. His steady state required the distribution of ownership of capital between classes to be constant. He also required to assume that the saving propensity of workers was less than the share of profits in income multiplied by the capitalist's propensity to save.

This last condition has given rise to an extended controversy (Samuelson and Modigliani [10], Robinson [8], Kaldor [3], Pasinetti [6]) which is too lengthy to reproduce. Mr. Sato's paper makes the point rather shortly. The point, of course, is that the economy may have two steady states: one where both classes own a constant positive fraction of the capital stock per man, and one where the fraction of this capital stock per man owned by capitalists becomes zero (which, of course, does not mean that they own no capital). The third possibility, that the fraction of the capital stock owned by workers become zero, is not possible. If, then, the Pasinetti condition is violated, there is effectively only one class, and so the steady state is again of the Harrod–Domar variety. However, Samuelson and Modigliani were not only concerned to establish this latter possibility but also convergence to this steady state. This cannot be shown for complicated von Neumann-type models, and they relied rather heavily on macro-economic production function-type arguments which cannot be shown to be generally valid. This, however, in no way invalidates their main point, which has nothing whatever to do with " neoclassical " arguments. This main point is very simple: even when there are fixed coefficients everywhere, the value-capital-output ratio is not given by technology but by market conditions combined with technology. The Pasinetti condition depends on this ratio which is not independently given. Hence as far as logic and steady states are concerned, one steady-state solution has as much claim on our attention as another. Nor is it hard, say, for a Leontief technology to show that both solutions may exist for specified thriftiness conditions. All this has nothing to do with an allegedly inverse relationship between capital per man and the rate of profit—and that relation may be as irregular as we care to make it.

This, of course, does not mean that for particular (" realistic ") saving propensities and technologies, the Pasinetti steady state may not turn out to be the proper one.

Before leaving this matter it may be worth while to note a related matter. The line which runs from von Neumann through Kaldor to Pasinetti is undoubtedly of importance and establishes an impressive, possible, direct and simple relationship between the rate of growth and the rate of profit. However, it is not a theory of relative shares. This requires one to know the investment-output and so the capital-output ratio in value terms which for any economist is an unknown of the model. To find its steady-state value requires a theory of the choice of techniques by investors. This may be of the von Neumann kind, it may be " parable-macro-economic " or it may be the pay-off period convention. But some micro-theory is required before we can say that we have a theory of relative shares.

Returning to the main line of steady-state theory, one cannot leave it without remarking how little Keynesian economics has any bearing on it. This is not surprising, since steady-state theories have been concerned with the question: what must be postulated in order that steady state be possible? Mostly the situation to be analysed was to be one of full employment, although steady states with a constant fraction of unemployed have also been discussed. But the ideal tranquillity of steady state perforce excludes most of the interesting features of a Keynesian analysis. Moreover, since no casual story is told, questions such as " Does investment determine saving or the other way round.? " have no meaning. When it comes to an inquiry into whether there are forces driving an economy to the steady state, matters are, of course, different. Although in recent years an attempt has been made to take account of monetary assets in steady-state theory (Johnson [1] and Tobin [12]), what has emerged has not surprisingly had no relevance to the matters which occupied Keynes.

Of course, one can conceive of steady-state theory which seeks to show that no steady state exists. This was precisely Harrod's intention, and he is one of the few growth theorists (Mrs Robinson is another) to remain faithful to Keynes. His view that the warranted and natural rates of growth may always be unequal was based on the Keynesian view that it would not be possible, for monetary reasons, to sustain a rate of return on investment as low as would be required by a capital-output ratio which is needed by the natural rate of growth. Almost everything written since has been a headlong retreat from this point of view. Whether it is the suggestion that permanent inflation or smooth substitutability or variability in thriftiness through variability in income distribution would allow one to argue that the two rates can coincide, the final outcome has always been essentially non-Keynesian: permanent, steady, full-employment growth is possible. This, of course, does not mean that one should judge these propositions adversely. But they serve to emphasise that modern steady-state theory is not about a world of disappointed expectations, unwanted capacity and speculative hoarding. It is like the theory of the equilibrium of a frictionless pendulum, a theory which, it should be remarked, physicists have found it useful to study.

III

The natural development of Harrod's "Keynesian" approach to growth was the development of cyclical theories: if steady state was not possible and if the main economic variables are bounded above and below, you are naturally left with cyclical behaviour. On the other hand, those theorists, and they were the majority, who sought to show that steady states were possible, were equally naturally taken to the next more difficult stage of telling a story of economic forces driving the economy towards the steady state from arbitrary initial points

Some of these stories have already appeared in some of the papers in this volume which I have discussed. Thus in a brilliant *tour de force*, Solow *et al.* show that in their " clay-clay " economy the supposition that the economy is at all times in equilibrium leads it to pursue a path which takes it arbitrarily close to the steady state. In the context of their assumptions this is a hard result to establish, and it is a beautiful result to have. However, the reader should carefully note the following points: (i) since there is no choice of technique, the expectations of investors concerning the path of real wages play no part in the analysis (in a putty-clay model this causes difficulties); (ii) the behaviour of asset prices on the path is not discussed and the behaviour is irrelevant to their analysis, since there is always full employment, savings always match investment and all machines yielding a product per man in excess of the real wage are used; (ii) it would be almost certainly very hard to extend the result to a many-sector economy.

The result just discussed extends the Solow " putty-putty " work of 1956 to the much more difficult case of fixed proportions and embodied technical progress. The two-sector work of Uzawa and Inada (and of many others) extends it to the "putty-putty" world of one comsumer and one capital good. As far as steady-state theory is concerned, the distinction between the consumer and investment good, in this simple context, introduces no difficulties and nothing that is essentially new.[1] However, difficulties were encountered

[1] Except the possibility that the steady-state value-capital-output ratio with proportional savings need not uniquely determine a rate of profit on this technique.

in analysing the behaviour of equilibrium paths. The chief of these was the observation that if savings behaviour depended on the distribution of income, then a given set of initial conditions may be consistent with a number of different momentary equilibria. The problem here is quite analogous to that caused in static analysis by intersecting community indifference curves. It has, of course, the consequence that the equilibrium path cannot be traced, given initial conditions, and this has been christened " causal indeterminacy ". In its absence the equilibrium paths do seek the steady state.

To avoid " causal indeterminacy ", a number of sufficient conditions were suggested. They share the characteristic that there is no good reason why they should be satisfied.

It has turned out that the neoclassical putty-putty story is not readily generalisable to a world with many capital goods, and the papers by Kurz and myself are concerned with this. The chief points are these: (i) if there is a variety of assets and one is concerned with equilibrium paths, the agents must at all times be in asset equilibrium; (ii) knowledge of saving behaviour is insufficient to determine the composition of new investment—this as well as asset equilibrium depends on the expected course of relative prices; (iii) if expectations are to be fulfilled, then, once initial expectations are given, a path of the economy can be traced; (iv) in general there is only one set of initial expectations which will lead the economy to the steady state, and there is no reason to suppose that they will rule.

It was noted (Shell and Stiglitz [11]) that certainly in a number of cases paths not leading to the steady state would eventually become infeasible. If therefore an economy is to have expectations fulfilling paths for ever, only those leading to the steady state will qualify. This observation brings out very well the main difficulties. In Solow (56), the future had no effect on the present since neither savings, investment nor choice of technique today depended on the values of variable tomorrow. This is not true if there are many capital goods (or if savings are governed by " lifetime " utility maximisation). However, there are not available sufficient current markets for future goods to make it at all sensible to suppose that all future transactions can be decided upon " now ". That being the case, and in any event it also being assured that all assets are always tradable, current behaviour will be governed by " myopic " expectations with the results already noted.

It should be emphasised that the discussion here—as in all " equilibrium dynamics " —is not a description of the world. Indeed, it should rather be taken as confirmation that this methodology is not very sensible. However, the connection with the planning-like nature of the problem is well brought out by Kurz. In the context of a Leontief model, the problem of multi-sectoral stability is further explored by Jorgenson.

A further point is worthy of brief notice. It can be shown that it is not generally true that permitting the degree of disequilibrium implied by "static expectations " will lead the resulting paths to the steady state. The reason is connected with a matter which has been of much concern to Professor Robinson: there is not necessarily a well-behaved relationship to be found between an aggregate index of capital and the rate of profit [7]. (The rate of profit is well defined with static expectations even out of steady state.)

Mr. Atkinson investigates the time taken by the various paths discussed before they are "near enough" to steady state. The result is not exactly encouraging to this kind of theory.

The forces driving an economy to the steady state have received rather different treatment from Kaldor, and the paper by Meade is a contribution to this discussion. As is known, Kaldor relies on changes in profit margins as one of the major mechanisms of adjustment. The spirit is quite different from that of the earlier construction discussed and makes it a much more hopeful approach to a theory which could actually be confronted with the facts. He has, however, been perhaps too keen to argue that his mechanism always performs in the desired way. Where there is excess demand, not only prices but money wages will tend to rise. Where the profit margin does rise, and so the rate of profit on investment, not only may savings be higher but so may be investment. Professor Meade shows that the final outcome depends on the relative strengths of the forces at work, and that is how it should be.

The whole problem of actual as opposed to warranted paths is still largely a matter of conjecture. The theorist has a great choice of behavioural postulates and so needs facts. It is only when attention is confined to equilibrium paths that this is not the case, and that is no doubt the reason why they have proved so popular. But to read some of the literature one is led to fear that should the world once again experience considerable unemployment it would be as unexpected and unexplained as it was in the thirties. Of course, this is not so; much of what is writtten here must have been done with tongue in cheek.

IV

The last remark leads to what I wish to say in conclusion. It would be as philistine and silly to write off modern growth theory as it would be to take it as a completed theory of the world. When an economist shows that all warranted paths seek the steady state he is not wishing to argue, say, that the U.S. economy is following such a path. He is aware of all that has been left out; he does his exercise in the hope that it will eventually help in more ambitious undertakings.

The student, therefore, should approach the literature not in the expectation that he will learn all about economic change and growth, but rather that he will see rather good minds struggling with the most elementary aspects of what may become such a theory. Even so he should find a good deal to enjoy and to admire.

F. H. HAHN.

REFERENCES

[1] Johnson, H. G. " The Neo-Classical One-Sector Growth Model: A Geometrical Exposition and Extension to a Monetary Economy ", *Economica*, Vol. 33 (1966).
[2] Jorgenson, D. W. and Griliches, Z. " The Explanation of Productivity Change ", *Review of Economic Studies*, Vol. XXXIV(3) (1967).
[3] Kaldor, N. " Marginal Productivity and the Macro-Economic Theories of Distribution ", *Review of Economic Studies*, Vol. XXXIII(4) (1966).
[4] Kemeny, J. G., Morgenstern O., and Thompson, G. L. " A Generalisation of the von Neumann Model of an Expanding Economy ", *Econometrica*, Vol. 24 (1956).
[5] Morishima, M. *Equilibrium, Stability and Growth* (Oxford University Press, 1964).
[6] Pasinetti, L. L. " New Results in an Old Framework ", *Review of Economic Studies*, Vol. XXXIII(5) (1966).
[7] Robinson, J. *The Accumulation of Capital* (Macmillan, 1956).
[8] ——, " Comment on Samuelson and Modigliani ", *Review of Economics Studies*, Vol. XXXIII(4) (1966).
[9] Rose, H., " On the Non-Linear Theory of the Employment Cycle ",
[10] Samuelson, P. A. and Modigliani, F. " The Pasinetti Paradox in Neo-Classical and More General Models ", *Review of Economic Studies*, Vol. XXXIII(4) (1966).
[11] Shell, K. and Stiglitz, J. E. " The Allocation of Investment in a Dynamic Economy ", *Quarterly Journal of Economics* (Nov. 1967).
[12] Tobin, Jonas. " Money and Economic Growth,", *Econometrica*, Vol. 33 (1965).

1 A Model of General Economic Equilibrium[1]

J. VON NEUMANN

The subject of this paper is the solution of a typical economic equation system. The system has the following properties:

(1) Goods are produced not only from "natural factors of production," but in the first place from each other. These processes of production may be circular, i.e. good G_1 is produced with the aid of good G_2, and G_2 with the aid of G_1.

(2) There may be more technically possible processes of production than goods and for this reason "counting of equations" is of no avail. The problem is rather to establish which processes will actually be used and which not (being "unprofitable").

In order to be able to discuss (1), (2) quite freely we shall idealise other elements of the situation (see paragraphs 1 and 2). Most of these idealisations are irrelevant, but this question will not be discussed here.

The way in which our questions are put leads of necessity to a system of inequalities (3)—(8′) in paragraph 3 the possibility of a solution of which is not evident, i.e. *it cannot be proved by any qualitative argument*. The mathematical proof is possible only by means of a generalisation of Brouwer's Fix-Point Theorem, i.e. by the use of very fundamental *topological* facts. This generalised fix-point theorem (the "lemma" of paragraph 7) is also interesting in itself.

The connection with topology may be very surprising at first, but the author thinks that it is natural in problems of this kind. The immediate reason for this is the occurrence of a certain "minimum-maximum" problem, familiar from the calculus of variations. In our present question, the minimum-maximum problem has been formulated in paragraph 5. It is closely related to another problem occurring in the theory of games (see footnote 1 in paragraph 6).

A direct interpretation of the function $\phi(X, Y)$ would be highly desirable. Its rôle appears to be similar to that of thermodynamic potentials in phenomenological thermodynamics; it can be surmised that the similarity will persist in its full phenomenological generality (independently of our restrictive idealisations).

Another feature of our theory, so far without interpretation, is the remarkable duality (symmetry) of the monetary variables (prices y_j, interest factor β) and the technical variables (intensities of production x_i, coefficient of expansion of the economy α). This is brought out very clearly in paragraph 3 (3)—(8′) as well as in the minimum-maximum formulation of paragraph 5 (7**)—(8**).

Lastly, attention is drawn to the results of paragraph 11 from which follows, among other things, that the normal price mechanism brings about—if our assumptions are valid—the technically most efficient intensities of production. This seems not unreasonable since we have eliminated all monetary complications.

The present paper was read for the first time in the winter of 1932 at the mathematical seminar of Princeton University. The reason for its publication was an invitation from Mr. K. Menger, to whom the author wishes to express his thanks.

1. Consider the following problem: there are n goods $G_1, \ldots, G_n$ which can be produced by m processes $P_1, \ldots, P_m$. Which processes will be used (as "profitable") and what prices of the goods will obtain? The problem is evidently

[1] This paper was first published in German, under the title *Über ein Ökonomisches Gleichungssystem und eine Verallgemeinerung des Brouwerschen Fixpunktsatzes* in the volume entitled *Ergebnisse eines Mathematischen Seminars*, edited by K. Menger (Vienna, 1938). It was translated into English by G. Morgenstern. A commentary note on this article, by D. G. Champernowne, is printed below.

non-trivial since either of its parts can be answered only after the other one has been answered, i.e. its solution is implicit. We observe in particular:

(*a*) Since it is possible that $m > n$ it cannot be solved through the usual counting of equations.

In order to avoid further complications we assume:

(*b*) That there are constant returns (to scale);

(*c*) That the natural factors of production, including labour, can be expanded in unlimited quantities.

The essential phenomenon that we wish to grasp is this: goods are produced from each other (see equation (7) below) and we want to determine (*i*) which processes will be used; (*ii*) what the relative velocity will be with which the total quantity of goods increases; (*iii*) what prices will obtain; (*iv*) what the rate of interest will be. In order to isolate this phenomenon completely we assume furthermore:

(*d*) Consumption of goods takes place only through the processes of production which include necessities of life consumed by workers and employees.

In other words we assume that all income in excess of necessities of life will be reinvested.

It is obvious to what kind of theoretical models the above assumptions correspond.

2. In each process P_i ($i = 1, \ldots, m$) quantities a_{ij} (expressed in some units) are used up, and quantities b_{ij} are produced, of the respective goods G_j ($j = 1, \ldots, n$). The process can be symbolised in the following way:

$$P_i: \sum_{j=1}^{n} a_{ij} G_j \rightarrow \sum_{j=1}^{n} b_{ij} G_j \qquad (1)$$

It is to be noted:

(*e*) Capital goods are to be inserted on both sides of (1); wear and tear of capital goods are to be described by introducing different stages of wear as different goods, using a separate P_i for each of these.

(*f*) Each process to be of unit time duration. Processes of longer duration to be broken down into single processes of unit duration introducing if necessary intermediate products as additional goods.

(*g*) (1) can describe the special case where good G_j can be produced only jointly with certain others, viz. its permanent joint products.

In the actual economy, these processes P_i, $i = 1, \ldots, m$, will be used with certain *intensities* x_i, $i = 1, \ldots, m$. That means that for the total production the quantities of equations (1) must be multiplied by x_i. We write symbolically:

$$E = \sum_{i=1}^{m} x_i P_i \qquad (2)$$

$x_i = 0$ means that process P_i is not used.

We are interested in those states where the whole economy expands without change of structure, i.e. where the ratios of the intensities $x_1 : \ldots : x_m$ remain unchanged, although $x_1, \ldots x_m$ themselves may change. In such a case they are multiplied by a common factor α per unit of time. This factor is the *coefficient of expansion of the whole economy*.

3. The numerical unknowns of our problem are: (*i*) the *intensities* $x_1, \ldots, x_m$ of the processes $P_1, \ldots, P_m$; (*ii*) the *coefficient of expansion* of the whole economy α; (*iii*) the *prices* $y_1, \ldots, y_n$ of goods $G_1, \ldots, G_n$; (*iv*) the interest factor β ($= 1 + \frac{z}{100}$, z being the rate of interest in % per unit of time. Obviously:

$$x_i \geqq 0, \qquad (3) \qquad\qquad y_j \geqq 0, \qquad (4)$$

and since a solution with $x_1 = \ldots = x_m = 0$, or $y_1 = \ldots = y_n = 0$ would be meaningless:

$$\sum_{i=1}^{m} x_i > 0, \ldots\ldots\ldots\ldots\ldots (5) \qquad \sum_{j=1}^{n} y_j > 0, \ldots\ldots\ldots\ldots\ldots (6)$$

The economic equations are now:

$$\alpha \sum_{i=1}^{m} a_{ij}\, x_i \leqq \sum_{i=1}^{m} b_{ij}\, x_i, \ldots\ldots\ldots\ldots\ldots (7)$$

and if in (7) $<$ applies, $y_j = 0$ .... (7′)

$$\beta \sum_{j=1}^{n} a_{ij}\, y_j \geqq \sum_{j=1}^{n} b_{ij}\, y_j, \ldots\ldots\ldots\ldots\ldots (8)$$

and if in (8) $>$ applies, $x_i = 0$ .... (8′)

The meaning of (7), (7′) is: it is impossible to consume more of a good G_j in the total process (2) than is being produced. If, however, less is consumed, i.e. if there is excess production of G_j, G_j becomes a free good and its price $y_j = 0$.

The meaning of (8), (8′) is: in equilibrium no profit can be made on any process P_i (or else prices or the rate of interest would rise—it is clear how this abstraction is to be understood). If there is a loss, however, i.e. if P_i is unprofitable, then P_i will not be used and its intensity $x_i = 0$.

The quantities a_{ij}, b_{ij} are to be taken as given, whereas the x_i, y_j, α, β are unknown. There are, then, $m + n + 2$ unknowns, but since in the case of x_i, y_j only the ratios $x_1 : \ldots : x_m$, $y_1 : \ldots : y_n$ are essential, they are reduced to $m + n$. Against this, there are $m + n$ conditions (7) + (7′) and (8) + (8′). As these, however, are not equations, but rather complicated inequalities, the fact that the number of conditions is equal to the number of unknowns does not constitute a guarantee that the system can be solved.

The dual symmetry of equations (3), (5), (7), (7′) of the variables x_i, α and of the concept "unused process" on the one hand, and of equations (4), (6), (8), 8′) of the variables y_j, β and of the concept "free good" on the other hand seems remarkable.

4. Our task is to solve (3)—(8′). We shall proceed to show:

Solutions of (3)—(8′) *always exist*, although there may be several solutions with different $x_1 : \ldots : x_m$ or with different $y_1 : \ldots : y_n$. The first is possible since we have not even excluded the case where several P_i describe the same process or where several P_i combine to form another. The second is possible since some goods G_j may enter into each process P_i only in a fixed ratio with some others. But even apart from these trivial possibilities there may exist—for less obvious reasons—several solutions $x_1 : \ldots : x_m$, $y_1 : \ldots : y_m$. Against this it is of importance that α, β should have the same value for all solutions; i.e. α, β *are uniquely determined.*

We shall even find that α and β can be directly characterised in a simple manner (see paragraphs 10 and 11).

To simplify our considerations we shall assume that always:

$$a_{ij} + b_{ij} > 0 \ldots\ldots\ldots\ldots\ldots (9)$$

(a_{ij}, b_{ij} are clearly always $\geqq 0$). Since the a_{ij}, b_{ij} may be arbitrarily small this restriction is not very far-reaching, although it must be imposed in order to assure uniqueness of α, β as otherwise W might break up into disconnected parts.

Consider now a hypothetical solution x_i, α, y_j, β of (3)—(8′). If we had in (7) always $<$, then we should have always $y_j = 0$ (because of (7′)) in contradiction to (6).

If we had in (8) always > we should have always $x_i = 0$ (because of (8′)) in contradiction to (5). Therefore, in (7) $\leqq$ always applies, but = at least once; in (8) $\geqq$ always applies, but = at least once.

In consequence:

$$\alpha = \underset{j=1,\ldots,n}{\text{Min.}} \left[\frac{\sum_{i=1}^{m} b_{ij}\, x_i}{\sum_{i=1}^{m} a_{ij}\, x_i} \right] \qquad \text{(10)},$$

$$\beta = \underset{i=1,\ldots,m}{\text{Max.}} \frac{\sum_{j=1}^{n} b_{ij}\, y_j}{\sum_{j=1}^{n} a_{ij}\, y_j} \qquad \text{(11)}.$$

Therefore the x_i, y_j determine uniquely α, β. (The right-hand side of (10), (11) can never assume the meaningless form $\frac{0}{0}$ because of (3)—(6) and (9)). We can therefore state (7) + (7′) and (8) + (8′) as conditions for x_i, y_j only:

$y_j = 0$ for each $j = 1, \ldots, n$, for which:

$$\frac{\sum_{i=1}^{m} b_{ij}\, x_i}{\sum_{i=1}^{m} a_{ij}\, x_i}$$

does not assume its minimum value (for all $j = 1, \ldots, n$) . . . (7*).

$x_i = 0$ for each $i = 1, \ldots, m$, for which:

$$\frac{\sum_{j=1}^{n} b_{ij}\, y_i}{\sum_{j=1}^{n} a_{ij}\, y_i}$$

does not assume its maximum value (for all $i = 1, \ldots, m$) . . . (8*).

The $x_1, \ldots, x_m$ in (7*) and the $y_1, \ldots, y_n$ in (8*) are to be considered as given. We have, therefore, to solve (3)—(6), (7) and (8) for x_i, y_j.

5. Let X' be a set of variables $(x'_1, \ldots, x'_m)$ fulfilling the analoga of (3), (5):

$$x'_i \geqq 0, \qquad \text{(3′)} \qquad \sum_{i=1}^{m} x'_i > 0, \qquad \text{(5′)}$$

and let Y' be a series of variables $(y'_i, \ldots, y'_n)$ fulfilling the analoga of (4), (6):

$$y'_j \geqq 0, \qquad \text{(4′)} \qquad \sum_{j=1}^{n} y'_j > 0, \qquad \text{(6′)}$$

Let, furthermore,

$$\phi(X'_i, Y'_i) = \frac{\sum_{i=1}^{m} \sum_{j=1}^{n} b_{ij}\, x'_i\, y'_j}{\sum_{i=1}^{m} \sum_{j=1}^{n} a_{ij}\, x'_i\, y'_j} \qquad \text{(12)}$$

Let $X = (x_1, \ldots, x_m)$, $Y = (y_1, \ldots, y_n)$ the (hypothetical) solution, $X' = (x'_i, \ldots, x'_m)$, $Y' = (y'_1, \ldots, y'_n)$ to be freely variable, but in such a way that (3)—(6) and (3′)—(6′) respectively are fulfilled; then it is easy to verify that (7*) and (8*) can be formulated as follows:

$\phi(X, Y')$ assumes its minimum value for Y' if $Y' = Y$.....(7**).

$\phi(X', Y)$ assumes its maximum value for X' if $X' = X$.....(8**).

The question of a solution of (3)—(8′) becomes a question of a solution of (7**), (8**) and can be formulated as follows:

(*) *Consider* (X', Y') *in the domain bounded by* (3′)—(6′). *To find a saddle point* $X' = X$, $Y' = Y$, *i.e. where* (X, Y') *assumes its minimum value for* Y', *and at the same time* (X', Y) *its maximum value for* Y'.

From (7), (7*), (10) and (8), (8*), (11) respectively, follows:

$$\alpha = \frac{\sum_{j=1}^{n}\left[\sum_{i=1}^{m} b_{ij}\, x_i\right] y_j}{\sum_{j=1}^{n}\left[\sum_{i=1}^{m} a_{ij}\, x_i\right] y_j} = \phi(x, y) \text{ and } \beta = \frac{\sum_{i=1}^{m}\left[\sum_{j=1}^{n} b_{ij}\, y_j\right] x_i}{\sum_{i=1}^{m}\left[\sum_{j=1}^{n} a_{ij}\, y_j\right] x_i} = \phi(x, y)$$

respectively.

Therefore:

(**) *If our problem can be solved, i.e. if* $\phi(X', Y')$ *has a saddle point* $X' = X$, $Y' = Y$ *(see above), then*:

$\alpha = \beta = \phi\,(X,Y) =$ *the value at the saddle point*............(13)

6. Because of the homogeneity of $\phi\,(X', Y')$ (in X', Y', i.e. in $x', \ldots, x_m'$ and $y_1', \ldots y_m'$) our problem remains unaffected if we substitute the normalisations

$\sum_{i=1}^{m} x_i = 1$,...............(5*) $\sum_{j=1}^{n} y_j = 1$,..............(6*)

for (5′), (6′) and correspondingly for (5), (6). Let S be the X' set described by:

$x_i' \geqq 0$,...............(3′) $\sum_{i=1}^{m} x_i' = 1$,...............(5*)

and let T be the Y' set described by:

$y_j' \geqq 0$, ...(4′) $\sum_{j=1}^{n} y_j' = 1$,...............(6*)

(S, T are simplices of, respectively, $m - 1$ and $n - 1$ dimensions).

In order to solve[1] we make use of the simpler formulation (7*), (8*) and combine these with (3), (4), (5*), (6*) expressing the fact that $X = (x_1, \ldots, x_m)$ is in S and $Y = (y_1, \ldots, y_n)$ in T.

7. We shall prove a slightly more general lemma: Let R_m be the m-dimensional

[1] The question whether our problem has a solution is oddly connected with that of a problem occurring in the Theory of Games dealt with elsewhere. (Math. Annalen, 100, 1928, pp. 295–320, particularly pp. 305 and 307–311). The problem there is a special case of (*) and is solved here in a new way through our solution of (*) (see below). In fact, if $a_{ij} \equiv 1$, then $\sum_{i=1}^{m} \sum_{j=1}^{n} a_{ij}\, x'_i\, y'_j = 1$ because of (5*), (6*). Therefore $\phi\,(X', Y') = \sum_{i=1}^{m} \sum_{j=1}^{n} b_{ij}\, x'_i\, y'_j$, and thus our (*) coincides with loc. cit., p. 307. (Our $\phi\,(X', Y')$, b_{ij}, x'_i, y'_j, m, n here correspond to $h\ (\xi, \eta)$, a_{pq}, ξ_p, η_q, $M + 1$, $N + 1$ there).

It is, incidentally, remarkable that (*) does not lead—as usual—to a simple maximum or minimum problem, the possibility of a solution of which would be evident, but to a problem of the saddle point or minimum-maximum type, where the question of a possible solution is far more profound.

space of all points $X = (x_1, \ldots, x_m)$, R_n the n-dimensional space of all points $Y = (y_1, \ldots, y_n)$, R_{m+n} the $m + n$ dimensional space of all points $(X, Y) = (x_1, \ldots x_m, y_1, \ldots, y_n)$.

A set (in R_m or R_n or R_{m+n}) which is *not empty, convex closed and bounded* we call a set C.

Let S°, T° be sets C in R_m and R_n respectively and let $S^\circ \times T^\circ$ be the set of all (X, Y) (in R_{m+n}) where the range of X is S° and the range of Y is T°. Let V, W be two closed subsets of $S^\circ \times T^\circ$. For every X in S° let the set $Q\ (X)$ of all Y with (X, Y) in V be a set C; for each Y in T° let the set $P\ (Y)$ of all X with (X, Y) in W be a set C. Then the following lemma applies.

Under the above assumptions, V, W have (at least) one point in common.

Our problem follows by putting $S^\circ = S$, $T^\circ = T$ and $V =$ the set of all $(X, Y) = (x_1, \ldots, x_m, y_1, \ldots, y_n)$ fulfilling (7*), $W =$ the set of all $(X, Y) = (x_1, \ldots, x_m, y_1, \ldots, y_n)$ fulfilling (8*). It can be easily seen that V. W are closed and that the sets $S^\circ = S$, $T^\circ = T$, $Q\ (X)$, $P\ (Y)$ are all simplices, i.e. sets C. The common points of these V, W are, of course, our required solutions $(X, Y) = (x_1, \ldots, x_m, y_1, \ldots, y_m)$.

8. To prove the above lemma let S°, T°, V, W be as described before the lemma.

First, consider V. For each X of S° we choose a point $Y^\circ\ (X)$ out of $Q\ (X)$ (e.g. the centre of gravity of this set). It will not be possible, generally, to choose $Y^\circ\ (X)$ as a continuous function of X. Let $\epsilon > 0$; we define:

$$w^\epsilon\ (X, X') = \text{Max.}\ (0, 1 - \frac{1}{\epsilon}\ \text{distance}\ (X, X')) \quad \ldots\ldots\ldots\ldots \quad (14)$$

Now let $Y^\epsilon\ (X)$ be the centre of gravity of the $Y^\circ\ (X')$ with (relative) weight function $w^\epsilon\ (X, X')$ where the range of X' is S°. I.e. if $Y^\circ\ (X) = (y_1{}^\circ\ (x), \ldots, y_n{}^\circ\ (x))$, $Y^\epsilon\ (X) = (y_1{}^\epsilon\ (x), \ldots, y_n{}^\epsilon\ (x))$, then:

$$y_j{}^\epsilon\ (X) = \int_{S^\circ} w^\epsilon\ (X, X')\ y_j{}^\circ\ (X')\ dX' / \int_{S^\circ} w^\epsilon\ (X, X')\ dX', \ldots. \quad (15)$$

We derive now a number of properties of $Y^\epsilon\ (X)$ (valid for all $\epsilon > 0$):

(*i*) $Y^\epsilon\ (X)$ is in T°. Proof: $Y^\circ\ (X')$ is in $Q\ (X')$ and therefore in T°, and since $Y^\epsilon\ (X)$ is a centre of gravity of points $Y^\circ\ (X')$ and T° is convex, $Y^\epsilon\ (X)$ also is in $T^\bullet$.

(*ii*) $Y^\epsilon\ (X)$ is a continuous function of X (for the whole range of S°). Proof: it is sufficient to prove this for each $y_j{}^\epsilon\ (X)$. Now $w^\epsilon\ (X, X')$ is a continuous function of X, X' throughout; $\int_{S^\circ} w^\epsilon\ (X, X')\ dX'$ is always > 0, and all $y_j{}^\circ\ (X)$ are bounded (being co-ordinates of the bounded set S°). The continuity of the $y_j{}^\epsilon\ (X)$ follows, therefore, from (15).

(*iii*) For each $\delta > 0$ there exists an $\epsilon_0 = \epsilon_0\ (\delta) > 0$ such that the distance of each point $(X, Y^{\epsilon_0}\ (X))$ from V is $< \delta$. Proof: assume the contrary. Then there must exist a $\delta > 0$ and a sequence of $\epsilon_\nu > 0$ with $\lim_{\nu \to \infty} \epsilon_\nu = 0$ such that for every $\nu = 1, 2, \ldots$ there exists a X_ν in S° for which the distance $(X_\nu, Y^{\epsilon_\nu}\ (X_\nu))$ would be $\geqq \delta$. A fortiori $Y^{\epsilon_\nu}\ (X_\nu)$ is at a distance $\geqq \frac{\delta}{2}$ from every $Q\ (X')$, with a distance $(X_\nu, X') \leqq \frac{\delta}{2}$.

All X_ν, $\nu = 1, 2, \ldots$, are in S° and have therefore a point of accumulation X^* in S°; from which follows that there exists a subsequence of X_ν, $\nu = 1, 2, \ldots$, converging towards X^* for which distance $(X_\nu, X^*) \leqq \frac{\delta}{2}$ always applies. Substituting this subsequence for the ϵ_ν, X_ν, we see that we are justified in assuming: $\lim X_\nu = X^*$, distance $(X_\nu, X^*) \leqq \frac{\delta}{2}.$ Therefore we may put $X' = X^*$ for every $\nu = 1, 2, \ldots,$ and in consequence we have always $Y^{\epsilon_\nu}(X_\nu)$ at a distance $\geqq \frac{\delta}{2}$ from $Q(X^*)$.

$Q(X^*)$ being convex, the set of all points with a distance $< \frac{\delta}{2}$ from $(Q(X^*)$ is also convex. Since $Y^{\epsilon_\nu}(X_\nu)$ does not belong to this set, and since it is a centre of gravity of points $Y^\circ(X')$ with distance $(X_\nu, X') \leqq \epsilon_\nu$ (because for distance $(X_\nu, X') > \epsilon_\nu$, $w^{\epsilon_\nu}(X_\nu, X') = 0$ according to (14)), not all of these points belong to the set under discussion. Therefore: there exists a $X' = X_\nu$ for which the distance $(X_\nu, X'_\nu) \leqq \epsilon_\nu$ and where the distance between $Y^\circ(X'_\nu)$ and $Q(X^*)$ is $\geqq \frac{\delta}{2}.$

Lim $X_\nu = X^*$, lim distance $(X_\nu, X'_\nu) = 0$, and therefore lim $X'_\nu = X^*$. All $Y^\circ(Y_\nu)$ belong to T° and have therefore a point of accumulation Y^*. In consequence, (X^*, Y^*) is a point of accumulation of the $(X_\nu, Y^\circ(X_\nu))$ and since they all belong to V, (X^*, Y^*) belongs to V too. Y^* is therefore in $Q(X^*)$. Now the distance of every $Y^\circ(Y_\nu)$ including from $Q(X^*)$ is $\geqq \frac{\delta}{2}.$ This is a contradiction, and the proof is complete.

(*i*)—(*iii*) together assert: for every $\delta > 0$ there exists a continuous mapping $Y_\delta(X)$ of S° on to a subset of T° where the distance of every point $(X, Y_\delta(X))$ from V is $< \delta$. (Put $Y_\delta(X) = Y^\epsilon(X)$ with $\epsilon = \epsilon_0 = \epsilon_0(\delta)$.)

9. Interchanging S° and T°, and V and W we obtain now: for every $\delta > 0$ there exists a continuous mapping $X_\delta(Y)$ of T° on to a subset of S° where the distance of every point $(X_\delta(Y), Y)$ from W is $< \delta$.

On putting $f_\delta(X) = X_\delta(Y_\delta(X))$, $f_\delta(X)$ is a continuous mapping of S° on to a subset of S°. Since S° is a set C, and therefore topologically a simplex[1] we can use L. E. J. Brouwer's Fix-point Theorem[2]; $f_\delta(X)$ has a fix-point. I.e., there exists a X^δ in S° for which $X^\delta = f_\delta(X^\delta) = X_\delta(Y_\delta(X^\delta))$. Let $Y^\delta = Y_\delta(X^\delta)$, then we have $X^\delta = X_\delta(Y^\delta)$. Consequently, the distances of the point (X^δ, Y^δ) in R_{m+n} both from V and from W are $< \delta$. The distance of V from W is therefore $< 2\delta$. Since this is valid for every $\delta > 0$, the distance between V and W is $= 0$. Since V, W are closed and bounded, they must have at least one common point. This proves our lemma completely.

10. We have solved (7^*), (8^*) of paragraph 4 as well as the equivalent problem $(^*)$ of paragraph 5 and the original task of paragraph 3: the solution of (3)—(8′). If the x_i, y_j (which were called X, Y in paragraphs 7—9) are determined, α, β follow from (13) in $(^{**})$ of paragraph 5. In particular, $\alpha = \beta$.

We have emphasised in paragraph 4 already that there may be several solutions x_i, y_j (i.e. X, Y); we shall proceed to show that there exists only one value of α (i.e. of β). In fact, let $X_1, Y_1, \alpha_1, \beta_1$ and $X_2, Y_2, \alpha_2, \beta_2$ be two solutions. From (7^{**}), (8^{**}) and (13) follows:

$$\alpha_1 = \beta_1 = \phi(X_1, Y_1) \leqq \phi(X_1, Y_2),$$

$$\alpha_2 = \beta_2 = \phi(X_2, Y_2) \geqq \phi(X_1, Y_2),$$

therefore $\alpha_1 = \beta_1 \leqq \alpha_2 = \beta_2$. For reasons of symmetry $\alpha_2 = \beta_2 \leqq \alpha_1 = \beta_1$, therefore $\alpha_1 = \beta_1 = \alpha_2 = \beta_2$.

[1] Regarding these as well as other properties of convex sets used in this paper, cf., e.g., Alexandroff and H. Hopf, *Topologie*, vol. I, J. Springer, Berlin, 1935, pp. 598-609.

[2] Cf., e.g., loc. cit. footnote 1 p. 480.

We have shown:

At least one solution X, Y, α, β exists. For all solutions:

$$\alpha = \beta = \phi\ (X,\ Y) \qquad (13)$$

and these have the same numerical value for all solutions, in other words: The interest factor and the coefficient of expansion of the economy are equal and uniquely determined by the technically possible processes $P_1, \ldots, P_m$.

Because of (13), $\alpha > 0$, but may be $\gtreqless 1$. One would expect $\alpha > 1$, but $\alpha \leqq 1$ cannot be excluded in view of the generality of our formulation: processes $P_1, \ldots, P_m$ may really be *unproductive*.

11. In addition, we shall characterise α in two independent ways.

Firstly, let us consider a state of the economy possible on purely technical considerations, expanding with factor α' per unit of time. I.e., for the intensities $x_1, \ldots, x_m$ applies:

$$x_i \geqq 0 \qquad (3') \qquad \sum_{i=1}^{m} x_i' > 0 \qquad (5') \text{ and}$$

$$\alpha' \sum_{i=1}^{m} a_{ij}\ x_i' \leqq \sum_{i=1}^{m} b_{ij}\ x_i' \qquad (7'')$$

We are neglecting prices here altogether. Let $x_i, y_j, \alpha = \beta$ be a solution of our original problem (3)—(8′) in paragraph 3. Multiplying (7″) by y_j and adding $\sum_{j=1}^{n}$ we obtain:

$$\alpha' \sum_{i=1}^{m} \sum_{j=1}^{n} a_{ij}\ x_i'\ y_j \leqq \sum_{i=1}^{m} \sum_{j=1}^{n} b_{ij}\ x_i'\ y_j,$$

and therefore $\alpha' \leqq \phi\ (X',\ Y)$. Because of (8**) and (13) in paragraph 5, we have:

$$\alpha' \leqq \phi\ (X',\ Y) \leqq \phi\ (X,\ Y) = \alpha = \beta \qquad (15).$$

Secondly, let us consider a system of prices where the interest factor β' allows of no more profits. I.e. for prices $y_1', \ldots y'_n$ applies:

$$y'_j \geqq 0, \qquad (4') \qquad \sum_{j=1}^{n} y'_j > 0, \qquad (6') \text{ and}$$

$$\beta' \sum_{j=1}^{n} a_{ij}\ y'_j \geqq \sum_{j=1}^{n} b_{ij}\ y'_j. \qquad (8'')$$

Hereby we are neglecting intensities of production altogether. Let $x_i, y_j, \alpha = \beta$ as above. Multiplying (8″) by x_i and adding $\sum_{i=1}^{m}$ we obtain:

$$\beta' \sum_{i=1}^{m} \sum_{j=1}^{n} a_{ij}\ x_i\ y'_j \leqq \sum_{i=1}^{m} \sum_{j=1}^{n} b_{ij}\ x_i\ y'_j$$

and therefore $\beta' \geqq \phi\ (X,\ Y')$. Because of (7**) and (13) in paragraph 5, we have:

$$\beta' \geqq \phi\ (X,\ Y') \geqq \phi\ (X,\ Y) = \alpha = \beta. \qquad (16)$$

These two results can be expressed as follows:

The greatest (purely technically possible) factor of expansion α' *of the whole economy is* $\alpha' = \alpha = \beta$, *neglecting prices.*

The lowest interest factor β' *at which a profitless system of prices is possible is* $\beta' = \alpha = \beta$, *neglecting intensities of production.*

Note that these characterisations are possible only on the basis of our knowledge that solutions of our original problem exist—without themselves directly referring to this problem. Furthermore, the equality of the maximum in the first form and the minimum in the second can be proved only on the basis of the existence of this solution.

Princeton, N.J. J. v. NEUMANN.

2 A Note on J. von Neumann's Article on "A Model of Economic Equilibrium"[1]

D. G. CHAMPERNOWNE

SCOPE OF THE PAPER

The supreme merit of this paper lies in the elegance of the mathematical solution of a highly generalised problem in theoretical economics. But the paper is of considerable interest to economists as well as to mathematicians, because it deals simultaneously with questions on several fields of economics, which until this paper was first read, (in 1932) had seldom been considered together as parts of one problem. For example, in this short paper the author considers which goods will be free goods, and the determination of the prices of goods which are not free : at the same time he examines which productive processes and scales of production will be optimum and which will be unprofitable : he also examines the degree in which each optimum process will be used and the relative amounts of different goods that will be produced. At the same time he demonstrates the mechanism which determines the rate of interest and the rate of expansion of the whole economy.

Approaching these questions as a mathematician, Dr. Neumann places emphasis on rather different aspects of the problem than would an economist. Whereas he takes great care to give an absolutely rigorous mathematical argument and to state his assumptions completely and without ambiguity, he develops his points with the minimum of descriptive explanation. The paper is logically complete and admirably concise. In contrast to the convention among mathematical writers of reducing explanations to a minimum and stating assumptions as concisely as possible, economists more usually provide illustrative examples and repetitions of their argument to ease the reader's task of comprehension. Those accustomed to these less austere conventions may therefore be interested to read the following discursive commentary which develops some of the points of economic interest in Dr. Neumann's classic article.

By adopting extremely artificial assumptions, the author rendered his problem soluble and concentrated attention on some very interesting properties of the actual economic system. But at the same time this process of abstraction inevitably made many of his conclusions inapplicable to the real world : others could be applied only after considerable modifications. It is interesting to enquire how far the properties in his simplified model do correspond to similar phenomena in the real world.

THE APPROACH TO THE PROBLEM

Prof. v. Neumann's method is the familiar one of examining the conditions of equilibrium of his simplified model of the economic world. The first point is to get clear what is meant by equilibrium. The definition of equilibrium is very similar to that of the economist's stationary state : but in v. Neumann's article equilibrium differs from a stationary state's equilibrium in the vital respect that a uniform expansion of the whole system is allowed under equilibrium. Such a state of equilibrium may be called a quasi-stationary state, although v. Neumann does not in fact use this term.

From the point of view of the mathematician, the most important result of the article is the proof that under the simplified conditions there assumed, it will be possible for the model to have any equilibrium position at all, in the sense in which equilibrium

[1] This note is the outcome of conversations with Mr. N. Kaldor, to whom many of the ideas in it are due. I am also indebted to Mr. P. Sraffa of Cambridge and to Mr. Crum of New College, Oxford, for instruction in subjects discussed in this article.

is there defined. This may seem rather surprising, as one is rather apt to investigate conditions of equilibrium without bothering first of all to find out whether any equilibrium position need actually exist at all : one is liable to assume that some equilibrium position is possible. The fact that it is necessary to prove the existence of an equilibrium position before finding out the properties of such a position may be illustrated by the following consideration. Although v. Neumann defines equilibrium to be that of a quasi-stationary state, which may be expanding, he might perhaps have chosen to define equilibrium to be that of a stationary state without expansion or contraction. It so happens that the simplifying assumptions made about his economic model make it impossible in general for it to settle down to a state of stationary equilibrium : if, therefore, he had assumed that such a stationary equilibrium position was possible and had investigated the various conditions which the system must satisfy when in equilibrium, he would evidently have arrived at ridiculous results. For similar reasons, it was therefore necessary for him to prove that there was at least one possible position of quasi-stationary state equilibrium, before it was of any use investigating the properties which the system must have in such an equilibrium position.

Although, to the mathematician, the most interesting part of this paper will be that which proves the existence of at least one equilibrium position ; for the economist the most interesting part is that which analyses the properties of the system when it is in equilibrium. Fortunately, once the existence of an equilibrium position has been demonstrated, the arguments demonstrating the nature of this equilibrium are of quite an elementary nature, and it is possible to translate the rigorous mathematics of this part of the article into a somewhat looser form of words more readily digestible by those who are unused to thinking in terms of symbols.

Before turning to these arguments, it is useful to examine the manner in which v. Neumann approaches the economic problem. As we have seen, he is concerned not with short period problems but with the properties of the economic system when it has settled down to an equilibrium position which may be described as a quasi-stationary state. In such a state, all prices remain constant, the production of all goods remains in the same proportion although a uniform geometric rate of growth is allowed to the whole system. Thus if in any period the output of one particular good doubles, so then does the output of every other good double in that period, and the population and quantity of each kind of capital equipment double also in the same period. Thus in equilibrium there is no progress or change in production per head of population : growth merely consists of replication and the economic system expands like a crystal suspended in a solution of its own salt. The composition of any given volume of the crystal is at all times the same. To describe a system with uniform expansion of this kind we have introduced the term quasi-stationary state.

The model, being concerned only with a quasi-stationary state, can throw no direct light on problems of economic development and changes in the standard of living. The model has only one advantage over the strictly stationary state and that is that the community has an outlet for its savings in providing for the uniform expansion of the community and its stock of equipment.

In order to make it possible for quasi-stationary state equilibrium to exist in the model, several drastic simplifying assumptions had to be introduced. Constant returns were assumed in the sense that any economic process could be carried out at half, double, or in general x times its given scale, without any increase in costs per unit of output. Conditions of perfect competition in the long period were also assumed, and it was supposed that the natural factors of production (including labour) were available in unlimited quantities. One other very important assumption was implied, although it was nowhere very clearly stated : this was that no saving was carried out by the workers whereas the propertied class saved the whole of their income. These various simplifying assumptions, although necessary if a rigorous proof of the existence of equilibrium was to be possible, evidently render the model unsuitable for examining problems connected with monopoly, economies of mass production, technical progress, or with land.[1] Since monetary problems are also assumed away, the reader may begin to wonder in what way the model has interesting relevance to conditions in the real world.

Prof. v. Neumann's model does however exhibit certain features of a competitive capitalist economy which tend to be obscured in the more traditional approach and can deal with the consequences of the circular nature of the production process (*i.e.* that commodities are largely produced out of each other) in a way that is not possible under it. By reducing the role of the worker-consumer to that of a farm animal, he can focus attention on those parts of the mechanism determining prices and the rate of interest, which depend on supply conditions alone and not on the tastes of consumers. This emphasis is important because the orthodox analysis has distributed attention evenly between marginal utility and conditions of supply ; since supply is often more elastic than demand, prices in the long run do over a wide field reflect contrasts in cost rather than conditions of consumers' demands: a price-theory focussing attention on costs can give a very clear and yet an approximately true account. We may first consider v. Neumann's approach to the problem of prices.

Consider a good which may be manufactured out of a lot of other goods : in the simplified conditions of the model the cost price of the good will consist of the values of the goods of which it is composed plus an interest charge on the fixed and working capital involved in the process. If a good is a joint product, then the value of the other products must be subtracted from the cost in arriving at the cost price of the good. Competition will ensure that where a good may be produced by many different processes, its cost price will correspond to the costs in the cheapest process.

Wage costs are not considered as such, for labourers are not separately considered any more than are farm animals. It is supposed that they will do their work in return for rations of shelter, fuel, food and clothing, just as a horse works when it is fed and cared for. The costs of labour thus consist of the goods which maintain the workers, just as the costs of a horse's work consist of his fodder, stabling, etc. The essential point about v. Neumann's theory of prices is that goods are made out of goods alone and that the cost price of any good or collection of goods consists of the value of the goods from which they are made plus an interest charge.

Prof. v. Neumann's approach to the theory of the rate of interest is interesting. He makes no reference to marginal products or to the marginal efficiency of capital : nor does he regard the rate of interest as depending on the relative efficiency of production processes involving different " periods of production " : the rate of interest is not determined as the supply price of waiting, abstinence or saving, for it is assumed that the propertied class save all their income and that the working class consume all theirs. Nor is the rate of interest determined as the measure of liquidity preference, for money as such plays no part in v. Neumann's article. The rate of interest appears as the natural and optimum rate of organic expansion[2] of the system, and depends on the technical processes of production which are available. If these processes enable the system to expand at 5 per cent per annum at most, then 5 per cent per annum will be the rate of interest.

In its concern with a quasi-stationary state, in its theory of prices as determined

[1] By assuming both constant returns and perfect competition, v. Neumann also implies that the division of the total output (by means of a given process) between firms (using that process) is indeterminate.

[2] See pp. 14–15 for a fuller explanation of this concept.

by the minimum cost of goods made from other goods alone, and in its theory of the rate of interest determined by the greatest possible rate of expansion of the economic system, this paper approaches the problems of economics in an extremely original and stimulating fashion : it can claim, quite apart from the beautiful mathematical proof of the existence of an equilibrium position, to make a substantial contribution to the economic theory of interest, prices and production.

THE PROOF OF THE PROPERTIES OF THE SYSTEM IN EQUILIBRIUM

It would not be profitable to comment on the large part of the paper which deals with the proof of the existence of an equilibrium, since the argument is essentially one of advanced mathematics which cannot be economically expressed in words. But those readers who prefer to think in words rather than symbols may be interested in the following comments on v. Neumann's proof of the properties of the economic system in equilibrium.

Prof. v. Neumann defines a process of production as an operation lasting for one unit of time which converts one bundle of goods into another bundle of goods. He includes the fixed capital equipment used both in the bundle of goods which is converted and again in the bundle of goods which emerges from the operation. He supposes that there are available always a very large number of possible production processes, and that constant returns prevail in the sense that any operation can be carried out at any scale without affecting the relation of the output to the input. In any given process of production, the relative quantities of goods put in are absolutely fixed, and so are the relative quantities of the goods emerging from it : thus the only way in which an entrepreneur can alter the proportions between the goods which he uses is to change from one process of production to another : similarly he must do this in order to change the proportion of goods in his output. What would normally be regarded as two different forms of the same process of production, the one involving slightly different proportions of the factors of production than the other, is thus treated by v. Neumann as being two different processes of production.

It is fairly obvious that with given prices, some production processes are likely to be more profitable than others, in the sense that they could afford to pay a higher rate of interest without making losses. One of v. Neumann's conditions for equilibrium is in fact that every process in use should make zero profits : for under perfect competition, positive profits would attract competitors to use the same process and negative profits would deter people from using the process at all. He thus obtains the following rule for equilibrium :

> *Profitability Rule.*—Only those processes will be used which, with the actual prices and rate of interest, yield zero profits after payment of interest. These processes will be the most profitable ones available.

The second part of the rule follows from the fact that if there were any processes which could earn positive profits they would not have continued out of use under competition.

The usual point of view in economic theory is that free goods play no part in the economic system : but part of v. Neumann's problem is to determine which goods will be free goods in equilibrium. It is an essential property of his equilibrium that the physical outputs of all goods, whether free or not, remain in the same proportions to each other throughout time : so do the physical inputs. Suppose that the system in equilibrium is expanding by k per cent per unit of time : then the input of each good at any moment must be exactly k per cent greater than the input for the previous unit of time. Clearly this can only continue indefinitely if the output of every good is at least k per cent greater than the input of every good, since the source of the input at any moment is simply the output of the previous unit of time. But there may be goods for which the output exceeds the input by more than k per cent : there will then be more than enough of these goods to supply the input of the next moment of time, and if the equilibrium continues it is clear that in the case of these goods, larger and larger surplus stocks will be built up. v. Neumann concludes that the prices of these goods can only remain in equilibrium if they have become free goods in the sense that these prices are zero. Hence he obtains his rule about free goods :

> *Free goods rule.*—In an equilibrium production system, those goods whose output exceeds their input by more than the expansion rate of k per cent will be free goods. Only those goods whose output exceeds their input by the minimum, namely k per cent, will have prices (other than zero).

Prof. v. Neumann is also able to tell us quite a lot about the relative intensities with which the various profitable processes will be used. We may refer to the organisation of processes of production in any given proportions as being a system of production. We may define the expansion rate of any given system of production in terms of the relation of the output to the input of the various goods. We may, in short, define the rate of expansion of the system to be equal to the least rate of expansion of any good involved in the system. For instance, if there is a good whose output under the system exceeds its input by 2 per cent, and if there is no good whose output under the system exceeds its input by less than 2 per cent, then we say that the rate of expansion under this system is 2 per cent. Thus defined, the term rate of expansion may be applied to any production system whether it is in equilibrium or not.

Prof. v. Neumann obtains the following remarkable rule :

> *System of production rule.*—In equilibrium, the system of production actually used will have the greatest rate of expansion of all possible productive systems.

It should be noticed that this comprehensive rule does not involve prices at all : it shows that the system of production actually used has a maximum property depending only on what processes of production are in fact available.

A little reflection will confirm the validity of the rule. The reason for it is roughly this : if any system of production with a higher expansion rate were available, then it would pay all entrepreneurs to adopt this other system in place of the processes they are supposed to be using in equilibrium, and in this case the equilibrium could not continue. This point requires further explanation. In the conditions of the model, the input of any process is the same as the capital involved in the process : interest payments have to be made out of the excess of the value of output over the value of input. A little reflection will confirm that the rate of interest which any process can afford to pay per unit of time must therefore be the percentage by which the value of its output exceeds the value of its input. In equilibrium, we know that each process makes zero profits and hence that each process used can just afford to pay the actual rate of interest. It follows that in every process actually used the value of output exceeds the value of input by exactly the rate of interest. From this it follows in turn that the value of output for the system as a whole in equilibrium exceeds the value of input by a proportion equal to the rate of interest : in other words, the rate of expansion of the system is equal to the rate of interest. This equilibrium rate of interest is, as we have seen, the maximum rate of interest which the equilibrium system can afford to pay. Suppose that there were some other system with a larger rate of expansion, then it is clear that it could afford to pay a higher rate of interest : since it is open to any entrepreneur to adopt this other production system, he would be able to make a profit by so doing because he would then be able to afford more than the actual rate of interest : equilibrium would therefore be impossible if there were any other production system with a rate of expansion greater than that of the actual production system. That is why in equilibrium the actual production system must have the greatest possible rate of expansion, as stated in the system-of-production rule.

In the course of this argument we have incidentally demonstrated another of v. Neumann's results which may be summed up in the following rule :

> *Rate of interest rule.*—In equilibrium, the rate of interest equals the rate of expansion.

We still need to obtain a rule for determining the system of prices under equilibrium. The only result about prices which we have so far considered is that which gives the price of one good in terms of the prices of other goods : this in itself is not immediately helpful if we suppose the prices of all goods to be unknown. In order to understand the rule which prices must obey in equilibrium, it is useful to consider a new concept. This concept is the rate of interest possible under a given system of prices. With given prices, any particular production process will be able to pay a rate of interest equal to the percentage excess of the value of its output with those prices over the value of its input. In particular, with these prices, there will be one or more production processes which can afford to pay a rate of interest higher than can any other production processes. This particular rate of interest will be called the rate of interest possible under the given system of prices. The rule for determining prices may be set out in the following terms* :

> *Price system rule.*—The price system in equilibrium will have a possible rate of interest smaller than or as small as that of any other price system.

The reader will notice that this rule is closely analogous to the production system rule. Its validity may be confirmed by the following argument. In equilibrium, we have seen that the production system actually used must have an expansion rate equal to the actual rate of interest : it follows that the actual production system could afford to pay at least the actual rate of interest, whatever system of prices were ruling.[1] *A fortiori*, whatever the price system might be, at least one of the production processes actually used would be able to afford at least the actual rate of interest. This implies that no price system can have a possible rate of interest less than the actual rate of interest ruling in an equilibrium position. This result is embodied in the price system rule given above.

ECONOMIC IMPLICATIONS OF THE RESULTS

Since v. Neumann's results only relate to a quasi-stationary state, the utmost caution is needed in drawing from them any conclusions about the determination of prices, production or the rate of interest in the real world. Since, in the real world, land is limited in supply, the only possible quasi-stationary state is a strictly stationary state (or conceivably a contracting state[2]) : for an expanding quasi-stationary state would eventually be confronted with a shortage of land and its equilibrium would be destroyed. Hence v. Neumann's " quasi-stationary " state does not in fact bring his model any nearer to reality than would be the case with a strictly stationary state.

In spite of this v. Neumann's results are highly suggestive ; and it is interesting to explore in what respects the operation of his model may be relevant to the real world.

* Prof. v. Neumann does not use this particular rule in his article: He does, however, use the property that given the equilibrium intensities of the processes of production, the ratio of the value of the system's output to that of its input will be a minimum with respect to prices.

[1] This follows almost immediately from the definition of the expansion rate of a production system.

[2] Allowing for the existence of exhaustible resources, *e.g.* minerals, or for a system unable to provide the subsistence wages of the workers except by using up its stocks.

(1) As a first example, we may take the property that competition will ensure that equilibrium can only be reached if the maximum technically possible rate of expansion is achieved. This may immediately suggest an argument in favour of free enterprise in the real world. But quite apart from the point already mentioned that in a world with non-augmentable resources like land the maximum rate of expansion that is ultimately possible is zero (and hence competition would merely lead to an equilibrium position with no growth or contraction and with a zero rate of interest) the claim is strictly valid only if, as in v. Neumann's model, there is a slave-system and the object of production is mere enlargement without any advance in the standard of living. v. Neumann's model certainly does not suggest that competition secures the highest possible standard of living or the greatest possible rate of advance for living standards: for, on the assumptions of his model, the living standard is simply the minimum needed to persuade people to work.

(2) This point brings us to a second interesting implication of v. Neumann's results. He has successfully constructed an economic model in which the equilibrium level for real wages is simply whatever is needed to persuade people to work: it does not apparently depend on what industry can "afford to pay". Suppose that the working-class effectively insists on a higher real wage, then this has the effect of increasing the input needed in any process (to secure a given output) by the amount of the extra fodder which the workers demand. Hence, there will be a change in the equilibrium conditions, and the position of quasi-stationary equilibrium will change to one with a lower rate of interest and a lower rate of expansion. This might suggest an argument for vigorous trade union activity: for in the model the result of standing out for higher real wages is to secure higher living standards at the expense of the owners of property: it is true that it is also at the expense of the rate of expansion of the system, but that is because in the model it is assumed that the propertied class save the whole of their income; in the real world, where the propertied class also consume, it may be obtained at the expense of the consumption of the propertied class. Such an argument is suggested, but it is not certain whether it could be developed by means of any simple extension of the model.

(3) The question of consumption by the propertied class is also relevant to the theory of the rate of interest. The rate of interest will be determined as the greatest rate of expansion possible if all income from property is saved. A *rigorous* proof of this proposition is only possible if we assume that all income from property is in fact saved: this could happen, for example, if all property was owned by the State. On the other hand, even if part of the income from property were spent on consumption, and not saved, the rate of interest would not necessarily be much affected: it might still be *approximately* equal to the greatest expansion rate that *would* have been possible *if* all income from property had been saved. At the same time, the spending of part of the income from property would, of course, reduce the actual rate of expansion of the system; this would now be well below the rate of interest and the maximum possible expansion rate.[1]

(4) An interesting feature of the model is that both prices and the outputs of the individual commodities are determined solely by the technical conditions of production. As was explained above, v. Neumann has proved (*a*) that competition will allow the system to be in equilibrium only if the five rules given above on pp. 13–15 are satisfied: these five rules of competitive equilibrium determine both the intensities of production of the individual commodities and their relative prices where all production processes

[1] The equality of the rate of interest and the rate of expansion in the model is, in fact, (once the existence of an equilibrium is proved) fairly obvious on the assumption that workers spend all their income and capitalists save all theirs.

are given. The model, it is true, ignores the possibility of increasing returns in the production of individual commodities, and does not allow for consumers' choice as an independent factor in the direction of productive activity. There is no room in the theory for an increase in population to make books cheaper and for a shift in demand from cotton to wool and from mutton to beef to send wool prices up and mutton prices down. But the important point is that these may conveniently be considered as the "special cases" of price-theory, to be introduced in the *second approximation*; and not, as is common in traditional economics, at the centre of the theory. For the basic influences determining equilibrium prices v. Neumann's model provides a novel approach; here, perhaps for the first time, is a self-contained theory of the determination of prices, ignoring the second approximation.

The role played by consumers' tastes in the determination of prices is suggested by considering how consumers' choice may be introduced into v. Neumann's model. The method is to allow several alternative production processes for obtaining "labour", each process requiring a different bundle of goods as "real wages", between which the labourer may be supposed indifferent. A change in the labourers' tastes will then be reflected in a change in the input required in the various processes producing "labour": this in turn will react on the equilibrium position of the system and hence on relative prices. But the latter effect may be trivial, even if the change in tastes is significant; and one is left with the impression that consumers' tastes play, in fact, a comparatively minor role in the determination of equilibrium prices.

It may be objected that the assumption that the propertied class save the whole of their income further restricts the scope which "marginal utility" can play in the determination of prices. This may be granted; but this restriction is not so serious as it may appear to be: indeed the novelty of the distribution of emphasis which it implies is, from some points of view, an advantage. For even in the actual world the great bulk of productive activity (as measured, for example, by the distribution of labour between industries) is devoted to the production of intermediary products of one sort or another, which are mainly used as inputs in a series of other products. The prices (and relative outputs) of these intermediary goods can best be explained in terms of the considerations covered in v. Neumann's model.[1]

(5) Land is assumed by v. Neumann to be available in unlimited quantities. It is, however, possible to introduce land into his model by including the land used both in the input and the output of each process using it. In this case, since the quantity of "land" cannot be increased (or decreased), equilibrium is only possible in a stationary state. In such a state, the rate of interest will be zero and the workers will get the whole income. This suggests that if the assumption that all property income is saved is abandoned, the equilibrium in a system containing land may be a stationary state with a positive rate of interest and all income consumed. During the approach to this equilibrium the rate of interest will presumably fall as the increasing scarcity of land lowers the *potential* rate of expansion, and the *actual* rate of expansion may fall even faster owing to monetary complications. These considerations take us however, outside the assumptions made by v. Neumann, and away from the possibility of rigorous proof.

(6) In a world where the scarcity of non-augmentable resources exerts a major influence on the productive system, v. Neumann's model ceases to be so interesting. But even ignoring the complications due to "land", there is still danger of another kind of complication. The rate of expansion of the system is determined, as we have

[1] And even in the case of final-consumers' goods, the prices (though not of course the relative intensities of production) are *largely* to be explained by the technical conditions of production, rather than "marginal utility". (The exceptions being joint products, or commodities with largely increasing or decreasing cost.)

seen, by the goods whose supply can be expanded least rapidly. These may well be those goods which are created largely out of themselves, (*i.e.* in whose production processes input and output mainly consist of the same commodities), as, for example, whales or mathematical wranglers. The point of these examples is that the commodities with the lowest rate of expansion may be trivial goods. Yet, if it is impossible for the expansion of these goods to keep pace with the rest of commodities, it is they who, on v. Neumann's model, will rule the roost and determine the rate of expansion of the whole system !

The reason for this unnatural result is that there is no room in the model for processes which do *not* involve whales and wranglers ! It is expressly assumed that every good is involved (either as input or as output) in every process. Hence it is not possible in the model to reduce below a certain proportion the part played in the economy by such goods as whales and wranglers, and eventually the expansion of the system must be slowed down to their own pace. v. Neumann states that his assumption that every good enters every process does not really matter because they may be supposed to do so in very small quantities ; nevertheless the implications of this assumption need bearing in mind.

(7) It should be noted that although in the model the equilibrium rate of interest is uniquely determined, the system of prices and outputs is not *uniquely* determined : there may be any number of possible equilibrium positions. But each must satisfy the rules set out in section 2 above.

The ease with which these rules could be established once the existence of an equilibrium position was known, was due to the choice of assumptions which enabled constant prices and stable relative outputs to exist together under competition. The whole process of mathematics would become greatly complicated if increasing returns or monopoly were introduced.

It will be noted, of course, that the " equilibrium " of v. Neumann's model is a very long run equilibrium ; it may take many decades or even centuries for the system to settle down to the rate of expansion of the least expandable goods ; and over this period, the basic assumption of known technical possibilities remaining unchanged loses all reality. An important question, therefore, is how far v. Neumann's results are applicable to systems which are only in an approach to equilibrium ; and any rigorous examination of the properties of such a system would be bound to be most complicated.

Yet it is in the problems of the approach to equilibrium that economists are most interested. How can a country acquire the equipment needed to achieve the best system of production ? What prices should be used in its accounting system by a planning authority seeking to make the best use of its resources ? Here is a fruitful field for extending the powerful methods developed in Prof. v. Neumann's paper.

Oxford. D. G. CHAMPERNOWNE.

3 On a Two-Sector Model of Economic Growth[1]

H. UZAWA

1. In the present paper we are interested in the growth process in a two-sector model of capital accumulation and show that balanced growth equilibria are globally stable under the neoclassical hypotheses.

The neoclassical model of economic growth, as it has been developed by Solow [5] and Swan [6], is formulated in terms of the aggregate production function. The aggregate production function specifies the relationship between output and factors of production, and output is assumed to be composed of homogeneous quantities identical with capital, or at least price ratios between output and capital are assumed constant. The economy we are concerned with in this paper, on the other hand, consists of two types of goods, investment-goods and consumption-goods, to be produced by two factors of production, capital and labor; prices of investment-goods and consumption-goods are determined so as to satisfy the demand requirements.[2] It will be assumed that capital depreciates at a fixed rate, the rate of growth in labor is constant and exogenously determined, capitalists' income is solely spent on investment-goods, that of laborers on consumption-goods, and production is subject to the neoclassical conditions. Under such hypotheses, then, it will be shown that the state of steady growth exists and the growth process, starting at an arbitrary capital and labor composition, approaches some steady growth. If the consumption-goods sector is always more capital-intensive than the investment-goods sector, then the steady growth is uniquely determined and it is stable in the small as well as in the large.

2. We consider an economic system consisting of investment-goods and consumption-goods sectors, labelled 1 and 2, respectively. It is assumed that in both sectors production is subject to constant returns to scale, marginal rates of substitution are positive and diminishing, and there exist neither joint products nor external (dis-)economies.

The production processes in each sector are summarized by specifying each sector's production function; let $F_1(K_1,L_1)$ be the production function for the investment-goods sector, and $F_2(K_2,L_2)$ for the consumption-goods sector. $F_1(K_1,L_1)$ represents the quantity of the investment-goods, Y_1, produced by employing capital and labor by the quantities K_1 and L_1; and similarly for the consumption-goods sector's production function, $F_2(K_2,L_2)$.

In terms of production functions, the assumptions indicated above may be formulated as:

(1) $F_i(\lambda K_i, \lambda L_i) = \lambda F_i(K_i, L_i)$, $F_i(K_i, L_i) > 0$, for all K_i, $L_i > 0$, and $\lambda > 0$;

[1] This work was in part supported by the Office of Naval Research under Task NR-047-004. I owe much to Professor Robert M. Solow and the referees for their valuable comments and suggestions.

[2] Shinkai [4] has investigated the structure of growth equilibria in a two-sector model of growth in which technical coefficients are all constant. Our two-sector model presented here is a neoclassical version of Shinkai's model.

(2) $F_i(K_i, L_i)$ is twice continuously differentiable;

(3) $\partial F_i/\partial K_i > 0,\ \partial F_i/\partial L_i > 0,\ \partial^2 F_i/\partial K_i^2 < 0,\ \partial^2 F_i/\partial L_i^2 < 0$ for all $K_i, L_i > 0$.

In view of the constant-returns-to-scale hypothesis (1), the output-labor ratio y_i is a function of the capital-labor ratio k_i:

(4) $y_i = f_i(k_i)$,

where

$$y_i = Y_i/L_i,\ k_i = K_i/L_i,\ f_i(k_i) = F_i(k_i, 1),\quad i = 1, 2.$$

The assumptions (2-3) are then equivalent to:

(5) $f_i(k_i)$ is twice continuously differentiable;

(6) $f_i(k_i) > 0,\ f_i'(k_i) > 0,\ f_i''(k_i) < 0$, for all $k_i > 0$.

3. Let K and L be the aggregate quantities of capital and labor at time t; these quantities of the two factors of production are allocated competitively among the two sectors, and prices of goods are determined so as to satisfy the demand conditions. In what follows, we assume that both capital and labor are always fully employed and both goods are produced in positive quantities.

Let K_i and L_i be the quantities of capital and labor allocated to the i-th sector, P_1 and P_2 the price of investment-goods and of consumption goods, and r and w the returns to capital and the wage rate, respectively. Then we have,

(7) $Y_i = F_i(K_i, L_i)$,

(8) $P_i \dfrac{\partial F_i}{\partial K_i} = r,\quad P_i \dfrac{\partial F_i}{\partial L_i} = w,\quad i = 1, 2.$

(9) $K_1 + K_2 = K,\quad L_1 + L_2 = L,$

(10) $P_1 Y_1 = rK,\qquad P_2 Y_2 = wL.$

The condition (8) is familiar marginal productivity conditions, and (10) formulates the hypothesis that labor does not save and capital does not consume.

Let

$$k = K/L$$
$$k_i = K_i/L_i,\ y_i = Y_i/L_i,\quad \rho_i = L_i/L,\quad i = 1, 2.$$
$$\omega = w/r.$$

Then conditions (7-10) may be reduced to:

(11) $y_i = f_i(k_i),\quad i = 1, 2.$

$$(12)\qquad \omega = \frac{f_i(k_i)}{f_i'(k_i)} - k_i, \quad i = 1, 2.$$

$$(13)\qquad \rho_1 k_1 + \rho_2 k_2 = k,$$

$$(14)\qquad \rho_1 + \rho_2 = 1,$$

$$(15)\qquad \rho_1 f_1(k_1) = f_1'(k_1)k.$$

Differentiating (12) with respect to k_i, we have:

$$(16)\qquad \frac{d\omega}{dk_i} = \frac{-f(k_i)\, f_i''(k_i)}{[f_i'(k_i)]^2}$$

which is always positive in view of (6). Hence: *For any wage-rentals ratio* ω, *the optimum capital-labor ratio* k_i *in each sector is uniquely determined by the relation* (12), *provided*:

$$(17)\qquad \underline{\omega}_i = \lim_{k_i \to 0} \left[\frac{f_i(k_i)}{f_i'(k_i)} - k_i\right] < \omega\ \overline{\omega}_i = \lim_{k_i \to \infty} \left[\frac{f_i(k_i)}{f_i'(k_i)} - k_i\right]$$

The optimum capital-labor ratio k_i corresponding to the wage-rentals ratio ω, uniquely determined by (12), will then be denoted by $k_i = k_i(\omega)$, $i = 1, 2$. The determination of the optimum capital-labor ratio $k_i(\omega)$ may be illustrated by the diagram:

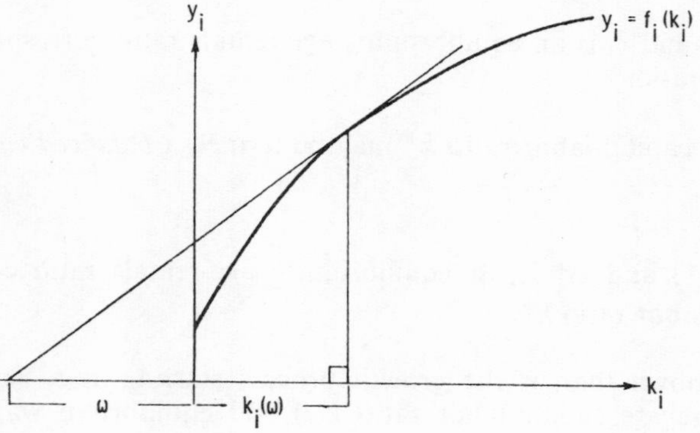

We have from (16) that:

$$(18)\qquad \frac{dk_i}{d\omega} = \frac{[f_i'(k_i)]^2}{-f_i(k_i)f_i''(k_i)} > 0,$$

with $k_i = k_i(\omega)$, $i = 1, 2$.

In view of (12), the labor allocation ρ_1 to the investment-goods sector, determined by (15), may be written as:

$$(19)\qquad \rho_1 = \frac{k}{\omega + k_1(\omega)}$$

Substituting (14) and (19) into (13) and rearranging, we have

$$k = \frac{\omega+k_1(\omega)}{\omega+k_2(\omega)}\, k_2(\omega) \tag{20}$$

The equilibrium wage-rentals ratio ω is obtained by solving the equation (20).

4. Let the rate of growth in labor be a positive constant, say λ, and μ be the instantaneous rate of depreciation in capital. Then the growth process in the two-sector model we have described is formulated by the following differential equations:

$$\frac{\dot{K}}{K} = \frac{r}{P_1} - \mu, \tag{21}$$

and

$$\frac{\dot{L}}{L} = \lambda, \tag{22}$$

where r is the equilibrium return to capital and P_1 the equilibrium price of the investment-goods, both at time t.

The equations (21) and (22), together with the equilibrium condition (8), imply that:

$$\frac{\dot{k}}{k} = f_1'(k_1) - \lambda - \mu, \tag{23}$$

where $k_1 = k_1(\omega)$ and ω is an equilibrium wage-rentals ratio corresponding to the aggregate capital-labor ratio.

An aggregate capital-labor ratio k^* may be termed a *balanced capital-labor ratio* if

$$f_1'(k_1^*) = \lambda + \mu, \tag{24}$$

where $k_1^* = k_1(\omega^*)$ and ω^* is an equilibrium wage-rentals ratio corresponding to the aggregate capital-labor ratio k^*.

It is easily shown that at the growth process starting at a balanced capital-labor ratio k^*, the aggregate capital-labor ratio $k(t)$ and equilibrium wage-rentals ratio ω(t) both remain constant.

5. Suppose that the consumption-goods sector is always more capital-intensive than the investment-goods sector;[1] namely,

$$k_1(\omega) < k_2(\omega), \text{ for all } \omega \text{ such that } \max[\underline{\omega}_1, \underline{\omega}_2] < \omega < \min[\bar{\omega}_1, \bar{\omega}_2]. \tag{25}$$

Let

$$\Psi(\omega) = \frac{\omega + k_1(\omega)}{\omega + k_2(\omega)}\, k_2(\omega).$$

[1] The concept of relative factor intensities was introduced by Samuelson in the context of international trade theory; see, e.g., [3], p.9.

Differentiating $\log \Psi(\omega)$ with respect to ω, we have

$$\frac{1}{\Psi(\omega)} \frac{d\Psi}{d\omega} = \frac{1 + \frac{dk_1}{d\omega}}{\omega + k_1(\omega)} - \frac{1 + \frac{dk_2}{d\omega}}{\omega + k_2(\omega)} + \frac{\frac{dk_2}{d\omega}}{k_2(\omega)}$$

$$= \left[\frac{1}{\omega + k_1(\omega)} - \frac{1}{\omega + k_2(\omega)}\right] + \frac{\frac{dk_1}{d\omega}}{\omega + k_1(\omega)}$$

$$+ \frac{dk_2}{d\omega}\left[\frac{1}{k_2(\omega)} - \frac{1}{\omega + k_2(\omega)}\right],$$

which, by (18) and (25), is always *positive*.

Therefore, we have

(26) $$\frac{d\Psi}{d\omega} > 0, \text{ for all } \omega \text{ satisfying } \max [\underline{\omega}_1, \underline{\omega}_2] < \omega < \min [\bar{\omega}_1, \bar{\omega}_2].$$

The equation (20) has a positive solution ω if and only if:

(27) $$\Psi(0) < k < \Psi(\infty),$$

and the solution ω is uniquely determined by k. The equilibrium factor-price ratio ω may be denoted by $\omega = \omega(k)$.

From (20) and (26), we have

(28) $$\frac{d\omega}{dk} > 0 \text{ for all } k \text{ satisfying (27).}$$

In view of conditions (6), (18), and (28), the function

$$f_1'[k_1(\omega(k))]$$

is a strictly decreasing function of the aggregate capital-labor ratio k.

Hence, the balanced capital-labor ratio k^* always exists and is uniquely determined if the following condition is satisfied :

(29) $$\lim_{k_1 \to 0} f_1'(k_1) > \lambda + \mu > \lim_{k_1 \to \infty} f_1'(k_1).$$

It is easily shown that, for the growth process starting at an arbitrary initial capital-labor composition, the capital-labor ratio $k(t)$ approaches the balanced capital-labor ratio k^*.[1]

The results in this section may be summarized as:

Existence Theorem: Let the consumption-goods sector be more capital-intensive than the investment-goods sector for all relevant factor-price ratios ω. *Then for any given aggregate capital-labor ratio* k, *the equilibrium factor-price ratio* $\omega = \omega(k)$, *the optimum capital-labor ratios* $k_1 = k_1(\omega)$ *and* $k_2 = k_2(\omega)$ *in both sectors, and the equilibrium outputs per head for investment-goods and consumption-goods,* $y_1 = y_1(k)$ *and* $y_2 = y_2(k)$, *are all uniquely determined, provided the aggregate capital-labor ratio* k *satisfies the relation* (29).

Stability Theorem: Let λ *and* μ *be respectively the growth rate in labor and the instantaneous depreciation in capital; and the balanced capital-labor ratio* k^* *exist. Then, for the growth process starting at an arbitrary initial position, the capital-labor ratio* $k(t)$ *approaches the balanced capital-labor ratio* k^* *as* t *tend to infinity.*

6. The uniqueness of the balanced capital-labor ratio and its stability crucially hinge on the hypothesis that the consumption-goods sector be more capital-intensive than the investment-goods sector. In this section, we shall construct an example of the two-sector growth model in which the capital-intensity hypothesis above is not satisfied and there is an unstable balanced capital-labor ratio.

Let the production functions be:

$$y_1 = f_1(k_1) = \frac{1}{1000}\,(k_1^{-3} + 7^{-4})^{\frac{1}{3}},\ y_2 = f_2(k_2) = (k_1^{-3} + 1)^{\frac{1}{3}}.$$

The optimum capital-labor ratios are then given by:

$$k_1 = k_1(\omega) = 7\omega^{\frac{1}{4}},\ k_2 = k_2(\omega) = \omega^{\frac{1}{4}};$$

hence,

$$k_1(\omega) > k_2(\omega), \text{ for all } \omega > 0.$$

For aggregate capital-labor ratio k the equilibrium factor-price ratio ω is determined by:

$$k = \frac{\omega + 7\omega^{\frac{1}{4}}}{\omega + \omega^{\frac{1}{4}}}\,\omega^{\frac{1}{4}};$$

hence,

$$\frac{1}{k}\frac{d\omega}{dk} = \frac{1 + \frac{7}{4}\omega^{-\frac{3}{4}}}{\omega + 7\omega^{\frac{1}{4}}} - \frac{1 + \frac{7}{4}\omega^{-\frac{3}{4}}}{\omega + \omega^{\frac{1}{4}}} + \frac{\omega}{\frac{1}{4}}.$$

Let us consider the case in which the sum $\lambda + \mu$ of the rate of growth in labor and the rate of depreciation is

$$\frac{7\sqrt[3]{7}}{1600} \doteq .8\%.$$

[1] See, e.g. Arrow and Hurwicz [2], p. 540.

Then $k^* = 4$ is a balanced capital-labor ratio and $\omega^* = 1$ is the corresponding wage-rentals ratio.

But

$$\left(\frac{1}{k}\ \frac{dk}{d\omega}\right)_{\omega=1} = -\tfrac{1}{32} < 0;$$

hence, the balanced capital-labor ratio $k^* = 4$ is not stable.

7.[1] Let us now consider the general case in which the capital-intensity hypothesis is not necessarily satisfied. In this case, the balanced capital-labor ratio may be no longer uniquely determined for given rates of labor growth and of depreciation; hence, there may exist unstable balanced capital-labor ratios, as was discussed in the previous section.

If, however, the conditions (29) and

(30) $f_1(0) = 0,\ f_2(0) = 0,$

are satisfied, then it is possible to show that the growth process represented by (21) and (22) is *globally stable* in the sense introduced by Arrow, Block and Hurwicz ([2], p. 85); namely, given any initial condition, the aggregate capital-labor ratio $k(t)$ converges to some balanced capital-labor ratio.

To see the global stability of the process (23), it suffices to show that[2]

(31) $\lim\limits_{k\to\infty} [f_1'(k_1) - \lambda - \mu] < 0,$

(32) $\lim\limits_{k\to 0} [f_1'(k_1) - \lambda - \mu] < 0.$

The relation (31) may be seen from the assumption (29) and the inequality:

$$k < \omega + k_1$$

which is derived from (20). On the other hand, to see the relation (32), let k tend to zero. Then the corresponding wage-rentals ratio ω converges to zero also; otherwise, the relation (20) would imply

$$0 = \frac{\bar{\omega} + k_1(\bar{\omega})}{\bar{\omega} + k_2(\bar{\omega})}\ k_2(\bar{\omega})$$

for some positive wage-rentals ratio $\bar{\omega}$, contradicting the assumption (30). Hence the corresponding capital-labor ratio $k_1 = k_1(\omega)$ converges to zero, again in view of (30). The relation (32) is then implied by the condition (29).

[1] This section has been written after I have read Professor Solow's note which suggests that the stability property of the growth equilibrium as discussed in the present paper may not depend on the capital-intensity hypothesis.

[2] See, e.g., Arrow and Hurwicz [2], p. 540.

We may summarize our results as:

Let the growth rate in labor λ and the depreciation rate in capital μ satisfy the conditions (29) *and* (30). *Then there exists at least one balanced capital-labor ratio, and, for the growth process starting an arbitrary initial capital-labor composition, the aggregate capital-labor ratio $k(t)$ converges to some balanced capital-labor ratio.*

Stanford. HIROFUMI UZAWA.

REFERENCES

[1] Arrow, K. J., H. D. Block, and L. Hurwicz. " On the Stability of the Competitive Equilibrium, II ", *Econometrica*, Vol. 27 (1959), pp. 82-109.

[2] Arrow, K. J., and L. Hurwicz. " On the Stability of the Competitive Equilibrium, I ", *Econometrica*, Vol. 27 (1958), pp. 522-552.

[3] Samuelson, P. A. " Prices of Factors and Goods in General Equilibrium," *Review of Economic Studies*, Vol. 21 (1953-54), pp. 1-20.

[4] Shinkai, Y. " On the Equilibrium Growth of Capital and Labor," *International Economic Review*, Vol. 1 (1960), pp. 107-111.

[5] Solow, R. M. " A Contribution to the Theory of Economic Growth," *Quarterly Journal of Economics*, Vol. 70 (1956), pp. 65-94.

[6] Swan, T. W. " Economic Growth and Capital Accumulation," *Economic Record*, Vol. 32 (1956), pp. 334-361.

4 Note on Uzawa's Two-Sector Model of Economic Growth

R. M. SOLOW

1. This Note has two objectives: one expository and one analytical. I am afraid that many readers will be put off by the apparent mathematical difficulty of Uzawa's paper. I say " apparent " advisedly, because the paper is in part very easy; it requires only a little arithmetic and the bare elements of the calculus of functions of one variable. Any economist who cannot read it ought at least to insist that his students do so. My first objective is to describe in plain English how the model works, because I think it is an interesting extension of earlier work in this branch of macro-economics.

2. My second objective is to try to elucidate the role of the crucial capital-intensity condition in Uzawa's model. He finds that his model economy is always stable (in the sense that full employment requires an approach to a state of balanced expansion) if the consumption-goods sector is more capital-intensive than the investment-goods sector. It seems paradoxical to me that such an important characteristic of the equilibrium path should depend on such a casual property of the technology. And since this stability property is the one respect in which Uzawa's results seem qualitatively different from those of my 1956 paper on a one-sector model, I am anxious to track down the source of the difference. Fortunately, I think plain English suffices for this too.

3. Uzawa's model works like this. There are two productive inputs: the services of a single grade of labor and of a single type of capital good depreciating at a rate μ. These two inputs are smoothly substitutable for each other in the production of consumer goods and in the separate industry which produces new machines; and labor and machines are freely transferable from one sector to the other. At any moment of time, an exogenously determined supply of labor is inelastically offered for employment. At any moment of time, the irrevocably existing stock of machines is inelastically offered for employment. What happens? The auctioneer calls off a value of the wage/rental ratio w/r. Each separate industry has a corresponding optimal machine/labor ratio: K_1/L_1 for the I-sector, K_2/L_2 for the C-sector. Since all the machines and all the labor must find employment,

and since $\dfrac{K}{L} = \dfrac{K_1 + K_2}{L_1 + L_2} = \dfrac{L_1}{L_1 + L_2}\left(\dfrac{K_1}{L_1}\right) + \dfrac{L_2}{L_1 + L_2}\left(\dfrac{K_2}{L_2}\right) = \dfrac{L_1}{L_1 + L_2}\left(\dfrac{K_1}{L_1}\right)$

$+\left(1 - \dfrac{L_1}{L_1 + L_2}\right)\dfrac{K_2}{L_2}$, the given value of w/r determines the division of the labor force

between the two sectors and thus also the division of machines and the two outputs. Both industries make optimal adjustments and these yield unit costs; competition then sets the price ratio P_2/P_1 for the two commodities equal to the ratio of unit costs. Thus any w/r determines an equilibrium P_2/P_1.

Uzawa makes the new-old assumption that wages are all spent on consumer goods and rentals (= profits) all spent on machines. Now given the auctioneer's w/r, given history's K/L, and given the just-deduced outputs Y_1 and Y_2, equilibrium on the commodity market also requires that $\frac{wL}{rK} = \frac{P_2Y_2}{P_1Y_1}$. This provides another independent relation between w/r and P_2/P_1. The auctioneer finds the unique wage/rental ratio for which both equilibrium conditions are satisfied. This miniature Walrasian general equilibrium fixes, among other things, the output of machines and hence the stock available in the next period. Since the labor supply is exogenous, the process can repeat itself.

4. The stability proposition says that if this process repeats itself (with the labor supply growing geometrically at rate λ), it will eventually approach a situation in which $k = \frac{K}{L}$ is constant, so that the stock of machines is also growing at rate λ, and indeed the whole economy changes only in scale. Now the basic law of motion of the system is easily deduced. By assumption $\frac{\triangle L}{L} = \lambda$. Since all rentals are spent on gross investment, $\triangle K = rK/P_1 - \mu K$. From competition r/P_1, the product-rental of machines in the machine sector, is equal to the marginal product of machines in the machine sector (Uzawa's $f_1'(k_1)$, since under constant returns to scale it depends only on $k_1 = K_1/L_1$). Combining these assertions, we find $\triangle k/k = \triangle K/K - \triangle L/L = f_1'(k_1) - \lambda - \mu$, Uzawa's equation (41). The stability proposition asserts that both sides of this equation tend to zero and to prove it we must prove that when k gets very high, $\triangle k/k$ becomes negative and when k gets very low, $\triangle k/k$ becomes positive.

Now the marginal product $f_1'(k_1)$ is of course a *decreasing* function of k_1. So what we must show is that k and k_1 always move in the same direction (for then when k rises, k_1 also rises, and $f_1'(k_1)$ decreases and ultimately becomes equal to or less than $\lambda + \mu$). There would seem to be a strong presumption that k and k_1 do always move in the same direction: not only does k_1 increase when and only when w/r increases, but so does k_2. That is, the machine-labor ratio rises in each industry whenever the wage/rental ratio rises. There is one way and only one way in which the association between k and k_1 can be broken and that is if, while the separate machine/labor ratios should be rising, the less machine-intensive industry should gain enough at the expense of the more machine-intensive one to permit a fall in the overall machine/labor ratio.

5. Enter the assumption that the C-sector is more machine-intensive than the I-sector. Suppose that at any w/r ratio, $K_2/L_2 > K_1/L_1$; then also $rK_2/wL_2 > rK_1/wL_1$. Under constant returns to scale and competition, it is rigorously provable (and everyone should know) that when w/r increases, the price ratio P_2/P_1 will increase or decrease according as the relative share of wages in Sector 2 is greater or smaller than in Sector 1. Thus in Uzawa's model, P_2/P_1 falls when w/r rises and *vice-versa*. Now from the assumption that wages are consumed and profits saved, we have $\frac{wL}{rK} = \frac{P_2Y_2}{P_1Y_1}$ and so $\frac{K}{L} = \frac{w}{r}\frac{P_1}{P_2}\frac{Y_1}{Y_2}$. Suppose w/r rises; so does P_1/P_2. Then K/L must rise unless Y_1/Y_2 falls. But if Y_1/Y_2 falls, there is a shift of output in favor of consumption goods, the *more* machine-intensive commodity. But from my earlier argument, with the machine/labor ratio increasing in both sectors and the machine-intensive sector gaining at the expense of the other, we know that K/L *must* rise. There is no way out: k_1 and k must move together and the stability proposition holds.

6. Note that the crucial condition about the *C*-sector being more machine-intensive is a *sufficient* condition for stability in this model, not a necessary one. Here is an example in which that condition is violated but stability occurs. Suppose both sectors have Cobb-Douglas production functions with elasticities of α_1 and $1-\alpha_1$ for K_1 and L_1, and α_2 and $1-\alpha_2$ for K_2 and L_2. Then $rK = \alpha_1 P_1 Y_1 + \alpha_2 P_2 Y_2$. But also $rK = P_1 Y_1$. Then $P_1 Y_1 = \dfrac{\alpha_2}{1-\alpha_1} P_2 Y_2$ and $\dfrac{P_1 Y_1}{P_2 Y_2} = \dfrac{\alpha_2}{1-\alpha_1}$. But $\dfrac{P_1 Y_1}{P_2 Y_2} = \dfrac{rK}{wL}$. So $\dfrac{rK}{wL} = \dfrac{\alpha_2}{1-\alpha_1}$. The right-hand side is a constant. Hence whenever r/w falls (so k_1 rises), K/L must rise. Once again k_1 and k move together and stability occurs, regardless of which sector is more machine-intensive (whether α_1 is bigger or smaller than α_2).

7. It is obvious from this mode of argument that the model works the way it does only because wages are spent entirely on consumption and profits on machines. This is an extraordinarily powerful assumption, more powerful than many of its users realize. Here is a cute example of just how powerful it is: Constant returns to scale, competition, machines produced by labor alone, consumables produced by machines alone, wages consumed, profits saved. Exercise: prove that the relative share of wages in national income is exactly 1/2!

8. In my 1956 paper (and in Swan's) this assumption is not made. We took saving as a fraction of aggregate income (at one point I permitted the savings ratio to depend on the rate of return on capital). If this assumption is carried into Uzawa's two-sector model, stability is no longer assured and the results become qualitatively more like the one-sector model.

Suppose that workers save a fraction S_w of their income and capitalists a fraction S_p of theirs. Then $P_1 Y_1 = S_w wL + S_p rK$ and $\triangle K = Y_1 - \mu K = S_w L \dfrac{w}{P_1} + S_p K \dfrac{r.}{P_1} - \mu K$. Using marginal productivity relations, $r/P_1 = f_1'(k_1)$ and $w/P_1 = f_1(k_1) - k_1 f_1'(k_1)$, we find $\dfrac{\triangle K}{K} = \dfrac{S_w}{k}(f_1 - k_1 f_1') + S_p f_1' - \mu$ and regrouping:

$$\frac{\triangle k}{k} = \frac{S_w}{k} f_1(k_1) + \left(S_p - S_w \frac{k_1}{k}\right) f_1'(k_1) - \lambda - \mu.$$

If $S_w = 0$, $S_p = 1$, this reduces to Uzawa's (41). If $S_w = S_p = S$, this reduces to

$$\triangle k = Sf_1(k_1) - (\lambda + \mu)k + S(k - k_1) f_1'(k_1).$$

This is more complicated than Uzawa's (41) and also than my analogous 1956 equation. If $k = k_1$ it reduces to something almost exactly like my 1956 equation. (Now that $P_1 Y_1 = S(wL + rK)$, it follows that $P_1 Y_1/P_2 Y_2 = S/1-S$ and from this we can already deduce that k and k_1 go up and down together. Because an increase in w/r will increase k_1 and k_2 and also increase P_1/P_2 if Sector 1 is more labor-intensive, hence decrease Y_1/Y_2, hence increase relatively the output of the machine-intensive sector.

It would not be easy to give a complete analysis of equilibrium paths for this model. But it seems highly likely from the first two terms on the right-hand side that it can give rise to behavior like that of the one-sector model; there may be equilibrium paths in which K/L increases without limit, for instance. It is also interesting to see the consequences if it should happen that the *C*-sector is more machine-intensive than the *I*-sector. Then $k - k_1$ would be positive. As k gets larger (along with k_1), $f_1'(k_1)$ would decrease. Whether the third term decreases or increases (thus contributing to stability or the reverse) would depend on whether $k - k_1$ increases faster or slower than $f_1'(k_1)$ and this in turn would depend on the shape of the two production functions.

Cambridge, Mass. ROBERT M. SOLOW.

Comment by R. M. SOLOW

Uzawa's article started a small literature on the two-sector model (most of it in the *Review*). It turned out that my instinct was right: the capital-intensity condition could be dispensed with and other, more plausible, sufficient conditions could be found for convergence of full-employment paths. For instance, with Uzawa's special assumption about saving it is enough if the sum of the elasticities of substitution in the two industries is not less than one. With arbitrary saving rates from wages and profits, it is enough if the elasticity of substitution in the consumer-goods industry is not less than one, or if the "overall elasticity of substitution" is not less than one (in the sense that a higher wage-rental ratio corresponds to a lower or unchanged share of wages). This last condition can be argued even more easily than the one in the Note: a higher w/r corresponds to a higher capital-labor ratio in each industry; it also corresponds to a lower value of wL/rK, therefore to a higher K/L; therefore k_1 and k move together. Any of these substitution conditions covers the Cobb-Douglas case in the Note.

It strikes me as lucky that not a lot hangs on the capital-intensity condition. Some Austrian residue in our minds makes it sound natural that the capital-goods industry should be labor-intensive. But if you think how much economic activity actually goes into intermediate goods (like metals, plastics, fuel, power) that then go indiscriminately into capital goods and consumer goods, it seems unlikely that you can count on any systematic difference in factor proportions. I suppose this is an argument in favor of the one-sector model.

I have received a certain amount of credit for pointing out that the two-sector model is really a tiny general-equilibrium system. This is one of the easier ways to get credit. But it suggests something: since we know that without *some* restrictive assumptions ordinary general-equilibrium systems need not have unique solutions and need not be stable, it is hardly surprising that something similar is true about the two-sector model (though convergence in one case is not exactly the same thing, nor the result of the same kind of process, as in the other).

5 On the Stability of Growth Equilibria in Two-Sector Models

K. INADA

1. In an ingenious paper [3], Uzawa has shown the global stability of the balanced growth equilibria in two-sector models of economic growth. Compared to the complex features of these models, the results are surprisingly simple and clear, and I believe that this is one of the most important contributions to the economic growth theories, and the structures of the models or equivalently the relationship between the assumptions and results in such an important work will be worth while to be studied in more detail. To the convenience for the following discussions, the results obtained by Uzawa shall be summarized here.

First, the savings-ratio of the gross national products is assumed to be constant, and the existence of some balanced growth equilibria and the global stability of the system are shown.[1] Moreover, *under the condition that the consumption-goods sector is always more capital intensive than the investment-goods sector*, the uniqueness of the balanced growth equilibrium is shown. We call this condition *the capital-intensity condition*.

Second, the rate of interest and its determination mechanism are introduced, and the savings-ratio is assumed to be dependent on *the rate of interest* and *the gross national products*. The existence of some balanced growth equilibria and the global stability are shown *under the capital-intensity condition*. The second model is an extended version of the simple model which is named by Uzawa a neoclassical economic growth model.

From these results, we see that the global stability is obtained *without the controversial capital-intensity condition* in the model of the *constant* savings-ratio, but *not* in the model of the *variable* savings-ratio. In the latter model, a new variable—the rate of interest and its determination mechanism are introduced into the model, and the savings-ratio is made dependent on the rate of interest and the gross national products. One or some of these complicated features require the compensating *strong sacrifice* such as the *capital-intensity condition* to get the same results as the simpler case.

It, therefore, may be interesting to study which newly introduced feature is responsible to require the compensating capital-intensity condition. In fact, such a study will clarify the structures of Uzawa models. The first purpose of this paper is to show that if the savings-ratio is made dependent on the gross national products but *not on the rate of interest*, the global stability is shown *without* the capital-intensity condition, and moreover, the uniqueness of the balanced growth equilibrium is shown under the capital-intensity condition. In Uzawa's extended model, the savings-ratio may be affected by the rate of interest. From our result, we see that this feature is responsible to require some condition such as the capital-intensity condition. But, the dependency of the savings-ratio on the rate of interest is not quite free in Uzawa's case. That is, he excludes the possibility that the savings-ratio is *negatively* affected by the rate of interest. This is, I believe, another controversial assumption. If so, we may go one step further to assume that the savings-ratio is *never* affected by the rate of interest. Then, we can dispense with the capital-intensity condition which is condemned by Solow [2] as a *casual* property of technology.

[1] Throughout this paper, we only concern with the non-trivial balanced growth equilibrium where the capital-labor ratio always remains at a certain *positive* level.

Only some empirical studies will be able to judge whether it is desirable or not to keep the restricted dependency of the savings-ratio on the rate of interest at the cost of the capital-intensity condition.

It is easily seen that the above-mentioned model is a generalization of Uzawa's constant savings-ratio model in one direction. For, the savings-ratio is made dependent on the gross national products. Now, we shall consider another direction of generalization.

Let's examine the economic implications of the constant savings-ratio. In this case, the income is expended on two types of commodities keeping the ratio of money term expenditure between them always constant. This type of savings-consumption pattern is derived when the social preference field is expressed by the utility index of the Cobb-Douglas type.

Let the social utility index be

$$u(y_C, y_I) \equiv A y_C^{1-s} y_I^s.$$

Here, y_C and y_I express the per capita amounts of the consumption goods and the investment goods, respectively.

Consider the following maximizing problem.

Maximize $\quad A y_C^{1-s} y_I^s,$

subject to $\quad y_C + p y_I = y.$

Here, p is the price of the investment goods in terms of the consumption goods. y is the per capita gross income. Employing the Lagrangean multiplier method,

$$(1-s) A y_C^{-s} y_I^s = \lambda,$$

$$s A y_C^{1-s} y_I^{s-1} = \lambda p.$$

Here, λ is the Lagrangean multiplier. From these,

(1.1) $$y_C / y_I = \frac{1-s}{s} p \equiv \alpha p,$$

or equivalently

(1.2) $$p y_I = s y.$$

This is Uzawa's saving function. We see from (1.1) that the elasticity of substitution between two commodities is one. Now, the pattern of saving-consumption expressed by (1.1) may be somewhat extreme.

As a first step to the more general case, we shall consider the case where the elasticity of substitution is a constant which may or may not be one. Such a pattern of saving-consumption is expressed by

$$y_C / y_I = \alpha p^\sigma.$$

Here, we assume that $0 \leqq \sigma \leqq 1$. It is easily seen that this relation is obtained when the social utility index is expressed by a function of the Constant Elasticity of Substitution [1]

$$u(y_C, y_I) = A(\delta y_C^{-\gamma} + (1-\delta) y_I^{-\gamma})^{-\frac{1}{\gamma}}.$$

Here, $$\gamma \equiv \frac{1-\sigma}{\sigma}.$$

[1] The production function of Constant Elasticity of Substitution includes the Cobb-Douglas and the Constant-Coefficient production function as special cases. The properties of the C. E. S. production function are extensively studied in [1].

We shall show the global stability of the system *without* the capital-intensity condition and the uniqueness of the balanced growth equilibrium *with* the capital-intensity condition. These are the results obtained by Uzawa for his constant savings-ratio model.

2. To avoid the duplication with Uzawa's arguments, we shall use his notation and results as far as possible.

Y: Gross national products in terms of the consumption goods
Y_I: Amount of the investment goods
Y_C: Amount of the consumption goods
K_I: Amount of capital allocated to the I-sector production
K_C: Amount of capital allocated to the C-sector production
K: Amount of capital
L_I: Amount of labor allocated to the I-sector production
L_C: Amount of labor allocated to the C-sector production
L: Amount of labor
p: Price of the investment goods in terms of the consumption goods
w: Wage rate
r: Rental rate
ρ: Rate of interest
s: Savings-ratio
μ: Depreciation rate
λ: Growth rate of labor population
$F_I(K_I, L_I)$: Production function of I-sector
$F_C(K_C, L_C)$: Production function of C-sector
$\varphi(v;\ r, k, y_I)$: Prospective returns v years ahead to the investment goods newly produced.

Define new variables as follows.

$$y \equiv Y/L,\ y_i \equiv Y_i/L,\ k_i \equiv K_i/L_i,\ l_i = L_i/L,$$
$$k = K/L,\ \omega \equiv w/r,\ F_i(k_i, 1) \equiv f_i(k_i). \qquad (i = I, C)$$

The model, which we are going to study in this section, is expressed by the following relations.

(2.1) $$y = y_C + p y_I,$$

(2.2) $$y_I = f_I(k_I) l_I = f_I l_I, \qquad (f_I(k_I) \equiv f_I)$$

(2.3) $$y_C = f_C(k_C) l_C = f_C l_C, \quad (f_C(k_C) \equiv f_C)$$

(2.4) $$k_I l_I + k_C l_C = k,$$

(2.5) $$l_I + l_C = 1,$$

(2.6) $$\omega = \frac{f_I}{f_I'} - k_I = \frac{f_C}{f_C'} - k_C,$$

(2.7) $$p = \frac{f_C'}{f_I'},$$

(2.8) $$p y_I = s y,$$

(2.9) $$s = g(y),$$

(2.10) $$\dot{k}/k = y_I/k - \lambda - \dot{\mu},$$

(2.11) $$p = \int_0^\infty \varphi(v;\ r, k, y_I)e^{-(\mu+\rho)v}dv.$$

The only one difference of this system from Uzawa's is the relation (2.9). If it is replaced by

$$s = g(\rho, y),$$

we get Uzawa's variable savings-ratio model.

System (2.1)—(2.9) expresses the miniature Walrasian general equilibrium system [1] for a given value of k. Relation (2.10) expresses the capital accumulation process and (2.11) the determination mechanism of the rate of interest. As is easily seen, system (2.1)—(2.10) does not depend on the rate of interest. Thus, the existence and the stability of the balanced growth equilibrium can be studied without paying any attention to relation (2.11). That is, the dependent relation between the rate of interest and other variables is one way.

First, suppose that s does not depend on y. System (2.1)—(2.8) has nine equations and eleven variables y, y_I, y_C, k_I, k_C, k, l_I, l_C, ω, s and p. Consider s and ω are independent and other variables, especially k_I, k_C, k and y are dependent. To show this explicitly, we write $k_I(\omega, s)$, $k_C(\omega, s)$, $k(\omega, s)$ and $y(\omega, s)$.

Now, Uzawa's relation (27) is

(2.12) $$\frac{1}{y}\frac{\partial y}{\partial \omega} = \frac{1}{\omega + k(\omega, s)} - \frac{1}{\omega + k_C(\omega, s)}\,.$$

From this,

$$\frac{\partial y}{\partial \omega} > 0 \text{ if } k_I(\omega, s) < k(\omega, s) < k_C(\omega, s),$$

$$\frac{\partial y}{\partial \omega} \leqq 0 \text{ if } k_I(\omega, s) \geqq k(\omega, s) \geqq k_C(\omega, s).$$

Next, consider that k and s are independent variables in system (2.1)—(2.8). Then, ω is dependent on k and s. Put this function $\omega(k, s)$. This is the inverse function of $k(\omega, s)$.

Uzawa's relation (30) is

(2.13) $$\frac{\partial \omega}{\partial s} = \left[\frac{1}{k_I + \omega} - \frac{1}{k_C + \omega}\right]$$
$$\div \left[\frac{s(k_I' + 1)}{(k_I + \omega)^2} + \frac{(1 - s)(k_C' + 1)}{(k_C + \omega)^2} - \frac{1}{(k + \omega)^2}\right].$$

Here, $k_i \equiv k_i(\omega, s)$ and $k_i' \equiv \dfrac{\partial k_i}{\partial \omega}$ $(i = I, C)$.

It should be noted that $k_I(\omega, s)$ and $k_C(\omega, s)$ are the functions defined above. Since ω is dependent on k and s, $k_I(\omega, s)$ and $k_C(\omega, s)$ are dependent, in turn, on k and s.

[1] This is named so by Solow [2].

The denominator of the right hand side of relation (2.13) is positive. This is shown by Uzawa as follows.

$$(2.14)\qquad \frac{s(k_I'+1)}{(k_I'+\omega)^2}+\frac{(1-s)(k_C'+1)}{(k_C+\omega)^2}-\frac{1}{(k+\omega)^2}$$

$$>\frac{s}{(k_I+\omega)^2}+\frac{1-s}{(k_C+\omega)^2}$$

$$-\frac{s^2}{(k_I+\omega)^2}-\frac{2s(1-s)}{(k_I+\omega)(k_C+\omega)}-\frac{(1-s)^2}{(k_C+\omega)^2}$$

$$=s(1-s)\left[\frac{1}{k+\omega}-\frac{1}{k_C+\omega}\right]^2\geqq 0.$$

For, as is shown by Uzawa,

$$(2.15)\qquad \frac{1}{k+\omega}=\frac{s}{k_I+\omega}+\frac{1-s}{k_C+\omega},$$

and

$$(2.16)\qquad k_i'=-\frac{(f_i')^2}{f_i f_i''}>0.\quad \text{(For it is assumed that } f_i''<0.)$$

From (2.13) and (2.14),

$$(2.17)\qquad 0<\frac{\partial\omega}{\partial s}<\left[\frac{1}{k_I+\omega}-\frac{1}{k_C+\omega}\right]\Big/s(1-s)\left[\frac{1}{k_I+\omega}-\frac{1}{k_C+\omega}\right]^2$$

$$=1/s(1-s)\left(\frac{1}{k_I+\omega}-\frac{1}{k_C+\omega}\right),\ \text{if } k_I<k_C.$$

$$(2.18)\qquad 0>\frac{\partial\omega}{\partial s}>\left[\frac{1}{k_I+\omega}-\frac{1}{k_C+\omega}\right]\Big/s(1-s)\left[\frac{1}{k_I+\omega}-\frac{1}{k_C+\omega}\right]^2$$

$$=1/s(1-s)\left(\frac{1}{k_I+\omega}-\frac{1}{k_C+\omega}\right),\ \text{if } k_I>k_C,$$

and

$$(2.19)\qquad 0=\frac{\partial\omega}{\partial s},\ \text{if } k_I=k_C.$$

Now, take into consideration relation (2.9). Then, only one independent variable in system (2.1)—(2.9) is k. s must be determined so as to satisfy the relation

$$s=g(y(\omega(s,k),k)).$$

We shall explain the reason why y can be written as $y(\omega(s,k),k)$. If s and k are fixed, ω is uniquely determined depending on these fixed values. It can be written as $\omega(k,s)$. When ω is determined, k_I and k_C are uniquely determined from (2.6), respectively. These can be written as $k_I(\omega(k,s))$ and $k_C(\omega(k,s))$, respectively. Then, from (2.7), p is uniquely determined and can be written as $p(\omega(k,s))$. From (2.4) and (2.5), l_I, and l_C are uniquely determined, respectively. These can be written as $l_I(\omega(k,s),k)$ and $l_C(\omega(k,s),k)$ respectively. From (2.2) and (2.3), y_I and y_C are uniquely determined and can be written as $y_I(\omega(k,s),k)$ and $y_C(\omega(k,s),k)$, respectively. From (2.1), y is uniquely determined, and can be written as $y(\omega(k,s),k)$.

Now, put

(2.20) $$\psi(s) = s - g(y(\omega(s, k), k)). \qquad (0 \leqq s \leqq 1)$$

Then,

(2.21) $$\frac{d\psi(s)}{ds} = 1 - \frac{dg}{dy}\frac{\partial y}{\partial \omega}\frac{\partial \omega}{\partial s}.$$

Uzawa assumed that

(2.22) $$0 \leqq \frac{dg}{dy} \leqq \frac{1-s}{y}.$$

Put $z = k + \omega,\ z_I = k_I + \omega$ and $z_C = k_C + \omega$.

First, consider the case where $\dfrac{dg}{dy}\dfrac{\partial y}{\partial \omega}\dfrac{\partial \omega}{\partial s} \neq 0$. In this case, $k_I \neq k_C$, and we get

(2.23) $$\frac{dg}{dy}\frac{\partial y}{\partial \omega}\frac{\partial \omega}{\partial s} < \frac{1-s}{y}\left(\frac{y}{z} - \frac{y}{z_C}\right)\Big/ s(1-s)\left(\frac{1}{z_I} - \frac{1}{z_C}\right)$$

$$= s(1-s)\left(\frac{1}{z_I} - \frac{1}{z_C}\right)\Big/ s(1-s)\left(\frac{1}{z_I} - \frac{1}{z_C}\right) = 1.$$

The first inequality is seen from (2.12), (2.17) or (2.18) and (2.22). The second equality can be seen as follows.

From (2.15),

$$\frac{1}{z} = \frac{s}{z_I} + \frac{1-s}{z_C}.$$

Then,

$$\frac{1}{z} - \frac{1}{z_C} = s\left(\frac{1}{z_I} - \frac{1}{z_C}\right).$$

From this,

$$\frac{1-s}{y}\left(\frac{y}{z} - \frac{y}{z_C}\right) = s(1-s)\left(\frac{1}{z_I} - \frac{1}{z_C}\right).$$

Then, we get

$$\frac{d\psi}{ds} = 1 - \frac{dg}{dy}\frac{\partial y}{\partial \omega}\frac{\partial \omega}{\partial s} > 1 - 1 = 0.$$

If $\dfrac{dg}{dy}\dfrac{\partial y}{\partial \omega}\dfrac{\partial \omega}{\partial s} = 0$, we also get

$$\frac{d\psi}{ds} = 1 - 0 = 1 > 0.$$

This shows that functions $s - g(y(\omega(s, k), k))$ is increasing is s. (Fig. 1.) Since it is assumed in Uzawa's paper that

$$0 < \varepsilon_1 < g(y) < 1 - \varepsilon_2$$

for some positive numbers ε_1 and ε_2, we get the unique value of s which satisfies relation

$$s = g(y(\omega(s, k), k)).$$

It is shown in Uzawa's paper that this is the only one thing to be proved for the global stability. Uzawa's variable savings-ratio model is more general than ours. In his model, it is proved under the capital-intensity condition that $\frac{d\psi}{ds} > 0$. Using only this property, Uzawa has shown the global stability of the system. That is, the capital-intensity condition is utilized only to get that $\frac{d\psi}{ds} > 0$. If this property is obtained without the capital-intensity condition, we get the global stability without this condition. This is our case.

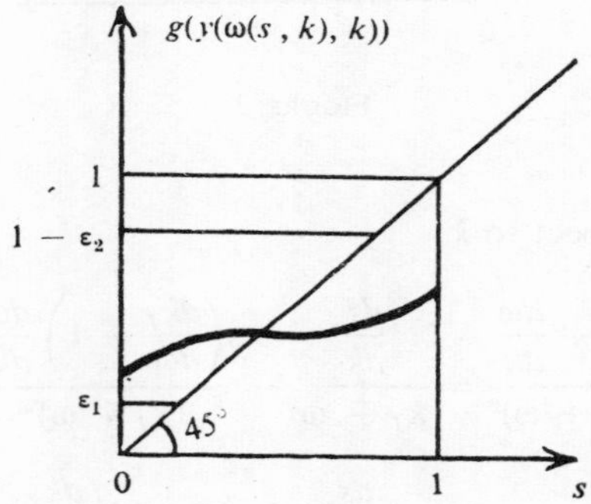

FIGURE 1

3. In this section, we shall show the uniqueness of the balanced growth equilibrium under the capital-intensity condition. First, we shall show that the short-term equilibrium wage-rentals ratio corresponding to k is an increasing function in k. Consider the function $g(y(k, s))$ in k. Here, s is fixed. If the capital-intensity condition is satisfied, we get from (2.15) that

$$k_I(\omega, s) < k(\omega, s) < k_C(\omega, s).$$

Then, from (2.12),

$$\frac{\partial y}{\partial \omega} > 0.$$

As is shown in Uzawa's constant savings-ratio model, ω is increasing in k. Thus,

$$\frac{\partial y}{\partial k} > 0$$

for any fixed value of s. Since g is non-decreasing in y, $g(y(k, s))$ viewed as a function in s shifts upwards when k increases. (Fig. 2.) Since $g(y(k, s))$ cuts the 45°-line from above, the value of s satisfying

$$s = g(y(k, s))$$

never decreases when k increases. That is,

$$\frac{ds}{dk} \geqq 0.$$

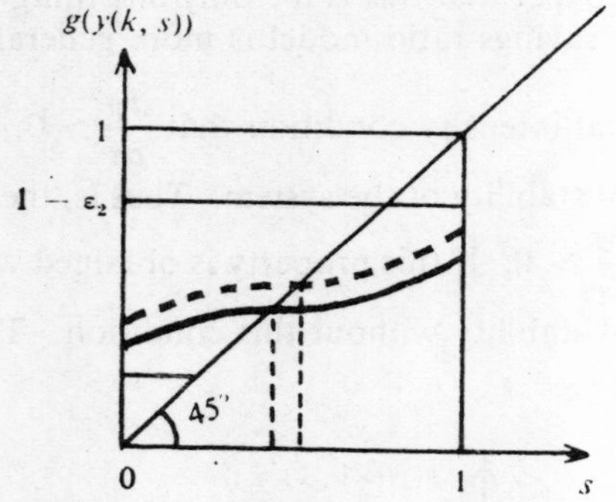

FIGURE 2

Differentiate (2.15) with respect to k.

$$-\frac{1+\dfrac{d\omega}{dk}}{(k+\omega)^2}=\frac{\dfrac{ds}{dk}}{k_I+\omega}-\frac{s\left(\dfrac{dk_I}{d\omega}+1\right)\dfrac{d\omega}{dk}}{(k_I+\omega)^2}$$

$$-\frac{\dfrac{ds}{dk}}{k_C+\omega}-\frac{(1-s)\left(\dfrac{dk_C}{d\omega}+1\right)\dfrac{d\omega}{dk}}{(k_C+\omega)^2}.$$

Then,

$$\frac{d\omega}{dk}\left[-\frac{1}{(k+\omega)^2}+\frac{s\left(\dfrac{dk_I}{d\omega}+1\right)}{(k_I+\omega)^2}+\frac{(1-s)\left(\dfrac{dk_C}{d\omega}+1\right)}{(k_C+\omega)^2}\right]$$

$$=\left[\frac{1}{k_I+\omega}-\frac{1}{k_C+\omega}\right]\frac{ds}{dk}+\frac{1}{(k+\omega)^2}.$$

The right-hand side of this relation is positive, and the term in [ ] in the left-hand side is positive from (2.14). Thus,

$$\frac{d\omega}{dk}>0.$$

Next, consider the capital accumulation process

$$\dot{k}/k=y_I/k-\lambda-\mu.$$

Our target is to show that y_I/k is decreasing in k. Now,

$$y_I/k=g(y(\omega))f_I'(k_I(\omega))\,\frac{k(\omega)+\omega}{k(\omega)}\equiv\varphi(\omega).$$

Here, ω should be considered as a function in k. But, as is shown above, ω is increasing in k. Thus, if y_I/k viewed as a function of ω is decreasing, we can see that y_I/k viewed as a function of k is decreasing.

Now, differentiate log $\varphi(\omega)$ with respect to ω.

$$
\begin{aligned}
(3.1)\qquad \frac{1}{\varphi}\frac{d\varphi}{d\omega} &= \frac{g'}{g}\frac{dy}{d\omega} + \frac{f''_I}{f'_I}\frac{dk_I}{d\omega} + \frac{1}{k+\omega} + \frac{1}{k+\omega}\frac{dk}{d\omega} - \frac{1}{k}\frac{dk}{d\omega} \\
&\leq \frac{1-g}{g}\left(\frac{1}{k+\omega} - \frac{1}{k_C+\omega}\right) - \frac{1}{k_I+\omega} + \frac{1}{k+\omega} + \left(\frac{1}{k+\omega} - \frac{1}{k}\right)\frac{dk}{d\omega} \\
&= \frac{1-g}{g}\left(\frac{g}{k_I+\omega} + \frac{1-g}{k_C+\omega} - \frac{1}{k_C+\omega}\right) - \frac{1}{k_I+\omega} + \frac{g}{k_I+\omega} \\
&\quad + \frac{1-g}{k_C+\omega} + \left(\frac{1}{k+\omega} - \frac{1}{k}\right)\frac{dk}{d\omega} \\
&= \left(\frac{1}{k+\omega} - \frac{1}{k}\right)\frac{dk}{d\omega} < 0.
\end{aligned}
$$

Here, the following relations are used.

(2.22), (2.12), (2.15) and (2.16).

4. In this section, we shall study the model in which the pattern of saving-consumption is expressed by

$$(4.1)\qquad y_C/y_I = \alpha p^{\sigma}.$$

That is, our model is expressed by the system of relations (2.1)—(2.11) is which (2.8) and (2.9) are replaced by (4.1).

From (2.4) and (2.5) [1]

$$(4.2)\qquad l_I = \frac{k_C - k}{k_C - k_I},$$

$$(4.3)\qquad l_C = \frac{k - k_I}{k_C - k_I}.$$

Then, from (2.2) and (2.3)

$$(4.4)\qquad y_I = f_I\frac{k_C - k}{k_C - k_I},$$

$$(4.5)\qquad y_C = f_C\frac{k - k_I}{k_C - k}.$$

From (4.1), (4.4), (4.5) and (2.7),

$$(4.6)\qquad \frac{f_C(k - k_I)}{f_I(k_C - k)} = \alpha\left(\frac{f'_C}{f'_I}\right)^{\sigma}.$$

Then,

$$(4.7)\qquad k = \frac{(f'_I)^{\sigma}f_Ck_I + \alpha(f'_C)^{\sigma}f_Ik_C}{(f'_I)^{\sigma}f_C + \alpha(f'_C)^{\sigma}f_I} = \frac{Mk_I + Nk_C}{M + N}.$$

Here, $M \equiv (f'_I)^{\sigma}f_C$, $N \equiv \alpha(f'_C)^{\sigma}f_I$, and every variable is considered as a function in ω.

[1] For the convenience of the calculation, it is assumed that $k_C \neq k_I$ below. The arguments can be reformulated even in the case where $k_C = k_I$ for some values of ω.

Calculate $\frac{dk}{d\omega}$. Define $M' \equiv \frac{dM}{d\omega}$ and $N' \equiv \frac{dN}{d\omega}$.

(4.8)
$$\frac{dk}{d\omega} = \frac{1}{(M+N)^2}(M'k_I + Mk_I' + N'k_C + Nk_C')(M+N)$$
$$- (Mk_I + Nk_C)(M' + N')]$$
$$= \frac{1}{(M+N)^2}[M^2k_I' + MN'k_C + MNk_C' + M'Nk_I$$
$$+ MNk_I' + N^2k_C' - MN'k_I - M'Nk_C]$$
$$= \frac{1}{(M+N)^2}[M^2k_I' + N^2k_C' + T].$$

Here, $T \equiv MN'k_C + MNk_C' + M'Nk_I + MNk_I' - MN'k_I - M'Nk_C$.

Now,
$$M' = \sigma(f_I')^{\sigma-1}f_I''k_I'f_C + (f_I')^\sigma f_C'k_C',$$
and
$$N' = \alpha\sigma(f_C')^{\sigma-1}f_C''k_C'f_I + \alpha(f_C')^\sigma f_I'k_I'.$$

Since
$$k_I' \equiv -\frac{(f_i')^2}{f_if_i''} \qquad (i = I, C),$$
we get
$$M' = -\sigma(f_I')^{\sigma+1}f_C/f_I + (f_I')^\sigma f_C'k_C',$$
and
$$N' = -\alpha\sigma(f_C')^{\sigma+1}f_I/f_C + \alpha(f_C')^\sigma f_I'k_I'.$$

Then,
$$T = -\alpha\sigma(f_I')^\sigma(f_C')^{\sigma+1}f_I(k_C - k_I)$$
$$+\alpha(f_C')^\sigma(f_I')^\sigma f_Cf_I'k_I'(k_C - k_I) + \alpha(f_I')^\sigma(f_C')^\sigma f_Cf_Ik_C'$$
$$+\alpha(f_I')^\sigma(f_C')^\sigma f_Cf_Ik_I' + \alpha\sigma(f_C')^\sigma(f_I')^{\sigma+1}f_C(k_C - k_I)$$
$$-\alpha(f_C')^\sigma(f_I')^\sigma f_C'k_C'f_I(k_C - k_I)$$
$$= -\alpha\sigma(f_I')^\sigma(f_C')^\sigma(k_C - k_I)(f_C'f_I - f_I'f_C) \quad \text{(First and fifth terms)}$$
$$+\alpha(f_C')^\sigma(f_I')^\sigma f_Cf_I'k_I'k_C$$
$$+\alpha(f_I')^\sigma(f_C')^\sigma f_Ck_I'(f_I - f_I'k_I)$$
$$+\alpha(f_C')^\sigma(f_I')^\sigma f_Ik_C'(f_C - f_C'k_C)$$
$$+\alpha(f_C')^\sigma(f_I')^\sigma f_C'k_C'f_Ik_I$$
$$= \alpha\sigma(f_I')^{\sigma+1}(f_C')^{\sigma+1}(k_C - k_I)^2$$
$$+\alpha(f_I')^\sigma(f_C')^\sigma f_Ck_I'f_I'(k_C + \omega)$$
$$+\alpha(f_I')^\sigma(f_C')^\sigma f_Ik_C'f_C'(k_I + \omega).$$

Here, the following relations are used.

$$f_i'\omega = f_i - k_i f_i', \ (i = I, C), \text{ (This is derived from (2.6)) and}$$

$$f_C' f_I - f_I' f_C = f_C' f_I' \left(\frac{f_I}{f_I'} - \frac{f_C}{f_C'} \right) = f_C' f_I'(k_I + \omega - k_C - \omega)$$
$$= -f_C' f_I'(k_C - k_I).$$

As is easily seen, the sum of the last three terms is positive. Thus,

$$T > 0.$$

From (4.8),

$$\frac{dk}{d\omega} > 0.$$

This shows that k is increasing in ω. Since k is a positively weighted average of k_I and k_C, we get that

$$\text{Min}\,\{k_I, k_C\} \leqq k \leqq \text{Max}\,\{k_I, k_C\}.$$

It is assumed by Uzawa that

$$f_i > 0,\ f_i' > 0,\ f_i'' < 0.$$

(4.9) $$f_i(0) = 0,\ f_i(\infty) = \infty,$$

$$f_i'(0) = \infty,\ f_i(\infty) = 0.$$

From these, we easily see that

$$\lim_{\omega \to \infty} k_i(\omega) = \infty \text{ and } \lim_{\omega \to 0} k_i(\omega) = 0,\ (i = I, C).$$

Then, we get

$$\lim_{\omega \to \infty} k(\omega) = \infty \text{ and } \lim_{\omega \to 0} k(\omega) = 0.$$

Thus, given any positive value of k, the short-term miniature Walrasian equilibrium system has a uniquely determined solution.

Next, consider the capital accumulation process.

$$\dot{k}/k = y_I/k - \lambda - \mu.$$

Put

$$y_I/k = f_I \frac{k_C - k}{(k_C - k_I)k}.$$

Our target is to show that y_I/k viewed as a function in k satisfies the following property

(4.10) $$\lim_{k \to 0} y_I/k = \infty \text{ and } \lim_{k \to \infty} y_I/k = 0.$$

As is shown above, ω is uniquely determined for any given value of k and is viewed as an increasing function in k. Now, consider the inverse function $k(\omega)$. Then, y_I/k can be viewed as a function in ω. Put this function $\varphi(\omega)$. As ω is increasing in k, it is necessary and sufficient for (4.10) to hold that the following property holds.

(4.11) $$\lim_{\omega \to 0} \varphi(\omega) = \infty \text{ and } \lim_{\omega \to \infty} \varphi(\omega) = 0.$$

Now,

$$\varphi(\omega) = y_I/k = f_I \frac{k_C - k}{(k_C - k_I)k} \tag{4.12}$$

$$= \frac{(f_I')^\sigma f_I f_C}{(f_I')^\sigma f_C k_I + \alpha (f_C')^\sigma f_I k_C}.$$

Here, relation (4.7) is used. From (4.12),

$$\frac{1}{\varphi(\omega)} = \frac{k_I}{f_I} + \alpha \frac{k_C}{f_C}\left(\frac{f_C'}{f_I'}\right)^\sigma. \tag{4.13}$$

From (4.9),

$$\lim_{\omega \to \infty} \frac{k_i}{f_i} = \infty, \ (i = I, C). \quad \text{(Fig. 3.)} \tag{4.14}$$

Thus,

$$\lim_{\omega \to \infty} \frac{1}{\varphi(\omega)} = \infty \text{ or } \lim_{\omega \to \infty} \varphi(\omega) = 0. \tag{4.15}$$

Next, from (4.9),

$$\lim_{\omega \to 0} \frac{k_I}{f_I} = 0. \quad \text{(Fig. 3.)} \tag{4.16}$$

On the other hand,

$$\frac{k_C f_C'}{f_C} = \frac{k_C}{k_C + \omega} < 1.$$

Thus,

$$\frac{k_C f_C'}{f_C (f_I')^\sigma (f_C')^{1-\sigma}} < \frac{1}{(f_I')^\sigma (f_C')^{1-\sigma}}.$$

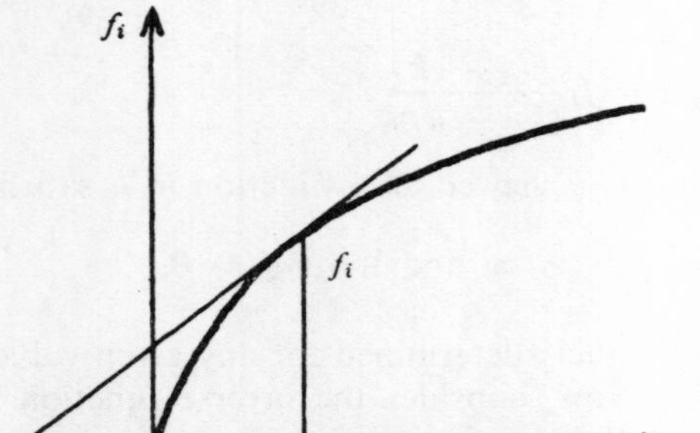

FIGURE 3

From (4.9),

$$\lim_{\omega \to 0} (f_I')^\sigma = \infty \text{ and } \lim_{\omega \to 0} (f_C')^{1-\sigma} = \infty, \tag{4.17}$$

provided $o < \sigma < 1$. If $\sigma = 0$ or 1, one of these relations holds. Thus, for any value of σ ($0 \leqq \sigma \leqq 1$), we get that

$$\lim_{\omega \to 0} \alpha \frac{k_C}{f_C} \left(\frac{f_C'}{f_I'} \right)^\sigma = 0. \tag{4.18}$$

Thus, from (4.16) and (4.18),

$$\lim_{\omega \to 0} \frac{1}{\varphi(\omega)} = 0. \tag{4.19}$$

From (4.15) and (4.19), we get (4.11) and thus, (4.10). As is easily seen from Fig. 4, the existence of some balanced growth equilibria and the global stability of the system are obtained.

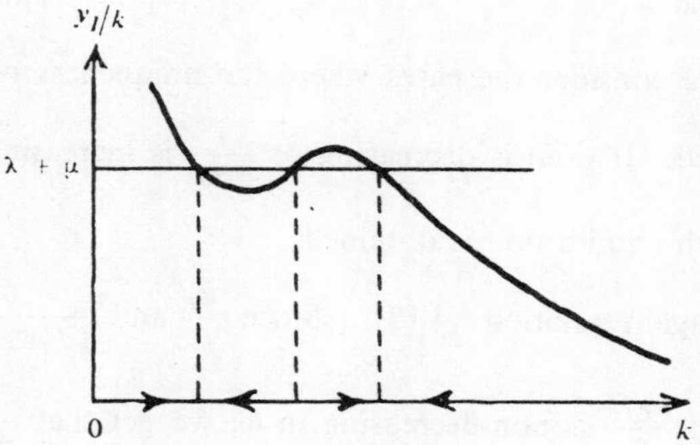

FIGURE 4

5. In the previous section, it is assumed that $0 \leqq \sigma \leqq 1$. If $\sigma > 1$ or equivalently the elasticity of substitution is larger than one, there may not exist any non-trivial balanced growth equilibria. For, in such a case, relation (4.17) may not hold and thus, y_I/k may not approach to infinity when k approaches to zero. (Fig. 5.) The reason will be explained as follows.

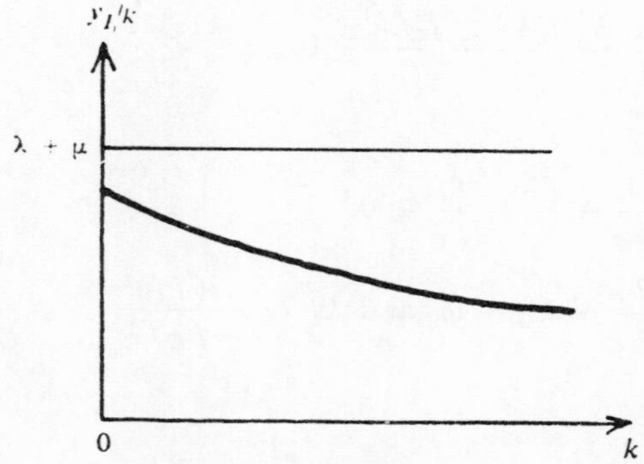

FIGURE 5

In the case where $\sigma > 1$, the expenditure on the investment goods may become zero, if its price in terms of the consumption goods becomes very high. For, the indifference curves may cut the coordinate axis in this case. (Fig. 6.) In contrast to this, in the case where $\sigma \leqq 1$, the expenditure on the investment goods never becomes zero, provided the income is positive. For, the indifference curves never cut the coordinate axis. (Fig. 7.)

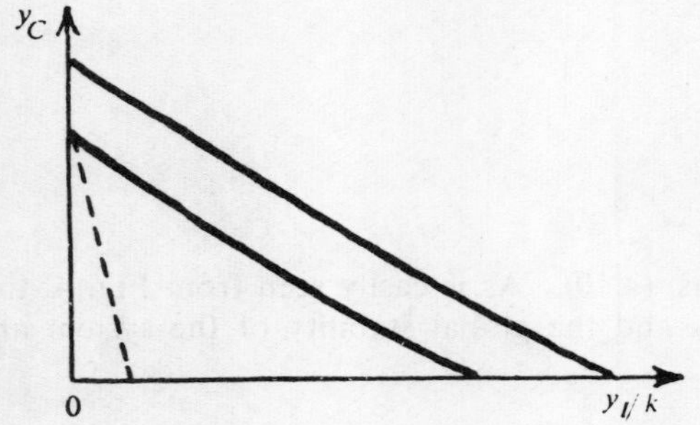

FIGURE 6

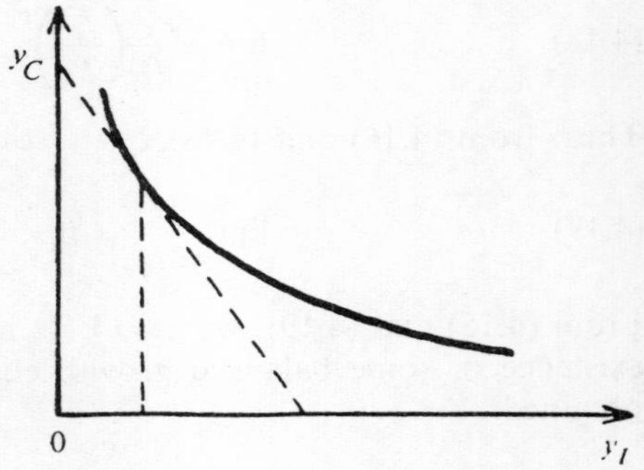

FIGURE 7

6. In this section, we consider the cases where the uniqueness of the balanced growth equilibrium is obtained. If $\varphi(\omega)$ is decreasing or $\dfrac{1}{\varphi(\omega)}$ is increasing in ω, the uniqueness of the balanced growth equilibrium is obtained.

Now, consider again relation (4.13). Since $\dfrac{k_I}{f_I}$ and $\dfrac{1}{(f'_I)^\sigma (f'_C)^{1-\sigma}}$ are increasing in ω $(0 \leqq \sigma \leqq 1)$, if $\dfrac{k_C f'_C}{f_C}$ is non-decreasing in ω, we get that $\dfrac{1}{\varphi(\omega)}$ is increasing in ω. For example, if the production function in C-sector is of the Cobb-Douglas type, $\dfrac{k_C f'_C}{f_C}$ is constant. Thus, the uniqueness of the balanced growth equilibrium is obtained.

Suppose $\dfrac{k_C f'_C}{f_C}$, or equivalently $\log \dfrac{k_C f'_C}{f_C}$ is non-decreasing in ω. Differentiate $\log \dfrac{k_C f'_C}{f_C}$ with respect to ω.

$$\frac{k'_C}{k_C} + \frac{f''_C k'_C}{f'_C} - \frac{f'_C k'_C}{f_C} \geqq 0.$$

Then,

$$\frac{1}{k_C} + \frac{f''_C}{f'_C} - \frac{f'_C}{f_C} \geqq 0.$$

Since
$$\frac{f_C}{f'_C} = k_C + \omega, \text{ and } k'_C = -\frac{(f'_C)^2}{f_C f''_C},$$

we get

$$\frac{1}{k_C} - \frac{1}{k'_C(k_C+\omega)} - \frac{1}{k_C+\omega} \geqq 0.$$

Then,

$$\frac{\omega}{k_C(k_C+\omega)} - \frac{1}{k'_C(k_C+\omega)} \geqq 0.$$

From this,

$$\frac{\omega}{k_C}\frac{dk_C}{d\omega} \geqq 1. \tag{6.1}$$

Conversely, if (6.1) holds, we see that $\frac{k_C f'_C}{f_C}$ is non-increasing in ω. Relation (6.1) shows that the elasticity of substitution in C-sector is not smaller than one. Thus, if the elasticity of substitution in C-sector is not smaller than one, the uniqueness of the balanced growth equilibrium is obtained.

Next, consider the case where the capital-intensity condition is satisfied. That is, suppose that $k_C(\omega) > k_I(\omega)$. Consider again relation (4.13). Since $\frac{k_i}{f_i}$ $(i = I, C)$ are increasing in ω, if we can show that $\left(\frac{f'_C}{f'_I}\right)$ is non-decreasing in ω, we see that $\frac{1}{\varphi(\omega)}$ is increasing in ω. Differentiate $\log\left(\frac{f'_C}{f'_I}\right)$ with respect to ω. Then,

$$\begin{aligned}\frac{d\log\left(\frac{f'_C}{f'_I}\right)}{d\omega} &= \frac{f''_C k'_C}{f'_C} - \frac{f''_I k'_I}{f'_I}\\ &= -\frac{f'_C}{f_C} + \frac{f'_I}{f_I}\\ &= \frac{1}{k_I+\omega} - \frac{1}{k_C+\omega} > 0.\end{aligned}$$

Thus, the uniqueness of the balanced growth equilibrium is obtained if the capital-intensity condition is satisfied. It is noted that the existence of the unique balanced growth equilibrium is also obtained for the case where $\sigma > 1$, if the capital-intensity condition is satisfied.

The above two cases refer to the condition on the production functions. Consider one sufficient condition on the utility index for the uniqueness of the balanced growth equilibrium. Suppose that $\sigma = 0$. Then, relation (4.13) reduces to

$$\frac{1}{\varphi(\omega)} = \frac{k_I}{f_I} + \alpha\frac{k_C}{f_C}.$$

Since $\frac{k_i}{f_i}$ $(i = I, C)$ are increasing in ω, $\frac{1}{\varphi(\omega)}$ is increasing in ω. The existence of the unique balanced growth equilibrium is obtained. The pattern of saving-consumption in this case is expressed by

$$\frac{y_C}{y_I} = \alpha.$$

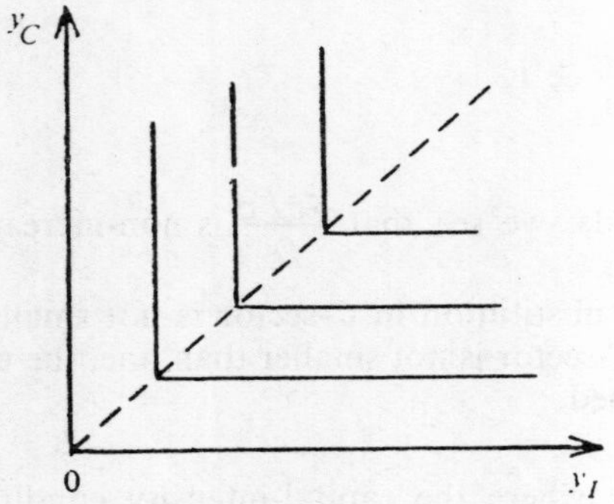

FIGURE 8

When the social utility index is expressed by the constant coefficient function

$$A \text{ Min} \{y_C/\alpha, \; y_I\},$$

we get this saving function. (Fig. 8.)

Tokyo Metropolitan University. KEN-ICHI INADA.

REFERENCES

[1] Arrow, K. J., H. B. Chenery, B. S. Minhas, and R. M. Solow. " Capital-Labor Substitution and Economic Efficiency ", *Review of Economics and Statistics*, Vol. XLIII (1961), 225-50.

[2] Solow, R. M. " Note on Uzawa's Two-Sector Model of Economic Growth ", *Review of Economic Studies*, Vol. 29 (1961-62), 48-50.

[3] Uzawa, H. " On a Two-Sector Model of Economic Growth, II ", *Review of Economic Studies*, Vol. 30 (1962-63), 105-118.

Comment by K. INADA

The results of my paper can be summarised as follows:

1. Global stability of balanced growth equilibrium is demonstrated without the capital-intensity condition, if the saving ratio is of the form $s(y)$. But balanced growth equilibrium is not necessarily unique.
2. Balanced growth equilibrium is shown to be unique if the capital-intensity condition is satisfied.
3. Where the saving-comsumption pattern is such that the elasticity of substitution is a non-negative constant not greater than one, global stability of balanced growth equilibrium is demonstrated. A constant saving ratio is a special case of this. Balanced growth equilibrium is not necessarily unique in this general case.
4. If the elasticity of substitution mentioned above is larger than one, there may exist no balanced growth equilibrium.
5. Regarding (3), some conditions sufficient for the uniqueness of balanced growth equilibrium are obtained. These conditions are: the elasticity of substitution in the consumption-goods sector is not less than one; the capital-intensity condition; and a consumption pattern implying that the ratio between consumption and investment, both measured in physical units, is a constant.

After my paper had been published in 1964, some of the above results were generalized in a paper, also published in the *Review of Economic Studies*, in 1965.[1] The results (1) and (3) above are generalized in the 1965 paper. Result (1) assumes a saving ratio of the form $s(y)$; while result (3) assumes a saving ratio $(1+\alpha p^{\alpha-1})$. In the 1965 paper a saving ratio of the form $s(p,y)$ is assumed which covers the two above assumptions as special cases. Also it was assumed in the 1964 paper that consumption goods and capital goods are produced separately, but in the 1965 paper joint production is not excluded. Furthermore, another generalization is included: the saving function is made dependent on the accumulated per capita quantity of all capital; i.e. the saving ratio is assumed to be a function of the form $s(p,y,k)$. In these generalized cases the global stability of balanced growth equilibrium is demonstrated.

The main purpose of the 1965 paper is to explain the basic structure of neoclassical two-sector models, but as by-products some generalizations as above are obtained. Another generalization is the following: the saving ratio is allowed to depend on the rate of interest, i.e. a saving function of the form $s(p,y,k,\dot{\rho})$ is assumed, where ρ is the rate of interest. Clearly the stability of balanced growth equilibrium is then demonstrated under the capital-intensity condition. This is a generalization of Uzawa's result in [3]. But in the 1965 paper no condition sufficient for the uniqueness of balanced growth equilibrium is given, i.e. results (1) and (3) of the 1964 paper are generalized in the 1965 paper but there is no attempt to generalize results (2), (4) and (5).

[1] K. Inada. " On Neoclassical Models of Economic Studies ", *Review of Economic Studies*, Vol. 32(2) (1965).

6 The Classification of Inventions

JOAN ROBINSON

In a discussion of the effect of changes in technique upon the position of long-period equilibrium, in my *Essays in the Theory of Employment*,[1] I made use of Mr. Hicks's classification of inventions, according to which an invention is said to be neutral when it raises the marginal productivities of labour and capital in the same proportion, and is said to be labour-saving or capital-saving according as it raises the marginal productivity of capital more or less than that of labour, the amounts of the factors being unchanged. I analysed the effect of an invention upon the relative shares of the factors in the total product, when the amount of capital is adjusted to the new technique (so that full equilibrium is attained, with zero investment), in terms of this classification of inventions and the elasticity of substitution, showing that, with a constant rate of interest, the relative shares are unchanged, in equilibrium, by an invention which is neutral in Mr. Hicks's sense provided that the elasticity of substitution is equal to unity, while if an invention is labour-saving or capital-saving in Mr. Hicks's sense, the relative shares are unchanged (in equilibrium, with a constant rate of interest) if the elasticity of substitution is correspondingly less or greater than unity.

Mr. Harrod [2] made some criticisms of my analysis which lead to the suggestion that it would be more convenient to use a classification in which an invention is said to be neutral when it leaves the relative shares of the factors unchanged, with a constant rate of interest, after the stock of capital has been adjusted to the new situation.[3] A method by which such a classification can be made is put forward in what follows. The argument is confined to the primitive stage at which it is assumed that there are only two factors of production, labour and capital, and that conditions of constant physical returns prevail. Draw AP_1 and AP_2, the average productivity curves of capital with a given amount of labour, before and after the invention, and the corresponding marginal productivity

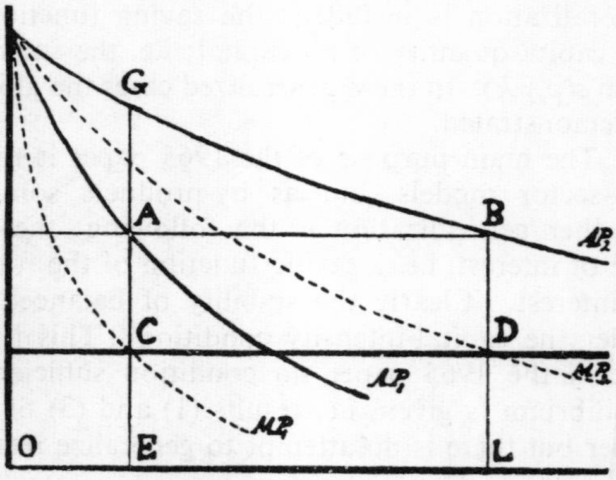

[1] Pp. 132–6.

[2] *Economic Journal*, June, 1937, p. 329.

[3] Mr. Harrod's criticisms were mainly concerned with the question of measuring the stock of capital. For our present purpose capital must be conceived in physical terms, that is, as a stock of capital goods, and it is most conveniently measured in terms of cost units. Two stocks of capital goods are said to be equal if they would cost the same sum to produce at a given date, in a given state of knowledge. An invention may introduce the knowledge of new types of capital goods, but it does not destroy the knowledge of the types of capital goods appropriate to the old technique; the date for measuring capital must therefore be chosen after the invention has taken place, and the cost of each stock of capital goods must be measured on the basis of whatever may be the most efficient method of producing it. By this means the major difficulties presented by the conception of a given stock of capital are evaded, though some ambiguous cases would still remain.

curves, MP_1 and MP_2. The amount of capital employed with the constant amount of labour is measured on the x axis, and product per unit of capital on the y axis. In full equilibrium before the invention, the marginal product of capital, CE, is equal to the rate of interest, the amount of capital employed with the given amount of labour being OE. The average product of capital is AE. Total product is equal to OE×AE, the income of capital to OE×CE, and the income of labour to OE×AC.

Now suppose that, when full equilibrium is restored after the invention, the amount of capital employed with the given amount of labour is OL and its marginal product DL, which is equal to CE, both being equal to the constant rate of interest. The average product of capital is now BL.

In the first position the ratio of the shares of labour and capital in the total product is AC : CE, and in the second position BD : DL. CE is equal to DL. Therefore the relative share of capital is increased or reduced by the invention according as BD is less or greater than AC. The relative share of capital is unchanged when, as in the diagram, BD is equal to AC.

Now, the elasticity of the curve AP_1 at A is equal to $\frac{AE}{AC}$[1] and the elasticity of the curve AP_2 at B is equal to $\frac{BL}{BD}$. Thus the share of capital is increased or reduced according as elasticity at B is greater or less than elasticity at A. In the diagram the two elasticities are equal and the share of capital is unchanged.

It thus appears that an invention which is neutral in the sense required by Mr. Harrod, that is, an invention which leaves the ratio of capital to product unchanged if the rate of interest is constant, raises the average productivity curve of capital iso-elastically.[2] A capital-saving invention, which reduces the ratio of capital to product, lowers the elasticity of the average productivity curve (at a given value of y) ; while a labour-saving, or more properly *capital-using*, invention, which increases the ratio of capital to product, raises the elasticity of the average productivity curve.

This classification of inventions lends itself more easily than that of Mr. Hicks's to realistic interpretation. An iso-elastic rise in the average productivity curve of capital means that there is a certain proportion, say k, such that if the amount of capital per unit of labour is increased by k, output also increases by k. Thus an invention which raises the average productivity curve iso-elastically, that is, a neutral invention in Mr. Harrod's sense, has the same effect as an increase in the supply of labour, in the ratio k, with unchanged technique. A neutral invention is thus seen to be equivalent to an all-round increase in the efficiency of labour. A capital-saving invention is one which improves efficiency in the higher stages of production relatively to efficiency at lower stages, and a capital-using invention is one which brings about a relative increase in efficiency in the lower stages. This corresponds to our general notions about the nature of inventions, wireless, for instance, being a capital-saving invention in this sense, and railways a capital-using one.

[1] See my *Economics of Imperfect Competition*, p. 36.
[2] Ibid., p. 42.

There is no inconsistency between this and my former method of analysis. The two concepts which I formerly used—the elasticity of substitution and the change, due to an invention, in the ratio of the marginal productivities of given amounts of the factors—merely represent two aspects of the productivity curves, and these aspects are equally well represented by the single concept of the change in the elasticity of the productivity curve brought about by an invention. The manner in which the two methods of analysis dovetail together can easily be seen.

Consider, for instance, the case in which an invention raises the average productivity curve of capital iso-elastically (so that the invention is neutral in Mr. Harrod's sense). In this case (with a constant rate of interest) the relative share of capital in the total product is unchanged by the invention ; it follows from my former analysis that if, in this case, the elasticity of substitution with the new technique is equal to unity, then the invention must be neutral in Mr. Hicks's sense, while if the elasticity of substitution is less or greater than unity, the invention must be capital-saving or labour-saving, to a corresponding extent, in Mr. Hicks's sense.

These relations can be demonstrated as follows : let GE be the average product of the original amount of capital, OE, with the new technique, and HE its marginal product. Then, with the new technique and the old amounts of the factors, total product is GE $\times$ OE, and the income of labour is GH $\times$ OE.

Now, if the elasticity of substitution is equal to unity over the relevant range, it follows that the ratio of the income of labour to the total product is independent of the amount of capital. Therefore $\frac{\text{GE}}{\text{GH}}$ is equal to $\frac{\text{BL}}{\text{BD}}$. Therefore the elasticity of the curve AP_2 at G is equal to its elasticity at B. But the elasticity of the curve AP_1 at A is also equal to the elasticity of AP_2 at B. Therefore the elasticity of AP_2 at G is equal to the elasticity of AP_1 at A. Therefore $\frac{\text{GE}}{\text{GH}}$ is equal to $\frac{\text{AE}}{\text{AC}}$. It follows that the marginal product of labour is raised by the invention (with a constant amount of capital) in the same proportion as total output, and the invention is neutral in Mr. Hicks's sense. Similarly, if the elasticity of substitution is less than unity, then $\frac{\text{GE}}{\text{GH}}$ is correspondingly greater than $\frac{\text{AE}}{\text{AC}}$ (as in the diagram) and the invention is labour-saving in Mr. Hicks's sense, while if the elasticity of substitution is less than unity, the invention is capital-saving, to a corresponding extent, in Mr. Hicks's sense.[1]

[1] This argument reveals an interesting property of the productivity function. The magnitude of the elasticity of substitution varies with the rate of change of the elasticity of the average productivity curve, being greater or less than unity according as the elasticity of the average productivity curve increases or decreases with an increase in the proportion of capital to labour.

Let $y = f(x)$ be the average productivity curve of capital, the amount of labour being constant. The elasticity of the average productivity curve is $\frac{-f(x)}{xf'(x)}$. The rate of change of this elasticity is $-\frac{x[f'(x)]^2 - f(x)[xf''(x) + f'(x)]}{[xf'(x)]^2}$. This is greater or less than zero, i.e. the elasticity

Thus there is no conflict between the system of analysis followed in my treatment of long-period equilibrium and the system suggested in this note, but the former is somewhat more cumbersome and less susceptible to realistic interpretation.

Cambridge. JOAN ROBINSON.

increases or decreases with an increase in the proportion of capital, according as

$$xf''(x)+f'(x) \gtrless \frac{x[f'(x)]^2}{f(x)},$$

or according as $xf''(x)+2f'(x) \gtrless \dfrac{f'(x)[f(x)+xf'(x)]}{f(x)}$ (1).

Now, the return per unit of capital is $f(x)+xf'(x)$, and the return per unit of labour is $-\dfrac{x^2}{L}f'(x)$, where L is the constant amount of labour.

It follows that the elasticity of substitution is

$$-x\left[\frac{2f'(x)+xf''(x)}{f(x)+xf'(x)} - \frac{2xf'(x)+x^2f''(x)}{x^2f'(x)}\right]$$
$$= \frac{f(x)[xf''(x)+2f'(x)]}{f'(x)[f(x)+xf'(x)]}$$

The elasticity of substitution is accordingly greater or less than unity according as

$$xf''(x)+2f'(x) \gtrless \frac{f'(x)[f(x)+xf'(x)]}{f(x)}$$

i.e. by (1) above, according as the elasticity of the average productivity curve increases or decreases with an increase in the proportion of capital.

Comment by JOAN ROBINSON

This note belongs to the period when Harrod was groping for his conceptions of the natural and warranted rates of growth and I was in a great state of confusion about the meaning of a " quantity of capital ". However, we seem to have hit upon the correct solution of our problem.

Comparing two equilibrium situations with different technologies and the same rate of profit, when the value of capital per man (in units of final output) is higher in the second situation in the same proportion as the value of output per man, the relative shares of wages and profits are unchanged. The improvement in technology then has the traditional characteristics of *neutrality*.

Harrod took up the suggestion of interpreting neutrality as an equal rise in output per head at all " stages of production " (we were both very vague about the time-pattern of inputs). His definition of neutrality does not, therefore, depend upon the rate of profit (or the rate of interest, as we were calling it) actually being constant. An improvement might be neutral in its technical nature, but if the real wage rate fails to rise in proportion to output per head, the rate of profit and the relative shares will not be constant.

In a simple case where the economy can be divided into a capital-good sector and a consumption-good sector, with a homogeneous labour force, neutrality means that output per unit of labour is raised equally in the two sectors, output in the capital-good sector being reckoned in units of productive capacity. Then, when the real wage rises in the same proportion as output per man, the rate of profit is constant; the value of capital per man is raised in the same proportion as output per man. In real life, of course, nothing is so simple. The criterion can be used only in a very rough way. When statistics over a run of years seem to show a fairly constant capital-output ratio, while output per head and the real wage rate are rising more or less in step and the relative share of wages and profits in net output is fairly constant, it seems likely that the overall rate of profit on capital has been fairly constant and that technical progress has been neutral on balance.

There is still a great deal of verbal confusion around this subject. Neutral improvements, and indeed all improvements except those which are merely time-saving, save labour in the sense that they increase output per head, but in spite of my plea the term " labour-saving " is still generally used for those which increase output per man by more than output per unit of " capital ". This is very awkward. It would be more perspicuous to adopt the convention that I proposed in this note of classifying improvements on either side of neutrality into *capital-saving* and *capital-using* types.

With Harrod's usage, a constant rate of profit makes it possible to compare two stocks of capital in terms of value. (The labour force and the composition of final output are supposed to be identical in the two situations.) The Hicks definition of neutrality was ambiguous, for it did not specify the meaning of a comparison between quantities of capital. It may be interpreted as comparing a larger and a smaller stock of some homogeneous substance (pieces of Meccano, putty, jelly, etc.). Each technology is then taken to be represented by a production function in terms of this substance and labour, showing the elasticity of substitution between them. The argument is then conducted in the way that I proposed.

I now think that it would be fairer to Hicks, as well as more comprehensible, to interpret his argument in terms of what I later called " real capital ", that is the value of capital in terms of " labour commanded "—its value, at a given rate of profit, in terms of product divided by the product-wage rate. When an improvement increases output per unit of capital, in this sense, in the same proportion as output per unit of labour, and the time-pattern of the stock of capital is unchanged, the Hicks and Harrod criteria of neutrality come to the same thing. The production functions and the elasticities of substitution are then seen to be unnecessary complications.

I set out the argument, following Pigovian tradition, in terms of a jump from one equilibrium to another. Harrod introduced it into the setting of a continuous process of technical progress and accumulation, which gives it much more sense.

7 Disembodied Technical Change in a Two-Sector Model[1]

P. A. DIAMOND

1. *Introduction*

There are two aspects of technical change that are essential for a description of the behavior of an economy over time. These are the rate of technical progress and the bias of the change. For a twice-differentiable production function, $F(K, L, t)$ homogeneous of the first degree, with positive marginal products and a diminishing marginal rate of substitution everywhere, where K is capital; L, labor; t, time; these two aspects can be characterized by two indices:[2]

(1) $$T = \frac{F_t}{F} = \frac{KF_{Kt} + LF_{Lt}}{KF_K + LF_L},$$

(2) $$D = \frac{\partial(F_K/F_L)}{\partial t} \bigg/ \frac{F_K}{F_L} = \frac{F_{Kt}}{F_K} - \frac{F_{Lt}}{F_L}.$$

Both indices, in general, are functions of both the capital-labor ratio, $k\left(=\frac{K}{L}\right)$, and time.

In a two-sector model the conditions necessary to preserve equilibrium in the factor markets can be expressed in terms of these aspects of the production functions of the two sectors. These conditions can then be used to characterize those types of technical change which permit steady exponential growth, in the labor force, and capital stock in both sectors.

2. *Economic Growth*

In order to describe the time profile of various economic variables, two standard characteristics of a production function will also be used. These are the elasticity of substitution, σ, and the share of capital, π; both of which, in general, are functions of both k and t.

(3) $$\sigma = -\frac{(dK/L)}{d(F_K/F_L)} \bigg/ \frac{K/L}{F_K/F_L} = \frac{F_K F_L}{FF_{KL}},$$

(4) $$\pi = \frac{F_K K}{F}.$$

A dot over a variable will denote its time derivative.

The definitions of T and D can be solved for F_{Kt} and F_{Lt} giving:

(5) $$\frac{F_{Kt}}{F} = T + (1-\pi)D, \quad \frac{F_{Lt}}{F_L} = T - \pi D.$$

[1] The author is indebted to Robert M. Solow for lengthy discussions on this paper. Financial support by the Ford Foundation is gratefully acknowledged. Views and remaining errors are solely the author's.

[2] These are the natural counterparts for a study of economic growth of the indices used to describe changes in unit costs in [5]. For other uses of similar indices see [1], [2].

From the definition of σ we have:

(6) $$\frac{\partial F_K}{\partial k}\Big/ F_K = -\frac{(1-\pi)}{\sigma k}, \quad \frac{\partial F_L}{\partial k}\Big/ F_L = \frac{\pi}{\sigma k}.$$

Equations (5) and (6) can now be combined to give the rate of growth of the marginal products in terms of the two indices of technical change and the rate of growth of the capital-labor ratio.

(7) $$\frac{\dot{F}_K}{F_K} = T + (1-\pi)D - \frac{(1-\pi)}{\sigma}\frac{\dot{k}}{k},$$

(8) $$\frac{\dot{F}}{F_L} = T - \pi D + \frac{\pi}{\sigma}\frac{\dot{k}}{k}.$$

From equations (7) and (8) can be derived the rates of growth of output and the share of capital.

(9) $$\frac{\dot{F}}{F} = T + \pi\frac{\dot{k}}{k} + \frac{\dot{L}}{L},$$

(10) $$\frac{\dot{\pi}}{\pi} = (1-\pi)\left(D + \left(1 - \frac{1}{\sigma}\right)\frac{\dot{k}}{k}\right).$$

These relationships between the indices of technical change and the rates of growth of output and marginal products will hold for a one-sector model or for any sector of a multi-sector model of an economy.

These equations can be used to examine the maintenance of factor market equilibrium. For the consumption good sector, let $C = F(K_1, L_1, t) = L_1 f(k_1, t)$, $f_k > 0$, $f_{kk} < 0$. For the investment good sector, let $I = G(K_2, L_2, t) = L_2 g(k_2, t)$, $g_k > 0$, $g_{kk} < 0$, both f and g twice differentiable. Let p be the price of the investment good in terms of the consumption good.[1] Preservation of equilibrium in the factor markets requires that the ratios of marginal products for the two sectors remain equal. Since $\frac{1}{\sigma}\frac{\dot{k}}{k} - D$ is the rate of change of this ratio, this condition is:

(11) $$\frac{1}{\sigma_1}\frac{\dot{k}_1}{k_1} - D_1 = \frac{1}{\sigma_2}\frac{\dot{k}_2}{k_2} - D_2.$$

Preservation of factor market equilibrium also requires that the wage in consumption units be the same in both sectors. This implies:

(12) $$\frac{\dot{p}}{p} = T_1 - T_2 + D_2(\pi_2 - \pi_1) - \frac{(\pi_2 - \pi_1)}{\sigma_2}\frac{\dot{k}_2}{k_2}.$$

[1] Note that the equations in this section will hold for any depreciation assumption for which the rate of depreciation is independent of the use of the capital.

From (9), (11), and (12), the remaining variables can be expressed:

(13) $$\frac{\dot{C}}{C} = \sigma_1\pi_1(D_1 - D_2) + \frac{\pi_1\sigma_1}{\sigma_2}\frac{\dot{k}_2}{k_2} + T_1 + \frac{\dot{L}_1}{L_1},$$

(14) $$\frac{\dot{I}}{I} = \pi_2\frac{\dot{k}_2}{k_2} + T_2 + \frac{\dot{L}_2}{L_2},$$

(15) $$\frac{\dot{(pI)}}{pI} = (\pi_2 - \pi_1)D_2 + \left(\frac{\pi_1 - \pi_2}{\sigma_2} + \pi_2\right)\frac{\dot{k}_2}{k_2} + T_1 + \frac{\dot{L}_2}{L_2}.$$

For the gross saving rate, $s = \dfrac{pI}{C + pI}$:

(16) $$\frac{\dot{s}}{s} = (1 - s)\left(\frac{\dot{p}}{p} + \frac{\dot{I}}{I} - \frac{\dot{C}}{C}\right)$$

$$= (1 - s)\left(\frac{\pi_1(1 - \sigma_1) - \pi_2(1 - \sigma_2)}{\sigma_2}\frac{\dot{k}_2}{k_2} + (\pi_2 - \pi_1)D_2 - \sigma_1\pi_1(D_1 - D_2) + \frac{\dot{L}_2}{L_2} - \frac{\dot{L}_1}{L_1}\right).$$

Thus, the difference in the rates of technical change of the two sectors is reflected in the changing price ratio, implying that the change in the value of new investment (in terms of consumption goods) and the change in the saving rate depend on the economy's decisions as to changes in k_2, L_1, and L_2 and the biases of the change in the two production functions but not the difference in the rates of technical progress.

3. " *Harrod* " *Neutrality*

In a two-sector model, the natural counterpart of Harrod neutrality, which will be called " Harrod " neutrality, is the constancy of the capital-output ratio in value terms at a constant rate of interest. For the economy, the capital-output ratio depends on the capital-output ratios in the two sectors and, except when the two ratios are equal, on the relative outputs of the two sectors. Expressed in terms of the share of capital

(17) $$\pi = (1 - s)\pi_1 + s\pi_2 \text{ where } s \text{, as above, equals } \frac{pI}{C + pI}.$$

Thus if π_1 and π_2 are unequal, π is not uniquely related to the rate of interest, but depends on r and a decision variable, s. Thus, as a definition of the character of technical change, " Harrod " neutrality cannot be applied to the entire economy, but must be applied to the two sectors separately.

From (7) and (11) the constancy of the rate of interest implies:

(18) $$\frac{\dot{k}_1}{k_1} = \frac{\sigma_1 T_2}{1 - \pi_2} + \sigma_1 D_1; \quad \frac{\dot{k}_2}{k_2} = \frac{\sigma_2 T_2}{1 - \pi_2} + \sigma_2 D_2.$$

From (10) the constancy of π_2 implies

(19) $$\frac{\dot{k}_2}{k_2} = -\frac{D_2}{1 - \frac{1}{\sigma_2}}, \text{ for } \sigma_2 \neq 1; \; D_2 = 0 \text{ for } \sigma_2 = 1.$$

Equating (18) and (19) gives the condition for " Harrod " neutrality in the investment good sector:

$$(20) \qquad \left(1 - \frac{1}{\sigma_2}\right)T_2 + (1 - \pi_2)D_2 = 0.$$

Since the rate of interest is the marginal product of capital in the investment good sector and since the capital-output ratio is the same in both value and physical units for this sector, equation (20) is the same as the condition for Harrod neutrality in a one-sector model (see [1]). This implies that $G(K, L, t)$ can be written as $H(K, A(t)L)$ and $\frac{T_2}{1 - \pi_2} = \frac{A'}{A}$. Harrod neutrality is equivalent to the independence of $\frac{T_2}{1 - \pi_2}$ of k.

For the consumption good sector the price of capital appears both in the equation relating the marginal product of capital and the interest rate and in the expression for the capital-output ratio in value terms. This causes the condition for " Harrod " neutrality for this sector to depend on the nature of the change in both sectors. The constancy of π_1 implies:

$$(21) \qquad \frac{\dot{k}_1}{k_1} = \frac{-D_1}{1 - \frac{1}{\sigma_1}}, \text{ for } \sigma_1 \neq 1, \ D_1 = 0 \text{ for } \sigma_1 = 1.$$

Equating (18) and (21) gives the condition for " Harrod " neutrality in the consumption good sector:

$$(22) \qquad \left(\frac{1}{1 - \sigma_1}\right)T_2 + (1 - \pi_2)D_1 = 0.$$

Thus, neutral technical change for the consumption good sector depends on characteristics of both production functions.

As an example consider the constant elasticity production functions:

$$C = (\beta_{1t}K_1{}^{-\rho_1} + \alpha_{1t}L_1{}^{-\rho_1})^{-\frac{1}{\rho_1}},$$

$$I = (\beta_{2t}K_2{}^{-\rho_2} + \alpha_{2t}L_2{}^{-\rho_2})^{-\frac{1}{\rho_2}}.$$

Then, for either sector:

$$T = -\frac{\dot{\beta}k^{-\rho} + \dot{\alpha}}{\rho(\beta k^{-\rho} + \alpha)},$$

$$D = \frac{\dot{\beta}}{\beta} - \frac{\dot{\alpha}}{\alpha},$$

$$\sigma = \frac{1}{1 + \rho},$$

$$\pi = \frac{\beta k^{-\rho}}{\beta k^{-\rho} + \alpha}.$$

Equation (20) becomes:

$$\dot{\beta}_2\left(k_2^{-\rho} + \frac{\alpha_2}{\beta_2}\right) = 0$$

which implies $\dot{\beta}_2 = 0$ for " Harrod " neutrality for all capital-labor ratios. This and (22) imply that $\frac{\rho_1}{\rho_2}\left(\frac{\dot{\alpha}_2}{\alpha_2}\right) + \frac{\dot{\beta}_1}{\beta_1} - \frac{\dot{\alpha}_1}{\alpha_1} = 0$ is the condition on the consumption good sector for " Harrod " neutrality in both sectors.

4. *Kennedy's Theorem*

Kennedy [3], [4], has shown the equivalence of Hicks neutrality in the consumption good sector, which is equivalent to $D_1 = 0$, and " Harrod " neutrality in that sector when there is no technical change in the investment good sector. The absence of technical change in the investment good sector implies that $T_2 = 0$. From equation (22) we see that $D_1 = 0$ is then the condition for both Hicks and " Harrod " neutral change. It is also seen from (22) that, except for the unit elasticity of substitution case, the presence of technical change in the investment good sector prevents the equivalence of the two types of change.

5. *Exponential Growth*

For a two-sector model to exhibit exponential growth, in addition to the equation relating the growth of the capital stock and the growth of output of the investment good sector, it is necessary to satisfy equation (11) relating the rates of growth of the capital-labor ratios of the two sectors. We will first consider the case where capital and labor grow at the same rates in both sectors with the rates independent of the initial conditions and then relax these assumptions.

Assume $\frac{\dot{L}_1}{L_1} = \frac{\dot{L}_2}{L_2} = \gamma$, $\frac{\dot{K}_1}{K_1} = \frac{\dot{K}_2}{K_2} = \rho$, and depreciation equals δ times the capital stock.[1]

Equation (11) expressing factor market equilibrium becomes:

$$(23) \qquad (\rho - \gamma) = \frac{\sigma_1(D_1 - D_2)}{1 - \frac{\sigma_1}{\sigma_2}} \text{ for } \sigma_1 \neq \sigma_2; \; D_1 = D_2 \text{ for } \sigma_1 = \sigma_2.$$

Equation (9) relating the growth of investment and capital good production is expressed as:

$$(24) \qquad (\rho - \gamma) = \frac{T_2}{1 - \pi_2}.$$

While growth is feasible for only certain initial capital-labor ratios, it is assumed that these equations hold for all initial capital-labor ratios, not just those with a sufficiently small capital-output ratio to permit growth.

Equation (24) imposes the same condition on the investment good production function as is imposed in a one-sector model for exponential growth in the case of a constant savings ratio. The independence of $\frac{T_2}{1 - \pi_2}$ of k_2 implies that the investment good production function is Harrod neutral $G(K, L, t) = \hat{G}(K, A(t)L)$. This permits the use of equation (20), the

[1] Any depreciation function independent of the use of the capital and not affecting the rate of growth of capital on the growth path could be used here; the one-hoss shay assumption for example.

equation for Harrod neutrality, which may be solved for D_2 in terms of T_2. Equating (23) and (24), using this substitution, gives the equation for " Harrod " neutrality in the consumption good sector, equation (22). Thus for an economy growing along such an exponential path, both production functions are " Harrod " neutral and, from (7), (20), and (24), the rate of interest and relative shares in both sectors are constant.

The rate of growth of the output of consumption goods can be derived from (13):

$$(25) \qquad \frac{\dot{C}}{C} = T_1 + (\rho - \gamma)\pi_1 + \gamma.$$

$\left(\text{For } \frac{\dot{C}}{C} \text{ to equal } \frac{\dot{I}}{I}\text{, this equation would imply Harrod neutrality, } F(K, L, t) = F(K, B(t)L),\right.$ $\left.\text{with } \frac{A'}{A} = \frac{B'}{B}\right).$

The change in the price ratio can be derived from (12):

$$(26) \qquad \frac{p}{\dot{p}} = T_1 - (1 - \pi_1)(\rho - \gamma) = T_1 - (1 - \pi_1)\frac{T_2}{1 - \pi_2}$$

$$= (1 - \pi_1)\left(\frac{T_1}{(1 - \pi_1)} - \frac{T_2}{(1 - \pi_2)}\right).$$

Thus, the sign of the price change depends on the relative rates of technical change, $\frac{T_1}{1 - \pi_1} - \frac{T_2}{1 - \pi_2}$. Thus, the amount of capital which may be purchased by the sacrifice of a unit of consumption changes over time with the changing input requirements for unit production.

This equation can also be used to derive the consumption stream which may be obtained by sacrificing one unit of consumption, at $t = 0$, for example. One unit of consumption purchases $\frac{1}{p_0}$ units of capital which gives a stream of $(r - \delta)\frac{1}{p_0}$ units of capital. This is worth $(p_t/p_0)(r - \delta)$ units of consumption at time t for all $t \geqq 0$. In the general case p_t changes irregularly over time. The instantaneous rate of return on a unit of consumption, that is the own rate of return of consumption goods, is $(r - \delta) + \frac{\dot{p}}{p}$, which, in general, will not equal the net interest rate, $(r - \delta)$.

Equations (25) and (26) imply that the gross savings rate, $s = \frac{pI}{C + pI}$, is constant. This constancy, and those of π_1 and π_2, imply constant relative shares for the entire economy. This also implies that the value of *GNP* in consumption units grows at the same rate as consumption.

From (8) the growth of the real wage, w, satisfies:

$$(27) \qquad \frac{\dot{w}}{w} = T_1 + \pi_1(\rho - \gamma).$$

Thus, the real wage rises at the same rate as the average product of labor in the consumption sector, which is also the rate of growth of consumption per head.

While still assuming $\frac{\dot{K}_1}{K_1} = \frac{\dot{K}_2}{K_2} = \rho$, we shall now assume $\frac{\dot{L}_1}{L_1} = \gamma_1$ and $\frac{\dot{L}_2}{L_2} = \gamma_2$, with γ_1 and γ_2 not necessarily equal. Equations (23) and (24) now become:

(28) $$(\rho - \gamma_1) = \sigma_1(D_1 - D_2) + \frac{\sigma_1}{\sigma_2}(\rho - \gamma_2);$$

(29) $$(\rho - \gamma_2) = \frac{T_2}{1 - \pi_2}.$$

If these two equations hold for all initial capital-labor ratios, equation (29) and the constancy of the growth rate again imply Harrod neutrality in the investment good sector. As before, the growth of the other variables can be derived.

Equating (28) and (29), using (22), gives:

(30) $$D_1 = \frac{1}{\sigma_1}(\rho - \gamma_1) - (\rho - \gamma_2).$$

For " Harrod " neutrality in the consumption sector D_1 would have to equal $\frac{1}{\sigma_1}(\rho - \gamma_2) - (\rho - \gamma_2)$. Thus, for $\gamma_1 \neq \gamma_2$, there is not " Harrod " neutrality in the consumption good sector.

As before, the interest rate and relative shares in the investment good sector are constant. The share of capital in the consumption good sector satisfies:

(31) $$\frac{\dot{\pi}_1}{\pi_1} = (1 - \pi_1)(\gamma_2 - \gamma_1).$$

Thus, the sign of the change depends on the relative rates of growth of labor inputs.

The equation for the growth in the output of consumption goods becomes:

(32) $$\frac{\dot{C}}{C} = T_1 + (\rho - \gamma_1)\pi_1 + \gamma_1.$$

(For $\frac{\dot{C}}{C} = \frac{\dot{I}}{I}$, this implies Harrod neutrality, $F(K, L, t) = \hat{F}(K, A(t)L)$, with $\frac{A'}{A} + \gamma_1 = \frac{B'}{B} + \gamma_2$.)

The price change equation remains essentially the same:

(33) $$\frac{\dot{p}}{p} = T_1 - (1 - \pi_1)(\rho - \gamma_2) = T_1 - \frac{(1 - \pi_1)}{(1 - \pi_2)} T_2.$$

The rate of change of the gross savings rate can be derived from (16), (32), and (33):

(34) $$\frac{\dot{s}}{s} = (1 - s)(1 - \pi_1)(\gamma_2 - \gamma_1).$$

Since the price ratio reflects the differences in technical change, the sign of the change in the savings rate depends on the difference in the growth of labor inputs.

The equation for the growth of the real wage becomes:

(35) $$\frac{\dot{w}}{w} = T_1 + \pi_1(\rho - \gamma_2).$$

Thus, the average and marginal products in the consumption good sector no longer grow at the same rate.[1, 2]

[1] If the rates of growth of the capital inputs are different for the two sectors, $\frac{\dot{I}}{I} \neq \frac{\dot{K}_2}{K_2}$. Let $\rho = \frac{\dot{I}}{I}$, $\rho_2 = \frac{\dot{K}_2}{K_2}$, $\gamma_2 = \frac{\dot{L}_2}{L_2}$. Then the relation between inputs and outputs in the investment good sector is:

$$(\rho_2 - \gamma_2) = \frac{T_2}{1 - \pi_2} + \frac{\rho_2 - \rho}{1 - \pi_2}.$$

This is similar to the expression for a one-sector model with a changing savings rate with $\rho_2' - \rho = \frac{\dot{s}}{s}$.

[2] As in a one-sector model, see [1], it is possible to describe the movement of the factor-price frontier over time. The frontier has the form $w = \psi(\varphi_1^{-1}(\varphi_2(g_k^{-1}(r))))$, where r is the interest rate, $\varphi_2(k_2) = \frac{g_k}{g - k_2 g_k}$, $\varphi_1(k_1) = \frac{f_k}{f - k_1 f_k}$, and $\psi(k_1) = f(k_1) - k_1 f_k(k_1) = w$. Over time the movement of the frontier along lines of constant interest rate satisfies $\frac{\dot{w}}{w} = T_1 + \frac{\pi_1 T_2}{1 - \pi_2}$ while the movement along radii through the origin satisfies $\frac{\dot{r}}{r} = \frac{\dot{w}}{w} = \frac{\pi_1 T_2 + (1 - \pi_2) T_1}{1 + \pi_1 - \pi_2}$.

University of California, Berkeley. PETER A. DIAMOND.

REFERENCES

(1) Diamond, P. A. " Disembodied Technical Change in a One-Sector Model ", unpublished.

[2] Fei, J. C. H. and Ranis, G. " Capital Accumulation and Economic Development ", *American Economic Review*, 53 (1963), pp. 283-313.

[3] Kennedy, C. " Harrod on ' Neutrality ' ", *Economic Journal*, 1962, pp. 249-250.

[4] Kennedy, C. " The Character of Improvements and of Technical Progress ", *Economic Journal*, 1962, pp. 899-911.

[5] Salter, W. E. G. *Productivity and Technical Change*, Cambridge, 1960.

8 Tentative Notes on a Two-Sector Model with Induced Technical Progress [1]

C. C. VON WEIZSÄCKER

In the last few years several authors have developed different theoretical models of induced technical progress. The two by now best known concepts are the technical progress function of Kaldor [5], [6] and the " learning by doing " function of Arrow [1]. A new type of technical progress function based on ideas of Fellner [3], [4] concerning the influence of factor markets on the direction of technical progress has recently been introduced by Kennedy [7], and the present author (in an unpublished paper ; cf. [8]).

In order to differentiate the product I shall approach the problem in a different way from that used by Kennedy and later by Drandakis-Phelps [2] in describing and using the technical progress function. But the basic idea is the same: there exists for every firm the possibility of substitution between labour augmenting and capital augmenting technical progress.

There are two outputs in the economy: consumption goods and capital goods. The latter we call machines. There are two direct inputs: machines and " direct " labour (what Marx calls productive labour). By direct labour we mean labour engaged directly in the production process. Every firm is able to produce both consumption goods and machines. At any given moment of time no firm is able to substitute on the input side men for machines or machines for men. But the firm can choose between different developments of the two input output coefficients over time. In other words substitution takes time and it can therefore not strictly be distinguished from technical progress (an assumption which also underlies Kaldor's technical progress function). But let us emphasize that not all changes in the input output ratios are due to increasing knowledge. It is important to keep this in mind, since it may happen that some of the input output ratios increase over time which only can be explained by substitution effects and not by an improved technology.

We first consider only a single firm. Afterwards we try to draw certain macro-economic conclusions from the analysis of the firm.

For a given firm let a_1 be the amount of labour input necessary for one unit of output of the consumption good. Let b_1 be the corresponding input of machines. Then a_2 and b_2 are the input coefficients for producing machines. For the present moment, denoted by $t = 0$, $a_1(0)$, $a_2(0)$, $b_1(0)$ and $b_2(0)$ are given. The firm engages in research and development in order to improve its productivity. We assume that the cost for research and development consists only of salaries for research workers, engineers, etc. This is of course another oversimplification of the model, but it will make computation easier.

We denote by λ the ratio of " indirect " labour to direct labour in the firm. Direct labour is equal to a_1C+a_2M where C and M stand for the outputs of consumption goods and machines in the firm. Indirect labour consists of the research team. The size of the

[1] Paper presented at the Rome Congress of the Econometric Society, September 1965. For comments on an earlier unpublished paper on induced technical progress I am indebted to Edmund Phelps, Paul Samuelson and Robert Solow. I wish especially to thank Paul Samuelson for his constructive criticisms which made me aware of the weaknesses of the concepts used in the former as well as in the present paper. For criticism of an earlier version of this paper I am indebted to Frank Hahn.

team in relation to direct labour is assumed to be a function of the planned rates of change of a_1, a_2, b_1, b_2:

$$\lambda = \lambda(\alpha_1, \alpha_2, \beta_1, \beta_2),$$

where

$$\alpha_1 = \dot{a}_1/a_1,\ \alpha_2 = \dot{a}_2/a_2$$
$$\beta_1 = \dot{b}_1/b_1,\ \beta_2 = \dot{b}_2/b_2.$$

A dot above a variable denotes the rate of change of that variable with respect to time. It is reasonable to assume that λ is a decreasing function of its four arguments as long as λ is positive. A high rate of technical progress reveals itself in a low (usually negative) rate of change of the input coefficients. A high rate of technical progress also requires a high λ.

Before we specify other properties of the function λ, let us consider the question of transmission of knowledge from one firm to another. It would clearly be unrealistic to treat every firm as an isolated entity such that its technical coefficients only depend on occurrences within the firm. We have to admit the possibility of outside influences on the rate of technical progress. This will be done in the model by introducing four additional arguments into the function determining the required value of λ. Let a_1^+ be the ratio of the amount of direct labour engaged in producing consumption goods and the amount of consumption goods produced in the whole economy. In other words, let a_1^+ be the inverse of labour productivity in producing consumption goods. Let a_2^+, b_1^+, b_2^+ be the corresponding ratios for labour and machines in producing consumption goods and machines. We assume that the firm is small in comparison to the economy. It is then approximately correct to assume that the time functions $a_1^+(t)$, $a_2^+(t)$, $b_1^+(t)$, $b_2^+(t)$ cannot be influenced by the single firm. We now assume that the required indirect labour ratio λ is a function of the planned rates of change α_1, α_2, α_1, β_2 and of the ratios of the firm's input coefficients to the input coefficients of the economy which we call

$$\hat{a}_1 = a_1/a_1^+, \quad \hat{a}_2 = a_2/a_2^+,$$
$$\hat{b}_1 = b_1/b_1^+, \quad \hat{b}_2 = b_2/b_2^+.$$

That is

$$\lambda = \lambda(\alpha_1, \alpha_2, \beta_1, \beta_2, \hat{a}_1, \hat{a}_2, \hat{b}_1, \hat{b}_2). \qquad \text{...(1)}$$

This function is meant to express the following idea. As time goes by, not only is new knowledge created in the laboratories of the firms, but also already existing knowledge is diffused into more and more firms. Assuming for the moment that no new knowledge is produced we would expect the existing knowledge to become more and more evenly distributed and hence in the end the input ratios to be the same in every firm of a given industry. Thus at a given moment of time we would expect that, other things being equal, the rate of growth of knowledge to be inversely related to the level of knowledge in the firm. Or more specifically, now again allowing for positive technical progress, we would expect α_1 to be an increasing function of $\hat{a}_1$, keeping the other arguments and λ constant. The worse the relative state of technology of the firm the better are its opportunities to substitute costless gains of information from other firms for own research efforts. Thus we assume that λ increases with increasing $\hat{a}_1$, $\hat{a}_2$, $\hat{b}_1$, $\hat{b}_2$. We then have

$$\lambda_1 < 0,\ \lambda_2 < 0,\ \lambda_3 < 0,\ \lambda_4 < 0$$
$$\lambda_5 > 0,\ \lambda_6 > 0,\ \lambda_7 > 0,\ \lambda_8 > 0. \qquad \text{...(2)}$$

Where λ_i, $i = 1, \ldots, 8$, is the partial derivative with respect to the ith argument in equation (1). The relations (2) apply to that part D of the domain where λ is positive. Furthermore we assume that λ is twice continuously differentiable in D and has the following property: for $\bar{\lambda} > 0$ the set $S(\bar{\lambda})$ of arguments such that $\lambda \leqq \bar{\lambda}$ is strictly convex.

It is perhaps appropriate to emphasize one of the motives that lies behind our assumptions about the technical progress function: they are chosen to enable us to cook a steady state of growth in the economy. They are unrealistic since they don't exhibit any increasing returns to scale effects. In reality induced inventions and learning effects are closely linked to increasing returns, as for example can be seen in Arrow's [1] model. I hope later to be able to build a model taking account of increasing returns to scale. I am not so sure, whether it will exhibit similar results to the present one. My excuse for omitting this problem is that I am in this paper mainly interested in the substitution of one kind of technical progress for another rather than the total effect of efforts to increase the rate of technical progress.

Having discussed the properties of the technical progress function we now have to consider the behaviour of the firm with respect to this function. Let us start from the assumption that the firm anticipates a certain output stream $C(t)$, $M(t)$ for the future. Its purpose is now to minimize the total discounted costs of producing this output stream, given the prices of machines $p(t)$, the wage rate for direct labour $w(t)$ and for indirect labour $v(t)$ and the discount rate $r(t)$. The firm also anticipates the average labour and machine input ratios $a_1^+(t)$ etc. Furthermore the initial values of its own input ratios, $a_1(0)$ etc. are given. Let us assume that machines depreciate exponentially at the rate m. At any moment of time the firm's expenditures equal

$$E(t) = w(t)L(t)+v(t)\lambda(t)L(t)+p(t)I(t)$$

where $L(t)$ is the amount of direct labour employed and $I(t)$ is the number of machines bought at that time. If the stock of machines is $X(t)$ we have of course

$$I(t) = \dot{X}(t)+mX(t).$$

But $X(t)$ can be determined by b_1, b_2, $C(t)$ and $M(t)$:

$$X(t) = b_1(t)C(t)+b_2(t)M(t)$$

hence

$$I(t) = \dot{b}_1C+b_1\dot{C}+\dot{b}_2M+b_2\dot{M}+m[b_1C+b_2M].$$

We also have

$$L(t) = a_1(t)C(t)+a_2(t)M(t).$$

Taking into account these last 2 equations we get a new expression for expenditures at t

$$\begin{aligned} E(t) = {} & [w+v\lambda][a_1C+a_2M] \\ & +p[\beta_1+m+\dot{C}/C]b_1C \\ & +p[\beta_2+m+\dot{M}/M]b_2M. \end{aligned}$$

The discounted sum of expenditures, Z, is given by

$$Z = \int_0^\infty e^{-\int_0^t r(z)dz} E(t)dt.$$

It has to be minimized with respect to all differentiable functions $a_1(t)$, $a_2(t)$, $b_1(t)$, $b_2(t)$ starting at $a_1(0)$, $a_2(0)$, $b_1(0)$, $b_2(0)$. Let us assume that the optimal path is such that $\lambda(t)$ is always positive. We then can apply the Euler equation of the calculus of variations and then get the following expressions, where E' represents the integrand (discounted expenditures at time t) and $R(t)$ is defined by

$$R(t) = e^{-\int_0^t r(z)dz}.$$

We have

$$\frac{\partial E'}{\partial a_1} = \frac{d}{dt}\frac{\partial E'}{\partial \dot{a}_1}, \text{ hence}$$

$$R(t)\left[(w+v\lambda)C+v\left(C+\frac{a_2}{a_1}M\right)(-\alpha_1\lambda_1+\hat{a}_1\lambda_5)\right]$$

$$= \frac{d}{dt}\left[R(t)v\left(C+\frac{a_2}{a_1}M\right)\lambda_1\right] \qquad \ldots(3)$$

and correspondingly for the other variables a_2, b_1, b_2

$$R(t)\left[(w+v\lambda)M+v\left(\frac{a_1}{a_2}C+M\right)(-\alpha_2\lambda_2+\hat{a}_2\lambda_6)\right]$$

$$= \frac{d}{dt}\left[R(t)v\left(\frac{a_1}{a_2}C+M\right)\lambda_2\right] \qquad \ldots(4)$$

$$R(t)\left[p(mC+\dot{C})+v\left(\frac{a_1}{b_1}C+\frac{a_2}{b_1}M\right)(-\beta_1\lambda_3+\hat{b}_1\lambda_7)\right]$$

$$= \frac{d}{dt}\left\{R(t)\left[v\left(\frac{a_1}{b_1}C+\frac{a_2}{b_1}M\right)\lambda_3+pC\right]\right\} \qquad \ldots(5)$$

$$R(t)\left[p(mM+\dot{M})+v\left(\frac{a_1}{b_2}C+\frac{a_2}{b_2}M\right)(-\beta_2\lambda_4+\hat{b}_2\lambda_8)\right]$$

$$= \frac{d}{dt}\left\{R(t)\left[v\left(\frac{a_1}{b_2}C+\frac{a_2}{b_2}M\right)\lambda_4+pM\right]\right\}. \qquad \ldots(6)$$

Here it is of course assumed that $r(t)$ is sufficiently large to make Z a well-defined finite expression for at least some set of functions $a_1(t)$, $a_2(t)$, $b_1(t)$, $b_2(t)$.

In this paper we shall not concern ourselves with the stability properties of the model and hence from now on we consider only macroeconomic equilibrium paths which are characterized by an exponential development of all variables that are exogenous from the viewpoint of the firm. In addition we assume that the ratio of direct to indirect labour in the whole economy is given and a constant. On a golden age path the two wage rates w and v will grow at the same exponential rate, which we call γ. Let $\dot{p}/p$ be denoted by π, let the discount rate r be a constant and let g_1 and g_2 be the rates of growth of the consumption goods and the machines produced by the firm.

Let us now also assume that all firms are alike and that every firm is in an equilibrium situation with respect to α_1, α_2, β_1, β_2, i.e. these variables are constant in time. Since every firm is alike we have $\hat{a}_1, \hat{a}_2, \hat{b}_1, \hat{b}_2 = 1$ and then all eight arguments of λ remain constant through time. Hence λ and all its derivatives remain constant through time. In addition we want to make the assumption that at $\hat{a}_1, \hat{a}_2, \hat{b}_1, \hat{b}_2 = 1$ the equation

$$\frac{\lambda_5}{\lambda_1} = \frac{\lambda_6}{\lambda_2} = \frac{\lambda_7}{\lambda_3} = \frac{\lambda_8}{\lambda_4} = -k(\alpha_1, \alpha_2, \beta_1, \beta_2) \qquad \ldots(7)$$

holds for some non-negative function k of $\alpha_1, \alpha_2, \beta_1, \beta_2$. In order to motivate the acceptance of these four additional equations we may point out that λ_2/λ_1 is the elasticity of substitution between the rate of change of labour productivity and the relative position of the firm with respect to labour productivity in the production of consumption goods. A similar interpretation applies to the other three ratios. The assumption that they are equal enables us to define an elasticity of substitution between the firm's total productivity and growth of total productivity which is independent of the relative weights of capital and labour and of the two outputs in this productivity index.

Since every firm is alike, any one firm exhibits the same proportions as the whole economy. Therefore, in particular on an equilibrium path, the labour inputs for the production of machines and for the production of consumption goods grow at the same rate. Also the machine inputs for the production of the two outputs grow at the same rate. This implies the following relations

$$\alpha_1+g_1 = \alpha_2+g_2 \qquad \text{...(8)}$$

$$\beta_1+g_1 = \beta_2+g_2. \qquad \text{...(9)}$$

Using (7), (8) and (9) we get from (3)-(6) the following equations. From (3):

$$e^{-rt}\left[(w+v\lambda)C+v\left(C+\frac{a_2}{a_1}M\right)(-\alpha_1-k)\lambda_1\right]$$

$$=\frac{d}{dt}\left(e^{-rt}v\left(C+\frac{a_2}{a_1}M\right)\lambda_1\right)=e^{-rt}(\gamma+g_1-r)v\left(C+\frac{a_2}{a_1}M\right)\lambda_1$$

or

$$(\gamma+g_1-r+\alpha_1+k)\lambda_1=\frac{(w+v\lambda)Ca_1}{v(a_1C+a_2M)}. \qquad \text{...(10)}$$

In a similar way from (4), using (8):

$$(\gamma+g_1-r+\alpha_1+k)\lambda_2=\frac{(w+v\lambda)Ma_2}{v(a_1C+a_2M)}. \qquad \text{...(11)}$$

From (5), using (7)-(9):

$$e^{-rt}\left[p(m+g_1)C+v\left(\frac{a_1}{b_1}C+\frac{a_2}{b_1}M\right)(-\beta_1-k)\lambda_3\right]$$

$$=\frac{d}{dt}\left\{e^{-rt}\left[v\left(\frac{a_1}{b_1}C+\frac{a_2}{b_1}M\right)\lambda_3+pC\right]\right\}$$

$$=[-r+\gamma+\alpha_1-\beta_1+g_1]e^{-rt}v\left(\frac{a_1}{b_1}C+\frac{a_2}{b_1}M\right)\lambda_3+(\pi+g_1-r)e^{-rt}pC$$

or

$$(\gamma+g_1-r+\alpha_1+k)\lambda_3=\frac{(r+m-\pi)pb_1C}{v(a_1C+a_2M)}. \qquad \text{...(12)}$$

In a similar way from (6):

$$(\gamma+g_1-r+\alpha_1+k)\lambda_4=\frac{(r+m-\pi)pb_2M}{v(a_1C+a_2M)}. \qquad \text{...(13)}$$

Let us now notice that even in equilibrium growth the single firm is not forced to stay on its equilibrium path characterized by an exponentially growing output of C and of M. Keeping the rates α_1, α_2, β_1, β_2 and hence λ constant the firm may vary $C(t)$ and $M(t)$ until it finds the profit maximum. Since $C(t)$ and $M(t)$ can be made arbitrarily large such a profit maximum only exists if there is no extra profit above the discount rate r. On the other hand, if there is positive output the profit rate cannot be smaller than the discount rate r. These considerations lead to the conclusion that the quasirent of a machine is given by

$$(r+m-\pi)p=\frac{1-a_1(w+\lambda v)}{b_1}=p\,\frac{1-a_2(w+\lambda v)}{b_2} \qquad \text{...(14)}$$

applying the usual formulas of capital theory. Notice that by keeping λ fixed the costs of indirect labour can be treated just like costs of direct labour. This is of course due to the special type of technical progress function where technical progress depends on the *ratio* between indirect and direct labour.

Equations (10)-(13) are of similar structure. By dividing any two of them we see that the ratios of the partial derivatives of λ correspond to the ratios of the costs of the corresponding inputs. Thus for example

$$\frac{\lambda_1}{\lambda_3} = \frac{(w+v\lambda)a_1}{(r+m-\pi)pb_1}. \qquad \ldots(15)$$

The numerator of the right-hand side is the unit labour cost of consumption goods and the denominator is the unit capital cost of consumption goods. The left-hand side can be interpreted as the marginal rate of substitution between labour augmenting and capital augmenting technical progress. Hence we arrive at similar results to those obtained by Kennedy under his assumption that firms minimize the instantaneous rate of change of unit costs. But it is important to realize that this coincidence only applies on equilibrium paths of growth.

Let us now state only one macroeconomic property of the model. Assuming that every firm is alike we are able to interpret our technical progress function (1) as a macroeconomic one. But now of course the four last arguments are equal to unity and hence we can write

$$\lambda = \lambda(\alpha_1, \alpha_2, \alpha_1, \alpha_2).$$

We then assume that λ is a constant parameter $\bar{\lambda}$. Hence our technical progress function is a relationship between the four rates of productivity growth. Assuming that the supply of labour grows at a constant geometric rate n, what is the highest equilibrium rate of growth of consumption in this model?

In equilibrium the proportion of labour used for the production of consumption goods is constant and therefore consumption grows at the rate $n-\alpha_1$, since $-\alpha_1$ is the rate of growth of labour productivity. The production of machines grows at the rate $n-\alpha_2$. A constant proportion of machines is used for the production of consumption goods. Hence $n-\alpha_2-\beta_1 = n-\alpha_1$ or $\alpha_1 = \alpha_2+\beta_1$. In addition the number of machines will only grow exponentially, if the productivity of machines in producing machines is constant, i.e. if $\beta_2 = 0$. Therefore our problem is to maximize $-\alpha_1$ subject to the constraint

$$\bar{\lambda}-\lambda(\alpha_1, \alpha_2, \alpha_1-\alpha_2, 0) = 0$$

which is equivalent to maximizing

$$-\alpha_1+\mu(\bar{\lambda}-\lambda(\alpha_1, \alpha_2, \alpha_1-\alpha_2, 0)).$$

It then follows

$$-1-\mu(\lambda_1+\lambda_3) = 0, \text{ hence } \mu \neq 0$$

and

$$\mu(\lambda_2-\lambda_3) = 0, \text{ hence } \lambda_2 = \lambda_3.$$

But this compared with (11) and (12) implies for every firm and therefore for the whole economy

$$(w+v\lambda)Ma_2 = (r+m-\pi)pb_1C \qquad \ldots(16)$$

where M now represents the number of machines produced in the economy and C the amount of consumption goods produced in the economy. We multiply (14) by b_1C and combine it with (16) in order to get

$$(w+v\lambda)(Ma_2+Ca_1) = (r+m-\pi)pb_1C+(w+v\lambda)Ca_1 = C. \qquad \ldots(17)$$

The left-hand side represents the wage bill, therefore (17) gives as a condition for maximizing the rate of growth of consumption that the wage bill is equal to consumption, i.e. the rate of profit is equal to the rate of growth of consumption. This I call the Second

Golden Rule of Accumulation as opposed to the first Golden Rule which refers to the maximization of the level of consumption at a given growth rate.

University of Heidelberg, Germany
Alfred Weber Institut.

C. C. von Weizsäcker.

REFERENCES

[1] Arrow, K. "The Economic Implications of Learning by Doing", *Review of Economic Studies*, Vol. XXIX, 1962.

[2] Drandakis, E. M. and Phelps, E. S. "A Model of Induced Invention, Growth and Distribution", *Cowles Foundation Discussion Papers*, No. 186, July 1965.

[3] Fellner, W. J. "Two Propositions in the Theory of Induced Innovations", *Economic Journal*, 71, 1961.

[4] Fellner, W. J. "Does the Market Direct the Relative Factor-Saving Effects of Technological Progress?" in *The Rate and Direction of Inventive Activity*, Princeton, 1962.

[5] Kaldor, N. "A Model of Economic Growth", *Economic Journal*, 67, 1957.

[6] Kaldor, N. and Mirrlees, J. A. "A New Model of Economic Growth", *Review of Economic Studies*, Vol. XXIX, 1962.

[7] Kennedy, C. "Induced Bias in Innovation and the Theory of Distribution", *Economic Journal*, 74, 1964.

[8] Samuelson, P. A. "A Theory of Induced Innovations along Kennedy-Weizsäcker Lines", *Review of Economics and Statistics*, 47, 1965.

9 Neoclassical Growth with Fixed Factor Proportions

R. M. SOLOW, J. TOBIN,
C. C. VON WEIZSÄCKER and M. YAARI

I INTRODUCTION

We analyze in this paper a completely aggregated model of production in which output is produced by inputs of homogeneous labor and heterogeneous capital goods, and allocated either to consumption or to use as capital goods. Allocations are irreversible: capital goods can never be directly consumed. Fixed coefficients rule: any concrete unit of capital has a given output capacity and requires a given complement of labor. Technological progress continuously differentiates new capital goods from old. But we assume that the " latest model " in capital goods has no smaller capacity and no higher labor requirement than any older-model capital goods with the same reproduction cost. Thus each instant's gross investment will take the form of the latest-model capital. There is no problem of the optimal " depth " of capital. The main effect of an *increase* in gross investment is to modernize the capital stock in use.

One normal consequence of technological progress will be a rising trend of the real wage rate. Since existing capital operates under fixed coefficients, there will eventually come a time in the life of every vintage of investment when the wage costs of using it to produce a unit of output will exceed one unit of output. At that instant the investment may be said to have become obsolete as a result of the competition of more modern capital; it will be retired from production—permanently, unless the real wage should temporarily fall.

We have several motives for wishing to analyze so special a model.

1. Capital theory seems—perhaps inevitably—to consist of a catalog of special models, distinguished by the different ways time and durable commodities enter the process of production. Since this simple, but not trivial, model has not been studied as a growth model before, we think it a worthwhile addition to the catalog.[1]

2. The model contributes something more than mere completeness to the catalog. It isolates the effects of what has been called " quickening "—hastening the practical introduction of newly-discovered techniques into production—from those of " deepening " of capital. " Widening " can also be analytically excluded by considering the special case of a constant labor force.

3. The literature sometimes suggests, or seems to suggest, that what are called " neo-classical " *modes of analysis*—we emphasize that we do not refer to assumptions of Say's Law—require for their validity or utility that capital and labor be directly and smoothly substitutable for one another. This paper provides a counterexample. Although there is no scope for substitution *ex post* or *ex ante*, we show that the basic neo-classical methods do function and give the expectable results. No use is made of any " generalized stock of capital ".

[1] The model was formulated and studied in detail by Salter [2], from a point of view which is somewhat different from ours.

4. What is true is that the basic neo-classical methods apply when and only when output is limited by the availability of resources, not by effective demand. Most of our argument is conducted under the assumption that full employment of labor is the bottleneck to production. This assumption may be regarded as appropriate to a planned economy, or to a decentralized economy with an effective fiscal policy. An important task of economic theory is to find some way of unifying the theory of production and the theory of effective demand. The model of this paper is, we believe, particularly suited for this purpose, precisely because it gives effect to the common casual-empirical belief that in the short run the scope for changing factor proportions is small. On the other hand, the model no doubt limits excessively the scope for changing factor proportions over long periods of time. Like all aggregate models, it must ignore the effects of inter-commodity shifts.

5. Finally, it is sometimes asserted that in modern industrial economies *ex ante* choice of techniques is in fact unimportant; that at any instant of time one technique—the latest one—effectively dominates all others for all thinkable configurations of factor prices. We do not know how nearly true this assertion is (particularly in macroeconomic terms). But the model of production studied in this paper is presumably the appropriate vehicle for studying the implications of the assertion.

II PHYSICAL RELATIONS

1. *Technological assumptions*

The model assumes fixed-coefficient technology with embodied technical progress. Once capital has been put into place, there is no possibility of substituting capital for labor or vice versa; the output-capital and output-labor coefficients are fixed for the life of the capital. Neither are there any effective possibilities of *ex ante* substitution between labor and capital. For a business investing in new capital, only one pair of these coefficients, the pair which will characterize this capital so long as it is operating, is available. (This is not strictly true, since an investing business could always use older technology characterized by different coefficients. But this is an empty qualification, because in the model an investor will never prefer older technology to new technology no matter what wage rate and interest rate he faces.) Technical progress consists of improvement in one or both of the output-input coefficients. But the improved coefficients apply only to new vintage capital, not to investments made in the past. Since the model has only one commodity, serving indifferently as capital good and consumer good, investment can be measured unambiguously in physical units equal to the opportunity cost of one unit of consumption.

Formally, let:

$Y(t, v)dv$	be the rate of gross output (physical units per year) at time t, produced on capital of vintage v, i.e. capital installed during a period $(v, v + dv)$, where necessarily $v \leq t$.
$I(v)$	the rate of gross investment (physical units per year) at time v.
$I(v)dv$	the amount of capital (physical units) installed in the period $(v, v + dv)$.
$N(t, v)dv$	the rate of employment of labor (men) at time t on capital of vintage v.
$\lambda(v)$	the technologically determined output per year per man producible on capital of vintage v.
$\mu(v)$	the technologically determined output per year producible with one unit of capital of vintage v.
$Y(t)$	total gross output per year, summed over all vintages of capital, at time t.
$N(t)$	total employment (men), summed over all vintages of capital, at time t.

$L(t)$ total labor supply at time t.

$w(t)$ the real wage rate (physical units per man-year).

$\rho(t, v)dv$ the quasi-rent earned at time t on one unit of capital of vintage v (a pure number).

$m(t)$ the age of the oldest capital in use at time t (years).

The assumptions about production outlined verbally above can be summarized in the following production function for output from capital of vintage v ($\leqq t$)

$$Y(t, v) = \text{Min}\,\{\lambda(v)N(t, v),\ \mu(v)I(v)\}. \tag{1}$$

This formulation ignores physical depreciation and assumes that capital is perfectly durable. This assumption has the advantage of simplicity, and it permits the model to bring out clearly the economics of obsolescence. Capital wears forever, but it is not in general used forever—better, more modern, capital displaces it. At the same time, physical depreciation of simple types can be allowed without essentially altering the behavior of the economy described by the model. In Part VII below, two kinds of physical depreciation are mentioned: (1) exponential evaporation or decay; (2) " one-hoss-shay " collapse after a fixed lifetime at full strength. At that point we will also indicate how the model can be generalized to allow the productive capacity of a unit of capital to decline with age while the capital remains physically in existence with its original labor requirements.

In general, we shall be interested in situations where, for vintages v in use:

$$Y(t, v) = \lambda(v)N(t, v) = \mu(v)I(v). \tag{2}$$

Unless this condition is met, capital of vintage v is not being efficiently used. It makes no sense to overman capital, and in a continuous-time model it will not be under-manned either. In a discrete time model, it would be conceivable that some but not all of the capital invested during period v might be in use at a later time t. This possibility does not arise here because there is not a finite mass of capital of any instantaneous vintage. If any vintage v capital is in use, all of it is. Note that there is no specifically " vintage v " labor. Any labor available at time t will do. One unit of vintage v capital employs $\mu(v)/\lambda(v)$ workers when it is in use.

2. *Kinds of technical progress*

The coefficients $\lambda(v)$ and $\mu(v)$ carry technical progress. We shall assume that each of these coefficients is a non-decreasing function of v. This guarantees that no earlier technology is ever preferred to the newest. The model does not explain the advance of technical knowledge; it is autonomous, requires no productive resources, and cannot be accelerated or retarded. A more complete model would relate progress not just to the passage of time but to production experience (as is done, for instance, by Arrow [1]) and to the use of resources in research and development (see, e.g., Uzawa [4]).

Three special kinds of technical progress are depicted in Figures 1A, 1B and 1C. Capital-labor isoquants are shown for a fixed rate of output under vintage v_0 technology, and under technology of a later vintage v_1. The arrows show in each case the direction in which technical progress moves the isoquant.

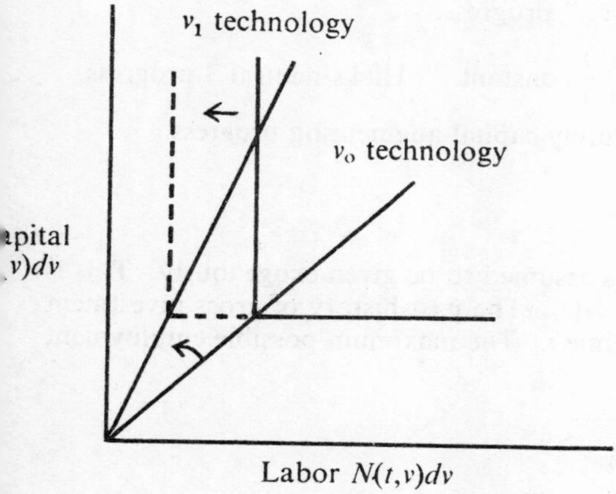

FIGURE 1A
Purely labor-augmenting technical progress, "Harrod-neutral". Capital-labor ratio increases

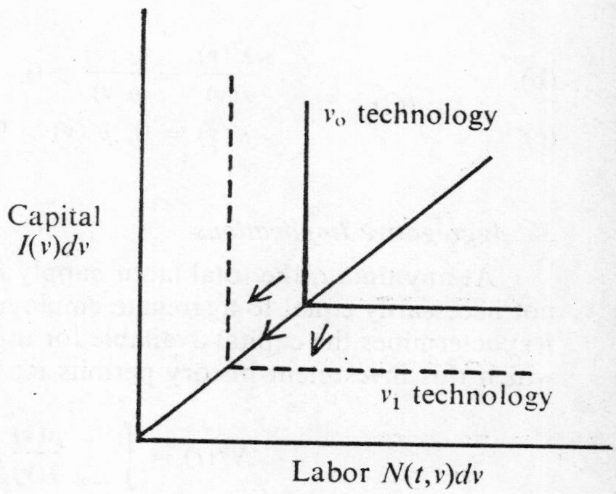

FIGURE 1B
"Hicks-neutral" Capital-labor ratio constant

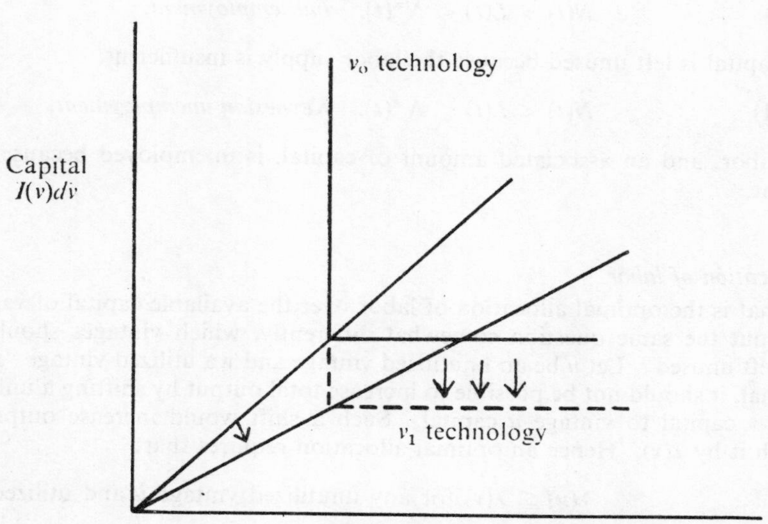

FIGURE 1C
Purely capital-augmenting technical progress. Capital-labor ratio falls

The three special cases are:

(a) $\lambda'(v) > 0, \mu'(v) = 0.$ Purely labor-augmenting or " Harrod-neutral " progress.

(b) $\dfrac{\lambda'(v)}{\lambda(v)} = \dfrac{\mu'(v)}{\mu(v)} > 0.$ $\dfrac{\lambda(v)}{\mu(v)}$ constant. " Hicks-neutral " progress.

(c) $\lambda'(v) = 0, \ \mu'(v) > 0.$ Purely capital-augmenting progress.

3. *Aggregative Implications*

At any time t, the total labor supply $L(t)$ is assumed to be given exogenously. This is not necessarily equal to aggregate employment $N(t)$. The past history of gross investment $I(v)$ determines the capital available for use at time t. The maximum possible employment which this investment history permits is:

$$N^*(t) = \int_{-\infty}^{t} \frac{\mu(v)}{\lambda(v)} I(v)dv$$

and this requires all (surviving) capital to be in use. The integral may diverge, in which case labor can never be in surplus. For simplicity we assume $N^*(t)$ finite. There are three important possible regimes:

(I) $L(t) \geq N^*(t) = N(t).$ *Labor surplus.*

All capital is in use. Labor is unemployed because of a shortage of capital. Or, when $L(t) = N^*(t)$, labor is just adequate to man all the capital.

(II) $N(t) = L(t) < N^*(t).$ *Full employment.*

Some capital is left unused because the labor supply is insufficient.

(III) $N(t) < L(t) \leq N^*(t).$ *Keynesian unemployment.*

Some labor, and an associated amount of capital, is unemployed because demand is insufficient.

4. *Allocation of labor*

What is the optimal allocation of labor over the available capital of various vintages? Or, to put the same question somewhat differently, which vintages should be used and which left unused? Let u be an unutilized vintage and v a utilized vintage. If an allocation is optimal, it should not be possible to increase total output by shifting a unit of labor from vintage v capital to vintage u capital. Such a shift would increase output by $\lambda(u)$ and diminish it by $\lambda(v)$. Hence an optimal allocation requires that:

(3) $\lambda(u) \leqq \lambda(v)$ for any unutilized vintage u and utilized vintage v.

Provided $\lambda'(v) > 0$, optimal allocation is very simple and obvious: $\lambda(u) < \lambda(v)$ if and only if $u < v$. No vintage should be left unutilized if an older vintage is in use. A rational planner allocating a given total employment $N(t)$ would first man the newest equipment, then the next newest, and so on until he runs out of labor (or out of equipment). This is also what the competitive market will do. As we shall see, except in the labor-surplus regime, the competitive real wage rate makes it unprofitable to operate the oldest equipment. Quasi-rents obtainable at time t vary inversely with the age of capital—highest for the most modern, zero for the " cut-off " age, and negative for economically obsolete vintages.

5. *The purely capital-augmenting case*

If technical progress is purely capital-augmenting—$\lambda'(v) = 0$, the third, (*c*), of the special cases listed above—the allocation of employment among competing vintages of capital is indeterminate. Technical progress lowers the real cost of a unit of productive capacity. But once the capacity is in being, the marginal and average variable cost of output is the same on every vintage. Therefore, this case is not very interesting. It reduces to these possibilities:

(a) In regime I, there is always ample labor to man the whole capital stock. When $\lambda(v) = \lambda$, this implies:

$$N(t) = N^*(t) = \frac{1}{\lambda} Y(t) = \frac{1}{\lambda} \int_{-\infty} \mu(v) I(v) dv. \tag{4}$$

Let $s(t)$ be the ratio of gross saving to gross output at time t. Correspondingly, $\frac{1}{\mu(t)}$ is the marginal or incremental capital requirement per unit of output. We have, therefore, the familiar Harrod-Domar equation for the rate of growth of output and employment:

$$\frac{N'(t)}{N(t)} = \frac{Y'(t)}{Y(t)} = \mu(t)s(t). \tag{5}$$

If labor is truly in excess supply, its marginal product is zero and so is its competitive real wage, or its shadow price in a planned economy. Correspondingly, the rent on capital of vintage v is its average product: $\mu(v)$. If $L(t)$ is just equal to $N(t)$, then the price of labor $w(t)$ is indeterminate between zero and its average product λ. Correspondingly, the quasi-rent $\rho(t, v)$ on vintage v capital is indeterminate between $\mu(v)$ and zero:

$$\rho(t, v) = \mu(v) \left(1 - \frac{w(t)}{\lambda}\right) \geqq 0. \tag{6}$$

(b) In the other two regimes, labor supply is not large enough to permit utilization of all vintages of capital. The marginal product of capital is zero, whatever its vintage. New capital has no advantage over old. If labor is fully employed, its real wage is λ, its average product. This situation may, of course, lead to Keynesian difficulties: full employment incomes might generate saving but, since profits are zero, not corresponding investment. Then the result would be under-utilization of both capital and labor, with the efficiency-prices of factors again indeterminate.

6. *Obsolescence and income distribution*

So much for purely capital-augmenting technical progress. In all other cases new vintages will always be preferred to older vintages. We disregard the labor surplus regime as atypical for advanced economies. In cases of interest, then, the age of the oldest capital in use, $m(t)$, is related to total employment by the equation

$$N(t) = \int_{t-m(t)}^{t} \frac{\mu(v)}{\lambda(v)} I(v) dv. \tag{7}$$

On the other hand, there is a relation between $m(t)$ and aggregate output:

$$Y(t) = \int_{t-m(t)}^{t} \mu(v) I(v) dv. \tag{8}$$

Employment of a unit of additional labor at time t would permit the use of capital just beyond the cutoff point $m(t)$, adding to total output the average product of labor on capital of this vintage. The marginal product of labor, therefore, is $\lambda(t - m(t))$. (This is the value of $\frac{\partial Y(t)}{\partial N(t)}$, as may be ascertained by differentiating (7) and (8) with respect to $N(t)$.) The marginal product of capital of any vintage may also be found. An additional unit of capital of an active vintage v (v greater than $t - m(t)$) would permit added output of $\mu(v)$. But it would require shifting $\frac{\mu(v)}{\lambda(v)}$ units of labor away from the oldest vintage capital, reducing output by $\frac{\mu(v)}{\lambda(v)}\lambda(t - m(t))$. An additional unit of capital of an idle vintage adds nothing to output.

Under competition, we can identify the marginal product of labor with the real wage and the marginal product of capital of any vintage with its quasi-rent:

$$w(t) = \lambda(t - m(t)), \tag{9}$$

$$\rho(t, v) = \begin{cases} 0 & \text{if } v \leq t - m(t) \\ \mu(v)\left(1 - \dfrac{\lambda(t - m(t))}{\lambda(v)}\right) & \text{if } v \geq t - m(t). \end{cases} \tag{10}$$

Together wages and quasi-rents exhaust the output of active capital.

The history of a particular investment is this: Its average product remains constant. At the beginning it earns a positive rent, because it is superior to earlier vintages. But as still better capital comes into existence, wages rise and the rents on the investment decline. Finally, wages are bid up so high by the owners of modern equipment that the rent on the investment vanishes. It is obsolete and ceases to operate.

7. *The growth of income*

The growth of income may be decomposed into a part attributable to the growth of the labor force and another part associated with new investment. Differentiating (7) and (8), we obtain:

$$N'(t) = \frac{\mu(t)I(t)}{\lambda(t)} - \frac{\mu(t - m(t))}{\lambda(t - m(t))} I(t - m(t))(1 - m'(t))$$

$$Y'(t) = \mu(t)I(t) - \mu(t - m(t))I(t - m(t))(1 - m'(t))$$

$$\lambda(t - m(t))N'(t) = \mu(t)\frac{\lambda(t - m(t))}{\lambda(t)} I(t) - \mu(t - m(t))I(t - m(t))(1 - m'(t))$$

$$Y'(t) = N'(t)\lambda(t - m(t)) + I(t)\mu(t)\left(1 - \frac{\lambda(t - m(t))}{\lambda(t)}\right) \tag{11}$$

$$= N'(t)w(t) + I(t)\rho(t, t)$$

$$\frac{Y'(t)}{Y(t)} = \left(\frac{w(t)N(t)}{Y(t)}\right)\frac{N'(t)}{N(t)} + \rho(t, t)\frac{I(t)}{Y(t)}\,. \tag{12}$$

This decomposition is analogous to the more conventional one for models with substitution.

In regime II, full employment, causation may be interpreted in this manner: $L(t) = N(t) \rightarrow m(t) \rightarrow Y(t)$ and $w(t)$. The first causal arrow stands for (7), the second for (8). In the Keynesian regime III, output is determined by effective demand. The causation then runs the other way: $Y(t) \rightarrow w(t)$ and $m(t) \rightarrow N(t) < L(t)$. Now the first arrow stands for (8), the second for (7). In this interpretation, one can easily allow for feedback effects of income distribution on effective demand. Equations (11) and (12) apply under either interpretation.

If aggregate demand falls, the model says that plants shut down in order of their age. Aside from the usual complications of aggregation, this is realistic enough. Its corollary, however, is that the average and marginal products of labor rise as labor is laid off from the oldest and least efficient plants. Cyclical statistics indicate the opposite, apparently because, in recessions believed to be temporary, employers continue to man, at least partially, facilities which they are not using (and/or because the right-hand side of (7) contains an " overhead " component independent of current output).

8. *Exponential Growth Under Full Employment: Labor-augmenting progress*

In what follows, both technical progress and labor force growth are assumed to be exponential:

$$(13)\qquad \begin{cases} L(t) = L_0 e^{nt} \\ \mu(v) = \mu_0 e^{\mu v} \\ \lambda(v) = \lambda_0 e^{\lambda v} \end{cases}$$

The *full employment* regime is analyzed first: the labor supply is fully used but is insufficient to man all physically surviving capital. Moreover, the simplest kind of technical progress is assumed—the purely labor-augmenting, " Harrod-neutral " variety, i.e., $\mu(v) = \mu_0$ for all v.

9. *Balanced growth paths*

Consider paths along which gross investment has been growing exponentially forever: $I(t) = I_0 e^{gt}$. From (7) and (13) we calculate:

$$L_0 e^{nt} = \frac{\mu_0 I_0}{\lambda_0 (g - \lambda)} e^{(g-\lambda)t}(1 - e^{-(g-\lambda)m(t)}) \text{ for all } t.$$

If $g = n + \lambda$, this equation can be satisfied with $m(t)$ constant. If $g \neq n + \lambda$, the equation can not be satisfied even with variable $m(t)$; for $g < n + \lambda$, the left-hand side must eventually outstrip the right while $g > n + \lambda$ implies that $m(t) \to 0$ which in turn implies that gross investment eventually exceeds gross output (see (18)). Therefore:

(i) $g = n + \lambda$, the usual formula for the " natural rate of growth " under Harrod-neutral technical progress; and

(ii) $m(t)$ is a constant, say m, satisfying

$$L_0 = \frac{\mu_0 I_0}{\lambda_0 n}(1 - e^{-nm}).$$

$$(14)\qquad m = -\frac{1}{n}\log\left(1 - \frac{\lambda_0 n L_0}{\mu_0 I_0}\right).$$

For this formula to make sense, it is necessary that $\lambda_0 n L_0 < \mu_0 I_0$. The meaning of this restriction is easily seen after it is rewritten:

$$nL_0 e^{nt} < \frac{\mu_0 I_0 e^{gt}}{\lambda_0 e^{\lambda t}}.$$

In this form it says that the increment to the labor force must be smaller than the labor required to man the brand new capital: the gap is to be filled with the labor that had been operating the capital (of age m) now being retired. If the inequality is not satisfied, the length of life of capital will have to be extended indefinitely and, if N^* is finite, labor will eventually become surplus. This puts a lower limit on I_0 (cf. (vi) below).

(iii) $\rho(t, t)$ is constant;

$$(15)\qquad \rho(t, t) = \mu_0(1 - e^{-\lambda m}).$$

(iv) $w(t)$ grows exponentially at rate λ;

(16) $$w(t) = (\lambda_0 e^{-\lambda m})e^{\lambda t};$$

(v) $Y(t)$ grows exponentially at rate g; from (8)

(17) $$Y(t) = \frac{\mu_0 I_0}{g}(1 - e^{-gm})e^{gt}.$$

(vi) From (17) it follows that the gross saving ratio, $s(t)$, defined as $I(t)/Y(t)$, is a constant depending on m:

(18) $$s = \frac{g}{\mu_0(1 - e^{-gm})} = \frac{I_0}{Y_0}.$$

If the saving rate thus calculated exceeds one, it means that even with consumption reduced to zero the economy is incapable of producing the minimal equipment required to employ the whole labor force, and eventually a labor surplus situation must emerge (cf. (ii) above)

10. *Alternative Saving Rates*

According to (18) the path corresponding to a high saving ratio is characterized by low m, quick obsolescence, modern capital. In the same sense, a low saving ratio means a long economic life for capital. Eliminating I_0 between (14) and (17) shows that a path with low m and high s has a high Y_0, as in Figure 2.

Not all values of s and m are consistent with balanced growth of this kind, at the " natural " rate $g = \lambda + n$. At one extreme, the lower limit on the saving ratio s is g/μ_0. This is the value of s for which m must be infinity in (18). It corresponds, therefore, to a situation in which, according to (14), the rate of investment is just sufficient to employ increments to the labor force without transferring any workers from obsolescent capital. $L(t)$ and $N(t)$ are equal to $N^*(t)$ and all are growing at rate n. But because full employment requires that infinitely old capital be left in use, the competitive equilibrium real wage, according to (16), must be zero!

Balanced Growth Paths

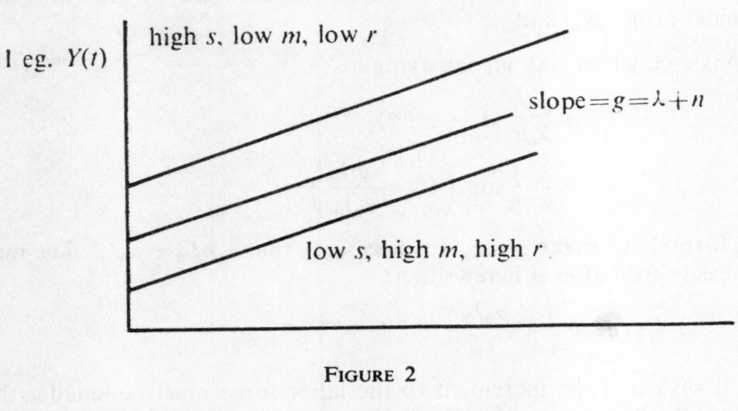

FIGURE 2

Suppose the saving ratio is still smaller, so that $s\mu_0$ is less than g. If no capital ever becomes obsolete, the stock of capital will grow at the rate $s\mu_0$. But with the number of workers growing at rate n and the number of workers required per machine falling at rate λ, the stock of capital must grow at rate g to provide enough places. If $s\mu_0 < g$, therefore, new investment is insufficient to employ the natural increase in the labor force, much less to require release of any labor from older capital. So long as any capital is unused, previously submarginal vintages will be brought into use. As labor goes to work on older and older vintages, the real wage falls. The limit, of course, is the labor surplus regime.

The highest conceivable saving ratio (in a closed economy) is 1, and the correspondingly shortest capital lifetime m is given by

$$1 = \frac{g}{\mu_0(1 - e^{-gm})}.$$

(This has a positive solution for m provided $g < \mu_0$; otherwise, as remarked above, the need for new capital surpasses total output.) But this path, which yields the highest output path in Figure 2, is obviously not the path of highest consumption.

11. *The Golden Rule Path*

There is indeed a " golden rule " path—the balanced growth path on which, given the development of the labor force $L(t)$, consumption is higher at every point in time than on any other balanced growth path. Along this path, (1) the saving ratio is equal to the share of capital in gross product; and (2) the rate of interest or marginal efficiency of capital is equal to the growth rate. These are familiar neo-classical or neo-neo-classical propositions, and it is of interest that they apply for the fixed-coefficient technology of the model under discussion here.

To prove the first proposition, it is necessary to show how the share of capital α depends on the obsolescence period m. The wage bill $N(t)w(t)$ is equal to $N(0)e^{nt}e^{\lambda(t-m)}$. Since $Y(t) = Y(0)e^{(n+\lambda)t}$, labor's share is constant over time along any path with exponential investment and, therefore, constant m and constant s:

$$1 - \alpha = \frac{N(t)w(t)}{Y(t)} = \frac{N(0)\lambda_0 e^{-\lambda m}}{Y(0)} \tag{19}$$

From (14) and (17) this becomes:

$$1 - \alpha = \frac{g(e^{-\lambda m} - e^{-gm})}{n(1 - e^{-gm})}. \tag{20}$$

From (20) it follows that α is an increasing function of m—running from zero for $m = 0$, i.e., when all input is current labor input, to 1 for $m = \infty$, i.e., when labor is in surplus.

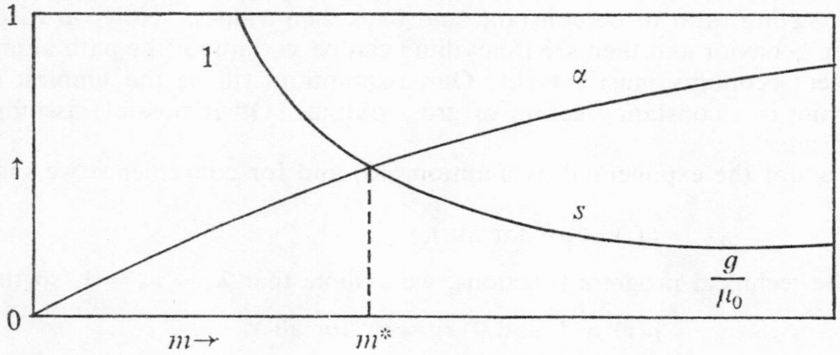

FIGURE 3

Balanced-Growth Paths

Relations of Capital Share α and

Saving Ratio s to Obsolescence Period m

Similarly (18) shows that s, the saving ratio, is a decreasing function of m. Both these relationships are shown in Figure 3. At m^*, $s = \alpha$. That is:

$$\frac{g}{\mu(1 - e^{-gm^*})} = \frac{n(1 - e^{-gm^*}) - g(e^{-\lambda m^*} - e^{-gm^*})}{n(1 - e^{-gm^*})}. \tag{21}$$

We must show that this value of m^* also maximizes $C(0)$.

$$C(0) = (1 - s)\,Y(0) = \frac{1 - s}{s} \cdot \frac{\lambda_0 n N(0)}{\mu_0(1 - e^{-nm})}.$$

For given $N(0)$, $C(0)$ will be maximized if

$$\frac{1 - s}{s(1 - e^{-nm})} \text{ is maximized,}$$

i.e., if $$\frac{\mu_0(1 - e^{-gm}) - g}{g(1 - e^{-nm})} \text{ is maximized with respect to } m.$$

The condition for the maximum,

$$g(1 - e^{-nm})\mu_0 g e^{-gm} = (\mu_0(1 - e^{-gm}) - g)gne^{-nm}, \tag{22}$$

reduces to (21), the condition for $\alpha = s$. Since this equation determines a unique local extremum, which is a maximum, the first formulation of the golden rule theorem is proved. The second version of the theorem states that along the balanced growth path with maximum consumption the rate of interest is equal to the growth rate. That statement is also true in this model, but the proof is postponed until the interest rate or marginal efficiency of capital has been introduced more formally.

III ASYMPTOTIC BEHAVIOR UNDER PURELY LABOR-AUGMENTING TECHNICAL PROGRESS WITH FULL EMPLOYMENT AT A CONSTANT SAVINGS RATIO

1. *Preliminaries*

Throughout the last few sections, we have been exploring the properties of full employment paths along which investment grows exponentially at the natural rate. We have observed in (14) and (18) that this restriction requires the economic lifetime of capital and the gross saving ratio to be constant, and fixes their values. Now we wish to postulate the saving behavior and then see if anything can be said about the path along which a full employment economy must travel.[1] Our assumption will be the simplest one, i.e., that gross saving is a constant fraction of gross output. Other possible assumptions will be discussed later.

We adopt the exponential assumption (13) and for convenience we shall let $L_0 = 1$, so that

$$L(t) = e^{nt} \text{ for all } t.$$

As for the technical progress functions, we assume that $\lambda_0 = \mu_0 = 1$, so that

$$\mu(v) = 1 \text{ and } \lambda(v) = e^{\lambda v} \text{ for all } v.$$

Finally, let s denote the (constant) savings ratio. These assumptions, which are merely choices of units, can be made without loss of generality.

Before our economy can proceed to evolve, it must be endowed with an *initial capital profile*. Let $t = 0$ be the point in time at which the economy begins to evolve. Then the

[1] Uzawa [3] studied this problem in the framework of the no-obsolescence vintage model.

initial capital profile is given by an arbitrary nonnegative real function, which we denote I, on the interval $(-\infty, 0)$. In other words, $I(t)$ is predetermined and arbitrary for all $t < 0$. As a matter of convenience we shall assume that there exists a real number $h^* < 0$ such that

$$I(v) = 0 \text{ for } v \leqq h^*,$$

$$I(v) > 0 \text{ for } v > h^*,$$

where $h^* = -\infty$ is permissible. Vintages later than h^* are all present in the initial capital profile in positive quantities. (We also assume that I is a function which can be integrated.)

Instead of using the function I for the initial capital profile, we shall use a transformed version. The reason for introducing this transformation will become apparent shortly. For every $t < 0$, define

$$f(t) = \frac{1}{s} I(t)e^{-(\lambda+n)t}.$$

Apart from the multiplier $\frac{1}{s}$, f is just the ratio of I to an exponential trend, so specifying f is equivalent to specifying I. Since $I(t)$ is intrinsically nonnegative, so is $f(t)$.

Starting at time $t = 0$, the economy proceeds under its own power. Its motion is determined by the following equations, which are obvious versions of (7) and (8).

(a) *Full employment of labor*

$$\int_{h(t)}^{t} e^{-\lambda v} I(v)dv = e^{nt} \text{ for all } t \geqq 0,$$

where $h(t)$ is the vintage of the oldest capital in use at time t, so that $h(t) + m(t) = t$.

(b) *Determination of output*

$$\int_{h(t)}^{t} I(v)dv = Y(t) \text{ for all } t \geqq 0.$$

(c) *Equality of gross saving and investment*

$$I(t) = sY(t) \text{ for all } t \geqq 0.$$

These three equations may be collapsed into two. For every $t \geqq 0$, let $f(t)$ be defined by

$$f(t) = e^{-(\lambda+n)t}Y(t);$$

$f(t)$ is output per efficiency unit of labor. This definition is consistent with the one already made for $t < 0$, so we can proceed to write the basic equations which govern the motion of the economy as follows:

$$\text{(7')} \qquad s\int_{h(t)}^{t} e^{-n(t-x)} f(x)dx = 1 \text{ for } t \geqq 0,$$

$$\text{(8')} \qquad s\int_{h(t)}^{t} e^{-(\lambda+n)(t-x)} f(x)dx = f(t) \text{ for } t \geqq 0.$$

It is sometimes more convenient to write these equations somewhat differently:

$$\text{(7'')} \qquad s\int_{0}^{m(t)} e^{-nx} f(t-x)dx = 1 \text{ for } t \geqq 0,$$

$$\text{(8'')} \qquad s\int_{0}^{m(t)} e^{-(\lambda+n)x} f(t-x)dx = f(t) \text{ for } t \geqq 0,$$

where $m(t)$ has its earlier meaning.

Remark 1: *$f(t) > 0$ for all $t \geqq 0$.*

Proof. It follows from equation (8′) that if $f(t_0) = 0$ for the first time at some $t_0 \geqq 0$, then either $f(t) = 0$ for *all* $t \leqq t_0$ or $h(t_0) = t_0$. In either case, equation (7′) cannot hold.

Remark 2: *The functions f and h are both continuous on the interval* $(0, \infty)$.

Proof. For $\lambda \geqq 0$, the integrand in (8′) is no greater than that in (7′). Hence $f(t) \leqq 1$. Since f is thus bounded and positive, the continuity of h follows from (7′) and then the continuity of f from (8′).[1]

Remark 3: *The functions f and h are, in fact, differentiable on* $(0, \infty)$.

Proof. Notice first that if h is differentiable, then it follows from equation (8′) that f is also differentiable. To see that h is differentiable, we write down equation (7′) twice, once for time t and once for time $t + \Delta t$, and then we subtract the latter from the former. This leads to

$$\int_{h(t)}^{h(t+\Delta t)} e^{nx} f(x)dx - \int_{t}^{t+\Delta t} e^{nx} f(x)dx = \frac{1}{s}\, e^{nt}(1 - e^{n\Delta t}).$$

Since f is continuous, we can use the mean value theorem and obtain, following division by Δt,

$$\frac{h(t+\Delta t) - h(t)}{\Delta t}\, e^{nx'} f(x') - e^{nx''} f(x'') = \frac{1}{s}\, e^{nt}\, \frac{1 - e^{n\Delta t}}{\Delta t}$$

where x' is between $h(t)$ and $h(t + \Delta t)$ and x'' is between t and $t + \Delta t$. Letting $\Delta t \to 0$, we see that

$$\lim_{\Delta t \to 0} \left\{ \frac{h(t+\Delta t) - h(t)}{\Delta t}\, e^{nx'} f(x') \right\}$$

must exist, since the other limits in the equation exist. Hence h is differentiable at t unless

$$\lim_{\Delta t \to 0} f(x') = 0.$$

But $\lim f(x') = f(h(t))$, by continuity of f and h. Now if $h(t) > h^*$, then $f(h(t)) > 0$. If $h(t) = h^*$ and $h'(t)$ does not exist, then equation (7′) cannot hold to the right of t, i.e., full employment ceases at t. This completes the proof.[2]

2. *Balanced growth paths*

At every point of time t, the values of the function f on the interval $(h(t), t)$ determine the immediate future of f. The values of f on the interval $(h(0), 0)$ are the *initial conditions* of the system. Our task in this section is to look for something analogous to an equilibrium point, namely for a set of self-sustaining initial conditions. In other words, we are looking for an initial capital profile which leads the function m to be constant and the function f to be periodic:

$$m(t) = m^* \text{ (a constant)} \qquad \text{for all } t \geqq 0,$$

$$f(t) = f(t - m^*) \qquad \text{for all } t \geqq 0.$$

A solution of equations (7′) and (8′) which satisfies these two requirements is called an *equilibrium solution.* An equilibrium solution for which f is in fact constant is called a *balanced growth* solution. The discussion in 11.10 of " replacement echoes " shows that if $n \neq 0$ the only equilibrium solutions are actually balanced growth solutions, because

[1] If we drop the assumption that the initial capital profile " has no holes " (i.e. the function I, once positive, remains positive) then h may cease to be continuous (although it is not difficult to trace its discontinuities) while f remains continuous throughout $(0, \infty)$.

[2] If the assumption that the initial capital profile " has no holes " were to be dropped, one would still have the differentiability of f and h in open intervals where h is continuous.

the " echoes " in the function $e^{-(\lambda+n)t}I(t)$ cannot be strictly periodic. In any case, even if $n = 0$ (which permits f to be strictly periodic) the saving ratio cannot be constant unless f is constant. In other words, the only equilibrium solutions are balanced growth solutions.

To find a balanced growth solution (if there is one) we must solve equations (7″) and (8″) under the assumption that f and m are both constant. Setting $f(t) = f^*$ and $m(t) = m^*$ for all t, where f^* and m^* are nonnegative real numbers, causes equations (7″) and (8″) to reduce to

$$sf^* \int_0^{m^*} e^{-nx}dx = \frac{sf^*}{n}(1-e^{-nm^*}) = 1$$

and

$$s\int_0^{m^*} e^{-(\lambda+n)x}dx = \frac{s}{\lambda+n}(1-e^{-(\lambda+n)m^*}) = 1$$

respectively. These equations have a unique solution, namely

$$m^* = -\frac{1}{\lambda+n}\log\frac{s-\lambda-n}{s} \tag{23}$$

and

$$f^* = \frac{n}{s(1-e^{-nm^*})} \tag{24}$$

provided that $s \geqq \lambda + n$. If $s = \lambda + n$, we have $m^* = +\infty$ and $f^* = n/s$, which we shall admit as a solution, provided $n > 0$. If $s > \lambda + n$, then m^* is finite and f^* exceeds n/s. If $s < \lambda + n$, full employment is in the long run impossible. This is another way of expressing the remarks made above in interpreting equation (14). Formally, (7″) and (8″) have no solution. To see this note that (8″) implies for every $t \geqq 0$

$$f(t) = s\int_0^{m(t)} e^{-(\lambda+n)x}f(t-x)dx \leqq s\int_0^{\infty} e^{-(\lambda+n)x}f(t-x)dx \leqq \frac{s}{\lambda+n}\bar{f}$$

where $\bar{f}$ is the supremum of f (finite by (7″)). If $\frac{s}{\lambda+n} < 1$, then either $\bar{f} = 0$ (whence $f(t)$ is identically zero) or, if $\bar{f} > 0$, a t_0 can be found for which $f(t_0) > \frac{s}{\lambda+n}\bar{f}$. The first contingency contradicts (7″), the second contradicts the inequality just derived.

Note that in this section the capital-output ratio $\mu_0 = 1$, so that s is Harrod's warranted rate of growth. Comparisons between s and $\lambda + n$ are comparisons between the warranted and natural rates.

3. *A Basic Differential Equation*

We return now to the general case where $f(t)$ and $m(t)$ need not be constant. Since we know that both f and m are differentiable, we may differentiate equations (7″) and (8″) and obtain, after some calculation, the differential equation:

$$f'(t) = (s-\lambda-n)f(t) - (sf(t)-n)e^{-\lambda m(t)}$$

for all $t > 0$. This is actually the differential equation which we have already seen in different guise, (11), expressing the rate of change of output in terms of marginal productivities and factor rewards. It can be usefully transformed with the help of (23) and (24), which imply that

$$s-\lambda-n = s\left(1-\frac{n}{sf^*}\right)e^{-\lambda m^*}.$$

We now have

$$f'(t) = s\left(1-\frac{n}{sf^*}\right)e^{-\lambda m^*}f(t) - (sf(t)-n)e^{-\lambda m(t)}.$$

But we have observed that $f(t) > 0$ for all t, so it is permissible to divide the second term by $f(t)$ and thus obtain

$$f'(t) = sf(t)\left\{e^{-\lambda m^*}\left(1 - \frac{n}{sf^*}\right) - e^{-\lambda m(t)}\left(1 - \frac{n}{sf(t)}\right)\right\} \tag{25}$$

for all $t > 0$.

This differential equation says something about the derivative of f in terms of the deviation of the system from balanced growth. Specifically,

$$\text{if} \quad m(t) \geqq m^* \text{ and } f(t) \leqq f^* \text{ then } f'(t) \geqq 0, \text{ and}$$
$$\text{if} \quad m(t) \leqq m^* \text{ and } f(t) \geqq f^* \text{ then } f'(t) \leqq 0.$$

4. *Asymptotic Behavior in the Case* $s \leqq \lambda + n$

Since the initial capital profile is, to a large extent, arbitrary, we cannot hope to characterize the solution of equations (7′) and (8′) fully. However, we can hope that as t becomes very large, the influence of the initial capital profile wanes, so that assertions can be made about the behavior of the economy for large t. This hope turns out to be realized. This section and the next are devoted to asymptotic analysis.

It has already been shown that if $s < \lambda + n$, continued full employment is not possible. The economy does not save enough to provide for the growing effective labor force. So we turn to the other cases, and first to the case $s = \lambda + n$.

For this case, we have the following differential equation:

$$f'(t) = (n - sf(t))e^{-\lambda m(t)}$$

which implies the following two statements:

$$f'(t) \gtreqqless 0 \quad \text{according as} \quad f(t) \lesseqqgtr \frac{n}{s}$$

and

$$f(t) \gtreqqless \frac{n}{s} \quad \text{according as} \quad f(o) \gtreqqless \frac{n}{s}.$$

In any case, f is monotone and bounded, and must therefore converge. We shall denote its limit δ. We now define a function F by

$$F(t) = s\int_{-\infty}^{t} e^{-(\lambda+n)(t-x)}f(x)dx \qquad \text{for } t \geqq 0.$$

$F(0)$ is finite if the stock of capital at time zero is finite. We assume this to be the case. Differentiating F, one obtains

$$F'(t) = sf(t) - (\lambda + n)F(t) = (\lambda + n)[f(t) - F(t)] \leqq 0.$$

Thus F is a non-increasing function. Since it is nonnegative, and therefore bounded below, it must converge. Now f is known to converge and therefore

$$\lim_{t\to\infty} [f(t) - F(t)]$$

exists. In other words, $\lim F'(t)$ exists, and since F converges, this limit must be equal to 0. Thus, f and F converge to the same limit. Comparison of the definition of F with (8′) now implies that $h(t) \to -\infty$ and, therefore,

$$\lim_{t\to\infty} m(t) = \infty.$$

For an arbitrary $\varepsilon > 0$, let T be defined by

$$\varepsilon = s\int_{T}^{\infty} e^{-nx}dx = \frac{s}{n}\, e^{-nT}.$$

It now follows from equation (7″) and the fact that $f \leqq 1$ that

$$1 - \varepsilon \leqq s \int_0^T e^{-nx} f(t - x)dx \leqq 1,$$

where the first inequality holds for all t, and the second inequality holds for large t (since $m(t) \to \infty$). Letting $t \to \infty$, we obtain

$$1 - \varepsilon \leqq \frac{s\delta}{n}[1 - e^{-nT}] \leqq 1,$$

$$1 - \varepsilon \leqq \delta\left[\frac{s}{n} - \varepsilon\right] \leqq 1.$$

But ε is arbitrary, so we must have $\delta = \frac{n}{s}$.

If $n = 0$, the proof must be modified slightly: in that case, for any arbitrary T,

$$s \int_0^T f(t - x)dx \leqq 1$$

provided t is sufficiently large. (This is true because $m(t)$ tends to ∞.) Letting $t \to \infty$, we obtain

$$s\delta T \leqq 1.$$

But T is arbitrary, so it must be true that $\delta = 0$. Thus, when $s = \lambda + n$, the functions f and n tend to the balanced growth values derived in (23) and (24).

5. *Convergence to Balanced Growth in the Case $s > \lambda + n$*

This section is devoted in its entirety to a proof of the following theorem:

If $s > \lambda + n$, then $\lim_{t\to\infty} f(t) = f^*$ and $\lim_{t\to\infty} m(t) = m^*$.

The proof is rather elaborate, but the techniques used may be of some interest. We shall develop the theorem in a series of lemmas.

Lemma 1. *There exists a t_0 such that*

$$f(t) \geqq \frac{n}{s} \textit{ for } t \geqq t_0.$$

Proof. It follows from the differential equation (25) that if $f(t) \leqq \frac{n}{s}$ then $f'(t) > 0$, so that if there exists a t_0 such that $f(t_0) \geqq \frac{n}{s}$, then $f(t) \geqq \frac{n}{s}$ for all $t \geqq t_0$. It remains to be shown, therefore, that $f(t) < \frac{n}{s}$ for *all* $t \geqq 0$ is an impossibility. Assume that in fact $f(t) < \frac{n}{s}$ for all $t \geqq 0$. Then

$$f'(t) > 0 \qquad \text{for all } t,$$
$$h'(t) < 0 \qquad \text{for all } t$$

where the second inequality follows from differentiation of equation (7′). Thus,

$$\lim_{t\to\infty} f(t)$$

exists. Call it δ. By assumption,

$$f(t) < \delta \leqq \frac{n}{s} \qquad \text{for all } t.$$

Substituting δ in equation (7″) we obtain

$$1 < \frac{s\delta}{n}(1 - e^{-nm(t)}) \leqq 1 - e^{-nm(t)}$$

whence

$$e^{-nm(t)} < 0,$$

an impossibility. This completes the proof.

Lemma 2. *If* $s > \lambda + n$, *then* $\lim_{t\to\infty} h(t) = \infty$.

Proof. Differentiating equation (7′) with respect to t leads to

$$se^{-nm(t)}f(h(t))h'(t) = sf(t) - n.$$

If $f(t) \geqq \frac{n}{s}$, then $h'(t) \geqq 0$. By Lemma 1, there exists a t_0 such that $f(t) \geqq \frac{n}{s}$ for $t \geqq t_0$, so we have $h'(t) \geqq 0$ for $t \geqq t_0$. Therefore,

$$\lim_{t\to\infty} h(t) = \infty$$

or

$$\lim_{t\to\infty} h(t) = K < \infty.$$

Assume the latter.[1] Multiply the first equation in the proof by e^{nt} and observe that $t - m(t) = h(t)$. Now integrate over t from 0 to ∞; if $h(t)$ has a limit the integral on the left is finite, so $\int_0^\infty e^{nt}(sf(t)-n)dt$ converges. This is not possible if f' is bounded away from zero. But (25) tells us (since $m(t)\to\infty$) that $\frac{f'}{f} \to (\delta-\lambda-n) > 0$, and thus, by Lemma 1, f' is bounded away from zero if $n > 0$. (A similar argument holds if $n = 0$.) When $n = 0$, the above argument shows that $f(t)\to 0$ from above, so that $f'(t) < 0$ for indefinitely large t. But $h(t)\to K$ implies $m(t)\to\infty$, in which case (25) implies $f'(t) > 0$ for all sufficiently large t, a contradiction.

What Lemma 2 tells us is that if $s > \lambda + n$ then every piece of capital is eventually discarded, never to be brought again into use.

Let t_0 be the point beyond which the function h is increasing. Such a point exists by Lemma 1. Since, by Lemma 2, $h(t) \to \infty$ as $t \to \infty$, we can divide the interval $[t_0, \infty)$ as follows: Let a sequence $\{t_n\}$ be defined by

$$h(t_{n+1}) = t_n \qquad n = 0, 1, \ldots$$

Thus, t_{n+1} is the time at which capital of vintage t_n becomes obsolete.

We shall now study the asymptotic behavior of the functions f and m by looking at successive intervals of the form $[t_k, t_{k+1})$.

Lemma 3. $\limsup_{t\to\infty} f(t) \leqq f^*$.

Proof. Suppose that we have been able to find a real number a_{n-1} such that for all $t \geqq t_{n-1}$,

$$f(t) \leqq a_{n-1}.$$

This means that if we take any $t \geqq t_n$, we have

$$f(t - x) \leqq a_{n-1} \qquad \text{for } 0 \leqq x \leqq m(t).$$

Consider an arbitrary $t \geqq t_n$ and fix it. We shall attempt to construct a real number a_n

[1] We acknowledge a useful suggestion from Kenneth Arrow at this point.

such that $a_n < a_{n-1}$ and $f(t) \leqq a_n$. For convenience, we shall refer to $f(t-x)e^{-nx}$ as $\varphi(x)$.

Problem. Among all real functions φ, defined on $[0, m(t)]$, and satisfying the two conditions

$$0 \leqq \varphi(x) \leqq a_{n-1}e^{-nx},$$

$$s\int_0^{m(t)} \varphi(x)dx = 1,$$

find a function φ^* which *maximizes* the quantity

$$s\int_0^{m(t)} e^{-\lambda x}\varphi(x)dx.$$

The solution of this maximization is given by the function φ which is as concentrated as possible near zero. In other words,

$$\begin{aligned} \varphi^*(x) &= a_{n-1}e^{-nx} && \text{for } 0 \leqq x < T \\ &= 0 && \text{for } T \leqq x \leqq m(t) \end{aligned}$$

where T is determined from

$$s\int_0^T a_{n-1}e^{-nx}dx = 1$$

which reduces to

$$T = -\frac{1}{n}\log\left(1 - \frac{n}{sa_{n-1}}\right).$$

Note that the inequality $T \leqq m(t)$ is assured because T is the *smallest* value which $m(t)$ could take on in equation (7′), with $f(t-x)$ satisfying the constraints. We may now write

$$\begin{aligned} \text{maximum} &= s\int_0^{m(t)} e^{-\lambda x}\varphi^*(x)dx \\ &= sa_{n-1}\int_0^T e^{-(\lambda+n)x}dx \\ &= \frac{sa_{n-1}}{\lambda+n}[1 - e^{-(\lambda+n)T}]. \end{aligned}$$

Using the expression for T, we have

$$\text{maximum} = \frac{sa_{n-1}}{\lambda+n}\left\{1 - \left(1 - \frac{n}{sa_{n-1}}\right)^{\frac{\lambda+n}{n}}\right\}$$

Let us call this last quantity a_n

$$a_n = \frac{sa_{n-1}}{\lambda+n}\left\{1 - \left(1 - \frac{n}{sa_{n-1}}\right)^{\frac{\lambda+n}{n}}\right\}.$$

Now a_n is the *largest* value which $f(t)$ could take on, with $f(t-x)$ satisfying the constraints for all x. In other words,

$$f(t) \leqq a_n.$$

It remains to be shown that $a_n < a_{n-1}$, which is equivalent to

$$\frac{s}{n} + n\left\{1 - \left(1 - \frac{n}{sa_{n-1}}\right)^{\frac{\lambda+n}{n}}\right\} < 1.$$

But $a_{n-1} > f^*$, or else there is nothing to prove. The left-hand side of the last inequality is *precisely* equal to 1 when $a_{n-1} = f^*$, so it is clearly *less* than 1 when $a_{n-1} > f^*$. Thus, we have produced a new upper bound for f, namely a_n, which is good for all $t \geqq t_n$. In the same fashion, we can produce still newer upper bounds, with the result that we shall have a sequence $\{a_k\}$ such that

$$f(t) \leqq a_k \qquad \text{for all } t \geqq t_k.$$

To complete the argument, we must find an a_0 such that $f(t) \leqq a_0$ for $t \geqq t_0$. But a brief look at equations (7′) and (8′) will reveal that $a_0 = 1$ will do nicely. Finally, it remains to be verified that the sequence $\{a_k\}$ converges to f^*. This follows immediately, from the definition of f^*, upon solving the equation for a_n under the condition $a_n = a_{n-1}$. Thus, the proof is complete.

Lemma 4. $\liminf_{t\to\infty} f(t) \geqq f^*$.

Proof. The proof is similar to that of Lemma 3, with one added complication. Suppose that we have found a real number c_{n-1} such that

$$f(t) \geqq c_{n-1} \qquad \text{for } t \geqq t_{n-1}.$$

Then, let t be an arbitrary number satisfying $t \geqq t_n$, and let $m(t)$ be denoted m for short. Note that m is restricted by

$$s\int_0^m c_{n-1}e^{-nx}dx \leqq 1$$

which reduces to

$$m \leqq -\frac{1}{n}\log\left(1 - \frac{n}{sc_{n-1}}\right).$$

We know that $c_{n-1} \leqq f(t-x) \leqq 1$ for all x in $[0, m]$. Let us refer to $e^{-nx}f(t-x)$ as $\varphi(x)$ and consider the following problem: Among all functions φ on $[0, m]$, which satisfy

$$c_{n-1}e^{-nx} \leqq \varphi(x) \leqq e^{-nx} \qquad \text{for all } x$$

$$s\int_0^m \varphi(x)dx = 1,$$

find the function φ^* which *minimizes* the quantity

$$s\int_0^m e^{-\lambda x}\varphi(x)dx.$$

The solution is given by

$$\begin{aligned} \varphi^*(x) &= c_{n-1}e^{-nx} && \text{for } 0 \leqq x < T \\ &= e^{-nx} && \text{for } T \leqq x \leqq m \end{aligned}$$

where T is determined from

$$s\int_0^T c_{n-1}e^{-nx}dx + s\int_T^m e^{-nx}dx = 1,$$

which can be written

$$\frac{s}{n}\{c_{n-1} + (1 - c_{n-1})e^{-nT} - e^{-nm}\} = 1.$$

We note for later reference that

$$\frac{dT}{dm} = \frac{e^{-n(m-T)}}{1 - c_{n-1}}.$$

Now let the minimum of the problem be denoted $f_l(t)$:

$$f_l(t) = s\int_0^m e^{-\lambda x}\varphi^*(x)dx$$

$$= \frac{s}{\lambda + n}\{c_{n-1} + (1 - c_{n-1})e^{-(\lambda+n)T} - e^{-(\lambda+n)m}\}.$$

We know that $f(t) \geqq f_l(t)$. But $f_l(t)$ depends on the unknown m, which is awkward. In order to get rid of this dependence upon m, let us evaluate

$$\frac{df_l(t)}{dm} = \frac{s}{\lambda + n}\left\{-(\lambda + n)(1 - c_{n-1})e^{-(\lambda+n)T}\frac{dT}{dm} + (\lambda + n)e^{-(\lambda+n)m}\right\}$$

$$= se^{-nm}\{e^{-\lambda m} - e^{-\lambda T}\} \leqq 0$$

since $T \leqq m$. Hence, if we let m become as large as it can be, we shall still have a lower bound on $f(t)$. But the largest m can get is given by

$$m = -\frac{1}{n}\log\left(1 - \frac{n}{sc_{n-1}}\right).$$

So, our new lower bound is obtained by setting m equal to this quantity in the definition of $f_l(t)$, whereupon T becomes equal to m. Doing this, one obtains a new lower bound, to be denoted c_n, where

$$c_n = \frac{sc_{n-1}}{\lambda + n}\left\{1 - \left(1 - \frac{n}{sc_{n-1}}\right)^{\frac{\lambda+n}{n}}\right\}.$$

From here on, the proof proceeds as in Lemma 3. We can choose $c_o = \frac{n}{s}$. The sequence of lower bounds, $\{c_n\}$, obtained in the manner described, is increasing and it converges to f^*.

Lemmas 3 and 4 together constitute the following theorem:

The function f converges and $\lim_{t\to\infty} f(t) = f^*$.

As an immediate corollary one now obtains that

The function m converges and $\lim_{t\to\infty} m(t) = m^*$.

IV COMPETITIVE VALUE RELATIONS

1. *Wages, quasi-rents, and marginal products*

The impossibility of direct substitution between labor and capital goods in this model means that there is no " intensive margin ". But there is an " extensive margin " at which, under competition, price relationships are determined. The elementary calculations have been made in section II, 6-7, and we recapitulate them here.

Capital goods of age $m(t)$ are on the verge of obsolescence; they are " no-rent " capital. If they earned a positive rent their owners would not be about to withdraw them from production under tranquil competitive conditions. Since wages are the only prime cost in this model, the real wage must equal the average product of labor on no-rent capital. This yields, as before,

(9) $$w(t) = \lambda(t - m(t)).$$

Younger capital goods are intra-marginal, and earn a differential quasi-rent equal to the difference between output and labor costs; older ones could not cover prime costs if they were operated. Thus, with $\rho(t, v)$ representing the real quasi-rent earned at time t by capital goods of vintage v,

$$\text{(10)} \qquad \begin{aligned} \rho(t, v) &= 0 & v &\leqq t - m(t) \\ &= \mu(v)\left(1 - \frac{\lambda(t - m(t))}{\lambda(v)}\right) & v &\geqq t - m(t). \end{aligned}$$

In II, 6-7 it is shown that the competitive real wage and quasi-rent play the role of social marginal product of labor and of capital goods of vintage v: $w(t)$ is the increase in aggregate output permitted by one extra unit of employment, and $\rho(t, v)$ is the increase in aggregate output permitted by the availability of one extra unit of vintage v capital.

2. *Capital values*

Under conditions near to steady growth, the economic lifetime of capital will not change very much and, therefore, $\rho(t, v)$ will fall through time for each fixed v. (In the short run a sharp increase in output and employment may require a sudden increase in $m(t)$ and bring about a temporary rise in the quasi-rents on existing capital. Even previously retired capital will be activated.) If $m(t)$ does not fluctuate much, it is reasonable to suppose that the market can foresee with fair accuracy the pattern of quasi-rents a unit of capital can be expected to earn. The market value of any existing unit of capital will be the present value of the expected quasi-rents, discounted at the market rate of interest. Let $P(t, v)$ be the price at time t of a unit of capital of vintage v, and let $r(t)$ be the rate of interest at time t. Then

$$\text{(26)} \qquad P(t, v) = \int_t^{\tau} \rho(u, v) e^{-\int_t^u r(z)dz} du = \mu(v) \int_t^{\tau} \left[1 - \frac{\lambda(u - m(u))}{\lambda(v)}\right] e^{-\int_t^u r(z)dz} du.$$

In this expression $\tau = \tau(v)$ is the root of the equation $\rho(\tau, v) = 0$; that is, it is the instant at which capital of vintage v will be retired.[1] If m is constant, then of course $\tau = v + m$, and in any case $\tau = v + m(\tau)$.

For existing capital (26) is all there is to be said. When $v = t$, (26) gives $P(t, t)$, the market price of a new machine at the moment of its construction. In tranquil competitive equilibrium, $P(t, t)$ must also equal the cost of production of a new machine of vintage t. ($P(t, t)$ can fall short of the cost of production if gross investment is zero, but we shall ignore that possibility.) Since this is a one-sector model we can, as mentioned in II, 1, measure capital goods in units identical with the unit of output. Thus $P(t, t) = 1$, and we have for every t

$$\text{(27)} \qquad 1 = \int_t^{\tau} \rho(u, t) e^{-\int_t^u r(z)dz} du \text{ [2]}$$

or

$$\text{(27')} \qquad 1 = \int_0^{m(\tau)} \rho(x + t, t) e^{-\int_t^{t+x} r(z)dz} dx.$$

From (26) we can extract the well-known equilibrium condition

$$\text{(28)} \qquad \rho(t, v) + \frac{\partial P(t, v)}{\partial t} = r(t)P(t, v).$$

[1] We assume for simplicity that it is correctly foreseen that capital, once retired, will never be called back into production by a "cyclical" increase in output and employment.

[2] This can be regarded as an integral equation for the unknown interest rate as a function of time. The substitution

$R(u) = \exp(-\int_0^u r(z)dz)$ throws (27) into the more familiar form

$R(t) = \int^{\tau(t)} \rho(u, t)R(u)du$. Similarly for (27').

The value of the stock of capital is

$$K(t) = \int_{t-m(t)}^{t} P(t, v)I(v)dv. \tag{29}$$

(Here we use again the assumption that the earnings of any particular investment fall eventually to zero and do not revive.) Now, by total differentiation with respect to t and use of (28) we find

$$I(t) - K'(t) = \int_{t-m(t)}^{t} \rho(t, v)I(v)dv - r(t)K(t). \tag{30}$$

$K'(t)$ can be identified as net investment and $r(t)K(t)$ as net profits. Thus the difference between gross investment and net investment is the same as the difference between gross quasi-rents and net profits. Both can be identified as " true depreciation "; since we have ignored physical depreciation, only " obsolescence " remains. We can let $Z(t)$ stand for net output and $C(t)$ for consumption and write the accounting identities

$$Y(t) = C(t) + I(t) = w(t)N(t) + \int_{t-m(t)}^{t} \rho(t, v)I(v)dv,$$

$$Z(t) = C(t) + K'(t) = w(t)N(t) + r(t)K(t).$$

Equipped with these definitions and relations we can experiment with hypotheses that make net saving depend in one way or another on net income or net profits. But not much can be accomplished at this level of generality, so we turn to our standard special case.

3. *Harrod-neutrality and balanced growth: the interest rate*

Under the assumptions of section II, 9 technical progress is purely labor-augmenting and gross investment grows exponentially. Along such a path, as we saw, $m(t)$ is constant. From (10) and (13)

$$\begin{aligned} \rho(t, v) &= 0 && \text{if } v \leqq t - m, \\ &= \mu_0(1 - e^{\lambda(t-v-m)}); && \text{if } v \geqq t - m. \end{aligned} \tag{31}$$

(27) becomes

$$1 = \mu_0 \int_{t}^{t+m} (1 - e^{\lambda(u-t-m)}) e^{-\int_t^u r(z)dz} du. \tag{32}$$

Solution of this integral equation gives the equilibrium interest-rate as a function of time on a balanced-growth path. Experience with Harrod-neutrality and balanced growth in other models suggests that the interest rate will be constant. Since the interest rate is required to discount to unity the stream of quasi-rents expected from any newly-built item of capital, and since (31) shows that the current quasi-rent depends only on the age $(t - v)$ of a unit of capital, it is indeed hard to see how any non-constant interest rate can do the trick. In fact, none can.

Substitution of $r(z) = r$ in (32) and integration yields

$$\begin{aligned} 1 &= \frac{\mu_0}{r}(1 - e^{-rm}) - \frac{\mu_0}{r - \lambda}(e^{-\lambda m} - e^{-rm}) \\ &= F(r). \end{aligned} \tag{33}$$

It is easily seen that $F(-\infty) = \infty$ and $F(\infty) = 0$; since $F(r)$ is continuous, (33) has at least one root. Since $F'(r) < 0$ (best seen directly from (32)) there is exactly one root. (That root may be negative; but not if the undiscounted sum of quasi-rents exceeds unity.) Thus if technical progress is Harrod-neutral there is one and only one constant interest rate compatible with competitive equilibrium along a path of steady growth.

It is more complicated to prove that the interest rate *must* be constant. In the form (27′) the basic integral equation can be written

$$1 = \mu_0 \int_0^m (1 - e^{\lambda(x-m)}) e^{-\int_t^{t+x} r(z)dz} dx = \int_0^m g(x) e^{-\int_t^{t+x} r(z)dz} dx$$

where $g(x) > 0$ for $x < m$ and $g(m) = 0$. The substitution $R(-t) = e^{-\int_0^t r(z)dz}$ transforms the equation into

$$R(t) = \int_0^m g(x)R(t-x)dx. \tag{27''}$$

$R(t)$ is, from its definition, intrinsically positive. We will show that the only positive solution of (27″) valid for all t is $R(t) = e^{rt}$, where r satisfies (33). Constancy of the interest rate follows.

We observe first that it is only necessary to settle the case $\int_0^m g(x)dx = 1$ (i.e. the case in which the constant interest rate is zero). If $\int_0^m g(x)dx \neq 1$, there is a unique constant h such that $\int_0^m e^{-hx}g(x)dx = 1$; and it is easily checked that $R^*(t) = R(t)e^{-ht}$ satisfies $R^*(t) = \int_0^m R^*(t-x)g^*(x)dx$ with $g^*(x) = e^{-hx}g(x)$. We will show that if $\int_0^m g(x)dx = 1$, the only positive solutions of (27″) are constant, whence h is the constant rate of interest, as it should be.

We begin by showing that any bounded solution of (27″) is constant. Let $R(t)$ be a bounded solution. Then for any fixed z, $D(t; z) = R(t) - R(t-z)$ is also a uniformly bounded solution of (27″). Let $M = \sup_t D(t; z)$. One can find a sequence t_k such that $D(t_k; z)$ converges to M. Now define the sequence of functions $D_k(t; z) = D(t+t_k; z)$; the D_k are an equicontinuous family of solutions to (27″). There is a subsequence converging uniformly in any bounded interval to a limit solution $D^*(t; z)$ which is continuous and bounded above by M. Moreover,

$$D^*(0; z) = \lim D(t_k; z) = M = \int_0^m D^*(-x; z)g(x)dx.$$

Since $g(x) > 0$, $D^*(t; z) = M$ for all t between 0 and $-m$. Working backward one finds $D^*(t; z) = M$ for all $t \leqq 0$. Therefore there is a k such that $D_k(t; z) = D(t+t_k; z) > M/2$ for t in any long but finite interval to the left of the origin, so $D(t; z) > M/2$ for t in any long but finite interval to the left of t_k. Therefore $R(t) - R(t-z) > M/2$ in the same interval. If $M > 0$, $R(t)$ can be made to exceed any preassigned bound by taking the interval long enough. If $M \leqq 0$, let $M' = \inf_t D(t; z) \leqq 0$. A similar argument then shows that $R(t) - R(t-z) < M'/2$ or $R(t-z) > R(t) - M'/2$ in a similarly long interval, and if $M' < 0$ $R(t)$ can be made to exceed any preassigned bound by making the interval long enough and going far enough back. Hence $M = M' = 0$ and $R(t) = R(t-z)$ for any z, so $R(t)$ is constant.[1]

[1] This lemma has a checkered history. We began by depending on a more or less heuristic argument resting on the expansion of $R(t)$ in an infinite sum of fundamental solutions of (27″). Not knowing how to make that rigorous, we constructed a direct " proof ". We are indebted to Kenneth Arrow for catching an error that vitiated the argument. He also gave us a reference to S. Karlin, " On the Renewal Equation ", *Pacific Journal of Mathematics*, 5 (1955), lemma 4 on page 242, where the lemma is proved using deep analytical arguments. It seemed to us that more elementary methods must suffice for this proposition; it is easy in discrete time, for example. The proof given in the text is intricate but elementary.

The rest of the argument we owe to Professor Frank Stewart of Brown University. Define $S(x) = \int_0^x R(t)dt$. From (27″)

$$S(x) = \int_0^x \int_0^m R(t-s)g(s)dsdt = \int_0^m \int_0^x R(t-s)g(s)dtds$$

$$= \int_0^m S(x-s)g(s)ds - \int_0^m S(-s)g(s)ds.$$

Let
$$c = \frac{\int_0^m S(-s)g(s)ds}{\int_0^m sg(s)ds},$$

so $c < 0$ if $R(t) > 0$, and define $T(x) = S(x) + cx$. It is easily verified that $T(t)$ satisfies (27″). Moreover $T'(x) = S'(x) + c = R(x) + c \geqq c$, so $T(t)$ is a solution of (27″) whose derivative is bounded below. In turn this entails the boundedness of $T(t)$. Let $M_n = \max R(t)$ and $m_n = \min R(t)$ on the interval $(n-1)m \leqq t \leqq nm$. If T were unbounded $M_n - m_n$ would become arbitrarily large as $n \to -\infty$. One could then find an n for which $M_n - m_{n+1} > -2mc$. $T(t)$ thus falls by more than $-2mc$ in an interval no larger than $2m$; by the mean value theorem $T'(t) < c$ at some intermediate point, a contradiction. It follows that $T(t)$ is a bounded solution of (27″). It is therefore constant. Thus $T'(t) = R(t) + c = 0$ and $R(t) = -c$ for every t.

We have established that, with exponential, purely labor-augmenting technical progress, the only competitive equilibrium interest rate compatible with a permanent path of balanced growth is a constant interest rate, namely the unique real root of (33). Since the instantaneous interest rate is constant, the yield curve or term structure of interest rates is flat.

According to (33) r depends on μ_0, λ and m; through (18) r depends also on the other parameters, n and the gross saving ratio s. Holding μ_0 and λ constant, one can calculate that $\frac{\partial r}{\partial m} > 0$; if one compares two steady-growth paths with the same μ_0 and λ but with different m, the path with longer lifetime for capital will be the one with higher interest rate. This sounds " un-Austrian "; indeed the mechanism is very different from the economics of roundaboutness. From (18), a higher m is associated with a lower s; with lower s, full employment requires the break-even margin to be pushed back to older machines. Thus a lower saving rate implies a higher m, which implies a higher rate of interest. This result is entirely conventional. Similarly (18) shows that, with given s $\frac{\partial m}{\partial g} > 0$. Since $g = n + \lambda$, a steady-growth path with higher n will have higher m and higher r; other things equal, faster growth in the labor force favors a higher rate of profit. (Remember that full employment, or at least a constant unemployment rate, is simply assumed.)

The relation between r and λ, for given s, is more complicated because λ appears directly in (32) or (33). Nevertheless, it can be shown from (32) and (18) that $\frac{\partial r}{\partial \lambda} > 0$. In this model faster Harrod-neutral technical progress with unchanged saving ratio always implies a higher rate of interest. The key to this result is that, from (18), $\frac{\partial m}{\partial \lambda} = \frac{1}{g}\left(\frac{1}{s\mu_0 - g}\right) - m$; and, again from (18), $s\mu_0 - g = \frac{g}{1 - e^{-gm}} - g = \frac{g}{e^{gm} - 1} < \frac{1}{m}$. Thus

$\frac{\partial m}{\partial \lambda} > 0$; with given s, a faster rate of technical progress actually lengthens the economic lifetime of capital. The greater initial productivity advantage of new capital must outweigh the more rapid rate of improvement of capital still to come.

By letting $r \to 0$ in (33), we find the m corresponding to a zero rate of interest. This m_1 satisfies

$$\lambda = \mu_0(\lambda m_1 - 1 - e^{-\lambda m_1}).$$

Since the right-hand side increases monotonically from zero at $m = 0$ to $+\infty$ as $m \to \infty$, there is always a lifetime short enough to reduce the rate of interest to zero. From II, 11, however, the shortest m, say m_2, attainable by a closed economy in balanced growth is associated with $s = 1$, and satisfies $\mu_0(1 - e^{-gm_2}) = g$. Depending on the other parameters, m_1 may exceed, equal, or fall short of m_2. In the first case, $r = 0$ for some saving rate less than unity; in the second case $r = 0$ for $s = 1$; in the third case, the rate of interest remains positive even if all of output is saved and invested.

At the other end of the spectrum, as $m \to \infty$, $r \to \mu_0$ and this is the highest profit rate the technology can generate. For then the real wage is zero and investment of one unit of output earns a perpetuity of μ_0 units of output per unit time. The saving rate corresponding to infinite lifetime is $s = \frac{g}{\mu_0}$.

4. *The Golden Rule path once more*

In II, 12 it was shown that a steady-growth path on which gross investment is always equal to gross quasi-rent generates the highest consumption path among all steady-growth paths. We can now see that the other standard characterization of the " Golden Rule ", that the rate of interest equals the rate of growth, also holds in this model. It is only necessary to put $r = g$ in (33) and observe that the resulting equation is the same as (21) or (22).

5. *Harrod-neutrality and balanced growth: capital values*

Using (26) and (31), for Harrod-neutral balanced growth, it is easy to calculate that

$$P(t, v) = \frac{\mu_0}{r}(1 - e^{r(t-v-m)}) - \frac{\mu_0}{\lambda - r}(e^{r(t-v-m)} - e^{\lambda(t-v-m)}).$$

(Putting $v = t$ and $P(t, t) = 1$ gives the equation for the rate of interest.) With this formula and (29), another straightforward calculation gives

$$K(t) = I_0 e^{gt}\mu_0\left\{\frac{1}{rg} - \frac{\lambda e^{-rm}}{r(\lambda - r)(g - r)} + \frac{e^{-\lambda m}}{(\lambda - r)(g - \lambda)} - \frac{\lambda e^{-gm}}{g(g - r)(g - \lambda)}\right\}. \tag{34}$$

$K(t)$ is a value; to be exact it is the competitive market value (in units of the single commodity) of the stock of diverse capital goods in existence at time t. Since we are limited, in any case, to paths of steady growth, the foresight involved in this valuation is no extra strain on the imagination. The ratio $K(t)/I(t)$ will be constant along a steady-growth path. Its value depends on all the main parameters of the model λ, g, and μ_0, as well as on m and r, and therefore on s.

Knowledge of $K(t)$ permits the calculation of various *net* magnitudes. To begin with, since $K' = gK$, (34) gives the ratio of net to gross investment as

$$\frac{K'}{I} = \frac{gK}{I} = \mu_0\left\{\frac{1}{r} - \frac{\lambda g e^{-rm}}{r(r - \lambda)(r - g)} - \frac{g e^{-\lambda m}}{(r - \lambda)(g - \lambda)} + \frac{\lambda e^{-gm}}{(r - g)(g - \lambda)}\right\} \tag{35}$$

$$= 1 - \lambda\mu_0\left\{\frac{e^{-rm}}{(r - \lambda)(r - g)} + \frac{e^{-\lambda m}}{(r - \lambda)(g - \lambda)} - \frac{e^{-gm}}{(r - g)(g - \lambda)}\right\}.$$

(The last equality is obtained with the aid of (33).) Now if we define $\omega = 1 - \frac{K'}{I} =$ depreciation as a fraction of gross investment, we have

$$\begin{aligned} \omega &= \lambda\mu_0 \left\{\frac{e^{-rm}}{(r-\lambda)(r-g)} + \frac{e^{-\lambda m}}{(r-\lambda)(g-\lambda)} - \frac{e^{-gm}}{(r-g)(g-\lambda)}\right\}, \\ &= \frac{\lambda\mu_0}{r-\lambda}\left\{\frac{e^{-\lambda m}(1-e^{-nm})}{n} - \frac{e^{-gm}(1-e^{-(r-g)m})}{r-g}\right\}. \end{aligned} \tag{36}$$

Net output is gross output minus depreciation: $Z = Y - \omega I$; but $I/Y = s$, so $Z = \left(\frac{1}{s} - \omega\right)I$. Thus the ratio of net investment to net output is

$$\sigma = \frac{\dot{K}}{Z} = \frac{(1-\omega)I}{(\frac{1}{s}-\omega)I} = \frac{s - s\omega}{1 - s\omega}.$$

Since ω is nonnegative, $\sigma \leq s$. It would be interesting to know whether σ is a monotone function of s on steady-growth paths, i.e. whether, as between steady-growth paths alike in all parameters except s, the one with higher s always has higher σ. We have not settled this question; so far as we know, it may be that the higher gross saving ratio, associated with a shorter lifetime, may so accelerate depreciation as to result in a smaller net saving rate. It is clear, however, that " on the average " a higher s is associated with a higher σ. From the discussion in V.3, the lowest gross saving rate compatible with full employment is $s = \frac{g}{\mu_0}$ (we must assume $\mu_0 > g$ else continued full employment is not possible at all). Along such a path $\omega = 0$, since $m = \infty$ and $r \to \mu_0 > g$; hence $\sigma = s$. (Intuitively, as $m \to \infty$, the real wage tends to zero, and there is no obsolescence. Since we have ruled out physical depreciation, $\omega = 0$. If there were physical depreciation-by-evaporation, ω would tend to the rate of depreciation and σ would be at its minimum when s is at its minimum.) At the other extreme, when $s = 1$, $\sigma = 1$, so the net and gross saving rates reach their maxima together. But we do not know whether their overall positive association is broken for some values of s.

The symbol α has already been introduced for the share of gross quasi-rents in gross output. Let Π be the share of net profits in net output. Then

$$\Pi = \frac{\alpha Y - \omega I}{Y - \omega I} = \frac{\alpha - \omega s}{1 - \omega s} = \alpha - \frac{\omega\sigma(1-\alpha)}{1-\omega}.$$

Thus $\Pi < \alpha$. Also, when $\alpha = s$, $\Pi = \sigma$; the maximal-consumption or golden-rule path can be characterized in still a third way: net savings equal net profits.

6. *Harrod-neutrality and balanced growth: alternative savings functions*

So far we have parametrized saving-investment behavior by the ratio of gross investment to gross output along full employment balanced-growth paths. The equations describing any such path may be collected:

$$L_0 = \frac{\mu_0 I_0}{\lambda_0 n}(1 - e^{-nm}), \tag{14}$$

$$w(t) = \lambda_0 e^{-\lambda m} e^{\lambda t}, \tag{16}$$

$$s = \frac{g}{\mu_0(1 - e^{-gm})} = \frac{I_0}{Y_0}, \tag{18}$$

$$1 = \frac{\mu_0}{r}(1 - e^{-rm}) - \frac{\mu_0}{r - \lambda}(e^{-\lambda m} - e^{-rm}). \tag{33}$$

If we treat s, the gross savings ratio, as a parameter, then the given constants in these equations are L_0, μ_0, λ_0, n, λ, g and s. The unknowns are I_0, Y_0, w, m, and r, and they are uniquely determined (subject to the restriction $\frac{g}{\mu_0} \leq s \leq 1$). These equations " decompose " in a particular way. We can say that (18) alone determines m, (14) determines I_0, (16) determines w, and the " no-pure-rent " equation (33) determines the rate of interest or rate of profit r.

The gross savings ratio is not the only possible parametrization of saving behavior. It is convenient because, in this one-commodity model at least, it is a purely " physical " description independent of all value considerations. But for that very reason it may also be inappropriate in an economy in which the capitalist motivations play a role. Alternative descriptions have been proposed; the commonest are to make net saving proportional to net income, or to net profit, or to make gross or net saving a linear function of the wage bill and gross or net profits. Which of these alternative saving functions is the true one is an important descriptive question. They have different consequences in many ways. But they do not introduce any new growth paths. It is clear from (33) and (36) that along a steady-growth path a constant s is accompanied by constant ω, constant σ, and constant Π. But different ways of characterizing saving behavior lead to different " decompositions " of the *equivalent* equilibrium conditions and therefore, from a superficial point of view, to different " theories " of interest and profit. Since this is sometimes misunderstood, we make some remarks here.

The most interesting alternative to consider from this point of view is the assumption that net saving is proportional to net profit:

$$K' = \sigma_r \Pi Z.$$

It can be verified that (18), (20), (33), and (34) imply that $\Pi Z = rK$, as they should, since both sides define net profits. It is obvious that along any balanced-growth path K is a constant times I, so that $K' = gK$. It now follows that with the present savings function

$$r\sigma_r = g. \tag{37}$$

This equation replaces the first equality in (18) among the equilibrium conditions for steady growth.

Full employment and competition in the labor market continue to imply (14) and (16). These two equations, plus the second equality in (18) and the newly-derived (37), are one equation short of determining all the unknowns along a steady-growth path. There seem to be two and only two consistent ways of completing the system. One is to adopt (33) as a market equilibrium condition: the rate of interest must equalize the present value of future quasi-rents from a new capital good to its cost of production. The other requires that the uses of gross output exhaust gross output: $Y = I + wN + (1 - \sigma)\Pi Z$. But this requirement together with the other four equations just stipulated *entails* (33). So there is only one way to complete the system and we might as well let (33) stand.

The path just defined, with a particular value of σ_r given, is of course the same as one of the paths defined earlier, namely the one with $s = \dfrac{g}{\mu_0(1 - e^{-gm})}$. But the new equilibrium equations decompose differently and so lend themselves to another interpretation. Now (37) involves only one unknown, r. Thus we must say that *it* determines the rate of interest/profit, the " no-pure-rent " condition (33) determines m, and the rest goes as before. Thriftiness conditions and the rate-of-return conditions have exchanged roles. However (33) still holds, though the " causal " interpretation has changed.

The inessential character of the change is revealed by considering yet another assumption about saving, that net saving is proportional to net income: $K' = \sigma Z$. The determinate system of equilibrium conditions now consists of (14), (16), the second equality of

(18), (33), and the new equation, which can be written

$$(38) \qquad 1 - \omega = \sigma \left(\frac{\mu_0(1 - e^{-gm})}{g} - \omega \right)$$

where ω is the ratio of depreciation to gross investment given in (36). Once again, the paths thus described are the same as those described earlier; they are merely characterized via a different parameter. But now the equations do not " decompose " at all. There is no one-at-a-time solution possible. Instead (33) and (38) must be solved *simultaneously* for r and m, after which the other unknowns follow as before. (Something similar is the case if the propensities to save wages and profits are positive but different.)

The only safe statement, therefore, is that the rate of interest is determined, in general, both by thriftiness conditions and by " marginal " conditions. This result is not only safe, but satisfying.

V THE INTEREST RATE AND THE SOCIAL RATE OF RETURN ON INVESTMENT

1. *Definitions and preliminaries*

In this part of the paper we revert to the more general assumptions of Part II. To be precise, we assume $\mu(v)$ and $\lambda(v)$ to be continuous positive functions of v, with $\lambda(v)$ strictly increasing. The object of this part is to relate the competitive equilibrium interest rate defined in (27) to what we shall call the social rate of return on saving or investment. The point of the analogy is suggested by the fact that in a perfect capital market the ruling rate of interest functions as the private rate of return on savings.

Consider a person who disposes of a certain amount of wealth, $W(0)$, at time zero and who is obliged for some reason to pursue a saving program such that his wealth at some given later time T is equal to a given amount $W(T)$. His wealth at time zero may consist of a current stock plus the sum of his discounted wage income in the time interval $[0, T]$. This person is free to choose any stream of consumption $c(t)$, which has a present value equal to $W(0)$ minus the present value of $W(T)$ or, in a formula,

$$(39) \qquad \int_0^T e^{-\int_o^t r(u)du} c(t)dt = W(0) - e^{-\int_o^T r(t)dt} W(T).$$

Hence, as before, $r(t)$ is the instantaneous interest rate ruling in the market at time t. If we compare any two such programs $c_1(t)$ and $c_2(t)$ and define $\Delta c(t) = c_1(t) - c_2(t)$ we get from (39)

$$(40) \qquad \int_0^T e^{-\int_o^t r(u)du} \Delta c(t)dt = \int_0^T e^{\int_o^t r(u)du} [c_1(t) - c_2(t)]dt = 0.$$

Because of (40) it is natural to refer to the expression $e^{\int_o^t r(u)du}$ as the rate of transformation between consumption at time t and consumption at time zero. Giving up one unit of present consumption permits $e^{\int_o^t r(u)du}$ additional units of consumption at time t. Thus the instantaneous rate of return on savings is the geometric rate of change of the transformation rate as t varies. Especially, as t approaches zero we get

$$(41) \qquad e^{\int_o^t r(u)du} \simeq 1 + r(o)t.$$

If we choose the time unit small enough, we can say that $r(o)$ expresses the net gain in total consumption, if consumption is reduced by one unit at time zero and correspondingly increased after one period. The same interpretation will be given to the social rate of return on savings.

2. *The social rate of return on saving*

Under competitive conditions, the private rate of return on savings is independent of the individual's decisions. Like any price, however, the social rate of return depends on the aggregate of investment decisions. It can only be determined after the whole investment path (for the past as well as for the future) has been decided. Let us call this predetermined path $I^*(t)$. The development of the labor force, $L(t)$, is also given. We can now compute the corresponding values for $Y^*(t)$ and $C^*(t)$.

$$Y^*(t) = \int_{t-m^*(t)}^{t} \mu(v) I^*(v) dv, \tag{42}$$

$$C^*(t) = Y^*(t) - I^*(t), \tag{43}$$

where the age of the oldest capital in operation at time t, expressed by $m^*(t)$, is given by the now familiar equation

$$L(t) = \int_{t-m^*t}^{t} \frac{\mu(v)}{\lambda(v)} I^*(v) dv. \tag{44}$$

As in II, 3, our assumptions about the technology entail that the economy is efficient in the sense that $Y^*(t)$ is the capacity output of the economy at each instant of time. Without a change in the investment path $I^*(t)$, no higher gross output than $Y^*(t)$ is possible for any t. In other words, in order to achieve a higher volume of gross output in the future the economy has to increase the current rate of accumulation, which means that it has to reduce current consumption.

The concept of a social rate of return on savings makes sense only in the case of efficient paths. For if $Y(t)$ were limited not by the capacity to produce but by effective demand, then a rise in consumption today could be effected without changing the future capacity to produce consumption goods. But for efficient paths $Y^*(t)$ the social rate of return on investment links small changes in $I(t)$ to small changes in $C(t)$ for given $L(t)$, just as the marginal productivity of labor relates small changes in $L(t)$ to the resulting small changes in $C(t)$ for given $I(t)$.

There are of course infinitely many ways in which marginal changes of the function $I^*(t)$ can be introduced. $\Delta I(t)$, the difference between the old and the new investment path, may be almost any function of time, as long as t lies in the interval $[0, T]$, which we are considering. Since the past is history, $\Delta I(t) = 0$ for $t < 0$. We will confine ourselves to the effects of variations in the finite period from zero to some arbitrary T $(0 < T < \infty)$, and assume that $\Delta I(t) = 0$ for $t > T$. Let us write $\Delta I(t) = \varepsilon\psi(t)$ where ε is a constant and $\psi(t)$ is any bounded function of t for $0 \leq t \leq T$ and equal to zero otherwise. Note that $I(t)$ itself is not entirely arbitrary. It must be nonnegative and no bigger than $Y(t)$. To be sure of room to introduce small changes of $I^*(t)$ in either direction, we assume that

$$\inf_{0 \leq t \leq T} I^*(t) > 0 \text{ and } \inf_{0 \leq t \leq T} [Y^*(t) - I^*(t)] > 0. \tag{45}$$

Also, as will be seen, we have to assume that $I^*(t)$ is such that

$$\lim_{t \to \infty} \left(t - m^*(t) \right) = \infty. \tag{46}$$

(See III, 5 Lemma 2 for the case of constant s.)

This innocuous assumption means that along the original path the volume of investment is adequate to ensure that the economic lifetime of capital remains finite (or becomes infinite slowly). We now have

$$I(t) = I^*(t) + \varepsilon\psi(t); \tag{47}$$

for ε sufficiently close to zero $I(t)$ is a feasible investment program, differentiable with respect to ε at the point $\varepsilon = 0$. From (47) we infer

$$L(t) = \int_{t-m(t)}^{t} [\mu(v)/\lambda(v)][I^*(v) + \varepsilon\psi(v)]dv \tag{48}$$

which is an equation for $m(t)$, and

$$Y(t) = \int_{t-m(t)}^{t} \mu(v)[I^*(v) + \varepsilon\psi(v)]dv \tag{49}$$

which determines Y after $m(t)$ has been computed from (48). Now we can differentiate both sides of (48) and (49) with respect to ε for $\varepsilon = 0$. Then we get from (48), since $L(t)$ does not depend on ε,

$$0 = \frac{\partial L(t)}{\partial \varepsilon}\bigg|_{\varepsilon=0} = \int_{t-m^*t}^{t} [\mu(v)/\lambda(v)]\psi(v)dv + \frac{\mu(t-m^*(t))}{\lambda(t-m^*(t))} I^*(t-m^*(t)) \frac{\partial m(t)}{\partial \varepsilon}\bigg|_{\varepsilon=0}$$

or, since $I^*(t) > 0$ and $\dfrac{\mu(t-m^*(t))}{\lambda(t-m^*(t))} > 0$

$$\frac{\partial m(t)}{\partial \varepsilon}\bigg|_{\varepsilon=0} = -\frac{\displaystyle\int_{t-m^*(t)}^{t} [\mu(v)/\lambda(v)]\psi(v)dv}{\dfrac{\mu(t-m^*(t))}{\lambda(t-m^*(t))} I^*(t-m^*(t)).} \tag{50}$$

Differentiation of (49) yields

$$\frac{\partial Y(t)}{\partial \varepsilon}\bigg|_{\varepsilon=0} = \int_{t-m^*(t)}^{t} \mu(v)\psi(v)dv + \mu(t-m^*(t))I^*(t-m^*(t)) \frac{\partial m(t)}{\partial \varepsilon}\bigg|_{\varepsilon=0}$$

But $\dfrac{\partial m(t)}{\partial \varepsilon}\bigg|_{\varepsilon=0}$ is given by (50). So we have

$$\frac{\partial Y}{\partial \varepsilon}\bigg|_{\varepsilon=0} = \int_{t-m^*(t)}^{t} \mu(v)\psi(v)dv - \lambda(t-m^*(t)) \int_{t-m^*(t)}^{t} \frac{\mu(v)}{\lambda(v)} \psi(v)dv. \tag{51}$$

If we subtract $\dfrac{\partial I(t)}{\partial \varepsilon}\bigg|_{\varepsilon=0} = \psi(t)$ from (51) we get an expression for the marginal change in $C(t)$, which we may call $\delta C^*(t)$

$$\delta C^*(t) = \frac{\partial C(t)}{\partial \varepsilon}\bigg|_{\varepsilon=0} = \int_{t-m^*(t)}^{t} \psi(v)\mu(v)[1 - \frac{\lambda(t-m^*(t))}{\lambda(v)}]dv - \psi(t). \tag{52}$$

Comparison with (10) in II, 6 shows that the marginal change in consumption at time t is equal to the competitive quasi-rents earned at time t by the incremental investment less the current cost of incremental investment. If we consider very small ε, we can write

$$C(t) \approx C^*(t) + \varepsilon\delta C^*(t).$$

Hence in the neighbourhood of $C^*(t)$, $\varepsilon\delta C^*(t)$ plays the same role as $\Delta C(t)$ in the case of the private individual. In that case there existed a discount factor

$$e^{\int_o^t r(u)du},$$

such that any admissible $\Delta C(t)$ satisfied

$$\int_o^T e^{\int_o^t r(u)du} \Delta C(t)dt = 0.$$

Can we find a corresponding function $r^*(t)$ such that $\varepsilon\delta C^*(t)$ must satisfy a similar equation? Observe that $\psi(t) = 0$ for $t > T$ and that because of (46) there exists a T_1 such that $t - m^*(t) > T$ for $t > T_1$. Therefore after T_1 the economy is no longer affected by the perturbation function $\psi(t)$. This means that we have to look for a function $r^*(t)$ (depending on $I^*(t)$ but not on $\psi(t)$) with

$$(53) \qquad \varepsilon \int_0^{T_1} e^{-\int_0^t r^*(u)du} \delta C^*(t)dt = 0$$

for any $\delta C^*(t)$, which can be generated by some admissible $\psi(t)$. If such a function exists, we may call $e^{\int_0^t r^*(u)du}$ the marginal *social* rate of transformation between consumption at time zero and consumption at time t. For any fixed t society could increase $\delta C^*(t)$ by $e^{\int_0^t r^*(u)du}$ units, if it were to reduce $\delta C^*(0)$ by one unit (this change would be achieved by changing the function $\psi(t)$). It is then natural to call $r^*(t)$ the social rate of return on savings. For a small unit period we could express the marginal rate of transformation between consumption now and consumption t periods later by

$$e^{\int_0^t r^*(u)du} \simeq 1 + r^*(0)t.$$

By giving up one unit of consumption today society could gain $1 + r^*(0)$ additional units of consumption after one period.

3. *Equality of private and social rates of return*

We proceed now to prove that in the model of this paper for any given $I^*(t)$ (fulfilling the requirements (45) and (46)) there exists a function $r^*(t)$ such that (53) holds. Moreover we shall see that this unique social rate of return $r^*(t)$ is equal to the instantaneous rate of interest $r(t)$, which in turn, of course, depends on the particular reference path $I^*(t)$.

Substituting (52) into (53) and cancelling the ε on the left hand side of (53) produces the following double integral

$$(54) \qquad 0 = \int_0^{T_1} \left[e^{-\int_0^t r^*(u)du} \left\{ \int_{t-m^*(t)}^{t} \psi(v)\mu(v) \left[1 - \frac{\lambda(t - m^*(t))}{\lambda(v)}\right] dv - \psi(t) \right\} \right] dt.$$

Now we introduce a set function $X^*(v)$ defined by

$$X^*(v) = \{t : t - m^*(t) \leq v \leq t\}.$$

$X^*(v)$ has a simple economic interpretation: it is the set of all instants t at which machines of vintage v are operating. From this interpretation of $X^*(v)$ we can infer the equation

$$(55) \qquad \int_{X^*(v)} \mu(v)\left[1 - \frac{\lambda(t - m^*(t))}{\lambda(v)}\right] e^{-\int_v^t r(u)du} dt = 1.$$

This is merely (27) of IV, 2 in a slightly altered notation. We write $\rho^*(t, v)$ for the quasi-rent at time t of a capital good of vintage v along the reference path $I^*(t)$.

We define the set $X^*_S(v)$ as

$$X^*_S(v) = \{t : t \varepsilon X^*(v),\ 0 \leq t \leq S\}.$$

$X^*_S(v)$ is the set $X^*(v)$ restricted to the time interval $[0, S]$. Now, by some calculation, for any $S \geq 0$,

$$\int_O^S \left\{ e^{-\int_o^t r^*(u)du} \int_{t-m^*(t)}^t \psi(v)\rho^*(t, v)dv \right\} dt =$$

$$\text{(56)} \qquad \int_{-m^*(o)}^S \left\{ e^{-\int_o^v r^*(u)du} \psi(v) \int_{X^*_S(v)} e^{-\int_v^t r^*(u)du} \rho^*(t, v)dt \right\} dv.$$

To prove (56), it is enough to reverse the order of integration and observe that $\int_0^t r^*(u)du = \int_0^v + \int_v^t$. (We are indebted to Professor Kenneth Arrow for simplifying the argument here.)

If we take into account that $\psi(v) = 0$ for $v < 0$ and $v > T$ (56) turns into

$$\int_0^{T_1} \left\{ e^{-\int_o^t r^*(u)du} \int_{t-m^*(t)}^t \psi(v)\rho^*(t, v)dv \right\} dt =$$

$$\text{(60)} \qquad \int_0^{T_1} \left\{ e^{-\int_o^v r^*(u)du} \psi(v) \int_{X^*(v)} e^{-\int_v^t r^*(u)du} \rho^*(t, v)dt \right\} dv.$$

This is so, because for the relevant v's ($0 \leq v \leq T$) we have $X^*_{T_1}(v) = X^*(v)$. Now we can substitute (60) into (54):

$$\text{(61)} \qquad 0 = \int_0^{T_1} e^{-\int_o^v r^*(u)du} \psi(v) \left[\int_{X^*(v)} e^{-\int_v^t r^*(u)du} \rho^*(t, v)dt - 1 \right] dv.$$

For (61) to be true for all admissible functions $\psi(v)$ it is a necessary and sufficient condition that

$$\text{(62)} \qquad \int_{X^*(v)} e^{-\int_v^t r^*(u)du} \rho^*(t, v)dt = 1$$

for all v in the interval $[0, T]$. (The left-hand side must be equal to unity at least for a dense subset of $[0, T]$. But it can easily be shown to be a continuous function of v, whence it must be equal to unity everywhere.)

Comparison of (62) with (17) or (27) of V, 2 shows that $r^*(t)$ satisfies the same integral equation as $r(t)$, whose solution is known to be unique. It follows that $r^*(t) = r(t)$, as was to be proved.

VI THE KEYNESIAN CASE: OUTPUT LIMITED BY EFFECTIVE DEMAND

1. *Output and Employment*

Up to now we have dealt only with the case of full employment. Without inquiring into the causal mechanism, we have assumed that employment could be identified with the exogenous supply of labor. This is a double assumption (a) that at each moment of time the stock of surviving capital is adequate to employ the whole labor force, and (b) that effective demand is always adequate to buy the output producible at full employment from the existing stock of capital. Thus we have placed ourselves in the second of the three regimes mentioned in II, 3: output is limited by the supply of labor.

Regime I, in which output is limited by a shortage of capital while labor is redundant, has no application to an advanced industrial economy, though it may be relevant for the advanced sector of a developing economy. We turn in this part of the paper to the third, or Keynesian, regime, when both capital and labor are unemployed, and output is limited not by scarce resources but by effective demand.

The basic equations (7) and (8) continue to hold, but their interpretation is different. In the full-employment regime, $N(t)$ is replaced by $L(t)$, $m(t)$ is determined by (7) and $Y(t)$ by (8). That is: the margin separating active from idle capital is fixed by the requirement that the entire labor force find employment; and output is whatever they are capable of producing. This would presumably be true in a planned economy, or in one where a flexible fiscal policy regulated aggregate demand accurately. Pre-Keynesian neo-classical economics relied on a market mechanism: so long as there was unemployment the real wage would fall; older and older vintages of capital would be able to earn positive quasi-rents; as they entered production, employment would rise. Modern short-run income analysis rests on the presumption that this cannot or does not happen, or does not happen quickly enough to matter. The causal structure in (7) and (8) is reversed. If we take aggregate demand $Y(t)$ as given (in the simplest case, from exogenous investment via the multiplier), (8) determines $m(t)$ and (7) determines $N(t)$. That is: the margin separating active from idle capital is fixed by the requirement that output just match real effective demand; and employment is whatever is necessary to man that capital. If the division of output between consumption and investment is determined, a model like this is clearly able to generate its own future time-path.

2. *Aggregate Supply and Demand*

There must, of course, be a market mechanism underlying a Keynesian economy, though it cannot be the same as the neo-classical mechanism. For one thing, a Keynesian economy must have at least one more asset, money, and therefore one more price, the money wage, than the neo-classical aggregative model we have been discussing. Otherwise there is no explanation for over-saving. Without the attraction of some other store of value, investors would simply increase consumption whenever capital accumulation became unattractive. Nor is there, without money, any opening for the trouble that may arise from stickiness of money wages and prices. A mechanism close to that described in *The General Theory* itself is the following. Suppose $W(t)$, the money wage, is given in the short-run; $W(t)$ or its rate of change may depend on past unemployment, but for the current instant it is given. Now equation (9) can be rewritten

$$P(t) = \frac{W(t)}{\lambda(t - m(t))} \tag{9'}$$

where $P(t)$ is the money price level. Together (8) and (9′) define an aggregate supply curve, giving $Y(t)$ as a function of $P(t)$. Any $P(t)$ determines, via (9′), an $m(t)$. That $m(t)$, inserted in (8), yields the corresponding $Y(t)$. More descriptively, with a sticky money wage, any arbitrary price level fixes the margin between those vintages of capital which can operate at a profit and those which cannot; the corresponding supply of output is the capacity of the profitable vintages. Obviously $Y(t)$ is an increasing function of $P(t)$.

A detailed treatment of aggregate demand would be out of place in this essay. One limiting possibility is that real aggregate demand is independent of the price level for a given money wage. More generally, real demand might depend on the price level through the distribution of income, through the real volume of cash balances, or in other ways. In any case, the intersection of the aggregate demand and supply curves determines the price level and real output.

This is a perfectly-competitive Keynesian model, with (9′) doing the work of a marginal-product-of labor equation. Here—as in the full employment model—it is possible to allow for imperfectly-competitive pricing. Then (9′) can be altered to

$$P(t) = (1 + \eta)\ \frac{W(t)}{\lambda(t - m(t))}\ ; \tag{9''}$$

η is the percentage by which price is marked up over prime costs on *no-rent capital.* So long as η is roughly constant the theory can be worked out as before, though the results differ in more or less predictable ways. (Of course the equality of private and social rates of return is broken.) It should be realized that in short-run equilibrium the real wage may be at its competitive level for the current level of employment. Real-wage rigidity means only that unemployment does not make the real wage fall.

VII EXTENSIONS AND OPEN QUESTIONS

1. *Depreciation and loss of productivity*

It is quite straightforward to make allowance for age-dependent physical depreciation within our simple technology. Let $\delta(x)$ be the proportion of an instant's gross investment that survives to age x. Then the fundamental employment and output equations become

$$N(t) = \int_{t-m(t)}^{t} \frac{\mu(v)}{\lambda(v)} \delta(t-v)I(v)dv,$$

$$Y(t) = \int_{t-m(t)}^{t} \mu(v)\delta(t-v)I(v)dv.$$

The easy special case is, of course, depreciation-by-evaporation: $\delta(x) = e^{-\delta x}$. The results are generally predictable. The case of " one-hoss-shay " depreciation is mixed. If θ is the physical lifetime of capital, $\delta(x) = \begin{cases} 1 & 0 \leqq x < \theta \\ 0 & \theta \leqq x \end{cases}$. Whenever the economic facts require $m(t) \leqq \theta$, the physical lifetime is irrelevant, and the analysis is exactly as in the body of the paper. But when the economic facts would make $m(t) > \theta$, the physical lifetime has primacy and shortage of capital supervenes. It is laborious to piece the two regimes together but it can be done.

Related to, but not identical with, the idea of physical depreciation is the notion that capital goods lose productivity (or require increasing maintenance) over their lifetime. Suppose, for concreteness, that plant constructed at time v has a capacity at time $t \geqq v$ of $\mu(t, v)$ units of output. It is now complicated to say what " technological progress " means, since it may well be desirable to have capital goods which are less productive when new but lose productivity more slowly with age. It is unambiguously progress if $v' > v$ implies $\mu(v' + x, v') > \mu(v + x, v)$ for all $x \geqq 0$ (and labor requirements are not higher on vintage v' capital). But this is unnecessarily strong. The simple special case is $\mu(t, v) = \psi(t-v)\mu(v)$. Then one has

$$N(t) = \int_{t-m(t)}^{t} \frac{\mu(v)}{\lambda(v)} \delta(t-v)I(v)dv,$$

$$Y(t) = \int_{t-m(t)}^{t} \psi(t-v)\mu(v)\delta(t-v)I(v)dv.$$

The distinction between the phenomenon and depreciation is that half-depreciated capital is assumed to require only half the labor it did when new; but capital that has lost half its productivity is assumed to retain its original labor requirement. (There is a symmetric hypothesis; output capacity remains but labor requirement increases with age.) It is not hard to see that—ignoring depreciation again—the real wage must be $\psi(m)\lambda(t-m)$ where, as usual, m is the economic lifetime of capital. It follows that

$$\rho(t, v) = \mu(v)[\psi(t-v) - \frac{\psi(m)\lambda(t-m)}{\lambda(v)}].$$

If we revert to the exponential Harrod-neutral case and put $\psi(x) = e^{-\Psi x}$, it turns out that equilibrium paths have constant m and a constant interest rate satisfying

$$1 = \mu_0 \frac{1 - e^{-(r+\Psi)m}}{r + \psi} - \frac{\mu_0}{r - \lambda}(e^{-(\Psi+\lambda)m} - e^{-(\Psi+r)m}) .$$

Comparing this equation with (33) one sees that if the triple (r^*, λ^*, m^*) satisfies (33), then the triple ($r^* - \psi$, $\lambda^* - \psi$, m^*) satisfies the equation above.

2. *Partially capital-augmenting technical progress*

Although the basic model is quite general—within its fixed coefficient limitations—we have concentrated very heavily on the case of Harrod-neutral or purely-labor-augmenting technical progress. There are two reasons for this. First, only in this case can we get clear and simple analytical results. Second, it may be that the broad outlines of economic history—in particular, the apparent long-run trendlessness of the marginal efficiency of capital—suggest Harrod-neutrality more than they suggest any other simple hypothesis about technical progress. Recent research, however, casts considerable doubt on this reading of the facts.

Under Harrod-neutrality, constant m and constant s go together. When there is any capital-augmenting technical progress—including the other standard case of Hicks-neutrality—we must choose between them. In general a constant gross saving ratio requires $\lim_{t\to\infty} m(t) = 0$ [1] and therefore, a rate of interest falling toward zero. On the other hand, if $m(t)$ is constant, then output will grow at the usual natural rate while the gross saving ratio will fall exponentially and the rate of interest will rise. We illustrate these remarks by sketching the Hicks-neutral case.

Let $\lambda(v) = \lambda_0 e^{\lambda v}$ and $\mu(v) = \mu_0 e^{\mu v}$, and let employment be $N_0 e^{nt}$. Then the fundamental equations for employment and output are

$$N(t) = N_0 e^{nt} = \frac{\mu_0}{\lambda_0} \int_{t-m(t)}^{t} e^{(\mu-\lambda)v} I(v) dv,$$

$$Y(t) = \mu_0 \int_{t-m(t)}^{t} e^{\mu v} I(v) dv;$$

$\mu = 0$ returns us to Harrod-neutrality, while $\mu = \lambda$ gives Hicks-neutrality. On a path with gross investment growing exponentially at the rate g,

$$N_0 e^{nt} = \frac{\mu_0}{\lambda_0(\mu - \lambda + g)} I_0 e^{(\mu-\lambda+g)t}(1 - e^{-(\mu-\lambda+g)m(t)}),$$

$$Y(t) = \frac{\mu_0}{g + \mu} I_0 e^{(\mu+g)t}(1 - e^{-(\mu+g)m(t)}).$$

If $m(t)$ is to be constant along this path, it is necessary that the rate of growth of investment

$$g = n + \lambda - \mu.$$

In that case

$$N_0 = \frac{\mu_0 I_0}{n\lambda_0}(1 - e^{-nm}),$$

$$Y(t) = Y_0 e^{(n+\lambda)t} = \frac{\mu_0 I_0}{n + \lambda} e^{(n+\lambda)t}(1 - e^{-(n+\lambda)m});$$

[1] We owe Mr. George Akerlof of M.I.T. the observation that this is so if there is any capital-augmenting progress.

thus output must grow at the rate $n + \lambda$. Constant economic lifetime for capital is not compatible with a constant gross savings ratio; indeed

$$\frac{I(t)}{Y(t)} = \frac{n + \lambda}{\mu_0(1 - e^{-(n+\lambda)m})} e^{-\mu t};$$

the gross savings rate must fall at the rate of capital-augmenting technical progress. Output grows more rapidly than investment. When there is some capital-augmentation, our one-sector model begins to strain at the seams. The same gross output and the same consumption at two different times mean two different things, because the " same " remaining gross investment generates more capacity at the later time. The classical problem of the definition of " income " arises. As Arrow has pointed out, for some possible definitions, the ratio of " saving " to " income " is at least asymptotically constant.

Even if $m(t)$ is permitted to vary in time, a constant ratio of gross investment to gross output is incompatible with exponentially-growing gross investment and exponentially growing employment. The fundamental equation for output implies

$$m(t) = -\frac{1}{\mu + g} \log\left(1 - \frac{\mu + g}{s\mu_0} e^{-\mu t}\right).$$

Thus $m(t) \to \infty$ as t decreases to $\frac{1}{\mu}\log\left(\frac{s\mu_0}{\mu + g}\right)$. Even for larger values of t, substitution of this equation for $m(t)$ into the fundamental equation for employment leads to

$$N_0 = \frac{\mu_0 I_0}{\lambda_0(\mu - \lambda + g)} e^{(\mu-\lambda+g-n)t} \left[1 - \left(1 - \frac{\mu + g}{s\mu_0} e^{-\mu t}\right)^{\frac{\mu-\lambda+g}{\mu+g}}\right]$$

which is an impossibility if $\mu > 0$.

Akerlof has pointed out the following line of argument which proves that $m(t) \to 0$ whenever $\mu > 0$ and s is constant. Although we know that the investment and output paths are not exponential, we can be sure that the output path corresponding to $\mu > 0$ is no lower than the output path corresponding to $\mu = 0$ and the same values for all the other parameters. Therefore, it follows from the theorem of III, 5 that for sufficiently large t $Y(t) \geqq c\, e^{(\lambda+n-\varepsilon)t}$ where c is a constant and ε is any positive constant, however small. Gross investment, then, eventually exceeds $sce^{(\lambda+n-\varepsilon)t}$. Each unit of new gross investment provides employment equal to $\frac{\mu_0}{\lambda_0} e^{(\mu-\lambda)t}$. Thus current gross investment provides employment in excess of $\frac{s\mu_0}{\lambda_0} c\, e^{(n+\mu-\varepsilon)t}$. If ε is chosen to be less than μ, employment on currently-produced capital will eventually grow faster than an exponential itself growing faster than the labor force. From what has been said about constant-m paths, it is clear that $m(t)$ can have no positive lower limit. So $\lim_{t\to\infty} m(t) = 0$.

If we turn to the price relationships, (10) says that

$$\rho(t, v) = \mu_0 e^{\mu v} (1 - e^{\lambda(t-m-v)}),$$

no longer a function only of the age of capital.

If the saving rate behaves so as to keep m constant, it is clear that the quasi-rent on capital $t - v$ years old grows exponentially with v. This is true for the whole stream of quasi-rents from $t = v$ to $t = v + m$. Hence the rate of interest must be rising with calendar time in order to keep the present value of quasi-rents from new investment always equal to 1. On the other hand, if the saving ratio is constant, or falls slowly enough so that $m(t) \to 0$, the shortening of the length of life offsets the rising trend of quasi-rents. The result may be a constant or falling rate of interest.

For the equilibrium interest rate one can apply (27′) along a path with constant m to get

$$1 = \mu_0 e^{\mu t} \int_0^m (1 - e^{\lambda(x-m)})\, e^{-\int_t^{t+x} r(z)dz}\, dx.$$

Trial shows that the interest rate cannot be constant, i.e., the maturity structure of interest rates cannot be flat. The equation for $r(t)$ can be transformed by differentiating it with respect to t. The result, after some rearrangement is

$$r(t) + \lambda\mu_0 e^{\mu t} \int_t^{t+m} e^{-\int_t^u r(z)dz}\, du = \mu_0 e^{\mu t}(1 - e^{-\lambda m}) + \lambda - \mu.$$

We have not been able to solve this equation.

Massachusetts Institute of Technology.
Cowles Foundation for Research in Economics, Yale University.
Institut für Bildungsforschung, Berlin.

R. M. SOLOW, J. TOBIN, C. C. VON WEIZSÄCKER, M. YAARI.

REFERENCES

[1] Arrow, K. J. " The Economic Implications of Learning by Doing ", *Review of Economic Studies* 29, 3; 1962.

[2] Salter, W. E. G. *Productivity and Technical Change*. Cambridge; 1960.

[3] Uzawa, H. " A Note on Professor Solow's Model of Technical Progress ", *The Economic Studies Quarterly* 14, 3; 1964.

[4] ———————. " Optimum Technical Change in an Aggregative Model of Economic Growth ", *International Economic Review* 6, 1; 1965.

10 On Putty-Clay [1]

C. J. BLISS

I. INTRODUCTION

1. *The Model*

Following on the work of Johansen [3] and Salter [8] a number of writers (e.g. [2], [4], [6], [7] and [10]) have investigated various properties of a model of economic growth which is characterized by a variable capital-labour ratio at the moment that investment occurs (putty), and a fixed capital-labour ratio thereafter (clay). Technical progress takes the form of a flow of new ideas for the construction of investments, but it does not include any new ideas for the more efficient employment of existing investments. In the now standard terminology, technical change is all " embodied ". The term " putty-clay ", coined by Phelps [7], neatly describes these assumptions. The aim of this paper is to provide a fairly complete and rigorous treatment of the balanced and the efficient growth paths of the model without recourse to unnecessarily restrictive assumptions such as Cobb-Douglas. This task, among others, has already been completed by Solow, Tobin, von Weizsäcker and Yaari [9] for the case in which the capital-labour ratio is fixed even at the moment of investment. Such a case is a limiting and special case of the model of this paper, so that the results of Solow and his colleagues have provided a useful check on my results. The same is true of Phelps' results on the Cobb-Douglas case.

It turns out that there are certain problems to be faced in a rigorous treatment whose existence has not been noted in the literature. For example, even under the usual assumption of " diminishing returns ", the relation between the rate of profit and the balanced growth state need not be one-to-one; indeed, unless some care is taken with assumptions and proof, there may be no balanced growth path at all for some values of the rate of profit. This will all be demonstrated below. In the remainder of this introduction the assumptions are carefully stated, and critically evaluated. Then the notion of balanced growth is introduced, and certain consequences of the definition noted. Next comes an intensive examination of the state of a balanced growth economy at one moment of time, a discussion of the existence and uniqueness of profit maximizing investment choices, and an existence theorem. In balanced growth conditions there is a known relationship between the capital intensity of an investment designed to employ one man and the difference between its present value and its cost (the net present value). If net present value has a maximum for a unique investment decision then, in competitive conditions with perfect foresight, the type of investment is uniquely determined. But, unfortunately, there is nothing to guarantee a unique net present value maximizing decision, and the discussion has to take account of this fact. If the reader bears this in mind he will more readily follow where the argument is going. After the existence theorem, the proof of which is given in an appendix, there is a general discussion of comparative dynamics results under a special uniqueness assumption designed to eliminate the above problem. Finally there is a section on efficient growth paths in which the usual relation between efficiency and equilibrium under a shadow price system is shown to hold in the putty-clay model.

2. *Assumptions*

There is only one kind of output flow, whose level at time t is denoted $Y(t)$. This is divided into consumption, $C(t)$, and gross investment, $I(t)$. Thus

$$Y(t) = C(t)+I(t). \qquad \ldots(1)$$

[1] I am greatly indebted to D. G. Champernowne, F. M. Fisher, F. H. Hahn and J. A. Mirrlees for helpful advice and criticism of earlier drafts. None of these bear any responsibility for errors in this version.

Total output is the sum of outputs obtained from investments of various " vintages ", or past dates. Let $X(t, \theta)$ be the amount of output obtained at time t from investments initiated at, of vintage, θ. Then

$$Y(t) = \int_{-\infty}^{t} X(t, \theta) d\theta. \qquad \ldots(2)$$

$X(t, \theta)$ depends upon four things: the level of gross investment at time θ, the extent to which this investment has survived physically to time t, the amount of employment which investments of vintage θ were designed to offer (represented, given $I(\theta)$, by the investment-employment ratio), and the amount of labour applied to these investments at time t. Let us dispose of the problem of physical depreciation of capital by supposing that none occurs. This is unrealistic; but the inclusion of physical depreciation would not greatly enrich the model, while its exclusion serves to highlight important features of this vintage technology, in particular the central role of economic obsolescence. Let $L(t, \theta)$ be the amount of labour applied at time t to investments of vintage θ. Assume that at the instant at which an investment is undertaken it is fully manned, so that $L(\theta, \theta)$ represents the employment-capacity of investments of vintage θ. Later it will be seen that this assumption is justified under competition or on an efficient path. Now $X(\theta, \theta)$ is the capacity-output of investments of vintage θ and, assuming away gestation lags for investment, this is related to gross investment and capacity-employment by a production function.

$$X(\theta, \theta) = F[I(\theta), L(\theta, \theta), \theta]. \qquad \ldots(3)$$

In fact writing $X(\theta, \theta)$ as a function of $I(\theta)$, $L(\theta, \theta)$ and θ, as in (3), involves an important, so far unstated, assumption. This is that at most one kind of investment is constructed at θ, i.e. all investments of vintage θ share a common investment-labour ratio. Although it seems to be widely assumed that this will always be the case in a competitive economy with perfect foresight about future wage and interest costs, there is in fact no reason why investments of a particular vintage need be homogeneous in this manner. This will become clear below. Fortunately, there is no need to introduce a more general expression for $X(\theta, \theta)$, for the equations derived on the assumption of a unique investment-labour ratio turn out to be valid anyway. Where multiple investment-labour ratios occur the equations will have multiple solutions.

It is now necessary to specify the short-run, or ex-post, relation between labour input and output on existing investments—the utilization function. The easiest assumption, and the one that will be adopted, is that this relation is linear up to the employment-capacity. Then on applying any fraction, less than one, of capacity-labour to an investment one obtains the same fraction of capacity-output. Thus

$$X(t, \theta) = X(\theta, \theta) \frac{L(t, \theta)}{L(\theta, \theta)}; \qquad \ldots(4)$$

$$\left.\begin{array}{ll} L(t, \theta) \leqq L(\theta, \theta) & t \geqq \theta \\ L(t, \theta) = 0 & t < \theta \end{array}\right\}. \qquad \ldots(5)$$

However, convenient though it is, this assumption should not be allowed to pass unnoticed. There is no reason why there has to be constant-returns in this sense, anymore than there is ever any reason why there has to be constant returns-to-scale. Suppose, for example, that plant warmed up during use and operated more efficiently when hot. Then if a fraction of capacity-labour were applied to an investment by operating the plant for a fraction of the normal working day, (which might be the only feasible way of having labour below capacity), the plant would operate at a lower average temperature and might produce less than the given fraction of capacity output. The utilization function would, in this case, be strictly convex. In the present continuous time formulation this question is not critically involved because $L(t, \theta)$ will be equal either to $L(\theta, \theta)$ or to zero almost everywhere. But in a more realistic discrete time model one might have to modify (4).

Let $N(t)$ denote total employment at time t, and note that

$$N(t) = \int_{-\infty}^{t} L(t, \theta) d\theta. \qquad \ldots(6)$$

Finally, define $s(t)$, the gross saving-investment ratio, as

$$s(t) = I(t)/Y(t) \qquad \ldots(7)$$

and $k(t)$, *per capita* investment at time t, as

$$k(t) = I(t)/L(t, t). \qquad \ldots(8)$$

3. *Returns-to-Scale*

Equations (1) to (7) make no assertion about, and do not in any way depend upon, the homogeneity of degree one of the production function F. However, we must at some stage concern ourselves with the question of returns-to-scale. There are at least two ways in which increasing, or decreasing, returns-to-scale could be represented in this model, plus another which my formulation has virtually excluded. The latter is considered first. The technology is specified as though investment consisted entirely of the construction of a number of plants each completely independent of all existing plant. This formulation makes it hard to find a way of representing the kinds of returns-to-scale which neo-classical writers have had in mind when suggesting that the aggregate production function might exhibit increasing returns; namely the view that there may be returns-to-scale associated with the level of activity in the whole economy. Such returns-to-scale might derive from those of individual firms, or they might be Marshallian external economies. But they are not associated with the size of investment projects of particular dates. Yet such returns-to-scale may be of considerable importance.

The scale effects that might be more readily considered are of two types. One that has been discussed already is convexity of the utilization function of a particular plant. A different kind of increasing returns would be present if (3) were to exhibit increasing returns-to-scale. This would mean that there are returns to designing and building a large plant; or, more accurately, there are returns to having a large current investment project.

Thus there are numerous possibilities, and it should by now be clear that the whole question of returns-to-scale is very much more complex in the case of vintage models than it is in the straight non-vintage theory. Having said all this I shall from now on assume that (3) is homogeneous of degree one. Balanced growth theory requires, at the very least, homogeneity, not necessarily of degree one. The interested reader will however be able to confirm that my theorem on efficient paths of economic growth can easily be restated and proved, by the same methods, for the case of increasing returns.

There is another property of the production function that has to be considered. This is what is usually called diminishing returns. Suppose the amount of labour to be allocated to new investments (of one type) is fixed at a certain level. This eliminates pure scale effects. The capacity output of these investments now depends only upon *per capita* gross investment. Let

$$X(\theta, \theta)/L(\theta, \theta) = f(k(\theta), \theta). \qquad \ldots(9)$$

The function f will be said to satisfy the property of diminishing returns if it is a strictly concave function of k. Later a slightly stronger condition proves to be useful.

Definition 1. The function $f(k(\theta), \theta)$ will be said to be regularly strictly concave if for each $h>0$ there exists a value of k, denoted k_h, such that $f(k_h, \theta)<h.k_h$.

This is equivalent to saying that the investment output ratio increases without limit as $k \to \infty$. A sufficient condition for this is the right-hand Inada condition:

$$\lim_{k \to \infty} \frac{\partial f}{\partial k} = 0. \qquad \ldots(10)$$

Another condition sufficient to guarantee that Definition 1 be satisfied, due to Koopmans [5], is that the production function be strictly concave and that positive output cannot be produced without labour. An example of a function that is strictly concave, but not regularly strictly concave, is provided by the function:

$$f(k, \theta) = \frac{k(k+5)}{2(k+1)}. \qquad \ldots(11)$$

4. *Competitive Equilibrium and Efficiency*

Consider a time path of the economy satisfying equations (1) to (7), where $N(t)$ is a given function of time. Such a path will be said to be feasible.

Definition 2. A growth path of the economy will be said to be efficient if it is feasible and if there exists no other distinct feasible growth path, with consumption stream $C'(t)$, such that $C'(t) \geqq C(t)$, and $C'(t) > C(t)$ on a set of t whose measure is not zero.

The definition has of necessity to admit cases in which $C'(t)$ exceeds $C(t)$ at moments of time so sparse that they can be neglected for the purpose of integration. With that proviso, Definition 2 states that, essentially, no other feasible path dominates the efficient path with consumption stream $C(t)$.

On an efficient path investments are manned up in descending order of output per man. Thus if $f[k(\theta), \theta] > f[k(\theta'), \theta']$, then $L(t, \theta') > 0$ at $t \geqq \theta$ only if $L(t, \theta) = L(\theta, \theta)$. This leads naturally to the following definitions

$$S_t = \{x \mid x = f[k(\theta), \theta] \text{ for } \theta \leqq t \text{ such that } L(t, \theta) < L(\theta, \theta)\},$$
$$S'_t = \{x \mid x = f[k(\theta), \theta] \text{ for } \theta \leqq t \text{ such that } L(t, \theta) = L(\theta, \theta)\}. \qquad \ldots(12)$$

S_t is the set of all *per capita* outputs of investments that are not fully manned at time t. S'_t is the set of all *per capita* outputs of investments that are fully manned at time t. If a small amount of extra labour were to be made available to the economy and found employment then output could increase at a rate indicated by the least upper bound of S_t, while if labour available fell then output would decrease at a rate indicated by the greatest lower bound of S'_t. The shadow wage rate is a function satisfying at each t the following condition.

$$\sup S_t \leqq w(t) \leqq \inf S'_t. \qquad \ldots(13)$$

In most of the cases that we shall want to study S_t and S' will contain every value in a certain interval, in which case the sup and the inf of (13) will be equal, and $w(t)$ will be unique. But that cannot be guaranteed in general, and the definition has to cover the general case.

Definition 3. The function $r(t)$ will be said to be the rate of return on an efficient growth path if it satisfies the relation

$$-k(\theta) + \int_\theta^\infty \{f[k(\theta), \theta] - w(t)\} \frac{L(t, \theta)}{L(\theta, \theta)} \exp\left(-\int_\theta^t r(z)dz\right) dt = 0. \qquad \ldots(14)$$

for some $w(t)$ satisfying (13). (14) says that the investment cost of one man-place is equal to the value of all future quasi-rents discounted at an instantaneous rate which is $r(t)$ at time t. The existence and uniqueness of $r(t)$ will be established below. The fact that the path is required to be efficient plays no part in the definition, but the rate of return as defined would not correspond to the ordinary notion of a rate of return were the path inefficient.

Definition 4. A growth path of the economy will be said to be a competitive equilibrium if there exists $r(t)$ such that, for each θ, and for each type of investment constructed,

$$-k(\theta)+\int_{\theta}^{\infty}\{f[k(\theta),\theta]-w(t)\}\frac{L(t,\theta)}{L(\theta,\theta)}\exp\left(-\int_{\theta}^{t}r(z)dz\right)dt$$

$$=\max_{\substack{k\\L(t,\theta)}}\left[-k+\int_{\theta}^{\infty}\{f(k,\theta)-w(t)\}\frac{L(t,\theta)}{L(\theta,\theta)}\exp\left(-\int_{\theta}^{t}r(z)dz\right)dt\right]=0. \qquad \ldots(15)$$

This corresponds to the ordinary notion of an intertemporal competitive equilibrium. The capital intensity of each type of investment and the plan for manning it are chosen so as to maximize the net present value of an investment designed to employ one man (one man-place), and this present value is zero; there is no pure profit.

There are two conditions that are clearly necessary for (15) to be satisfied for a positive k. In the first place, $L(t, \theta)$ should be zero whenever $f(k, \theta)<w(t)$ (neglecting cases where this condition is violated on sets of t of zero measure). This simply states that present value cannot be maximized if the investment is manned when the output produced is not sufficient to pay shadow wage costs. The second condition is that the derivative of (15) with respect to k should vanish; net present value should be stationary with respect to variations in capital intensity alone. In certain cases these two necessary conditions may together be sufficient for (15), but they are not in general sufficient for a maximum of net present value. This is a basic problem of which our analysis has to take account. It is therefore useful to have to hand a piece of terminology to cover the case in which we know that necessary conditions for a maximum of net present value are satisfied, but we do not wish to prejudge the question as to whether (15) is satisfied.

Definition 5. A growth path of the economy will be said to be a first-order competitive equilibrium if there exists $r(t)$ such that (14) is satisfied and such that

$$L(t,\theta)=0 \text{ whenever } f[k(\theta),\theta]<w(t);$$

$$\frac{\partial f}{\partial k}\int_{\theta}^{\infty}\frac{L(t,\theta)}{L(\theta,\theta)}\exp\left(-\int_{\theta}^{t}r(z)dz\right)dt-1=0 \qquad \ldots(16)$$

for each θ, and for each type of investment constructed.

II. BALANCED GROWTH

1. *Definition*

The economy is in a state of balanced growth if all the variables grow through time at constant exponential rates, some of which are zero. This idea is given a precise formulation in the following definition.

Definition 6. A growth path will be said to be a balanced growth path if there exist scalars a and b such that: (i) b is positive; (ii) Y and I both grow at exponential rate $a+b$; (iii) N and $L(t, t)$ both grow at exponential rate a.

An immediate consequence of Definition 6 is that s, the gross saving-investment share is also a constant.

Theorem 1. *If Definition* 6 *is satisfied by an efficient path one of the following conditions is satisfied:* either *all investments, however old, are in use;* or *there exists* T, *a constant, such that an investment of vintage* θ *is in use if and only if* $t \leqq \theta+T$.

Proof. The definition of balanced growth clearly implies technical progress, rather than regress, since Y increases faster than N and $L(\theta, \theta)$. Thus the *per capita* output of investments is a monotonically increasing function of θ, the date of the investment. Hence, at any t, either all investments are in use or there exists a T satisfying the requirement of the theorem. It is only necessary to show that this T is invariant with time. Note that

$$N(t) = \int_{t-T(t)}^{t} L(\theta, \theta)d\theta = L_0 \int_{t-T(t)}^{t} e^{a\theta}d\theta = L_0 e^{at} \frac{1-e^{-aT(t)}}{a}; \qquad \text{...(17)}$$

$$\dot{N}(t) = L(t, t) - L(t-T, t-T)[1-\dot{T}(t)]$$
$$= L_0 e^{at}[1-e^{-aT(t)} + \dot{T}(t)e^{-aT(t)}]. \qquad \text{...(18)}$$

From which it follows at once that N is growing at rate a only if $\dot{T} = 0$.

2. *Existence of Balanced Growth Paths*

Balanced growth is only possible if technical change takes a particular form. Even if technical change is such as to permit balanced growth, such growth will not be possible if the labour supply does not expand or contract in such a manner as to permit balanced growth. Finally, even if the labour supply grows at a constant exponential rate it may grow so rapidly that it does not all find employment. There is no need to discuss all these questions in this paper. The condition for balanced growth with full employment of the labour force to be possible has been derived by Solow and colleagues [9] for the fixed investment-labour ratio model as

$$s \geqq \frac{g}{\mu_0(1-e^{-gT})} \qquad \text{...(19)}$$

where $g = a+b$ and μ_0 is the given constant output-investment ratio. (19) has to hold for some $T \leqq +\infty$. In the present model the condition is clearly the same with μ_0 interpreted as the supremum of the set of output-investment ratios available. Less obvious perhaps is the following theorem.

Theorem 2. *Balanced growth is technically possible, given sufficient labour supply, if and only if technical progress is Harrod-neutral at a constant positive exponential rate.*

Proof. (i) Sufficiency. Without loss of generality, let technical change be Harrod-neutral at rate 1. This is a choice of time units. Then the production function takes the form

$$X(\theta, \theta) = F[I(\theta), L(\theta, \theta)e^{\theta}]. \qquad \text{...(20)}$$

$L(\theta, \theta)$ grows at rate a. Then if $I(\theta)$ grows at rate $a+1$, and given the homogeneity of degree one of F, $X(\theta, \theta)$ will grow at rate $a+1$. But

$$Y(t) = \int_{t-T}^{t} X(\theta, \theta)d\theta, \qquad \text{...(21)}$$

where T is to be read as " $+\infty$ " if all investments are in use. Thus Y grows at rate $a+1$ and growth is balanced as required.

(ii) Necessity. Without loss of generality write the production function in the form

$$X(\theta, \theta) = F[I(\theta), L(\theta, \theta)e^{\theta}, \theta], \qquad \text{...(22)}$$

where units for time have been chosen so as to make b of Definition 6 equal 1. Derivatives with respect to various arguments of F will be denoted F_1, F_2 and F_3 to avoid confusion. Then

$$\dot{X}(\theta) = F_1(\theta)\dot{I}(\theta) + F_2(\theta)[\dot{L}(\theta, \theta)e^{\theta} + L(\theta, \theta)e^{\theta}] + F_3(\theta) \qquad \text{...(23)}$$
$$= (1+a)F_1(\theta)I(\theta) + (1+a)F_2(\theta)L(\theta, \theta)e^{\theta} + F_3(\theta). \qquad \text{...(24)}$$

But $\dot{X}(\theta) = (1+a)X(\theta)$ and, by constant returns-to-scale

$$X(\theta) = F_1(\theta)I(\theta)+F_2(\theta)L(\theta, \theta)e^{\theta}. \qquad ...(25)$$

Hence

$$F_3(\theta) = (1+a)X(\theta)-(1+a)F_1(\theta)I(\theta)-(1+a)F_2(\theta)L(\theta, \theta)e^{\theta} = 0. \qquad ...(26)$$

So that, at least at the point at which balanced growth takes place, the production function has the Harrod-neutral form. If balanced growth could take place on a whole range of values of the investment-output ratio at the same rate then technical change is Harrod-neutral everywhere on this range. The proof of Theorem 2 is now complete.

3. *Competitive Balanced Growth*

Consider now balanced growth paths that are also competitive equilibria in the sense of Definition 4. A balanced path is fully characterised by its state at time zero and by the numbers a and b. From now on units for measuring time will always be chosen so as to make b equal to 1. Thus technical progress is Harrod-neutral at rate 1. The shadow wage rate grows at the same rate as output per man on new investments which is the same as the rate of technical progress which is 1. It is first shown that if a balanced path satisfies Definition 4 then $r(t)$ must be a constant. From now on attention is confined to the case when T is finite.[1]

A necessary condition for positive k and non-negative $L(t, \theta)$ to maximize the present value expression (15) is that (15) be at a maximum for k taken alone, and for this a necessary condition is (16). If growth is balanced (15) and (16) reduce to

$$-k_0e^{\theta}+\int_{\theta}^{\theta+T}\{f_0e^{\theta}-w_0e^{t}\}e^{-\int_{\theta}^{t}r(z)dz}\,dt = 0 \qquad ...(27)$$

and

$$f'(\theta)\int_{\theta}^{\theta+T}e^{-\int_{\theta}^{t}r(z)dz}\,dt-1 = 0, \qquad ...(28)$$

where $f'(\theta)$ denotes the partial derivative of $f[k(\theta), \theta]$ with respect to $k(\theta)$, and where $f_0e^{\theta} = w_0e^{\theta+T}$. The relations (27) and (28) hold identically in θ. Thus the first derivative of (27) with respect to θ is zero.

$$-k_0e^{\theta}-[f_0e^{\theta}-w_0e^{\theta}]+f_0e^{\theta}\int_{\theta}^{\theta+T}e^{-\int_{\theta}^{t}r(z)dz}\,dt+r(\theta)\int_{\theta}^{\theta+T}\{f_0e^{\theta}-w_0e^{t}\}e^{-\int_{\theta}^{t}r(z)dz}\,dt = 0. \qquad ...(29)$$

Taking into account (27) and (28) this reduces to

$$-k_0e^{\theta}-[f_0e^{\theta}-w_0e^{\theta}]+\frac{f_0e^{\theta}}{f'(\theta)}+r(\theta)k_0e^{\theta} = 0, \qquad ...(30)$$

or

$$r(\theta) = 1+\frac{f_0-w_0}{k_0}-\frac{f_0}{k_0f'(\theta)}. \qquad ...(31)$$

Since $f'(\theta)$ is a constant on a balanced path it follows that $r(\theta)$ is a constant.

Since a balanced growth path is characterized, given a and b, by its state at time zero it is sufficient for many purposes to develop the theory of competitive investment behaviour at time zero. Competitive behaviour by decision-makers is taken to entail the following; (i) they are price-takers who expect the real wage rate to rise at exponential rate 1, and the rate of discount to remain constant at r, (ii) they choose the capital intensity

[1] My proof that $r(t)$ must be a constant is an alternative proof to that of Solow and colleagues in [9], which would serve as well for this model. Their proof is superior to the present one in that no appeal is made to the maximisation of present value. However, it is also more intricate than the simple proof which a variable proportions model allows.

of new investments so as to maximize the present value, discounting at rate r, of one " man-place ", i.e, an investment designed to employ one man, and (iii) in order to achieve a maximum of present value they plan to retire investments when the cost of manning them has just reached their capacity output level. The maximum net present value is zero. From now on a variable without a time argument will denote the value of that variable at time zero, e.g. $X = X(0, 0)$, and

$$\frac{X}{L} = f[k(0), 0] = f(k). \qquad \ldots(32)$$

Consider an investor at time zero making a decision as to the type of investment to construct. For the moment it is assumed that only one kind of investment is constructed, and its type is fully specified by the investment-labour ratio k. This investment is one man-place. Suppose that the planned economic lifetime of the investment is T years. Then the net present value net of investment outlay is the following

$$-k+\int_0^T f(k)e^{-rt}dt-\int_0^T we^te^{-rt}dt = -k+f(k)\frac{1-e^{-rT}}{r}-w\frac{1-e^{-(r-1)T}}{r-1}. \qquad \ldots(33)$$

The expression $\frac{1-e^{-rT}}{r}$ is the discounted value of a stream of one unit of output lasting for T periods of time, the discount rate being r. It is useful to have a shorthand for expressions of this kind, and the following is introduced

$$\text{dis}\,(r, T) = \frac{1-e^{-rT}}{r}. \qquad \ldots(34)$$

Then the right-hand side of (33) can be written more compactly as

$$-k+f(k)\,\text{dis}\,(r, T)-w\,\text{dis}\,(r-1, T). \qquad \ldots(35)$$

If the optimal retirement condition is satisfied we also have

$$f(k) = we^T \text{ or } T = \max\,[\log_e\{f(k)/w\}, 0]. \qquad \ldots(36)$$

The max operator in (36) reminds us that if an investor were foolish enough to build an investment that could not produce enough to cover wage costs even at their low initial level, then it would be optimal to retire it at once.

Now, given r and w, and taking into account (36), the net present value can be written as a function of k alone. Since the net present value is to be maximised it would be desirable, though by no means necessary, if this function were to be concave on the range of values of k such that $f(k) \geqq w$. Better still, it might be strictly concave. Of course a failure of this function to be concave would mean that on a range on which there was not concavity the net present value of investments in this range could be bettered by convex combinations of investments outside the range. This is illustrated in Fig. 1. On the range AB the net present value of a man-place of capital intensity k, denoted $P(k)$, is non-concave. But the net present value of a convex combination of machines of capital intensity k_A and k_B is clearly the same convex combination of their net present values. Thus the " dip " in the function can always be filled in by building investments of less than one man-place and of differing capital intensities and " mixing " them. Furthermore, as is to be expected, the maximum net present value can always be obtained, given any r and w, with one kind of investment; but that may not be the unique way of obtaining it.

There are two things that I have not yet demonstrated. The first is that the kind of case illustrated in Fig. 1 can in fact arise when the ex-ante production function is subject to the diminishing returns requirement $f''(k)<0$. The second is that this case, should it arise, could occur in the instance that the values of r and w were values consistent with equilibrium, i.e. such that the maximum net present value was zero, and that further there might be more than one equilibrium value of k associated with a particular value of r. All these possibilities occur in the following example.

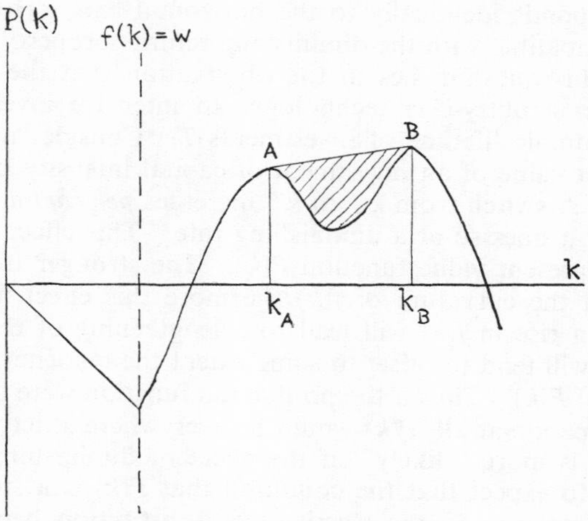

FIGURE 1

Let $r = 0{\cdot}25$ and $w = 1$. Since the production function is monotonic we can work just as well with the inverse of $f(k)$ as with $f(k)$ itself. Thus let $k = f^{-1}(x)$. The function f^{-1} gives the amount of *per capita* investment that is required to obtain a *per capita* output of x. The requirement that $f(k)$ be a strictly concave function now translates into the requirement that f^{-1} be a strictly convex function; the inverse of a monotonic strictly concave function is strictly convex. Now consider this case:

$$k = f^{-1}(x) = \tfrac{4}{3}(1-4x^{0{\cdot}75}+3x). \qquad \text{...(37)}$$

This function is not very well behaved for low x, but the example does not depend upon the properties of the function for $x<1 = w$. So the function could be modified so as to make it a better text-book production function for low values of x. As it stands $f^{-1}(1) = 0$ so that some output is obtainable with no investment at all, but again it could be easily modified, while still remaining convex, to remove this feature. That the function (37) is indeed strictly convex on the relevant range can be seen as follows.

$$\left.\begin{aligned} \frac{dk}{dx} &= 4(1-x^{-0.25})>0 \text{ for } x>1, \\ \frac{d^2k}{dx^2} &= x^{-1.25}>0. \end{aligned}\right\} \qquad \text{...(38)}$$

Thus f^{-1} is the inverse of a well-behaved production function, at least for x greater than some number greater than one. Now, substituting into (33), obtain the following expression for the net present value as a function of x.

$$-k+x\,\frac{1-e^{-rT}}{r} - \frac{1-e^{-(r-1)T}}{r-1} = -f^{-1}(x)+x\,\frac{1-e^{-0.25\log_e x}}{0{\cdot}25} + \frac{1-e^{0.75\log_e x}}{0{\cdot}75}, \qquad \text{...(39)}$$

where T has been eliminated from (36). Simplifying (39) one obtains

$$-f^{-1}(x)+4x(1-x^{-0.25})+\tfrac{4}{3}(1-x^{0.75}) = -f^{-1}(x)+\tfrac{4}{3}(1-4x^{0.75}+3x), \qquad \text{...(40)}$$

which is identically zero from (37). Here then is the ultimate case of multiple equilibrium solutions corresponding to one value of r. If the production function is the inverse of $\frac{4}{3}(1-4x^{0\cdot 75}+3x)$ then at $r = 0\cdot 25$ every choice of technique such that x exceeds unity is an equilibrium, as is every possible mix of choices on this range, for the net present value function corresponds identically to the horizontal axis. How do such cases arise and how are they compatible with the diminishing returns property of $f(k)$?

The answer to this question lies in the observation that the capital stock has two distinct dimensions in a putty-clay technology, an intensive investment-labour ratio k, and an extensive economic lifetime of investments T. Consider now an investor who is comparing the present value of an investment of capital intensity k^- to one with a larger capital intensity k^+. A switch from k^- to k^+ increases *per capita* output but, because of the concavity of $f(k)$, it does so at a diminishing rate. This effect taken alone makes for concavity of the net present value function $P(k)$. The stronger the effect of diminishing returns manifested in the curvature of $f(k)$ the more this effect makes for concavity in $P(k)$. But, given w, a rise in $f(k)$ will lead to a lengthening of the economic lifetime of investments and this will tend to offset to some extent the tendency of diminishing returns to lead to concavity of $P(k)$. Thus if the production function were linear, so that diminishing returns did not operate at all, $P(k)$ would be everywhere strictly convex. So, in some sense, non-concavity is more " likely " if the effect of diminishing returns is weak, and this would lead one to expect that the condition that $P(k)$ is a strictly concave function will be related in some way to the elasticity of substitution between employment and investment, denoted by σ, at the relevant point. This is indeed the case as the following argument demonstrates.

$P(k)$ is locally concave (strictly concave) if and only if its second derivative is non-positive (negative).[1] From (33) one obtains the first two derivatives of $P(k)$ noting that T is a function of k through (36).

$$\frac{dP(k)}{dk} = -1+f'(k)\,\frac{1-e^{-rT}}{r} +(f(k)-we^{T})e^{-rT}\frac{f'(k)}{f(k)}$$

$$= -1+f'(k)\left[\frac{1-e^{-rT}}{r} +e^{-rT}\right] - we^{-(r-1)T}\,\frac{f'(k)}{f(k)}, \qquad \ldots(41)$$

where, from (36), I have obtained the relation $\dfrac{dT}{dk} = \dfrac{f'(k)}{f(k)}$. Next note that,

$$\frac{d^2P(k)}{dk^2} = f''(k)\left(\frac{1-e^{-rT}}{r} +e^{-rT}\right) - we^{-(r-1)T}\frac{f''(k)f(k)-f'(k)^2}{f(k)^2}$$

$$+f'(k)\left[e^{-rT} - re^{-rT} + (r-1)e^{-(r-1)T}\,\frac{w}{f(k)}\right]\frac{f'(k)}{f(k)}. \qquad \ldots(42)$$

From (36) the last term is zero. Hence,

$$\frac{d^2P(k)}{dk^2} = f''(k)\left[\frac{1-e^{-rT}}{r} +e^{-rT} - e^{-rT}\right] + e^{-rT}\frac{f'(k)^2}{f(k)}$$

$$= f''(k)\,\frac{1-e^{-rT}}{r} +e^{-rT}\frac{f'(k)^2}{f(k)}, \qquad \ldots(43)$$

[1] This statement requires a regularity condition to justify the necessity for the second derivative to be negative. A function can be strictly concave at a point at which its second derivative vanishes provided that higher order derivatives, should they exist, satisfy the requirement that the lowest order non-vanishing derivative that exists be of even order and negative. An example is provided by the function $-x^m$, where m is a positive even integer, at $x = 0$.

$$\frac{d^2P}{dk^2} = \frac{f'(k)\{f(k)-kf'(k)\}}{kf(k)}\left[-\frac{1}{\sigma}\left(\frac{1-e^{-rT}}{r}\right)+\frac{kf'(k)}{f(k)-kf'(k)}e^{-rT}\right], \qquad \text{...(44)}$$

where σ, the elasticity of substitution, is given by the usual formula

$$\sigma = -\frac{f'(k)\{f(k)-kf'(k)\}}{kf(k)f''(k)}. \qquad \text{...(45)}$$

Thus $P(k)$ will fail to be locally concave when

$$\sigma > \frac{1-e^{-rT}}{re^{-rT}}\left[\frac{f(k)-kf'(k)}{kf'(k)}\right]. \qquad \text{...(46)}$$

This is a very important condition, and one that will turn up again in later discussion. It depends of course not simply upon the technology as specified by $f(k)$, but also upon the factor prices r and w.

4. *Existence of Competitive Balanced Growth Paths*

The ground has now been cleared for the existence theorem for a competitive balanced growth equilibrium. The foregoing discussion has given warning that there are certain problems which must be taken into account in the construction of this proof. In the first place we know already that we cannot hope to establish the uniqueness of the competitive equilibrium values corresponding to a particular value of r. But the existence theorem will claim to establish no more than the proposition that to each r within a given range there corresponds at least one competitive equilibrium. More important, the argument must take account of the fact that $P(k)$ cannot be assumed in advance to be concave at any particular point. Fortunately, this does not give rise to any great analytical problems.

We are here concerned with the following limited question: given suitable values of w, can the equations expressing the conditions of equilibrium in the investment market (profit maximization and free entry) be satisfied by admissible values of r, k and T? The production function $f(k)$ will be assumed to satisfy the property of regular strict concavity, i.e., for each $h>0$ there exists k_h such that $f(k_h)-hk_h<0$.

Theorem 3. *Either, for each positive w less than a given w_0, or for each positive w, there exists a unique positive r, and positive k and T (not necessarily unique), such that the right-hand side of* (33) *achieves its maximum value for positive k and T, and this maximum value is zero.*

The proof of Theorem 3 is given in the Appendix, together with a discussion of why each requirement on w may be necessary. The essence of Theorem 3 is the assertion that the putty-clay model has a factor-price frontier relating r to w. The factor-price frontier may or may not meet the axes.

5. *Comparative Dynamics of Balanced Growth*

The following is the only comparative dynamic result which has general validity.

Theorem 4. *Let w' and w'' be less than w_0 of Theorem* 3, *if such a bound on w exists, and let r' and r'' be such that the requirements of Theorem* 3 *are satisfied, i.e., at r' and w' the maximum net present value is zero, and the same is true at r'' and w''. Then $w'>w''$ implies $r'<r''$.*

Proof. The proof is almost implicit in the proof of Theorem 3. The right-hand side of (33) is, by inspection, a decreasing function of w. So a fall in w from w' to w'' will raise the net present value of every policy, hence raise the net present value of the most profitable policies, which must then be positive for $r = r'$. Also, the present value of every policy (every choice of k and T) is a monotonically decreasing function of r, the derivative of (33) with respect to r being

$$-\int_0^T \{f(k)-we^t\}te^{-rt}dt<0. \quad \ldots(47)$$

Suppose now that $r' \geqq r''$. Then the change from r' to r'' would further increase the net present value of every policy, or at least leave it unchanged. Then the most profitable policy at $w = w''$ would have a positive net present value, so that r'' and w'' would not satisfy the requirements of Theorem 3, contrary to assumption.

The possibility of multiple solutions for k and T given r and w seems to rule out the derivation of further comparative dynamic results. The situation is parallel to that which has emerged in the literature on neo-classical two-sector models, where the derivation of general comparative dynamic results depends upon assumptions sufficient to ensure the uniqueness of the solution to the model. In order to carry the discussion further I need the following assumption.

Uniqueness assumption. To each pair of values of r and w satisfying the requirements of Theorem 3 there correspond unique values of k and T such that the net present value function achieves its maximum.

It would no doubt be more desirable to have a condition, at least a sufficient one, for the uniqueness assumption to be valid. Such a condition is provided by the inequality (46). If this inequality is reversed we have a condition that $P(k)$ is locally strictly concave which, were it to hold everywhere, would guarantee that a unique k would produce a maximum of $P(k)$. The uniqueness of T would then follow from (36). However, (46) is not very satisfactory from this point of view because it is not a direct statement about the shape of $f(k)$ alone, but involves also the factor prices r, and, if T is eliminated, w also. So it is very difficult to apply (46) to some particular function to see if uniqueness can be guaranteed. I have however been unable to obtain a more transparent condition. If the uniqueness assumption, in its admittedly unsatisfactory form, is accepted there are some further comparative dynamic results available. I need the following Lemma. As with Theorem 3, the proof is relegated to the Appendix to avoid filling the text with lengthy arguments.

Lemma 5. *Let* $\frac{1}{w}\frac{dw}{dr}$ *be the proportional change in the wage rate associated with a change in* r. *Then the following inequality is satisfied identically.*

$$-\frac{rT+1-e^{rT}}{r^2} > -\frac{1}{w}\frac{dw}{dr}. \quad \ldots(48)$$

The equipment necessary to tackle the question of the relation between r, and k and T, is now to hand. Since net present value is at a maximum it must be stationary with respect to variations in k alone. Hence,

$$-1+f'(k)\,\frac{1-e^{-rT}}{r} = 0. \quad \ldots(49)$$

Taking the total derivative of (49) one obtains

$$-\frac{f''(k)}{f'(k)^2}\frac{dk}{dr} - e^{-rT}\frac{dT}{dr} - \frac{(rT+1)e^{-rT}-1}{r^2} = 0. \quad \ldots(50)$$

Similarly, net present value is at a maximum with respect to variations in T alone, so that

$$f(k)-we^T = 0, \quad \ldots(51)$$

and a total derivative of (51) gives

$$f'(k)\frac{dk}{dr} - e^{T}\frac{dw}{dr} - we^{T}\frac{dT}{dr} = 0. \qquad \text{...(52)}$$

Let $q = -\dfrac{1}{k}\dfrac{dk}{dr}$. Then (50) and (52) can be written

$$\frac{dT}{dr} = -\frac{f(k)-kf'(k)}{f'(k)f(k)}\frac{1}{\sigma}e^{rT}q - \frac{rT+1-e^{rT}}{r^2}, \qquad \text{...(53)}$$

$$\frac{dT}{dr} = -\frac{kf'(k)}{f(k)}q - \frac{1}{w}\frac{dw}{dr}, \qquad \text{...(54)}$$

where σ is the elasticity of substitution between investment and employment. (53) and (54) are two linear relations between $\dfrac{dT}{dr}$ and q, since at any particular equilibrium point r, k and T will all have known values. Clearly if one were to take two arbitrary linear relations between $\dfrac{dT}{dr}$ and q one could get no information at all about their signs, nor indeed about anything else. This approach is useful because we in fact have, already, two important restrictions on (53) and (54). Consider first the difference between their slopes, given by

$$-\frac{f(k)-kf'(k)}{f'(k)f(k)}\frac{1}{\sigma}e^{rT} + \frac{kf'(k)}{f(k)} \qquad \text{...(55)}$$

The sign of (55) is the same as the sign of

$$\sigma - \frac{f(k)-kf'(k)}{kf'(k)^2}e^{rT}. \qquad \text{...(56)}$$

At an equilibrium, taking into account (49), this can be written

$$\sigma - \frac{f(k)-kf'(k)}{kf'(k)}\frac{1-e^{-rT}}{re^{-rT}}. \qquad \text{...(57)}$$

Now compare this to the concavity condition (46). If local strict concavity, and hence the uniqueness assumption, is not to be violated (57) must be negative. Thus the uniqueness assumption guarantees that the slope of (53) will be less than the slope of (54). Next consider the relationship between the vertical intercepts of these two lines; these are

$$-\frac{rT+1-e^{rT}}{r^2} \quad \text{and} \quad -\frac{1}{w}\frac{dw}{ar}.$$

But Lemma 5 is concerned with the relationship between these two expressions and it asserts that the first is strictly greater than the second.

In Fig. 2 the lines (53) and (54) are illustrated taking into account the restrictions on slopes and intercepts already noted. The figure also illustrates the effect on the intersection of the two lines of changes in σ and the rotation of (53) through its intercept that results. A number of results that are obtained immediately from this Figure are collected together in the next theorem.

Theorem 6. *Let r, w, T and k be equilibrium values of the variables at time zero. Let the uniqueness assumption hold, and let* $\dfrac{dT}{dr}$ *be the slope of the function relating T to r evaluated at this equilibrium point, let* $\dfrac{dk}{dr}$ *be the slope of the function relating k to r evaluated at this equilibrium point, and let q be* $-\dfrac{1}{k}\dfrac{dk}{dr}$. *Then;*

(i) *q is positive for every positive value of σ consistent with the concavity condition, and hence the uniqueness assumption.*

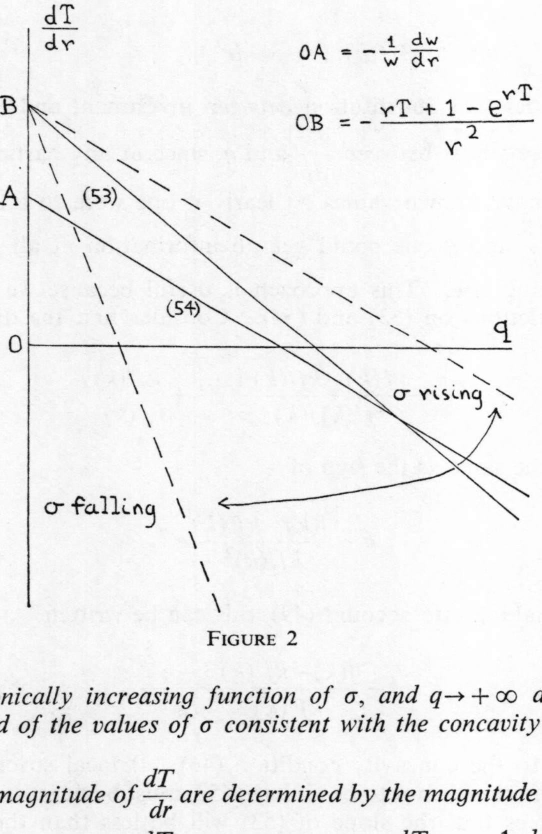

FIGURE 2

(ii) *q is a monotonically increasing function of σ, and* $q \to +\infty$ *as* $\sigma \to \sigma^*$, *where* σ^* *is the least upper bound of the values of σ consistent with the concavity condition.* $q \to 0$ *as* $\sigma \to 0$.

(iii) *The sign and magnitude of* $\dfrac{dT}{dr}$ *are determined by the magnitude of σ.* $\dfrac{dT}{dr}$ *is a monotonically decreasing function of σ.* $\dfrac{dT}{dr} \to -\infty$ *as* $\sigma \to \sigma^*$. $\dfrac{dT}{dr} \to -\dfrac{1}{w}\dfrac{dw}{dr}$ *as* $\sigma \to 0$.

Proof. Earlier arguments and inspection of Fig. 2.

While Theorem 6 provides us with a considerable amount of information about the form of the function relating T to r, and the dependence of that function upon the elasticity of substitution, it does not elucidate the global properties of that function. The following analysis shows what form the function relating T to r will take in various cases, always assuming the uniqueness assumption to hold. As is to be expected, the magnitude of σ plays a crucial role.

In equilibrium the present value of one man-place is zero.

$$-k+f(k)\,\text{dis}\,(r, T)-w\,\text{dis}\,(r-1, T) = 0. \qquad \ldots(58)$$

Multiplying (49) by $kf'(k)$ and adding the resulting equation to (58).

$$\{f(k)-kf'(k)\}\,\mathrm{dis}\,(r, T)-w\,\mathrm{dis}\,(r-1, T) = 0. \qquad \ldots(59)$$

Rearranging, and taking into account (36).[1]

$$\frac{f(k)-kf'(k)}{f(k)} = e^{-T}\frac{\mathrm{dis}\,(r-1, T)}{\mathrm{dis}\,(r, T)} \qquad \ldots(60)$$

The equation (60) is an extremely useful relation, because the left-hand side depends upon k only, while the right-hand side depends only on r and T. The right-hand side of (60) is graphed as a function of r, for various values of T, in Fig. 3. As the Figure shows it is a monotonically descreasing function of both r and T, and for all positive values of r and T it has a value between zero and one. The maximum value ($r = 0$) is $(1-e^{-T})/T$, and the limit as $r \to \infty$ is e^{-T}.

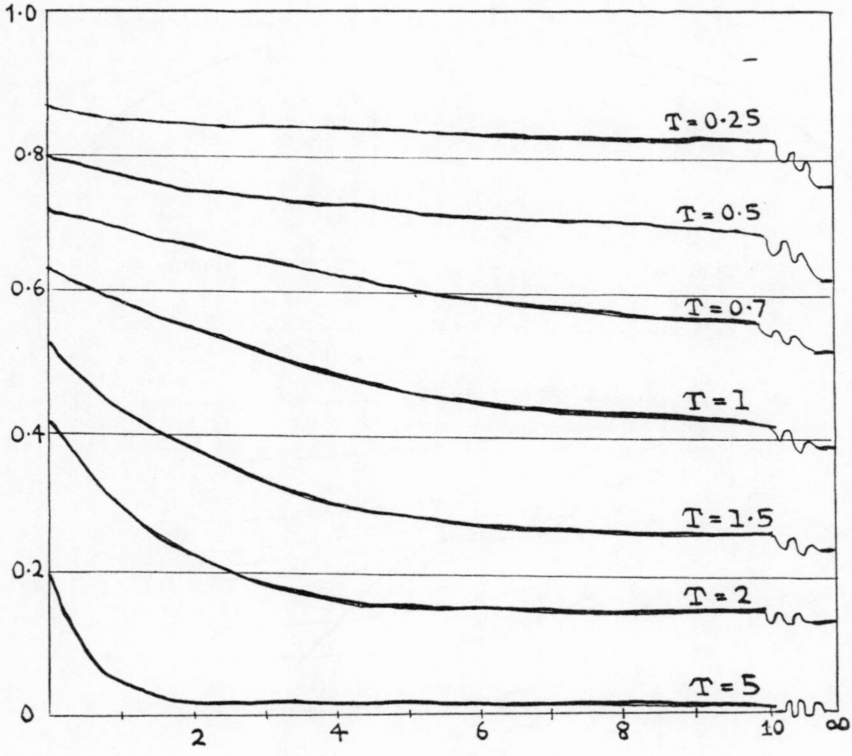

FIGURE 3

Graphs of the function $\frac{r}{r-1}\,e^{-T}\,\frac{1-e^{-(r-1)T}}{1-e^{-rT}}$

Now consider the left-hand side of (60) regarded as a function of r. From Theorem 6 we know that k is a decreasing function of r, i.e. q is positive. But the response of

$$\{f(k)-kf'(k)\}/f(k)$$

[1] The reader who knows R. C. O. Matthews' paper [6] will recognise the tactics that I am adopting here, and will appreciate the extent of my debt to that paper. His argument is open to certain objections on account of its lack of rigour, but the faults are fairly easily remedied. More seriously, the argument is conducted on the assumption that a rise in the gross saving-investment share will be associated with a fall in r. This is not in general true; not even if the elasticity of substitution is less than one.

to a fall in k depends upon the elasticity of substitution between employment and investment. There are numerous possibilities here, and I have selected three cases to present. They serve to demonstrate the richness of the model.

(i) The elasticity of substitution is greater than or equal to 1. Then k falls as r increases and the fall in k is associated with a rise, or no change at all, in $\{f(k)-kf'(k)\}/f(k)$.

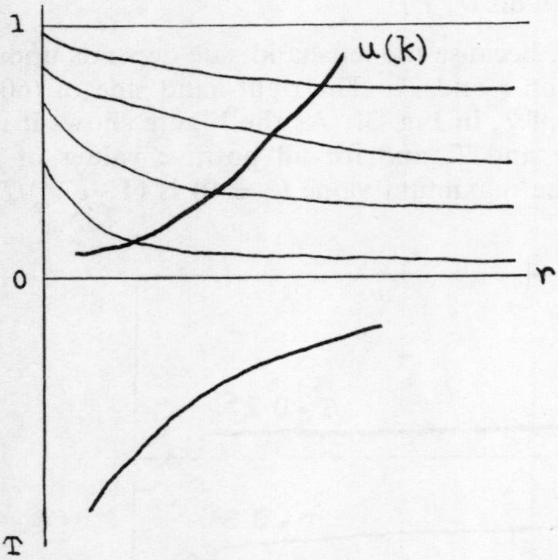

FIGURE 4a

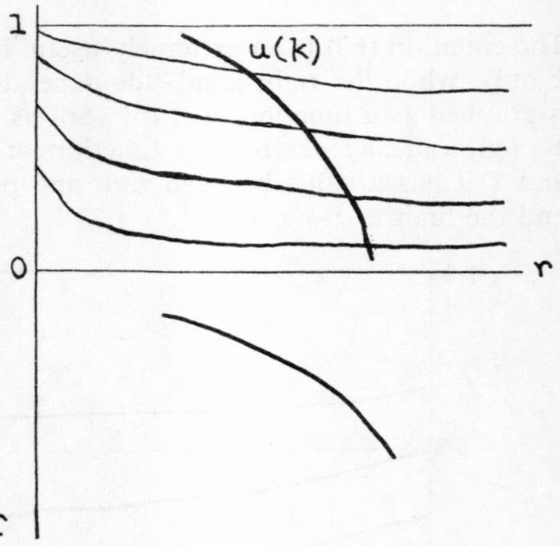

FIGURE 4b

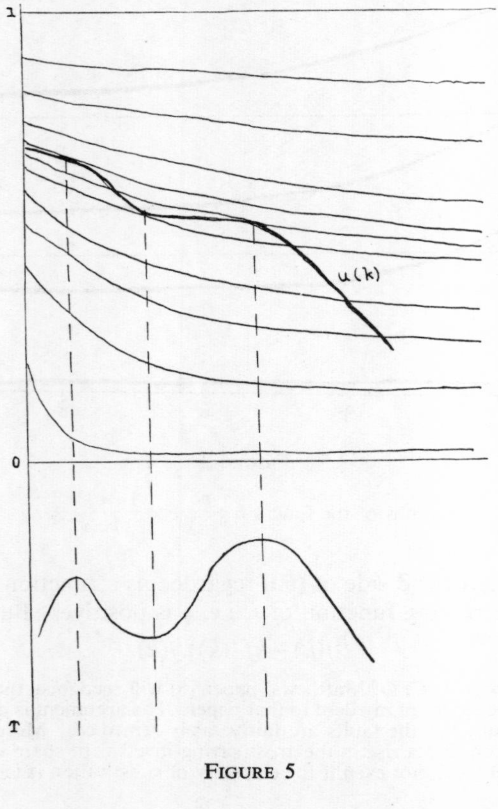

FIGURE 5

Moving along the r axis to the right one travels across curves corresponding to lower and lower values of T. Thus T is a monotonically decreasing function of r. This case is illustrated in Fig. 4(a) in which the function $\{f(k)-kf'(k)\}/f(k)$, denoted $u(k)$, is superimposed upon Fig. 3. In the lower quadrant the resulting relationship between r and T is illustrated.

(ii) The elasticity of substitution is close to zero. In this case k is not very responsive to changes in r, but even a small change in k results in a large movement of $u(k)$, which is an increasing function of k. Hence the curve $u(k)$ falls sharply to the right as one travels along the r-axis, cutting the curves of Figure 3 from above. T is a monotonically increasing function of r. Figure 4(b) illustrates this case.

(iii) The elasticity of substitution is less than one, but is not everywhere very small. Furthermore, it may vary with k, and it is not required to be a monotonic function of k. In this class of cases the curve $u(k)$ is falling as one travels to the right along the r-axis, but it may fall faster or slower than the curves of Figure 3. The slope of the function relating T to r may be either positive or negative, and T may oscillate as r increases. Such an oscillatory case is illustrated in Fig. 5.

Here then is a summary of the above analysis. The effect of a change in r upon T is the outcome of two offsetting influences: (i) a rise in r is associated with a fall in w and this, given $f(k)$, tends to lengthen the economic lifetime of investments, and (ii) a rise in r is associated with a fall in k and this, given w, tends to lower the economic lifetime of investments. The effect that a change in r has on w is independent of the elasticity of substitution (see the proof of Lemma 5), while the effect on k is larger the larger is σ. Hence the second effect tends to dominate when the elasticity of substitution is sufficiently large. In general oscillatory cases cannot be excluded.

6. *Balanced Growth and the Gross Saving-Investment Share*

The ratio of $I(t)$ to $Y(t)$, denoted s, is a constant on a balanced growth path. Let employment grow at rate a; then the natural rate of growth n is $1+a$. Note that

$$Y = Lf(k)\int_0^T e^{-nt}dt = Lf(k)\,\mathrm{dis}\,(n, T). \qquad \ldots(61)$$

Since $s = I/Y$, one has

$$k = \frac{sY}{L} = sf(k)\,\mathrm{dis}\,(n, T). \qquad \ldots(62)$$

Thus balanced growth is characterized by the equation

$$s = \frac{k}{f(k)}\frac{1}{\mathrm{dis}\,(n, T)} = \frac{k}{f(k)}\frac{n}{1-e^{-nT}}. \qquad \ldots(63)$$

Now given n the right-hand side of (63) is a function of r, since k and T depend, given the uniqueness assumption, uniquely on r. In this section I shall be mainly concerned with the following question: is the opposite true; i.e., does a knowledge of s uniquely determine r? Or the same question can be put in somewhat different ways. Is it true, for example, as has sometimes been assumed, that a rise in s will be associated, in a comparative dynamic sense, with a fall in r and a move to investments with a larger k? Rewrite (63) as

$$\frac{k}{f(k)} = s\,\frac{1-e^{-nT}}{n}. \qquad \ldots(64)$$

The left-hand side of (64) is a decreasing function of r. If the right-hand side were to be an increasing function of r it would follow that there was at most one balanced growth equilibrium consistent with a given value of s. This will be the case if the elasticity of substitution is less than 1 and small; for then, as has been seen, T will be an increasing function of r, and the right-hand side of (64) is an increasing function of T. But in no other case can uniqueness of r, given s, be guaranteed. For if $\sigma > 1$ we have seen that T will decrease with r; while if $\sigma < 1$ and large T may even oscillate, and in neither case can the possibility of multiple solutions be excluded. Clearly, if several disjoint values of the rate of return are consistent with one value of s, it must follow that s is not a monotonic function of r.

So far nothing has been said about the determinants of the gross saving-investment share s. This number has been treated as parameter, an approach commonly used, though with more justification, in treating the net saving-investment share in neo-classical growth models. Yet s may be affected by any of the variables of the model. The most important relation between s and other variables is likely to be the dependence of s upon the distribution of income between wages and gross profits. To demonstrate the consequences of such a relation I need an expression for the share of wages in gross output. Total employment at time zero is given by

$$N = L \int_0^T e^{-at} dt = L \operatorname{dis}(a, T). \qquad \ldots(65)$$

Hence the share of wages in gross output is given by

$$\frac{w.N}{Y} = w \frac{\operatorname{dis}(a, T)}{\operatorname{dis}(n, T)} \frac{1}{f(k)} = e^{-T} \frac{\operatorname{dis}(a, T)}{\operatorname{dis}(n, T)} = e^{-T} \frac{\operatorname{dis}(n-1, T)}{\operatorname{dis}(n, T)}. \qquad \ldots(66)$$

Now the right-hand side of (66) has precisely the functional form of the right-hand side of (60). Thus one can say at once, or by inspection of Fig. 3, that, given n, the share of wages in gross output is a decreasing function of T. This is not an unnatural result. Now suppose that s is a weighted average of a saving share for wages and a saving share for gross profits, the weights being the relative income shares. Suppose a larger share of gross profits is saved. Then s increases with r if and only if T increases with r. However, allowing s to vary with the distribution of income does not, of necessity, guarantee a unique balanced growth equilibrium. For take the extreme " classical " case, when all gross profits are saved and there is no saving of wage income. This case is surely most favourable to uniqueness of r if income distribution effects are favourable to uniqueness of r, since maximum power is given to these effects. The balanced growth state is now characterised by the condition that s shall be equal to the share of gross profit in gross output.

$$1 - e^{-T} \frac{\operatorname{dis}(n-1, T)}{\operatorname{dis}(n, T)} = \frac{k}{f(k)} \frac{1}{\operatorname{dis}(n, T)}, \qquad \ldots(67)$$

$$\frac{1-e^{-nT}}{n} - e^{-T} \frac{1-e^{-(n-1)T}}{n-1} = \frac{k}{f(k)}. \qquad \ldots(68)$$

The right-hand side of (68) is a decreasing function of r. The left-hand side depends upon T alone, given n, and its derivative with respect to T is

$$e^{-nT} - e^{-(n-1)T} e^{-T} + e^{-T} \frac{1-e^{-(n-1)T}}{n-1} = e^{-T} \frac{1-e^{-(n-1)T}}{n-1} > 0. \qquad \ldots(69)$$

So the left-hand side of (68) is an increasing function of T. For uniqueness to be guaranteed one would certainly want to have the left-hand side an increasing function of r. But this is only the case if T is an increasing function of r, as would be the case if σ were small. Otherwise we may again face the possibility that there will be more than one balanced growth equilibrium consistent with pure " classical " saving. If saving is related to net profits and is of the pure classical kind balanced growth equilibrium is unique by the usual argument that the rate of growth of the market value of capital is equal to n, which is equal to r. But even here the uniqueness assumption is still required.

III. EFFICIENT GROWTH

1. *A Theorem on Efficient Growth Paths*

Definition 2 introduced the concept of an efficient growth path.

Theorem 7. *A growth path of the economy is efficient only if it is a first-order competitive equilibrium.*

Proof. A necessary condition for a growth path to be efficient in the sense of Definition 2 is that the infinite integral

$$\int_0^\infty \{C'(t)-C(t)\}dt \qquad ...(70)$$

should achieve a maximum at zero for $C'(t) = C(t)$ when $C'(t)$ is constrained by the feasibility conditions (1) to (7), plus the requirement that

$$C'(t) \geqq C(t).^1 \qquad ...(71)$$

This is virtually a restatement of Definition 2. Thus an efficient path can be regarded as the solution to a problem in the variational calculus. The natural way to proceed now is to introduce the Lagrangean expression

$$\int_0^\infty \Bigg[C'(t)-C(t)+\eta(t)\{C'(t)-C(t)\} + \lambda(t)\left\{\int_{-\infty}^t f[k(\theta), \theta]L(t, \theta)d\theta - k(t)L(t, t) - C(t)\right\} + \mu(t)\left\{N(t) - \int_{-\infty}^t L(t, \theta)d\theta\right\} dt\Bigg]. \qquad ...(72)$$

Not all the feasibility constraints are incorporated into (72). For example, the requirement $L(t, \theta) \leqq L(\theta, \theta)$ is not included. A variation in one of the functions will be said to be admissible if it does not lead to a violation of any of the constraints not included. This is a common way of treating sign constraints in programming problems; they are not included in the Lagrangean, but care is taken to ensure that the variations considered do not lead to their violation. A necessary condition for (70) to achieve a maximum subject to the various constraints involved is that the Lagrangean expression (72) should be locally stationary for any admissible variation. Let $C^v(t)$, $k^v(t)$ and $L^v(t, \theta)$ be admissible variations in C', k and L.

Variations in $k(t)$

If (72) is to be stationary with respect to admissible variations in $k(t)$, and assuming $k(t)$ everywhere positive, so that any variation is admissible, one must have

$$\int_0^\infty \lambda(t)\left\{\int_{-\infty}^t f'[k(\theta), \theta]L(t, \theta)k^v(\theta)d\theta - L(t, t)k^v(t)\right\} dt = 0 \qquad ...(73)$$

for arbitrary $k^v(t)$. Let $k^v(t) = \max(h-t, 0)$, where h is a parameter.[2] Then (73) must be identically zero in h. Substituting one obtains

$$\int_0^h \left[\lambda(t)\left\{\int_{-\infty}^t f'[k(\theta), \theta]L(t, \theta)(h-\theta)d\theta - L(t, t)(h-t)\right\}\right] dt + \int_h^\infty \left[\lambda(t)\left\{\int_{-\infty}^h f'[k(\theta), \theta]L(t, \theta)(h-\theta)d\theta\right\}\right] dt = 0 \qquad ...(74)$$

[1] Both the statement that the maximum is achieved at $C'(t) = C(t)$, and the inequality (71), should be interpreted in the almost everywhere sense. I shall dispense with the tiresome reiteration of this qualification. Those who are annoyed by its absence will know where to insert it.

[2] This special variation approach is an adaptation of R. Courant's technique for deriving Euler's equation by special variations. An account of that method as applied to traditional variational problems can be found in [1], page 191.

identically in h. Hence, forming derivatives of (74) with respect to h, and identifying them with zero

$$\int_0^h \left[\lambda(t) \left\{ \int_{-\infty}^t f'[k(\theta), \theta] L(t, \theta) d\theta - L(t, t) \right\} \right] dt$$
$$+ \int_h^\infty \left[\lambda(t) \left\{ \int_{-\infty}^h f'[k(\theta), \theta] L(t, \theta) d\theta \right\} \right] dt = 0, \quad \text{...(75)}$$

all other terms being zero. Then the next derivative with respect to h is

$$-\lambda(h)L(h, h) + \int_h^\infty \lambda(t) f'[k(h), h] L(t, h) dt = 0, \quad \text{...(76)}$$

or, rearranging (76)

$$f'[k(h), h] \int_h^\infty \frac{\lambda(t)}{\lambda(h)} \frac{L(t, h)}{L(h, h)} dt - 1 = 0. \quad \text{...(77)}$$

Compare this to (16).

Variations in $L(t, \theta)$:

First note, by inspection of (72), that the Lagrange multiplier $\mu(t)$ must be equal, for each t, to $\lambda(t).w(t)$, where $w(t)$ is the shadow wage rate as defined in (13). Thus suppose, for example, that on a set of values of t we have $\mu(t) < \lambda(t)w(t)$. Then an increase in $L(t, \theta)$ on this set for vintages θ satisfying $f[k(\theta), \theta] = w(t)$ would increase the value of (72). Then a variation in $L(t, \theta)$ yields

$$\int_0^\infty \lambda(t) \left\{ \int_{-\infty}^t [f\{k(\theta), \theta\} - w(t)] L^v(t, \theta) d\theta - k(t) L^v(t, t) \right\} dt = 0 \quad \text{...(78)}$$

for all admissible variations $L^v(t, \theta)$. Now choose $L^v(t, \theta)$ to be

$$L^v(t, \theta) = \left\{ \begin{matrix} \min(\theta - h, 0) L(t, \theta) & \text{if } t \geq \theta \\ 0 & \text{if } t < \theta \end{matrix} \right\}. \quad \text{...(79)}$$

Then $L^v(t, \theta)$ is an admissible variation. For by definition it satisfies the restriction $L(t, \theta) = 0$ for all $\theta > t$. Furthermore, when $L(t, \theta)$ is zero, in which case one has to worry about variations that would decrease $L(t, \theta)$, $L^v(t, \theta)$ is zero by definition. Finally, when $L(t, \theta)$ is positive $L^v(t, \theta)$ is non-positive, so that there is no danger that the condition $L(t, \theta)$ not greater than $L(\theta, \theta)$ will be violated. Then (78) becomes

$$\int_0^h \lambda(t) \left\{ \int_{-\infty}^t [f(\theta) - w(t)](\theta - h) L(t, \theta) d\theta - L(t) L(t, t)(t - h) \right\} dt$$
$$+ \int_h^\infty \lambda(t) \left\{ \int_{-\infty}^h [f(\theta) - w(t)] L(t, \theta)(\theta - h) d\theta \right\} dt = 0, \quad \text{...(80)}$$

which is true identically in h. Then again all derivatives with respect to h must vanish, so that

$$-\int_0^h \lambda(t) \left\{ \int_{-\infty}^t [f(\theta) - w(t)] L(t, \theta) d\theta - k(t) L(t, t) \right\} dt$$
$$-\int_h^\infty \lambda(t) \left\{ \int_{-\infty}^h [f(\theta) - w(t)] L(t, \theta) d\theta \right\} dt = 0, \quad \text{...(81)}$$

all other terms being zero. And another derivative yields

$$k(h) L(h, h) \lambda(h) - \int_h^\infty \lambda(t) [f(h) - w(t)] L(t, h) dt = 0, \quad \text{...(82)}$$

or, rearranging (82)

$$-k(h)+\int_h^\infty \frac{\lambda(t)}{\lambda(h)}[f(h)-w(t)]\frac{L(t,h)}{L(h,h)}\,dt=0. \qquad \text{...(83)}$$

Compare this expression to (15). Now define $r(t)$ as

$$r(t)=-\frac{d}{dt}\log\lambda(t), \qquad \text{...(84)}$$

and the solution to this differential equation is

$$\frac{\lambda(t)}{\lambda(h)}=e^{-\int_h^t r(z)dz}. \qquad \text{...(85)}$$

Now substituting (85) into (77) and (83) the latter are seen to be the equations defining a first-order competitive equilibrium. This completes the proof of Theorem 7.

Now (16) by no means implies that the present value of investments is actually maximized on an efficient path. This has been demonstrated by the earlier discussion of the concavity of the net present value function. However, it is clear from general considerations of programming theory, and from the fact that (72) is concave in the choice functions, that in fact net present value must be maximized (not necessarily strictly) on an efficient path. Then the lesson to be drawn from the possibility of a locally non-concave net present value function is not that efficient growth may not involve the maximization of shadow net present values, but rather that the satisfaction of necessary conditions for the maximization of net present values may not be sufficient for efficient growth.

In order to make these points clear, I shall shift the formulation of the model to one to which standard theorems in programming can be more readily applied. Instead of continuous time let time be divided into discrete periods, numbered by t, $t = 0, 1, 2, \dots$ where period " 0 " is a fictitious period, beyond our control, whose history is such as to give the model suitable initial conditions. At each period of time there are only M types of investment to be constructed, numbered by m, $m = 1, 2, \dots, M$. The following notation is used.

$L_{m\theta t}$ = number of men assigned to investments of type m, vintage θ, at time period t.
I_{mt} = number of man places of type m constructed at t.
C_t = consumption at t.
$\bar{z}_{mt}$ = output required to construct one man-place of type m at t.
$\bar{x}_{mt}$ = output of one man-place of type m, vintage t.
$\bar{N}_t$ = total labour available at t.
$\bar{C}_t$ = actual consumption at t on an efficient path.
$C_t^* = C_t - \bar{C}_t$.

Then the analogue to the Lagrangean form (72) is

$$\sum_{t=1}^{\infty}\Bigg[C_t^*+\lambda_t\left\{\sum_{\theta=0}^{t-1}\sum_{m=1}^{M}L_{m\theta t}\bar{x}_{m\theta}-\sum_{m=1}^{M}I_{mt}\bar{z}_{mt}-C_t^*-\bar{C}_t\right\}$$
$$+\mu_t\left\{\bar{N}_t-\sum_{\theta=0}^{t-1}\sum_{m=1}^{M}L_{m\theta t}\right\}+\sum_{\theta=0}^{t-1}\sum_{m=1}^{M}\pi_{m\theta t}\{I_{m\theta}-L_{m\theta t}\}\Bigg]. \qquad \text{...(86)}$$

The choice variables are by definition non-negative, the non-negativity of C_t^* indicating that C_t must be chosen not less than $\bar{C}_t$. In (86) the constraints on the maximum amount of labour that can be allocated to an investment have been included explicitly. (86) is the Lagrangean form of a linear programme, though one with infinitely many variables and infinitely many constraints. However, if $\bar{C}_t$, $t = 1, 2, \dots$, is in fact an efficient feasible growth plan, then (86) has the value zero, and the usual programming theorems apply. In particular the derivative of (86) with respect to any variable is non-positive. Differentiation with respect to $L_{m\theta t}$ gives

$$\lambda_t \bar{x}_{m\theta} - \mu_t - \pi_{m\theta t} \leqq 0. \qquad ...(87)$$

A similar argument to that applied to (72) shows that $\mu_t = \lambda_t w_t$, where w_t is the shadow price of labour at t. Or note directly that $\pi_{m\theta t}$ is equal to the rate at which the value of the programme would increase as extra capacity of type m vintage θ became available at t. Then, necessarily,

$$\pi_{m\theta t} = \lambda_t \max(\bar{x}_{m\theta} - w_t, 0), \qquad ...(88)$$

which is equivalent to (87). Now the derivative of (86) with respect to $I_{m\theta}$ gives

$$-\lambda_\theta \bar{z}_{m\theta} + \sum_{t=\theta}^{\infty} \lambda_t \max(\bar{x}_{m\theta} - w_t, 0) \leqq 0, \qquad ...(89)$$

where (89) holds for all θ and all m. Hence, no feasible investment has a positive net present value, and an investment actually constructed has zero net present value. Thus profits, in the sense of net present values, are actually maximized by the efficient path.

Theorem 7, following Definitions 4 and 5, merely asserted the existence of one function $r(t)$ having the properties required of a competitive equilibrium. Will $r(t)$ be unique? The answer in general is no. In defining the shadow wage rate I have already had to take account of some rather pathological and awkward cases in which there is more than one possible shadow wage function. Clearly in such cases we cannot hope to have a unique $r(t)$. However, if the shadow wage function is unique, or anyway, given the shadow wage function, there exists a unique $r(t)$ such that any time function satisfying Definition 4 corresponds to $r(t)$ almost everywhere. Without being at all precise (the footnote points the way to a precise argument) form the derivative of (83) with respect to h to obtain, taking into account (77),[1]

$$-\dot{k}(h) - \{f(h) - w(h)\} + \dot{f}(h)/f'(h) - \frac{\dot{\lambda}(h)}{\lambda(h)} k(h) = 0. \qquad ...(90)$$

Thus,

$$r(h) = \frac{f(h) - w(h)}{k(h)} + \frac{\dot{k}(h)}{k(h)} - \frac{\dot{f}(h)}{k(h)f'(h)}. \qquad ...(91)$$

so that $r(h)$ is unique, as required. Further simplification is possible since

$$\dot{f}(h) = f'(h)\dot{k}(h) + f_h(h),$$

where $f_h(h)$ is the partial derivative of $f\{k(h), h\}$ with respect to its second argument. Then

$$r(h) = \frac{f(h) - w(h)}{k(h)} - \frac{f_h(h)}{k(h)f'(h)}. \qquad ...(92)$$

The first term on the right-hand side of (92) is the ratio of gross profit after paying shadow wage rate to the cost of investment at the instant that the investment starts production. It is sometimes called " the immediate rate of profit ". In an economy with a constant shadow wage rate it would be equal to the rate of profit as usually defined. A remarkable

[1] The lack of precision arises because $L(t, h)/L(h, h)$ is clearly not a differentiable function of h; yet in (90) the derivative of this function " under the integral " has been equated implicitly to zero. However, there is no difficulty in making this precise. There is a sense in which the derivative of $L(t, h)/L(h, h)$ is either zero, or a positive or negative δ-function; and in the latter case one must have $f(h) = w(t)$. So it is not surprising that the integral turns out to be zero. More simply, replace the range of integration by a set of closed intervals representing the set of t for which $f(h) \geqq w(t)$. The end-points of each of these intervals are continuous functions of h. If they are also differentiable functions of h we only have to note that the integrand vanishes by definition at every t which is an end-point, so that the derivative of the integral with respect to an end-point is zero. The set of end-points is at most countable if we exclude degenerate intervals. This is the basis of a precise argument.

consequence of (92) is the following.[1] Suppose there is no technical progress, so that $f_h(h)$ is zero. Then $r(h)$ is equal to the immediate rate of profit, i.e., at the instant that an investment starts production there is no depreciation, the instantaneous loss of value is zero. This must be the case if the rate of return net, r, is equal to the gross immediate rate of return. This result holds even if the shadow wage rate is changing, for example, even if capital deepening is going on.

The necessary conditions for an efficient growth path are by no means sufficient as the discussion of the next section will make clear.

2. *Efficient Balanced Growth*: *The Golden Rule*

Numerous writers in recent years have provided proofs of the following proposition in the context of various growth models: if there exists an equilibrium balanced growth path, with natural rate of growth n, and rate of return r equal to n, then no other feasible balanced growth path has a higher level of consumption per unit of labour measured in efficiency units. For references, see Hahn and Matthews [2]. The same proposition holds true also for the present model. I give two proofs, each of which is useful in showing the relation of the Golden Rule in this model to the same rule in other cases.

For the first proof, which is an extremely general proof that will do for virtually any model, prices for old investments are introduced. Let $p(x, t)$ be the price at time t of a man-place of productivity x. Then

$$p(x, t) = \int_t^\infty \{x - w(h)\} L(h) e^{-\int_t^h r(z)dz} dh, \qquad \ldots(93)$$

where $L(h)$ is the optimal amount of labour, not exceeding one unit, to employ on this investment at time h. For the discussion of balanced growth it is useful to work with a slightly different variable. Thus $p^*(x, t)$ is the price at time t of an investment employing one efficiency unit of labour ($e^{-\gamma t}$ natural units) and producing x units of output, while $q^*(x, t)$ is the number of such units available. On a balanced growth path $p^*(x, t)$ is then independent of t, since $w(t)$ grows at rate γ, while $q^*(x, t)$ grows at rate n. Consider a balanced growth path at time t, and suppose it to be a competitive equilibrium. Then the instantaneous costs of production must be equal to the value of output; the latter is the value of consumption output and the value of the addition to the capital stock.

$$W + r\int_0^\infty p^*(x, t) q^*(x, t) dx = n\int_0^\infty p^*(x, t) q^*(x, t) dx + C, \qquad \ldots(94)$$

where C and W are the output of consumption and the wage bill respectively. Now consider an alternative balanced growth path, offering at this instant of time the same total employment. Denote the quantities relevant to this path by the subscript "o". Then the instantaneous activities of this path cannot be more profitable to the decision-makers of the original path, given the prices that they face, than their own activities. Thus

$$W + r\int_0^\infty p^*(x, t) q_0^*(x, t) dx \geqq n\int_0^\infty p^*(x, t) q_0^*(x, t) dx + C_0. \qquad \ldots(95)$$

These two relations together yield

$$(r-n)\int_0^\infty p^*(x, t)[q^*(x, t) - q_0^*(x, t)] dx \leqq C - C_0. \qquad \ldots(96)$$

Now in the case of a balanced growth path for which $r = n$ it follows at once that $C \geqq C_0$. Notice that the argument shows that C is at a global maximum. Furthermore, if there

[1] I am indebted to J. A. Mirrlees for this interpretation of equation (92). Notice that under balanced growth conditions (92) implies (31).

exists an alternative balanced growth path with the same level of consumption as the Golden Rule path, then it must be equally profitable at the Golden Rule prices and, since r is unique to a path, it must itself be a Golden Rule path. Thus consumption is at a maximum if and only if $r = n$.

Another proof follows that provided by Solow and his colleagues [9], for their model with fixed coefficients. This proof has the advantage that it also establishes the proposition that the Golden Rule path can also be characterised by the condition that the gross saving-investment share should be equal to the share of profit in gross output. This result is already obtained by Solow and colleagues for the fixed coefficient case. It only remains to note that it is easily generalized. Choose an arbitrary level of k, investment per man at time zero, within the range of feasible values. Holding this k constant, consumption at time zero is a function of the gross saving share; this is the fixed coefficient case. Thus there exists a curve relating C, consumption at time zero, to s lying between 0 and 1. This curve has a unique maximum for some value of s, call it s_k^*. Now there exists one of these curves for each feasible value of k, and the relation between consumption and the gross saving share which is offered by the model without fixed coefficients is clearly given by the upper envelope of the class of curves corresponding to fixed values of k. Hence, because it is an envelope, it must achieve a maximum at the same value of x as does one of the fixed coefficient curves. It will of course be the curve corresponding to the value of k on the Golden Rule path. Now the maximum of this fixed coefficient curve is achieved when s_k^* is equal to the share of gross profits. This completes the proof. These results are collected together in the next theorem.

Theorem 8. *If there exists a balanced growth path satisfying either of the following properties,*

(i) *it is a competitive equilibrium with rate of return equal to the natural rate of growth,*

or (ii) *the share of gross profit in gross output is equal to the investment-saving share; then this path has a level of consumption per head not less than that of any feasible balanced growth path.*

In the one good neo-classical model the Golden Rule can also be regarded as an efficiency theorem. For a balanced growth path with rate of return less than the natural rate of growth can be readily shown to be inefficient. The same result can be obtained for the putty-clay model, and this will justify an earlier remark that competitive equilibrium is not a sufficient condition for efficiency.

Theorem 9. *A balanced growth path with rate of return r less than the natural rate of growth n is inefficient.*

Proof. It is sufficient to show that the result is true in the case of a fixed coefficient model. For if a balanced growth path is inefficient subject to the constraint that every other path shall have investments, at each t, of the same capital intensity, then it is inefficient *a fortiori* in the case in which this restriction is relaxed. In the discussion of balanced growth I was able to show that T, the economic lifetime of investments, is an increasing function of r in the fixed coefficients case. Then output, at a given t, is a decreasing function of r. The economy with a higher value of r has its labour spread out over a longer set of vintages so that average output, the weights being given, is lower. From this it follows that the economy with a high r has an economy utilization function (economy output related to efficiently allocated labour) which is dominated by the utilization function of the economy with the lower value of r. Suppose then that at a certain moment of time the gross saving share is switched to the Golden Rule gross saving share, and remains at this level thereafter. This entails a once-for-all fall in the saving share. Now, since output is initially higher than the Golden Rule level, investment is larger. Thus, at each t, more men are employed on the latest investments than would be the case on the

Golden Rule path. But then output remains above the Golden Rule level, and hence the same share of it going to consumption gives more consumption than on the Golden Rule path, and hence more than on the original path. So the original path with $r<n$ was certainly inefficient.

It can be easily shown that the path discussed above would in fact approach the Golden Rule path asymptotically; but that is incidental to the proof of Theorem 9, which is now complete.

Christ's College, Cambridge CHRISTOPHER BLISS.

REFERENCES

[1] Courant, R. *Calculus of Variations* (New York University, 1957) (mimeographed).

[2] Hahn, F. H. and Matthews, R. C. O. " The Theory of Economic Growth: A Survey ", *Economic Journal* (December 1964).

[3] Johansen, L. " Substitution versus Fixed Production Coefficients in the Theory of Economic Growth: A Synthesis ", *Econometrica* (April 1959).

[4] Kemp, M. C., and Thanh, P. C. " On a Class of Growth Models ", *Econometrica* (April 1966).

[5] Koopmans, T. C. " The Concept of Optimal Economic Growth ", Cowles Foundation Discussion Paper, No. 163.

[6] Matthews, R. C. O. " ' The New View of Investment ' : Comment ", *Quarterly Journal of Economics* (February 1964)

[7] Phelps, E. S. " Substitution, Fixed Proportions, Growth and Distribution ", *International Economic Review* (September 1963).

[8] Salter, W. E. G. *Productivity and Technical Change* (Cambridge University Press. 1960).

[9] Solow, R. M., Tobin, J., von Weizsäcker, C. C. and Yaari, M. " Neoclassical Growth with Fixed Factor Proportions ", *Review of Economic Studies* (April 1966).

[10] Solow, R. M. " Substitution and Fixed Proportions in the Theory of Capital ", *Review of Economic Studies* (June 1962).

APPENDIX

Theorem 3. *Either, for each positive w less than a given w_0, or for each positive w, there exists a unique positive r, and positive k and T (not necessarily unique), such that the right-hand side of* (33) *achieves its maximum value for positive k and T, and this maximum value is zero.*

Proof. It is first shown that for each positive r and positive w the right-hand side of (33), here denoted $P(k, T)$, has a maximum on the set of k and T satisfying

$$f(k) \geqq w \text{ and } T \geqq 0. \qquad ...(97)$$

The optimal retirement condition implies that

$$P(k, T) \leqq P(k, \max\{\log_e f(k)/w, 0\}) = P(k), \qquad ...(98)$$

so that $P(k, T)$ fails to achieve a maximum, subject to (97), if and only if $P(k)$ fails to achieve a maximum. But $P(k)$ is a continuous function of k, and as such achieves a maximum on every compact subset of its range. Thus it is enough to show that $P(k)$ is eventually a monotonically decreasing function of k. Now (33) can be rewritten as

$$-k+f(k)\frac{1-e^{-r\log_e f(k)/w}}{r}-w\,\frac{1-e^{-(r-1)\log_e f(k)/w}}{r-1}$$

$$=-k+\frac{f(k)}{r}\left[1-\left\{\frac{f(k)}{w}\right\}^{-r}\right]-\frac{w}{r-1}\left[1-\left\{\frac{f(k)}{w}\right\}^{-(r-1)}\right]. \quad \ldots(99)$$

Now (99) is the sum of the term

$$[f(k)-rk]/r \quad \ldots(100)$$

and terms that reduce to

$$\left\{\frac{f(k)}{w}\right\}^{-(r-1)}\left[\frac{w}{r(r-1)}\right]-\frac{w}{r-1}. \quad \ldots(101)$$

(101) is always a decreasing function of k, while (100) must eventually decrease with k by the regular strict concavity property of $f(k)$. Thus, for positive r and w, $P(k)$ has a maximum for k and T satisfying (47). Furthermore (100) goes to $-\infty$ as k goes to $+\infty$ so that $P(k)$ is certainly negative for all sufficiently large k.

I am now in a position to introduce the following definition.

$$Q(r, w)=\max_{f(k)\geqq w}\{P(k, \log_e[f(k)/w])\}. \quad \ldots(102)$$

From the above argument it is known that Q exists for each positive r and positive w.

It is next shown that $Q(r, w)$ is a continuous function of r on the positive r. Denote the net present value with optimal retirement by $P_r(k)$ to remind one of the dependence on r. Suppose that for each $\varepsilon>0$ there were to exist an $\alpha>0$ such that, for all k, $|r'-r|<\alpha$ implied $|P_r(k)-P_{r'}(k)|<\varepsilon$; that is, suppose $P_r(k)$ a continuous function of r uniformly with respect to k. Let $P_r(k_0)=Q(r, w)$ and $P_{r'}(k_0')=Q(r', w)$, and without loss of generality suppose $r'>r$. Then because, as has been noted, the net present value of every policy is a decreasing function of r, $Q(r, w)>Q(r', w)$. Next note that

$$Q(r, w)-Q(r', w)=P_r(k_0)-P_r(k_0')+P_r(k_0')-P_{r'}(k_0'). \quad \ldots(103)$$

The second difference on the right-hand side of (103) is $<\varepsilon$ by assumption if $|r'-r|<\alpha$, while the first difference is certainly non-positive by the definition of $Q(r, w)$. Thus $|Q(r, w)-Q(r', w)|<\varepsilon$ giving the required continuity with respect to r. It remains to show that $P_r(k)$ is continuous with respect to r uniformly with respect to k, as was assumed above. Now every continuous function of two variables is continuous with respect to one uniformly with respect to the second on a compact subset of its range. In the above argument on the continuity of $Q(r, w)$ the values of k with which the argument was concerned were both values at which $P_r(k)$ achieved a maximum for some value of r in a neighbourhood of the particular value of r at which continuity was to be established. Given any value of r, say $\bar{r}$, we can select a value of k, call it $\bar{k}$, such that for any value of r in an α-neighbourhood of $\bar{r}$, $P_r(k)$ is a monotonically decreasing function of k whenever $k>\bar{k}$. So values of k larger than $\bar{k}$ can be excluded without changing the argument in any way. One is then working on a compact subset of the values of k and r so that the required uniformity with respect to k of the continuity of $P_r(k)$ is obtained.

$Q(r, w)$ is now known to be a continuous monotonically decreasing function of r on the positive r. Then, on account of the monotonicity, one of two things can happen as $r\to 0$. Either $Q(r, w)$ approaches a finite limit from below, or $Q(r, w)$ increases without limit. If a finite limit exists it will be denoted $Q(0, w)$. Now define S_w as

$$S_w=\{w>0\mid Q(0, w)\geqq 0 \text{ or } \lim_{r\to 0} Q(r, w)=+\infty\}. \quad \ldots(104)$$

S_w is non-empty. For choose r and k such that $f(k) > rk$. Then, as $w \to 0$, $T \to \infty$, and

$$\lim_{w \to 0} P_r(k) = -k + \frac{f(k)}{r} > 0. \qquad \ldots(105)$$

Furthermore, if w' is in S_w then so is any positive $w < w'$, since a fall in w increases $Q(r, w)$. So S_w is an interval, and if it is bounded it is closed at its upper end-point. If this upper end-point exists, call it w_0. Next note that, for each positive w there exists a positive r such that $Q(r, w)$ is negative. For

$$\lim_{r \to \infty} \left\{ -k + f(k) \frac{1 - e^{-rT}}{r} - w \frac{1 - e^{-(r-1)T}}{r-1} \right\} = -k < 0. \qquad \ldots(106)$$

Thus $P_r(k)$ is negative eventually for each positive k. But $P_r(k)$ is negative anyway except on the interval $f^{-1}(w) \leqq k \leqq \bar{k}$, and the greatest lower bound of the values of r required to make $P_r(k)$ negative is a continuous function of k on this interval and as such has a maximum. Hence there exists an r that will make $P_r(k)$ everywhere negative, so that $Q(r, w)$ will be negative.[1]

The theorem is now complete. For each positive w we have seen that there exists an r such that $Q(r, w)$ is negative. But

$$\lim_{r \to 0} Q(r, w) > 0, \text{ for } w < w_0,$$

and $Q(r, w)$ is a continuous function of r. Hence there exists a value of r such that $Q(r, w) = 0$. Furthermore this r is unique, since $Q(r, w)$ is monotonic.

The proof of Theorem 3 has left open the question as to whether w_0 always exists; or, equivalently, whether it is possible to have equilibrium with $r = 0$. Equilibrium with $r = 0$ is certainly sometimes possible as, for example, when $f(k)$ is bounded above. But the assumption of regular strict concavity is not alone sufficient to guarantee it, as the following example shows. Let $x = f(k)$ and $k = f^{-1}(x) = g(x)$. Let $r = 0$. Then (33) becomes

$$-k + f(k)T - w(e^T - 1) = -g(x) + x(\log x - \log w) - x + w. \qquad \ldots(107)$$

Suppose

$$g(x) = \tfrac{1}{2} x \log(x+1). \qquad \ldots(108)$$

This is the inverse of an acceptable production function since

$$\left.\begin{aligned} g(0) &= 0, \\ \frac{dg}{dx} &= \tfrac{1}{2}\left[\log(x+1) + \frac{x}{x+1}\right], \\ \frac{d^2 g}{dx^2} &= \tfrac{1}{2}\left[\frac{1}{x+1} + \frac{1}{(x+1)^2}\right] \end{aligned}\right\}. \qquad \ldots(109)$$

Also

$$g(x) - hx = x[\tfrac{1}{2} \log(x+1) - h] \qquad \ldots(110)$$

is positive for x sufficiently large for each $h > 0$; i.e. $g(x)$ is regularly strictly convex, so that its inverse is regularly strictly concave. Then substituting (108) into (107) one obtains

$$-\tfrac{1}{2} x \log(x+1) + x(\log x - \log w - 1) + w$$
$$= \tfrac{1}{2} x \log x + \tfrac{1}{2} x \log \frac{x}{x+1} - x(\log w + 1) + w, \qquad \ldots(111)$$

which is unbounded regardless of the size of w.

[1] This statement is not of course true if we admit the case $w = 0$. For then the only lower bound on k is zero, and the argument fails at this point. It may then happen that however large the r chosen there exists a k sufficiently small to make $P(k)$ positive at $w = 0$. An example is provided by the Cobb-Douglas function.

Lemma 5. *Let* $\frac{1}{w}\frac{dw}{dr}$ *be the proportional change in the wage rate associated with a change in r. Then the following inequality is satisfied identically;*

$$-\frac{(rT+1)-e^{rT}}{r^2} > -\frac{1}{w}\frac{dw}{dr}. \qquad ...(112)$$

Proof. Differentiating the present value expression (33) totally with respect to r and equating the resulting expression to zero one obtains

$$\left[-1+f'(k)\frac{1-e^{-rT}}{r}\right]\frac{dk}{dr}+[f(k)-we^{T}]e^{-rT}\frac{dT}{dr}$$
$$-\left[\frac{1-e^{-(r-1)T}}{r-1}\right]\frac{dw}{dr}+\left[-f(k)\int_0^T te^{-rt}dt+w\int_0^T te^{-(r-1)t}dt\right]=0. \qquad ...(113)$$

But since k and T are chosen so as to maximize the present value of a man-place it follows that the terms multiplying $\frac{dk}{dr}$ and $\frac{dT}{dr}$ must be zero, and (113) reduces to

$$-\frac{1}{w}\frac{dw}{dr}=\frac{r-1}{1-e^{-(r-1)T}}\int_0^T te^{-rt}(e^T-e^t)dt, \qquad ...(114)$$

taking into account (36). Now note that

$$-\frac{rT+1-e^{rT}}{r^2}=-e^{rT}\frac{\partial}{\partial r}\left[\frac{1-e^{-rT}}{r}\right]=-e^{rT}\frac{\partial}{\partial r}\left[\int_0^T e^{-rt}dt\right]$$
$$=e^{rT}\int_0^T te^{-rt}dt. \qquad ...(115)$$

Thus the condition that is required can be written

$$\int_0^T te^{-rt}(e^T-e^t)dt<\frac{e^{rT}-e^T}{r-1}\int_0^T te^{-rt}dt, \qquad ...(116)$$

or

$$\int_0^T te^{-rt}\left(\frac{re^T-e^{rT}}{r-1}-e^t\right)dt<0. \qquad ...(117)$$

(117) would be established if it could be shown that

$$\frac{re^T-e^{rT}}{r-1}-e^t<0 \text{ for } 0<t\leqq T, \qquad ...(118)$$

and this would follow at once if it could be shown that

$$\frac{re^T-e^{rT}}{r-1}\leqq 1. \qquad ...(118)$$

It is this condition which will be established. Expanding the exponential expressions in (118),

$$\frac{1}{r-1}\left[r\left(1+T+\frac{T^2}{2\cdot 1}+...+\frac{T^j}{j!}+...\right)-\left(1+rT+\frac{r^2T^2}{2\cdot 1}+...+\frac{r^jT^j}{j!}+...\right)\right], \qquad ...(119)$$

and then,

$$1-r\left(\frac{T^2}{2.1}+\frac{T^3}{3.2.1}\frac{r^2-1}{r-1}+...+\frac{T^j}{j!}\frac{r^{j-1}-1}{r-1}+...\right)\leqq 1, \qquad ...(120)$$

as required.

11 The Economic Implications of Learning by Doing

K. J. ARROW

It is by now incontrovertible that increases in per capita income cannot be explained simply by increases in the capital-labor ratio. Though doubtless no economist would ever have denied the role of technological change in economic growth, its overwhelming importance relative to capital formation has perhaps only been fully realized with the important empirical studies of Abramovitz [1] and Solow [11]. These results do not directly contradict the neo-classical view of the production function as an expression of technological knowledge. All that has to be added is the obvious fact that knowledge is growing in time. Nevertheless a view of economic growth that depends so heavily on an exogenous variable, let alone one so difficult to measure as the quantity of knowledge, is hardly intellectually satisfactory. From a quantitative, empirical point of view, we are left with time as an explanatory variable. Now trend projections, however necessary they may be in practice, are basically a confession of ignorance, and, what is worse from a practical viewpoint, are not policy variables.

Further, the concept of knowledge which underlies the production function at any moment needs analysis. Knowledge has to be acquired. We are not surprised, as educators, that even students subject to the same educational experiences have different bodies of knowledge, and we may therefore be prepared to grant, as has been shown empirically (see [2], Part III), that different countries, at the same moment of time, have different production functions even apart from differences in natural resource endowment.

I would like to suggest here an endogenous theory of the changes in knowledge which underlie intertemporal and international shifts in production functions. The acquisition of knowledge is what is usually termed "learning," and we might perhaps pick up some clues from the many psychologists who have studied this phenomenon (for a convenient survey, see Hilgard [5]). I do not think that the picture of technical change as a vast and prolonged process of learning about the environment in which we operate is in any way a far-fetched analogy; exactly the same phenomenon of improvement in performance over time is involved.

Of course, psychologists are no more in agreement than economists, and there are sharp differences of opinion about the processes of learning. But one empirical generalization is so clear that all schools of thought must accept it, although they interpret it in different fashions: Learning is the product of experience. Learning can only take place through the attempt to solve a problem and therefore only takes place during activity. Even the Gestalt and other field theorists, who stress the role of insight in the solution of problems (Köhler's famous apes), have to assign a significant role to previous experiences in modifying the individual's perception.

A second generalization that can be gleaned from many of the classic learning experiments is that learning associated with repetition of essentially the same problem is subject to sharply diminishing returns. There is an equilibrium response pattern for any given stimulus, towards which the behavior of the learner tends with repetition. To have steadily increasing performance, then, implies that the stimulus situations must themselves be steadily evolving rather than merely repeating.

The role of experience in increasing productivity has not gone unobserved, though the relation has yet to be absorbed into the main corpus of economic theory. It was early observed by aeronautical engineers, particularly T. P. Wright [15], that the number of labor-hours expended in the production of an airframe (airplane body without engines) is a decreasing function of the total number of airframes of the same type previously produced. Indeed, the relation is remarkably precise; to produce the Nth airframe of a given type, counting from the inception of production, the amount of labor required is proportional to $N^{-1/3}$. This relation has become basic in the production and cost planning of the United States Air Force; for a full survey, see [3]. Hirsch (see [6] and other work cited there) has shown the existence of the same type of " learning curve " or " progress ratio," as it is variously termed, in the production of other machines, though the rate of learning is not the same as for airframes.

Verdoorn [14, pp. 433-4] has applied the principle of the learning curve to national outputs; however, under the assumption that output is increasing exponentially, current output is proportional to cumulative output, and it is the former variable that he uses to explain labor productivity. The empirical fitting was reported in [13]; the estimated progress ratio for different European countries is about ·5. (In [13], a neo-classical interpretation in terms of increasing capital-labor ratios was offered; see pp. 7-11.)

Lundberg [9, pp. 129-133] has given the name " Horndal effect " to a very similar phenomenon. The Horndal iron works in Sweden had no new investment (and therefore presumably no significant change in its methods of production) for a period of 15 years, yet productivity (output per manhour) rose on the average close to 2% per annum. We find again steadily increasing performance which can only be imputed to learning from experience.

I advance the hypothesis here that technical change in general can be ascribed to experience, that it is the very activity of production which gives rise to problems for which favorable responses are selected over time. The evidence so far cited, whether from psychological or from economic literature is, of course, only suggestive. The aim of this paper is to formulate the hypothesis more precisely and draw from it a number of economic implications. These should enable the hypothesis and its consequences to be confronted more easily with empirical evidence.

The model set forth will be very simplified in some other respects to make clearer the essential role of the major hypothesis; in particular, the possibility of capital-labor substitution is ignored. The theorems about the economic world presented here differ from those in most standard economic theories; profits are the result of technical change; in a free-enterprise system, the rate of investment will be less than the optimum; net investment and the stock of capital become subordinate concepts, with gross investment taking a leading role.

In section 1, the basic assumptions of the model are set forth. In section 2, the implications for wage earners are deduced; in section 3 those for profits, the inducement to invest, and the rate of interest. In section 4, the behavior of the entire system under steady growth with mutually consistent expectations is taken up. In section 5, the divergence between social and private returns is studied in detail for a special case (where the subjective rate of discount of future consumption is a constant). Finally, in section 6, some limitations of the model and needs for further development are noted.

1. The Model

The first question is that of choosing the economic variable which represents " experience ". The economic examples given above suggest the possibility of using cumulative output (the total of output from the beginning of time) as an index of experience, but this does not seem entirely satisfactory. If the rate of output is constant, then the stimulus to learning presented would appear to be constant, and the learning that does take place is a gradual approach to equilibrium behavior. I therefore take instead cumulative gross investment (cumulative production of capital goods) as an index of experience. Each new machine produced and put into use is capable of changing the environment in which production takes place, so that learning is taking place with continually new stimuli. This at least makes plausible the possibility of continued learning in the sense, here, of a steady rate of growth in productivity.

The second question is that of deciding where the learning enters the conditions of production. I follow here the model of Solow [12] and Johansen [7], in which technical change is completely embodied in new capital goods. At any moment of new time, the new capital goods incorporate all the knowledge then available, but once built their productive efficiency cannot be altered by subsequent learning.

To simplify the discussion we shall assume that the production process associated with any given new capital good is characterized by fixed coefficients, so that a fixed amount of labor is used and a fixed amount of output obtained. Further, it will be assumed that new capital goods are better than old ones in the strong sense that, if we compare a unit of capital goods produced at time t_1 with one produced at time $t_2 > t_1$, the first requires the co-operation of at least as much labor as the second, and produces no more product. Under this assumption, a new capital good will always be used in preference to an older one.

Let G be cumulative gross investment. A unit capital good produced when cumulative gross investment has reached G will be said to have *serial number G*. Let

$\lambda(G)$ = amount of labor used in production with a capital good of serial number G,
$\gamma(G)$ = output capacity of a capital good of serial number G,
x = total output,
L = total labor force employed.

It is assumed that $\lambda(G)$ is a non-increasing function, while $\gamma(G)$ is a non-decreasing function. Then, regardless of wages or rental value of capital goods, it always pays to use a capital good of higher serial number before one of lower serial number.

It will further be assumed that capital goods have a fixed lifetime, $\bar{T}$. Then capital goods disappear in the same order as their serial numbers. It follows that at any moment of time, the capital goods in use will be all those with serial numbers from some G' to G, the current cumulative gross investment. Then

$$(1) \qquad x = \int_{G'}^{G} \gamma(G)dG,$$

$$(2) \qquad L = \int_{G'}^{G} \lambda(G)dG.$$

The magnitudes x, L, G, and G' are, of course, all functions of time, to be designated by t, and they will be written $x(t)$, $L(t)$, $G(t)$, and $G'(t)$ when necessary to point up the dependence. Then $G(t)$, in particular, is the cumulative gross investment up to time t. The assumption about the lifetime of capital goods implies that

$$(3) \qquad G'(t) \geqq G(t - \bar{T}).$$

Since $G(t)$ is given at time t, we can solve for G' from (1) or (2) or the equality in (3). In a growth context, the most natural assumption is that of full employment. The labor force is regarded as a given function of time and is assumed equal to the labor employed, so that $L(t)$ is a given function. Then $G'(t)$ is obtained by solving in (2). If the result is substituted into (1), x can be written as a function of L and G, analogous to the usual production function. To write this, define

$$\Lambda(G) = \int \lambda(G)dG,$$

$$(4) \qquad \Gamma(g) = \int \gamma(G)dG.$$

These are to be regarded as indefinite integrals. Since $\lambda(G)$ and $\gamma(G)$ are both positive, $\Lambda(G)$ and $\Gamma(G)$ are strictly increasing and therefore have inverses, $\Lambda^{-1}(u)$ and $\Gamma^{-1}(v)$, respectively. Then (1) and (2) can be written, respectively,

$$(1') \qquad x = \Gamma(G) - \Gamma(G'),$$

$$(2') \qquad L = \Lambda(G) - \Lambda(G').$$

Solve for G' from (2′).

$$(5) \qquad G' = \Lambda^{-1}[\Lambda(G) - L].$$

Substitute (5) into (1′).

$$(6) \qquad x = \Gamma(G) - \Gamma\{\Lambda^{-1}[\Lambda(G) - L]\},$$

which is thus a production function in a somewhat novel sense. Equation (6) is always valid, but under the full employment assumption we can regard L as the labor force available.

A second assumption, more suitable to a depression situation, is that in which demand for the product is the limiting factor. Then x is taken as given; G' can be derived from (1) or (1′), and employment then found from (2) or (2′). If this is less than the available labor force, we have Keynesian unemployment.

A third possibility, which, like the first, may be appropriate to a growth analysis, is that the solution (5) with L as the labor force, does not satisfy (3). In this case, there is a shortage of capital due to depreciation. There is again unemployment but now due to structural discrepancies rather than to demand deficiency.

In any case, except by accident, there is either unemployed labor or unemployed capital; there could be both in the demand deficiency case. Of course, a more neo-classical model, with substitution between capital and labor for each serial number of capital good, might permit full employment of both capital and labor, but this remains a subject for further study.

In what follows, the full-employment case will be chiefly studied. The capital shortage case, the third one, will be referred to parenthetically. In the full-employment case, the depreciation assumption no longer matters; obsolescence, which occurs for all capital goods with serial numbers below G', becomes the sole reason for the retirement of capital goods from use.

The analysis will be carried through for a special case. To a very rough approximation, the capital-output ratio has been constant, while the labor-output ratio has been declining. It is therefore assumed that

(7) $\gamma(G) = a,$

a constant, while $\lambda(G)$ is a decreasing function of G. To be specific, it will be assumed that $\lambda(G)$ has the form found in the study of learning curves for airframes.

(8) $\lambda(G) = bG^{-n},$

where $n > 0$. Then

$$\Gamma(G) = aG,\ \Lambda(G) = cG^{1-n},\text{ where } c = b/(1-n) \text{ for } n \neq 1.$$

Then (6) becomes

(9) $$x = aG\left[1 - \left(1 - \frac{L}{cG^{1-n}}\right)^{1/(1-n)}\right] \text{ if } n \neq 1.$$

Equation (9) is always well defined in the relevant ranges, since from (2′),

$$L = \Lambda(G) - \Lambda(G') \leq \Lambda(G) = cG^{1-n}.$$

When $n = 1$, $\Lambda(G) = b \log G$ (where the natural logarithm is understood), and

(10) $x = aG(1-e^{-L/b})$ if $n = 1$.

Although (9) and (10) are, in a sense, production functions, they show increasing returns to scale in the variables G and L. This is obvious in (10) where an increase in G, with L constant, increases x in the same proportion; a simultaneous increase in L will further increase x. In (9), first suppose that $n < 1$. Then a proportional increase in L and G increases L/G^{1-n} and therefore increases the expression in brackets which multiplies G. A similar argument holds if $n > 1$. It should be noted that x increases more than proportionately to scale changes in G and L in general, not merely for the special case defined by (7) and (8). This would be verified by careful examination of the behavior of (6), when it is recalled that $\lambda(G)$ is non-increasing and $\gamma(G)$ is non-decreasing, with the strict inequality holding in at least one. It is obvious intuitively, since the additional amounts of L and G are used more efficiently than the earlier ones.

The increasing returns do not, however, lead to any difficulty with distribution theory. As we shall see, both capital and labor are paid their marginal products, suitably defined. The explanation is, of course, that the private marginal productivity of capital (more strictly, of new investment) is less than the social marginal productivity since the learning effect is not compensated in the market.

The production assumptions of this section are designed to play the role assigned by Kaldor to his " technical progress function," which relates the rate of growth of output per worker to the rate of growth of capital per worker (see [8], section VIII). I prefer to think of relations between rates of growth as themselves derived from more fundamental relations between the magnitudes involved. Also, the present formulation puts more stress on gross rather than net investment as the basic agent of technical change.

Earlier, Haavelmo ([4], sections 7.1 and 7.2) had suggested a somewhat similar model. Output depended on both capital and the stock of knowledge; investment depended on output, the stock of capital, and the stock of knowledge. The stock of knowledge was either simply a function of time or, in a more sophisticated version, the consequence of investment, the educational effect of each act of investment decreasing exponentially in time.

Verdoorn [14, pp. 436-7] had also developed a similar simple model in which capital and labor needed are non-linear functions of output (since the rate of output is, approximately, a measure of cumulative output and therefore of learning) and investment a constant fraction of output. He notes that under these conditions, full employment of capital and labor simultaneously is in general impossible—a conclusion which also holds for the present model, as we have seen. However, Verdoorn draws the wrong conclusion: that the savings ratio must be fixed by some public mechanism at the uniquely determined level which would insure full employment of both factors; the correct conclusion is that one factor or the other will be unemployed. The social force of this conclusion is much less in the present model since the burden of unemployment may fall on obsolescent capital; Verdoorn assumes his capital to be homogeneous in nature.

2. Wages

Under the full employment assumption the profitability of using the capital good with serial number G' must be zero; for if it were positive it would be profitable to use capital goods with higher serial number and if it were negative capital good G' would not be used contrary to the definition of G'. Let

$$w = \text{wage rate with output as numéraire.}$$

From (1′) and (7)

$$G' = G - (x/a) \tag{11}$$

so that

$$\lambda(G') = b\left(G - \frac{x}{a}\right)^{-n}. \tag{12}$$

The output from capital good G' is $\gamma(G')$ while the cost of operation is $\lambda(G')w$. Hence

$$\gamma(G') = \lambda(G')w$$

or from (7) and (12)

$$w = a\left(G - \frac{x}{a}\right)^{n}/b. \tag{13}$$

It is interesting to derive labor's share which is wL/x. From (2′) with $\Lambda(g) = cG^{1-n}$ and G' given by (11)

$$L = c\left[G^{1-n} - \left(G - \frac{x}{a}\right)^{1-n} \right],$$

for $n \neq 1$ and therefore

$$\text{(14)} \qquad wL/x = a\left[\left(\frac{G}{x} - \frac{1}{a}\right)^{n}\left(\frac{G}{x}\right)^{1-n} - \left(\frac{G}{x} - \frac{1}{a}\right)\right]/(1-n) \text{ for } n \neq 1,$$

where use has been made of the relation, $c = b/(1-n)$. It is interesting to note that labor's share is determined by the ratio G/x.

Since, however, x is determined by G and L, which, at any moment of time, are data, it is also useful to express the wage ratio, w, and labor's share, wL/x, in terms of L and G. First, G' can be found by solving for it from (2′).

$$\text{(15)} \qquad G' = \left(G^{1-n} - \frac{L}{c}\right)^{1/(1-n)} \text{ for } n \neq 1.$$

We can then use the same reasoning as above, and derive

$$\text{(16)} \qquad w = a\left(G^{1-n} - \frac{L}{c}\right)^{n/(1-n)}/b,$$

$$\text{(17)} \qquad \frac{wL}{x} = \frac{\left[\left(\frac{L}{G^{1-n}}\right)^{(1-n)/n} - \frac{1}{c}\left(\frac{L}{G^{1-n}}\right)^{1/n}\right]^{n/(1-n)}}{b\left[1 - \left(1 - \frac{L}{cG^{1-n}}\right)^{1/(1-n)}\right]}.$$

Labor's share thus depends on the ratio L/G^{1-n}; it can be shown to decrease as the ratio increases.

For completeness, I note the corresponding formulas for the case $n = 1$. In terms of G and x, we have

$$\text{(18)} \qquad w = (aG - x)/b,$$

$$\text{(19)} \qquad wL/x = \left(\frac{aG}{x} - 1\right) \log \frac{G/x}{(G/x) - (1/a)}.$$

In terms of G and L, we have

$$\text{(20)} \qquad G' = Ge^{-L/b},$$

$$\text{(21)} \qquad w = \frac{aG}{be^{L/b}},$$

$$\text{(22)} \qquad wL/x = \frac{L}{b(e^{L/b} - 1)}.$$

In this case, labor's share depends only on L, which is indeed the appropriate special case ($n=1$) of the general dependence on L/G^{1-n}.

The preceding discussion has assumed full employment. In the capital shortage case, there cannot be a competitive equilibrium with positive wage since there is necessarily unemployment. A zero wage is, however, certainly unrealistic. To complete the model, it would be necessary to add some other assumption about the behavior of wages. This case will not be considered in general; for the special case of steady growth, see Section 5.

3. Profits and Investment

The profit at time t from a unit investment made at time $v \leqq t$ is

$$\gamma[G(v)] - w(t)\ \lambda[G(v)].$$

In contemplating an investment at time v, the stream of potential profits depends upon expectations of future wages. We will suppose that looking ahead at any given moment of time each entrepreneur assumes that wages will rise exponentially from the present level. Thus the wage rate expected at time v to prevail at time t is

$$w(v)\ e^{\theta(t-v)},$$

and the profit expected at time v to be received at time t is

$$\gamma[G(v)]\ [1 - W(v)\ e^{\theta(t-v)}],$$

where

$$W(v) = w(v)\ \lambda[G(v)]/\gamma[G(v)], \tag{23}$$

the labor cost per unit output at the time the investment is made. The dependence of W on v will be made explicit only when necessary. The profitability of the investment is expected to decrease with time (if $\theta > 0$) and to reach zero at time $T^* + v$, defined by the equation

$$We^{\theta T^*} = 1. \tag{24}$$

Thus T^* is the expected economic lifetime of the investment, provided it does not exceed the physical lifetime, $\bar{T}$. Let

$$T = \min(\bar{T}, T^*). \tag{25}$$

Then the investor plans to derive profits only over an interval of length T, either because the investment wears out or because wages have risen to the point where it is unprofitable to operate. Since the expectation of wage rises which causes this abandonment derives from anticipated investment and the consequent technological progress, T^* represents the expected date of obsolescence. Let

$$\rho = \text{rate of interest}.$$

If the rate of interest is expected to remain constant over the future, then the discounted stream of profits over the effective lifetime, T, of the investment is

$$(26) \qquad S = \int_0^T e^{-\rho t}\, \gamma[G(v)]\, (1 - W e^{\theta t})dt,$$

or

$$(27) \qquad \frac{S}{\gamma[G(v)]} = \frac{1 - e^{-\rho T}}{\rho} + \frac{W(1 - e^{-(\rho-\theta)T})}{\theta - \rho}.$$

Let

$$(28) \qquad V = e^{-\theta T} = \max (e^{-\theta \bar{T}}, W),\ \alpha = \rho/\theta.$$

Then

$$(29) \qquad \frac{\theta\, S}{\gamma[G(v)]} = \frac{1 - V^{\alpha}}{\alpha} + \frac{W(1 - V^{\alpha-1})}{1-\alpha} = R(\alpha).$$

The definitions of $R(\alpha)$ for $\alpha = 0$ and $\alpha = 1$ needed to make the function continuous are:

$$R(0) = -\log V + W(1 - V^{-1}),\ R(1) = 1 - V + W \log V.$$

If all the parameters of (26), (27), or (29) are held constant, S is a function of ρ, and, equivalently, R of α. If (26) is differentiated with respect to ρ, we find

$$dS/d\rho = \int_0^T (-t)e^{-\rho t}\, \gamma[G(v)]\, (1 - W e^{\theta t})dt < 0.$$

Also

$$S < \gamma[G(v)] \int_0^T e^{-\rho t} dt = \gamma[G(v)]\, (1 - e^{-\rho T})/\rho$$

$$< \gamma[G(v)]/\rho.$$

Since obviously $S > 0$, S approaches 0 as ρ approaches infinity. Since R and α differ from S and ρ, respectively, only by positive constant factors, we conclude

$$dR/d\alpha < 0, \quad \lim_{\alpha \to +\infty} R(\alpha) = 0.$$

To examine the behavior of $R(\alpha)$ as α approaches $-\infty$, write

$$R(\alpha) = -\frac{(1/V)^{1-\alpha}}{(1-\alpha)^2}\, [(1-\alpha)V + \alpha\, W] \left(\frac{1-\alpha}{\alpha}\right) + \frac{1}{\alpha} + \frac{W}{1-\alpha}.$$

The last two terms approach zero. As α approaches $-\infty$, $1 - \alpha$ approaches $+\infty$. Since $1/V > 1$, the factor

$$\frac{(1/V)^{1-\alpha}}{(1-\alpha)^2}$$

approaches $+\infty$, since an exponential approaches infinity faster than any power. From (28), $V \geqq W$. If $V = W$, then the factor,

$$(1-\alpha)V - \alpha W = \alpha(W - V) + V,$$

is a positive constant; if $V > W$, then it approaches $+\infty$ as α approaches $-\infty$. Finally,

$$\frac{1-\alpha}{\alpha}$$

necessarily approaches -1. Hence,

(30) $R(\alpha)$ is a strictly decreasing function, approaching $+\infty$ as α approaches $-\infty$ and 0 as α approaches $+\infty$.

The market, however, should adjust the rate of return so that the discounted stream of profits equals the cost of investment, i.e., $S = 1$, or, from (29),

(31) $R(\alpha) = \theta/\gamma[G(v)]$.

Since the right-hand side of (31) is positive, (30) guarantees the existence of an α which satisfies (31). For a given θ, the equilibrium rate of return, ρ, is equal to $\alpha\,\theta$; it may indeed be negative. The rate of return is thus determined by the expected rate of increase in wages, current labor costs per unit output, and the physical lifetime of the investment. Further, if the first two are sufficiently large, the physical lifetime becomes irrelevant, since then $T^* < \bar{T}$, and $T = T^*$.

The discussion of profits and returns has not made any special assumptions as to the form of the production relations.

4. Rational Expectations in a Macroeconomic Growth Model

Assume a one-sector model so that the production relations of the entire economy are described by the model of section 1. In particular, this implies that gross investment at any moment of time is simply a diversion of goods that might otherwise be used for consumption. Output and gross investment can then be measured in the same units.

The question arises, can the expectations assumed to govern investment behavior in the preceding section actually be fulfilled? Specifically, can we have a constant relative increase of wages and a constant rate of interest which, if anticipated, will lead entrepreneurs to invest at a rate which, in conjunction with the exogenously given rate of interest to remain at the given level? Such a state of affairs is frequently referred to as "perfect foresight," but a better term is "rational expectations," a term introduced by J. Muth [10].

We study this question first for the full employment case. For this case to occur, the physical lifetime of investments must not be an effective constraint. If, in the notation of the last section, $T^* > \bar{T}$, and if wage expectations are correct, then investments will disappear through depreciation at a time when they are still yielding positive current profits. As seen in section 2, this is incompatible with competitive equilibrium and full employment. Assume therefore that

(32) $T^* \leqq \bar{T};$

then from (28), $W = V$, and from (29) and (31), the equilibrium value of ρ is determined by the equation,

(33) $$\frac{1 - W^{\alpha}}{\alpha} + \frac{W - W^{\alpha}}{1 - \alpha} = \frac{\theta}{a},$$

where, on the right-hand side, use is made of (7).

From (16), it is seen that for the wage rate to rise at a constant rate θ, it is necessary that the quantity,

$$G^{1-n} - \frac{L}{c},$$

rise at a rate $\theta(1 - n)/n$. For θ constant, it follows from (33) that a constant ρ and therefore a constant α requires that W be constant. For the specific production relations (7) and (8), (23) shows that

$$W = a\frac{\left(G^{1-n} - \frac{L}{c}\right)^{n/(1-n)}}{b} \frac{bG^{-n}}{a} = \left(1 - \frac{L}{cG^{1-n}}\right)^{n/(1-n)},$$

and therefore the constancy of W is equivalent to that of L/G^{1-n}. In combination with the preceding remark, we see that

(34) L increases at rate $\theta(1 - n)/n$, G increases at rate θ/n.

Suppose that

σ = rate of increase of the labor force,

is a given constant. Then

(35) $\theta = n\,\sigma/(1-n)$,

(36) the rate of increase of G is $\sigma/(1-n)$.

Substitution into the production function (9) yields

(37) the rate of increase of x is $\sigma/(1-n)$.

From (36) and (37), the ratio G/x is constant over time. However, the value at which it is constant is not determined by the considerations so far introduced; the savings function is needed to complete the system. Let the constant ratio be

(38) $G(t)/x(t) = \mu.$

Define

$g(t)$ = rate of gross investment at time $t = dG/dt$.

From (36), $g/G = \sigma/(1 - n)$, a constant. Then

$$(39) \qquad g/x = (g/G)(G/x) = \mu\,\sigma/(1-n).$$

A simple assumption is that the ratio of gross saving (equals gross investment) to income (equals output) is a function of the rate of return, ρ; a special case would be the common assumption of a constant savings-to-income ratio. Then μ is a function of ρ. On the other hand, we can write W as follows, using (23) and (13):

$$(40) \qquad W = a \frac{\left(G - \frac{x}{a}\right)^n}{b} \frac{bG^{-n}}{a} = \left(1 - \frac{x}{aG}\right)^n = \left(1 - \frac{1}{a\mu}\right)^n.$$

Since θ is given by (35), (33) is a relation between W and ρ, and, by (40) between μ and ρ. We thus have two relations between μ and ρ, so they are determinate.

From (38), μ determines one relation between G and X. If the labor force, L, is given at one moment of time, the production function (9) constitutes a second such relation, and the system is completely determinate.

As in many growth models, the rates of growth of the variables in the system do not depend on savings behavior; however, their levels do.

It should be made clear that all that has been demonstrated is the existence of a solution in which all variables have constant rates of growth, correctly anticipated. The stability of the solution requires further study.

The growth rate for wages implied by the solution has one paradoxical aspect; it increases with the rate of growth of the labor force (provided $n < 1$). The explanation seems to be that under full employment, the increasing labor force permits a more rapid introduction of the newer machinery. It should also be noted that, for a constant saving ratio, g/x, an increase in σ decreases μ, from (39), from which it can be seen that wages at the initial time period would be lower. In this connection it may be noted that since G cannot decrease, it follows from (36) that σ and $1-n$ must have the same sign for the steady growth path to be possible. The most natural case, of course, is $\sigma > 0$, $n < 1$.

This solution is, however, admissible only if the condition (32), that the rate of depreciation not be too rapid, be satisfied. We can find an explicit formula for the economic lifetime, T^*, of new investment. From (24), it satisfies the condition

$$e^{-\theta T^*} = W.$$

If we use (35) and (40) and solve for T^*, we find

$$(41) \qquad T^* = \frac{-(1-n)}{\sigma} \log\left[1 - \frac{1}{a\mu}\right]$$

and this is to be compared with $\bar{T}$; the full employment solution with rational expectations of exponentially increasing wages and constant interest is admissible if $T^* \leqq \bar{T}$.

If $T^* > \bar{T}$, then the full employment solution is inadmissible. One might ask if a constant-growth solution is possible in this case. The answer depends on assumptions about the dynamics of wages under this condition.

We retain the two conditions, that wages rise at a constant rate θ, and that the rate of interest be constant. With constant θ, the rate of interest, ρ, is determined from (31); from (29), this requires that

(42) W is constant over time.

From the definition of W, (23), and the particular form of the production relations, (7) and (8), it follows that the wage rate, w, must rise at the same rate as G^n, or

(43) G rises at a constant rate θ/n.

In the presence of continued unemployment, the most natural wage dynamics in a free market would be a decreasing, or, at best, constant wage level. But since G can never decrease, it follows from (43) that θ can never be negative. Instead of making a specific assumption about wage changes, it will be assumed that any choice of θ can be imposed, perhaps by government or union or social pressure, and it is asked what restrictions on the possible values of θ are set by the other equilibrium conditions.

In the capital shortage case, the serial number of the oldest capital good in use is determined by the physical lifetime of the good, i.e.,

$G' = G(t - \bar{T})$. From (43),

$$G(t - \bar{T}) = e^{-\theta\bar{T}/n}\, G.$$

Then, from (1′) and (7),

$$x = aG(1 - e^{-\theta\bar{T}/n}),$$

so that the ratio, G/x, or μ, is a constant,

(44) $$\mu = 1/a(1 - e^{-\theta\bar{T}/n}).$$

From (43), $g/G = \theta/n$; hence, by the same argument as that leading to (39),

(45) $$g/x = \theta/na(1 - e^{-\theta\bar{T}/n}).$$

There are three unknown constants of the growth process, θ, ρ, and W. If, as before, it is assumed that the gross savings ratio, g/x, is a function of the rate of return, ρ, then, for any given ρ, θ can be determined from (45); note that the right-hand side of (45) is a strictly increasing function of θ for $\theta \geqq 0$, so that the determination is unique, and the rate of growth is an increasing function of the gross savings ratio, contrary to the situation in the full employment case. Then W can be solved for from (31) and (29).

Thus the rate of return is a freely disposable parameter whose choice determines the rate of growth and W, which in turn determines the initial wage rate. There are, of course, some inequalities which must be satisfied to insure that the solution corresponds to the capital shortage rather than the full employment case; in particular, $W \leqq V$ and also the labor force must be sufficient to permit the expansion. From (2′), this means that the labor force must at all times be at least equal to

$$cG^{1-n} - c(G')^{1-n} = cG^{1-n}(1 - e^{-\theta(1-n)T/n});$$

if σ is the growth rate of the labor force, we must then have (46)

$$(46) \qquad \sigma \geqq \theta(1-n)/n,$$

which sets an upper bound on θ (for $n < 1$). Other constraints on ρ are implied by the conditions $\theta \geqq 0$ and $W \geqq 0$ (if it is assumed that wage rates are non-negative). The first condition sets a lower limit on g/x; it can be shown, from (45). that

$$(47) \qquad g/x \geqq 1/a\bar{T};$$

i.e., the gross savings ratio must be at least equal to the amount of capital goods needed to produce one unit of output over their lifetime. The constraint $W > 0$ implies an interval in which ρ must lie. The conditions under which these constraints are consistent (so that at least one solution exists for the capital shortage case) have not been investigated in detail.

5. Divergence of Private and Social Product

As has already been emphasized, the presence of learning means that an act of investment benefits future investors, but this benefit is not paid for by the market. Hence, it is to be expected that the aggregate amount of investment under the competitive model of the last section will fall short of the socially optimum level. This difference will be investigated in detail in the present section under a simple assumption as to the utility function of society. For brevity, I refer to the *competitive solution* of the last section, to be contrasted with the *optimal* solution. Full employment is assumed. It is shown that the socially optimal growth rate is the same as that under competitive conditions, but the socially optimal ratio of gross investment to output is higher than the competitive level.

Utility is taken to be a function of the stream of consumption derived from the productive mechanism. Let

$$c = \text{consumption} = \text{output} - \text{gross investment} = x - g.$$

It is in particular assumed that future consumption is discounted at a constant rate, β, so that utility is

$$(48) \qquad U = \int_o^{+\infty} e^{-\beta t} c(t)\,dt = \int_o^{+\infty} e^{-\beta t} x(t)\,dt.$$

$$- \int_o^{+\infty} e^{-\beta t} g(t)\,dt.$$

Integration by parts yields

$$\int_o^{+\infty} e^{-\beta t} g(t)\,dt = e^{-\beta t} G(t) \Big|_o^{+\infty} + \beta \int_o^{+\infty} e^{-\beta t} G(t)\,dt.$$

From (48),

(49) $$U = U_1 - \lim_{t \to +\infty} e^{-\beta t}G(t) + G(0),$$

where

(50) $$U_1 = \int_o^{+\infty} e^{-\beta t}[x(t) - \beta\, G(t)]dt.$$

The policy problem is the choice of the function $G(t)$, with $G'(t) \geqq 0$, to maximize (49), where $x(t)$ is determined by the production function (9), and

(51) $$L(t) = L_0 e^{\sigma t}.$$

The second term in (49) is necessarily non-negative. It will be shown that, for sufficiently high discount rate, β, the function $G(t)$ which maximizes U_1 also has the property that the second term in (49) is zero; hence, it also maximizes (49), since $G(0)$ is given.

Substitute (9) and (51) into (50).

$$U_1 = \int_o^{+\infty} e^{-\beta t}G(t) \left[a - \beta - a\left(1 - \frac{L_o e^{\sigma t}}{cG^{1-n}}\right)^{1/(1-n)}\right] dt.$$

Let $\bar{G}(t) = G(t)\ e^{-\sigma t/(1-n)}$.

$$U_1 = \int_o^{+\infty} e^{-\left(\beta - \frac{\sigma}{1-n}\right)t}\ \bar{G}(t)\left[a - \beta - a\left(1 - \frac{L_0}{c\bar{G}^{1-n}}\right)^{1/(1-n)}\right] dt.$$

Assume that

(52) $$\beta > \frac{\sigma}{1-n};$$

otherwise an infinite utility is attainable. Then to maximize U_1 it suffices to choose $\bar{G}(t)$ so as to maximize, for each t,

(53) $$\bar{G}\left[a - \beta - a\left(1 - \frac{L_0}{c\bar{G}^{1-n}}\right)^{1/(1-n)}\right].$$

Before actually determining the maximum, it can be noted that the maximizing value of $\bar{G}$ is independent of t and is therefore a constant. Hence, the optimum policy is

(54) $$G(t) = \bar{G}\ e^{\sigma t/(1-n)},$$

so that, from (36), the growth rate is the same as the competitive. From (52), $e^{-\beta t}G(t) \longrightarrow 0$ as $t \longrightarrow +\infty$.

To determine the optimal $\bar{G}$, it will be convenient to make a change of variables. Define

$$v = \left(1 - \frac{L_o}{c\bar{G}^{1-n}}\right)^{n/(1-n)}.$$

so that

(55) $$\bar{G} = \left[\frac{L_0}{(1 - v^{(1-n)/n})}\right]^{1/(1-n)}.$$

The analysis will be carried through primarily for the case where the output per unit capital is sufficiently high, more specifically, where

(56) $$a > \beta.$$

Let

(57) $$\gamma = 1 - \frac{\beta}{a} > 0.$$

The maximizing $\bar{G}$, or v, is unchanged by multiplying (53), the function to be maximized, by the positive quantity, $(c/L_0)^{1/(1-n)}/a$ and then substituting from (55) and (57). Thus, v maximizes

$$(1 - v^{(1-n)/n})^{-1/(1-n)}(\gamma - v^{1/n}).$$

The variable v ranges from 0 to 1. However, the second factor vanishes when $v = \gamma^n < 1$ (since $\gamma < 1$) and becomes negative for larger values of v; since the first factor is always positive, it can be assumed that $v < \gamma^n$ in searching for a maximum, and both factors are positive. Then v also maximizes the logarithm of the above function, which is

$$f(v) = -\frac{\log (1 - v^{(1-n)/n})}{1 - n} + \log (\gamma - v^{1/n}),$$

so that

$$f'(v) = \frac{v^{\frac{1}{n} - 2}}{n} \left[\frac{\gamma - v}{(1 - v^{(1-n)/n})(\gamma - v^{1/n})}\right].$$

Clearly, with $n < 1$, $f'(v) > 0$ when $0 < v < \gamma$ and $f'(v) < 0$ when $\gamma < v < \gamma^n$, so that the maximum is obtained at

(58) $$v = \gamma.$$

The optimum $\bar{G}$ is determined by substituting γ for v in (55).

From (54), L/G^{1-n} is a constant over time. From the definition of v and (58), then,

$$\gamma = \left(1 - \frac{L}{cG^{1-n}}\right)^{n/(1-n)}$$

for all t along the optimal path, and, from the production function (9),

(59) $$\gamma = \left(1 - \frac{x}{aG}\right)^n$$ for all t along the optimal path.

This optimal solution will be compared with the competitive solution of steady growth studied in the last section. From (40), we know that

(60) $$W = \left(1 - \frac{x}{aG}\right)^n$$ for all t along the competitive path.

It will be demonstrated that $W < \gamma$; from this it follows that *the ratio G/x is less along the competitive path than along the optimal path.* Since along both paths,

$$g/x = [\sigma/(1 - n)] (G/x),$$

it also follows that *the gross savings ratio is smaller along the competitive path than along the optimal path.*

For the particular utility function (48), the supply of capital is infinitely elastic at $\rho = \beta$; i.e., the community will take any investment with a rate of return exceeding β and will take no investment at a rate of return less than β. For an equilibrium in which some, but not all, income is saved, we must have

(61) $\rho = \beta.$

From (35), $\theta = n\sigma/(1 - n)$; hence, by definition (28),

(62) $\alpha = (1 - n)\beta/n\sigma.$

Since $n < 1$, it follows from (62) and the assumption (52) that

(63) $\alpha > 1.$

Equation (33) then becomes the one by which W is determined. The left-hand side will be denoted as $F(W)$.

$$F'(W) = \frac{1 - W^{\alpha-1}}{1 - \alpha}.$$

From (63), $F'(W) < 0$ for $0 \geqq W < 1$, the relevant range since the investment will never be profitable if $W > 1$. To demonstrate that $W < \gamma$, it suffices to show that $F(W) > F(\gamma)$ for that value of W which satisfies (33), i.e., to show that

(64) $F(\gamma) < \theta/a.$

Finally, to demonstrate (64), note that $\gamma < 1$ and $\alpha > 1$, which imply that $\gamma^\alpha < \gamma$, and therefore

$$(1 - \alpha) - \gamma^\alpha + \alpha\gamma > (1 - \alpha)(1 - \gamma).$$

Since $\alpha > 1$, $\alpha(1 - \alpha) < 0$. Dividing both sides by this magnitude yields

$$\frac{1 - \gamma^\alpha}{\alpha} + \frac{\gamma - \gamma^\alpha}{1 - \alpha} < \frac{1 - \gamma}{\alpha} = \frac{\theta}{a}$$

where use is made of (57), (28), and (61); but from (33), the left-hand side is precisely $F(\gamma)$, so that (64) is demonstrated.

The case $a \leqq \beta$, excluded by (56), can be handled similarly; in that case the optimum v is 0. The subsequent reasoning follows in the same way so that the corresponding competitive path would have $W < 0$, which is, however, impossible.

6. Some Comments on the Model

(1) Many writers, such as Theodore Schultz, have stressed the improvement in the quality of the labor force over time as a source of increased productivity. This interpretation can be incorporated in the present model by assuming that σ, the rate of growth of the labor force, incorporates qualitative as well as quantitative increase.

(2) In this model, there is only one efficient capital-labor ratio for new investment at any moment of time. Most other models, on the contrary, have assumed that alternative capital-labor ratios are possible both before the capital good is built and after. A still more plausible model is that of Johansen [7], according to which alternative capital-labor ratios are open to the entrepreneur's choice at the time of investment but are fixed once the investment is congealed into a capital good.

(3) In this model, as in those of Solow [12] and Johansen [7], the learning takes place in effect only in the capital goods industry; no learning takes place in the use of a capital good once built. Lundberg's Horndal effect suggests that this is not realistic. The model should be extended to include this possibility.

(4) It has been assumed here that learning takes place only as a by-product of ordinary production. In fact, society has created institutions, education and research, whose purpose it is to enable learning to take place more rapidly. A fuller model would take account of these as additional variables.

REFERENCES.

[1] Abramovitz, M., " Resource and Output Trends in the United States Since 1870," *American Economic Review, Papers and Proceedings of the American Economic Association*, 46 (May, 1956): 5-23.

[2] Arrow, K. J., H. B. Chenery, B. S. Minhas, and R. M. Solow, " Capital-Labor Substitution and Economic Efficiency," *Review of Economics and Statistics*, 43 (1961): 225-250.

[3] Asher, H., *Cost-Quantity Relationships in the Airframe Industry*, R-291, Santa Monica, Calif.: The RAND Corporation, 1956.

[4] Haavelmo, T. *A Study in the Theory of Economic Evolution*, Amsterdam: North Holland, 1954.

[5] Hilgard, E. R., *Theories of Learning*, 2nd ed., New York: Appleton-Century-Crofts, 1956.

[6] Hirsch, W. Z., " Firm Progress Ratios," *Econometrica*, 24 (1956): 136-143.

[7] Johansen, L., " Substitution vs. Fixed Production Coefficients in the Theory of Economic Growth: A Synthesis," *Econometrica*, 27 (1959): 157-176.

[8] Kaldor, N., " Capital Accumulation and Economic Growth," in F. A. Lutz and D. C. Hague (eds.), *The Theory of Capital*, New York: St. Martin's Press, 1961, 177-222.

[9] Lundberg, E., *Produktivitet och räntabilitet*, Stockholm: P. A. Norstedt and Söner, 1961.

[10] Muth, J., "Rational Expectations and the Theory of Price Movements," *Econometrica* (in press).

[11] Solow, R. M., "Technical Change and the Aggregate Production Function," *Review of Economics and Statistics*, 39 (1957): 312-320.

[12] Solow, R. M., "Investment and Technical Progress," in K. J. Arrow, S. Karlin, and P. Suppes (eds.), *Mathematical Methods in the Social Sciences*, 1959, Stanford, Calif.: Stanford University Press, 1960, 89-104.

[13] Verdoorn, P. J., "Fattori che regolano lo sviluppo della produttività del lavoro," *L'Industria*, 1 (1949).

[14] Verdoorn, P. J., "Complementarity and Long-Range Projections," *Econometrica*, 24 (1956): 429-450.

[15] Wright, T. P., "Factors Affecting the Cost of Airplanes," *Journal of the Aeronautical Sciences*, 3 (1936): 122-128.

Stanford. KENNETH J. ARROW.

12 Extensions of Arrow's "Learning by Doing"*

D. LEVHARI

In a recent paper[1] Arrow discusses the behavior of an economic model in which technological change is related to cumulated gross investment, or to the serial number of the machines used in production. Arrow uses a model of fixed proportions, and for a machine of specified vintage and serial number there is a fixed labor requirement for production. In the following paper we shall show that most of Arrow's results can be extended to any homogeneous production function of the first degree with the type of technological change discussed by him. The production function shows ordinary convexity. Here we shall distinguish two types of production function according to the properties of the marginal product of labor with zero labor input. In type I the marginal product of labor with zero input is finite and it is impossible to produce without labor (as an example we have the CES production function with elasticity of substitution smaller than 1). In type II the marginal product of labor with zero labor input is infinite, or it is possible to produce without labor input (as an example we have CES with elasticity of substitution greater than or equal to 1; if it is 1, we have of course the known Cobb-Douglas case). As we shall see, in type I, as in the fixed proportion case, there is discarding of capital. Capital is used up to the time when it is scrapped. We shall ignore physical wear and tear and assume that the economic life of machinery is shorter than its physical life. There is no difficulty, and none of the results would change, if we include an exponential force of mortality. In type II, where marginal productivity is infinite with zero labor input, there is of course no complete discarding. We shall start with type I production function, then we shall show briefly that all the results apply to type II, and finally, we shall discuss the Cobb-Douglas production function.

1. *The Model*

Let G_t = cumulative gross investment.

Q_t = total ouput at time t.

L_t = total labor force employed with machines.

$Q_{v,t}$ = output at time t produced by machines born at time v.

$L_{v,t}$ = labor allocated at time t, to machines born at v.

w_t = wage rate at time t.

I_v = $\dot{G}_v$, investment in new machines at time v.

$$G_t = \int_{-\infty}^{t} I_v dv.$$

Let $F(x, y)$ be a linear homogeneous production function with $\frac{\partial^2 F}{\partial y^2}; \frac{\partial^2 F}{\partial x^2} < 0$ and assume $\left.\frac{\partial F(x, y)}{\partial y}\right|_{y=0}$ is finite.

Output with machines of vintage v, I_v, at time t obeys the rule $Q_{v,t} = F(I_v, G_v^n L_{v,t})$, where $0<n<1$. Here we have the essence of Arrow's assumption: technological change

* I am indebted to R. M. Solow for many helpful comments.

[1] K. J. Arrow, "The Economic Implications of Learning by Doing", *Review of Economic Studies*, XXIX (1962), 155-173.

embodied in machines born at v is related to gross cumulated investment. Moreover, we have used his assumption about the type of technological change, that it is a labor-augmenting technological change; but instead of having some autonomous function of time, say $a(t)$ or $e^{\lambda t}$, showing the increased efficiency of labor on the new machines, it is here related to cumulated gross investment. We have also assumed the same functional form of technological change assumed by Arrow.[1] We assume the possibility of re-allocating and reshuffling labor so as to maximize production.[2] Discussing at present production functions of type I with discarding of capital, we denote by $m(t)$ the age of the oldest capital in use at time t. Then output at Q_t and $m(t)$ satisfy

$$Q_t = \int_{t-m(t)}^{t} F(I_v, G_v^n L_{v,t})dv, \qquad \ldots(1)$$

$$L_t = \int_{t-m(t)}^{t} L_{v,t}dv. \qquad \ldots(2)$$

The second of these equations shows us simply that total labor force, assumed exogenously given, is equal to labor used with machines of all vintages.

The first equation presents the sum of production with capital of all vintages using the fact that with production functions of type I, no output is contributed by machines older than $m(t)$. To maximize output—deliberately or by the operation of the "invisible hand" in a perfectly competitive situation—the marginal product of labor used with all vintages should be the same, i.e. $\dfrac{\partial F(I_v, G_v^n L_{v,t})}{\partial L_{v,t}} = w_t$ where w_t is marginal product of labor at t. Using the homogeneity of $F(x, y)$, we know that $\dfrac{\partial F(x, y)}{\partial y}$ is a function of $\dfrac{y}{x}$, and remembering the condition of decreasing returns, that it is a monotonic decreasing function of $\dfrac{y}{x}$. Call this function $h\left(\dfrac{y}{x}\right)$. h has an inverse H, which is also a monotonic decreasing function. So,

$$\frac{\partial F(I_v, G_v^n L_{v,t})}{\partial L_{v,t}} = G_v^n \frac{\partial F(I_v, G_v^n L_{v,t})}{\partial (G_v^n L_{v,t})} = G_v^n h\left(\frac{G_v^n L_{v,t}}{I_v}\right), \qquad \ldots(3)$$

and the condition for maximum output is

$$G_v^n h\left(\frac{G_v^n L_{v,t}}{I_v}\right) = w_t; \text{ i.e. } \frac{G_v^n L_{v,t}}{I_v} = H(G_v^{-n} w_t),$$

or

$$L_{v,t} = G_v^{-n} H(G_v^{-n} w_t) I_v. \qquad \ldots(4)$$

H is a monotonic decreasing function of its argument, and therefore an increasing function of G_v. G_v^{-n} is obviously a decreasing function of G_v, therefore it is generally not possible to make additional inferences about $\dfrac{\partial L_{v,t}}{\partial v}$ without further assumptions; as a

1 R. Solow, J. Tobin, C. von Weizsäcker and M. Yaari discuss the economic implications of a fixed coefficient labor-augmenting case. In their discussion, machines of vintage v produce a units of output and require a crew of $be^{-\lambda v}$. Their model is in many ways analogous to the Arrow model, although of course the introduction of technological change through cumulated gross investment brings some essential changes in behavior. ("Neoclassical Growth with Fixed Factor Proportions", *Review of Economic Studies*, this number.)

2 Here, of course, we follow R. M. Solow, "Investment and Technical Progress", in *Mathematical Methods in the Social Sciences* (ed. K. J. Arrow, S. Karlin and P. Suppes), 1959, Stanford, Stanford University Press, 1960, pp. 89-104, rather than L. Johansen, "Substitution vs Fixed Proportions in the Theory of Economic Growth: A Synthesis", *Econometrica*, XXVII (1959), 157-176.

matter of fact $L_{v,t}$ is not necessarily a monotonic function of v. For the vintages not used we must obviously find

$$\left.\frac{\partial F(I_v, G_v^n L_{v,t})}{\partial L_{v,t}}\right|_{L_{v,t}=0} \leqq w_t. \qquad ...(5)$$

In the oldest vintage used we must find equality.

Evaluating the marginal product of labor at $L(v, t) = 0$ one gets

$$\left.\frac{\partial F(I_v, G_v^n L_{v,t})}{\partial L_{v,t}}\right|_{L_{v,t}=0} = G_v^n h(0). \qquad ...(6)$$

For $t-m(t)$ we must therefore find

$$G_{t-m(t)}^n h(0) = w_t. \qquad ...(7)$$

Thus,

$$L_{v,t} = G_v^{-n} H[G_v^{-n} G_{t-m(t)}^n h(0)] I_v. \qquad ...(8)$$

Substituting (7) in (1) and (2) we get:

$$Q_t = \int_{t-m(t)}^{t} F\{1, H[h(0)G_v^{-n} G_{t-m(t)}^n]\} I_v dv, \qquad ...(9)$$

$$L_t = \int_{t-m(t)}^{t} G_v^{-n} H[h(0)G_v^{-n} G_{t-m(t)}^n] I_v dv. \qquad ...(10)$$

From equation (10) we get $m(t)$, the age of oldest machines used at t. The right-hand side is a monotonic increasing function of $m(t)$. First, by increasing $m(t)$ we decrease $w_t = G_{t-m(t)}^n h(0)$ and we therefore increase the labor allocated to each of the vintages used; moreover we start using older vintages. So from (10) we get a unique solution for $m(t)$, and substituting in (9) we find Q_t. At first glance it may seem that there is an essential difference between this model and the model discussed by Arrow. While in Arrow production Q is a function of G_t and L alone, in our case the time profile of I_v or G_v may enter into the production function; but (9) and (10) reveal that this is not so.

This can be shown by making the following substitution: $z = G_v$, $dz = I_v dv$ in (9) and (10). (9) and (10) are transformed into:

$$Q_t = \int_{G_{t-m(t)}}^{G_t} F\{1, H[h(0)z^{-n} G_{t-m(t)}^n]\} dz \qquad ...(9')$$

and

$$L_t = \int_{G_{t-m(t)}}^{G_t} z^{-n} H[h(0)z^{-n} G_{t-m(t)}^n] I_v dv. \qquad ...(10')$$

It is easily seen that the right-hand side of (10′) is a monotonic decreasing function of $G_{t-m(t)}$, and we can solve for $G_{t-m(t)}$ in terms of G_t and L_t. Using (9) we find a pseudo-production function $Q(G, L)$ of the same type as the one discussed by Arrow. Later, we shall carry out an explicit calculation in the Cobb-Douglas case. We can look on $Q(G, L)$ as on an ordinary production function and through knowing the shape of $Q(G, L)$, we can discuss all the properties of the system, such as the share of the wages, social and private returns, stability of exponential growth. We shall show this later with the Cobb-Douglas example. It is generally easier to prove the properties of the system indirectly, without performing the conversion to $Q(G, L)$. First of all it is easy to see the increasing returns to scale of the system. It should be remembered that since the time path of I_v is not important we can multiply G_t by λ by multiplying I_v by λ. From the right-hand side of (9) we get:

$$\int_{t-m(t)}^{t} F\{1, H[h(0)\lambda^{-n}G_v^{-n}\lambda^n G_{t-m(t)}]\}\lambda I_v dv = \lambda \int_{t-m(t)}^{t} F\{1, H[h(0)G_v^{-n}G_{t-m(t)}]\}I_v dv.$$

From the right-hand side of (10) we get:

$$\int_{t-m(t)}^{t} \lambda^{-n}G_v^{-n}H[h(0)\lambda^{-n}G_v^{-n}\lambda^n G_{t-m(t)}^n]\lambda I_v dv = \lambda^{1-n} \int_{t-m(t)}^{t} G_v^{-n}H[h(0)G_v^{-n}G_{t-m(t)}^n]I_v dv.$$

We see therefore that if we multiply our cumulated investment by λ, and our labor force by λ^{1-n}, we multiply production by λ. If we also multiply the labor force by λ, production will therefore be multiplied by more than λ. From this fact alone we know that it is impossible for both factors to be remunerated according to their marginal productivities. As we shall show later, if labor gets its marginal productivity $\dfrac{\partial Q(G, L)}{\partial L}$ capital is paid less than $\dfrac{\partial Q(G, L)}{\partial G}$, and if saving is related to returns to capital, the accumulation path may not be Pareto-optimal.

We shall consider many of the properties of $Q(G, L)$ indirectly through the properties of its defining equations. Differentiating equation (1) with respect to time, we get:

$$\dot{Q}_t = F(I_t, G_t^n L_{t,t}) + \int_{t-m(t)}^{t} \frac{\partial F(I_v, G_v^n L_{v,t})}{\partial L_{v,t}} \frac{\partial L_{v,t}}{\partial t} dv - F(I_t, G_{t-m(t)}^n L_{t-m(t),t})[1-m'(t)]. \quad \ldots(11)$$

The third term vanishes, and remembering that the condition for maximum product is $\dfrac{\partial F(I_v, G_v^n L_{v,t})}{\partial L_{v,t}} = w_t$ for all v, we get

$$\dot{Q}_t = F(I_t, G_t^n L_{t,t}) + w_t \int_{t-m(t)}^{t} \frac{\partial L_{v,t}}{\partial t} dv. \quad \ldots(12)$$

The second term is negative, if $\dot{w}_t > 0$, because of reshuffling in favor of new capital. This is seen by differentiating (4) with respect to t,

$$\frac{\partial L_{v,t}}{\partial t} = G_v^{-n} \frac{\partial H(w_t G_v^{-n})}{\partial w_t} I_v \dot{w}_t, \quad \ldots(13)$$

using the fact that H is a monotonic decreasing function, if $\dot{w}_t > 0$, $\dfrac{\partial L_{v,t}}{\partial t} < 0$. Differentiating equation (2) with respect to time we get:

$$\dot{L}_t = L_{t,t} + \int_{t-m(t)}^{t} \frac{\partial L_{v,t}}{\partial t} dv + L_{t-m(t)}[1-m'(t)]. \quad \ldots(14)$$

Substituting for $\displaystyle\int_{t-m(t)}^{t} \frac{\partial L_{v,t}}{\partial t} dv$ one finds

$$\dot{Q}_t = [F(I_t, G_t^n L_{t,t}) - w_t L_{t,t}] + w_t \dot{L}_t; \text{ or} \quad \ldots(15)$$

$$\dot{Q}_t = \frac{F(I_t, G_t^n L_{t,t}) - w_t L_{t,t}}{I_t} I_t + w_t \dot{L}_t. \quad \ldots(16)$$

Denote the rental at time t of capital born at time v by $r_{v,t}$. By definition

$$r_{v,t} = \frac{F(I_v, G_v^n L_{v,t}) - w_t L_{v,t}}{I_v}.$$

The growth of product is then

$$\dot{Q}_t = r_{t,t}\dot{G}_t + w_t \dot{L}_t. \qquad \ldots(17)$$

So by having an extra unit of new capital, output is increased by the instantaneous quasi-rent of the new capital; and by having an extra worker output is increased by w_t. Now if we differentiate $Q = Q(G, L)$ with respect to time we find $\dot{Q}_t = \frac{\partial Q}{\partial G}\dot{G} + \frac{\partial Q}{\partial L}\dot{L}$ and therefore $r_{t,t} = \frac{\partial Q}{\partial G}$, $w_t = \frac{\partial Q}{\partial L}$. So implicitly one finds the marginal productivities of the factors. We can express the quasi-rent of capital, $r_{v,t}$, using the optimum allocation of labor,

$$r_{v,t} = F\{1, H[h(0)G_v^{-n}G_{t-m(t)}^n]\} - h(0)G_v^{-n}G_{t-m(t)}^n H[h(0)G_v^{-n}G_{t-m(t)}^n], \qquad \ldots(18)$$

and

$$r_{t,t} = F\{1, H[h(0)G_t^{-n}G_{t-m(t)}^n]\} - h(0)G_t^{-n}G_{t-m(t)}^n H[h(0)G_t^{-n}G_{t-m(t)}^n], \qquad \ldots(19)$$

and $r_{v,t} < r_{t,t}$ for $v < t$.

2. *Exponential Growth*

Arrow pays special attention to the exponential growth situation. Assume that labor grows at a constant rate σ. Assume a constant savings rate s and an exponential history $G_t = G_0e^{gt}$, or $I_t = I_0e^{gt}$, or $Q_t = Q_0e^{gt}$, where g is the rate of exponential growth. On this path $gG_t = sQ_t$ and the capital-output ratio is $\frac{G_t}{Q_t} = \frac{s}{g}$. Let us first check the feasibility of an exponential solution to our integral equations (9) and (10).

On the exponential path we should have:

$$Q_0e^{gt} = sQ_0 \int_{t-m(t)}^{t} F[1, H\{h(0)e^{-ng[v-t+m(t)]}\}]e^{gv}dv, \qquad \ldots(20)$$

$$L_0e^{\sigma t} = \int_{t-m(t)}^{t} G_0^{-n}e^{-ngv}H\{h(0)e^{-ng[v-t+m(t)]}\}gG_0e^{gv}dv. \qquad \ldots(21)$$

Now let us substitute $v = u+t-m$ in both the above equations; after cancellation we find

$$1 = se^{-gm(t)} \int_0^{m(t)} F\{1, H[h(0)e^{-gnu}]\}e^{gu}du, \qquad \ldots(22)$$

and

$$L_0e^{\sigma t} = gG_0^{1-n}e^{-g(1-n)m(t)}e^{g(1-n)t} \int_0^{m(t)} H[h(0)e^{-ngu}]e^{g(1-n)u}du. \qquad \ldots(23)$$

In the first of these equations the left-hand side is independent of t, hence the right-hand side should be independent of t, and $m(t) \equiv m$ — a constant independent of time. From the second of these equations we then find that for exponential growth we need $g(1-n) = \sigma$ and $g = \frac{\sigma}{1-n}$.

Output, investment and cumulated gross investment are thus all growing at a common rate $\frac{\sigma}{1-n}$ and equations (9) and (10) are transformed to a time-free pair of equations:

$$1 = se^{-gm}\int_0^m F\{1, H[h(0)e^{-gnu}]\}e^{gu}du \qquad \text{...(24)}$$

$$L_0 = gG_0^{1-n}e^{-\sigma m}\int_0^m H[h(0)e^{-ngu}]e^{\sigma u}du. \qquad \text{...(25)}$$

On the exponential path $G_0 = \frac{s}{g}Q_0$, therefore

$$L_0 = g^n s^{1-n}Q_0^{1-n}e^{-\sigma m}\int_0^m H[h(0)e^{-ngu}]e^{\sigma u}du. \qquad \text{...(26)}$$

From equation (24) we find m, the constant economic life of machinery, and then we find the level of output, Q_0, from (26). The length of life of machinery and the level of output depend on the savings rate. We shall later show the nature of this dependence.

The condition for the existence of an exponential path—we shall show later that this is also the condition for stability of this path—is the existence of a solution m, Q_0 to equations (20) and (21) [or (24) and (25)]. For an exponential solution we then require the equation

$$1 = se^{-gt}\int_{t-m}^{t} F\{1, H[h(0)e^{-ng(v-t+m)}]\}e^{gv}dv \qquad \text{...(20')}$$

to possess a solution m. The right-hand side of (20′) is a monotonic increasing function of m. With $m = 0$ this right-hand side achieves the value 0 and for existence of a solution m we require that for large m the right-hand side achieve values greater than 1.

Letting $m \to \infty$ the right-hand side tends to

$$se^{-gt}\int_{-\infty}^{t} F[1, H(0)]e^{gv}dv = \frac{s}{g}F(1, \infty),$$

and the condition for the existence of an exponential path is $\frac{s}{g}F(1, \infty) > 1$.

3. *Wage Rate and Interest Rate in the Exponential Case*

In the exponential solution we find for the wage rate

$$w_t = h(0)G_{t-m}^n = h(0)G_0^{-n}e^{-ngm}e^{ngt}, \qquad \text{...(27)}$$

and

$$w_0 = h(0)G_0^{-n}e^{-ngm}. \qquad \text{...(28)}$$

The wage rate increases at a rate of $\frac{n}{1-n}\sigma$. The wage bill $w_t L_t$ is

$$h(0)G_0^n e^{-ngm}e^{ngt}L_0e^{\sigma t} = h(0)G_0^n L_0 e^{-ngm}e^{\frac{\sigma}{1-n}t},$$

i.e. it increases at the same rate as output. The labor share is $\frac{h(0)G_0^n L_0 e^{-ngm}}{Q_0}$; again it is a function of the savings rate and other parameters of the system, and to say something more about this dependence we need additional assumptions about the elasticity of substitution of the production function.

The wage rate in a competitive situation is equal to the marginal productivity of $\dfrac{\partial Q(G, L)}{\partial L}$.

To find the interest rate we have to assume something about expectations. Assume that entrepreneurs correctly anticipate the wage rate w_t and the interest rate profile. Denote the expected interest profile by ρ_t. In this world of no mistaken expectations the cost of producing an extra unit of capital should be equal to the present value of its stream of quasi-rents. So the interest rate profile should satisfy the functional equation

$$1 = \int_v^{v+m} r_{v,t} e^{-\int_v^t \rho_x dx} dt.$$

The quasi-rents are:

$$r_{v,t} = F\{1, H[e^{-ng(v-t+m)}h(0)]\} - h(0)e^{-ng(v-t+m)}H[h(0)e^{-ng(v-t+m)}]. \qquad \ldots(29)$$

We see that $r_{v,t}$ is a function only of $(t-v)$. It has been shown by Solow and others in an analogous case that $\rho_t \equiv \rho_0$, a constant, is the only solution of this functional equation.[1] So if ρ_0 is the constant interest rate it should satisfy

$$\int_0^m e^{-\rho_0 t} r_{0,t} dt = 1.$$

The left-hand side is a monotonic decreasing function of ρ_0. As $\rho_0 \to \infty$ it tends to zero and as $\rho_0 \to -\infty$ it tends to infinity; hence we find a unique ρ_0 for this equation. This ρ_0 is smaller than the marginal productivity of "capital" $\dfrac{\partial Q(G, L)}{\partial G}$. On the exponential path

$$\frac{\partial Q}{\partial G} = r_{t,t} = F\{1, H[h(0)e^{-gnm}]\} - h(0)e^{-gnm}H[h(0)e^{-gnm}] \qquad \ldots(30)$$

is independent of time. The instantaneous social rate of return to capital, ρ', i.e. the solution of the functional equation

$$\int_v^\infty \frac{\partial Q(G, L)}{\partial G} e^{-\int_v^u \rho'_x dx} du = \int_v^\infty r_{u,u} e^{-\int_v^u \rho'_x dx} du = 1$$

is a constant. That is, $1 = r_{0,0} \displaystyle\int_v^\infty e^{-\rho'(u-v)} du = \frac{r_{0,0}}{\rho'}$. Hence,

$$\rho' = r_{t,t} = r_{0,0}. \qquad \ldots(31)$$

Remembering that $r_{v,t} < r_{t,t} = r_{0,0}$ for all $v < t$,

$$\int_v^\infty r_{t,t} e^{-\rho_0(t-v)} dt > \int_v^{v+m} r_{t,t} e^{-\rho_0(t-v)} dt > \int_v^{v+m} r_{v,t} e^{-\rho_0(t-v)} dt = 1.$$

So $\dfrac{r_{0,0}}{\rho_0} > 1$ and $r_{0,0} = \rho' > \rho_0$. Capital, as is intuitively obvious, is underpaid compared with its marginal product or with the social rate of return. If we invest an extra unit of capital at time v, then in all future time, from v to infinity, production is increased in each t by $\dfrac{\partial Q(G, L)}{\partial G} = r_{t,t}$. But the private stream of rentals, because of obsolescence, decreases

[1] R. Solow, J. Tobin, C. von Weizsäcker and M. Yaari, *op. cit.*

continuously till $v+m$, when the machine is discarded. If capital is to get its marginal product, each investor should get $r_{t,t}$ per unit of time, regardless of whether the machine is still being fully operated as at the time of its manufacture, partly operated, or discarded. If savings and investment are related in a neoclassical way with the return to capital we shall of course get undersaving or underinvestment compared with what society prefers.

Assume that there is a tax-subsidy device which guarantees capital its marginal product $r_{t,t}$. Labor cannot of course then get its marginal product. We assume that labor continues to be optimally allocated, so that the marginal product of labor on all vintages is the same. Call this common marginal product W_t. Obviously if capital gets its marginal product $w_t < W_t$. We shall now prove that on exponential path $w_t = (1-n)W_t$. The share of capital then is $\frac{r_{t,t}G}{Q}$.

Looking at equation (17) we find

$$\frac{\dot{Q}}{Q} = r_{t,t}\frac{\dot{G}}{Q} + \frac{w_t L}{Q}\frac{\dot{L}}{L},$$

or

$$g = r_{t,t}s + \frac{w_t L}{Q}\sigma.$$

Again using $gG = sQ$ we find

$$1 - r_{t,t}\frac{s}{g} = 1 - \frac{r_{t,t}G}{Q} = (1-n)\frac{W_t L}{Q}. \qquad \text{...(32)}$$

On this path, this distribution is time-independent

$$1 - \frac{r_{0,0}G_0}{Q_0} = (1-n)\frac{W_0 L_0}{Q_0}. \qquad \text{...(33)}$$

So if capital is "properly" paid labor gets $(1-n)$ of its previous wage. To achieve this, we can tax proportion n of wages and transfer the proceeds to capital owners. Capital owners will be subsidized, the subsidy will increase with the age of the machine and equal $r_{t,t}$ when the machine is scrapped, for each unit of capital invested in the past.[1]

4. *Optimal Consumption Paths*

In this section we shall start with a proof of a golden rule for an exponential solution. As we have seen, exponential growth is characterized by the pair of equations

$$1 = se^{-gm}\int_0^m F\{1, H[h(0)e^{-ngu}]du, \qquad \text{...(36)}$$

$$L_0 = g^n s^{1-n} Q_0^{1-n} e^{-\sigma m}\int_0^m H[h(0)e^{-ngu}]du. \qquad \text{...(37)}$$

1 We can easily prove, for any path, that if capital gets its marginal product, labor gets $(1-n)$ *times* the marginal product of labor. We have already shown that (5) and (6) imply that multiplying G by λ and L by λ^{1-n} multiplies product by λ. This means that $Q(\lambda G, \lambda^{1-n}L) = \lambda Q(G, L)$. We differentiate both sides with respect to λ and obtain

$$\frac{\partial Q}{\partial \lambda G}G + \frac{\partial Q}{\partial \lambda^{1-n}L}(1-n)\lambda^{-n}L = Q(G, L).$$

Substituting $\lambda = 1$, we find:

$$\frac{\partial Q}{\partial G}G + (1-n)\frac{\partial Q}{\partial L}L = Q \qquad \text{...(34)}$$

or

$$\frac{(1-n)\frac{\partial Q}{\partial L}L}{Q} = 1 - \frac{\frac{\partial Q}{\partial G}G}{Q}. \qquad \text{...(35)}$$

(36) implicitly gives m, the life of capital, as a function of the savings rate s. (37) gives the level of output $Q_0(s)$ as a function of s and $m(s)$.

We implicitly differentiate (36) and (37) with respect to s and we find, respectively,

$$0=\frac{1}{s}-g\,\frac{dm}{ds}+sF\{1,\,H[h(0)e^{-gnm}]\}\,\frac{dm}{ds}, \qquad \text{...(38)}$$

$$0=(1-n)\,\frac{L_0}{s}+(1-n)L_0\,\frac{Q_0'(s)}{Q_0(s)}-\sigma L_0\,\frac{dm}{ds}+g^n s^{1-n}Q_0^{1-n}H[h(0)e^{-gnm}]\,\frac{dm}{ds}. \qquad \text{...(39)}$$

From the first of these equations we get:

$$\frac{dm}{ds}=\frac{1}{s}\,\frac{1}{g-sF\{1,\,H[h(0)e^{-gnm}]\}}; \qquad \text{...(40)}$$

after simplification we find:

$$\frac{Q_0'(s)}{Q_0(s)}=\frac{1}{s}\left[\frac{g-g^n\dfrac{s^{1-n}H[h(0)e^{-gnm}]Q_0^{1-n}}{(1-n)L_0}}{g-sF\{1,\,H[h(0)e^{-gnm}]\}}-1\right]. \qquad \text{...(41)}$$

To interpret these results we shall use the definition of $h(x)$ and $H(x)$. By definition $H[h(0)e^{-gnm}]=\dfrac{G_0^n L_{0,0}}{I_0}$, and $F\{1,\,H[h(0)e^{-gnm}]\}=\dfrac{Q_{0,0}}{I_0}$. We then obtain

$$\frac{dm}{ds}=\frac{1}{s}\,\frac{1}{g-s\left(\dfrac{Q_{0,0}}{I_0}\right)}=\frac{1}{s}\,\frac{1}{g-\dfrac{Q_{0,0}}{Q_0}}, \qquad \text{...(42)}$$

and

$$\frac{Q_0'(s)}{Q_0(s)}=\frac{1}{s}\left[\frac{g-g^n\dfrac{s^{1-n}Q_0^{1-n}\dfrac{L_{0,0}}{I_0}G_0^n}{(1-n)L_0}}{g-s\dfrac{Q_{0,0}}{I_0}}-1\right]. \qquad \text{...(43)}$$

Before proceeding to simplify these expressions we should discuss several relationships that hold on an exponential path. From the labor supply equation we find, as we have shown before, that

$$\dot{L}_t=L_{t,t}+\int_{t-m}^{t}\frac{\partial L_{v,t}}{\partial t}\,dv,$$

and on an exponential path

$$\sigma L_0 e^{\sigma t}=L_{t,t}+\int_{t-m}^{t}\frac{\partial L_{v,t}}{\partial t}\,dv,$$

and for $\quad t=0,\ \sigma L_0-L_{0,0}=\displaystyle\int_{-m}^{0}\frac{\partial L_{v,t}}{\partial t}\,dv.$

We know already that $w_t>0$ implies that

$$\int_{-m}^{0}\frac{\partial L_{v,t}}{\partial t}\,dv<0.$$

Using (17) we know that

$$\dot{Q}_t = (Q_{t,t} - W_t L_{t,t}) + W_t \dot{L}_t.$$

Solving for W_t we find on an exponential path

$$W_t = \frac{gQ_0 e^{gt} - Q_{t,t}}{\sigma L_0 e^{\sigma t} - L_{t,t}}, \qquad \text{...(44)}$$

and for $t = 0$

$$W_0 = \frac{gQ_0 - Q_{0,0}}{\sigma L_0 - L_{0,0}}. \qquad \text{...(45)}$$

We know $\sigma L_0 - L_{0,0} < 0$, $W_0 > 0$, and $gQ_0 - Q_{0,0} < 0$.

$$\frac{dm}{ds} = \frac{1}{s} \frac{1}{g - \dfrac{Q_{0,0}}{Q_0}} = \frac{1}{s} \frac{Q_0}{gQ_0 - Q_{0,0}} < 0, \qquad \text{...(46)}$$

i.e., as we feel intuitively, the economic life of capital is shorter whenever the rate of saving increases. Now let us proceed to interpret $\dfrac{Q_0'(s)}{Q_0(s)}$, the logarithmic derivative of the level of output, with respect to s.

Using $I_0 = sQ_0$ and $Q_0 = \dfrac{g}{s} G_0$ we find

$$\frac{Q_0'(s)}{Q_0(s)} = \frac{1}{s}\left[\frac{gQ_0 - g^n s^{-n} Q_0^{1-n} \dfrac{L_{0,0}}{(1-n)L_0} G_0^n}{gQ_0 - Q_{0,0}} - 1\right] \qquad \text{...(47)}$$

or

$$\frac{Q_0'(s)}{Q_0(s)} = \frac{1}{s}\left[\frac{\sigma L_0 - L_{0,0}}{gQ_0 - Q_{0,0}} \cdot \frac{Q_0}{(1-n)L_0} - 1\right] \qquad \text{...(48)}$$

but W_0 is $\dfrac{gQ_0 - Q_{0,0}}{\sigma L_0 - L_{0,0}}$ and we finally find:

$$\frac{Q_0'(s)}{Q_0(s)} = \frac{1}{s}\left[\frac{1}{\dfrac{(1-n)W_0 L_0}{Q_0}} - 1\right]. \qquad \text{...(49)}$$

$\dfrac{(1-n)W_0 L_0}{Q_0}$ is the share of labor when capital receives its marginal product. So the logarithmic derivative of $Q_0(s)$ is $\dfrac{1}{s}$ multiplied by the ratio of capital to labor shares when capital gets its marginal product $r_{t,t}$. Now among all exponential paths, the "golden rule" path, the path that maximizes the level of consumption $(1-s)Q_0(s)$, should satisfy $-Q(s) + (1-s)Q_0'(s) = 0$ or

$$\frac{Q_0'(s)}{Q_0(s)} = \frac{1}{1-s}. \qquad \text{...(50)}$$

From (10) we then easily find that on this golden rule path

$$s = 1 - \frac{(1-n)W_0 L_0}{Q_0}; \qquad \text{...(51)}$$

i.e. the profit share. Again we find that we get highest level of consumption with the savings rate equal to the share of capital when capital receives its marginal product.

On this path $\frac{r_{0,0}G}{Q} = s$, $gG = sQ$ and

$$r_{0,0} = r_{t,t} = g. \qquad \text{...(52)}$$

So on this path the social rate of return is equal to the rate of growth.

It is easy to see what happens if we have pure time preference at a rate of β and we want to maximize a functional of the type (discussed by Arrow) $\Omega = \int_0^\infty e^{-\beta t}C_t dt$, where C_t is the stream of consumption. For convergence we obviously need $\beta > g$. Now, on the optimal path the own rate of interest, $\frac{\partial Q(G, L)}{\partial G} = r_{t,t}$, should equal β. If $r_{t,t} > \beta$ we should save everything since we can consume later much more than the compensation we demand by our time preference. In the same way, if $r_{t,t} < \beta$ we should save nothing. So on the optimum path $r_{t,t} = \beta$, except for some initial adjustment. The fact that $r_{t,t}$ is a constant implies an exponential solution for the optimum path. On this exponential solution $r_{t,t}$ is a function of savings. Moreover, it can be proved that it is a monotonic decreasing function of the savings rate. So by solving $r_{t,t} = \beta$ we can find the optimal savings rate.

On the golden rule path $r_{t,t} = g$; on the optimal path $r_{t,t} = \beta > g$. Therefore the optimal savings rate with time preference is smaller than the savings rate on the golden rule path, as one would expect. Society is not ready to do the extra saving or refraining from consumption because of its time preference. Now, if there is no tax-subsidy mechanism then capital does not get its social return. Individuals with a time preference of β will save everything if $\rho_0 > \beta$, nothing if $\rho_0 < \beta$. They save part of their income only when $\rho_0 = \beta$.

Again for ρ_0 to be always a constant, we have an exponential solution and ρ_0 is a monotonic decreasing function of the saving rate s. From solving $\rho_0 = \beta$ we find the savings rate which will prevail. But on this path $\rho' = \rho_{t,t} > \rho_0 = \beta$. $r_{t,t}$ is a monotonic decreasing function of s and in the social optimal path $r_{t,t} = \beta$, and therefore investment falls short of what society considers the optimum.

5. *Stability of Exponential Growth*

Let us say that we start with some initial condition G_0 and that labor is growing exponentially so that $L_t = L_0 e^{\sigma t}$ and the gross savings rate is a constant s, we claim that there will then be convergence (in the relative sense) to exponential growth. In effect, we have the differential equation $\dot{G} = sQ(G, L)$ and we have to show that its solution converges asymptotically to $G_0 e^{\frac{\sigma}{1-n}t}$.[1]

[1] From (16) or (17) we get

$$\frac{\dot{Q}}{Q} = \frac{\frac{\partial Q}{\partial G}G}{Q}\frac{\dot{G}}{G} + \frac{\frac{\partial Q}{\partial L}L}{Q}\frac{\dot{L}}{L}.$$

As stated, $Q(\lambda G, \lambda^{1-n}L) = \lambda Q(G, L)$.

By differentiating with respect to λ and setting $\lambda = 1$ we get

(a) $$Q(L, G) = (1-n)\frac{\partial Q}{\partial L}L + \frac{\partial Q}{\partial G}G.$$

Substituting $\frac{\dot{L}}{L} = \sigma$ and $\frac{\partial Q}{\partial L}L$ from (a) we get

(b) $$\frac{\dot{Q}}{Q} = \frac{\sigma}{1-n} + \frac{\frac{\partial Q}{\partial G}G}{Q}\left(\frac{\dot{G}}{G} - \frac{\sigma}{1-n}\right).$$

So if $\frac{\dot{G}}{G} > \frac{\sigma}{1-n}$ then $\frac{\dot{Q}}{Q} > \frac{\sigma}{1-n}$ and $\dfrac{\frac{\dot{Q}}{Q} - \frac{\sigma}{1-n}}{\frac{\dot{G}}{G} - \frac{\sigma}{1-n}}$ is exactly the share of capital.

Recalling that $Q(\lambda G, \lambda^{1-n}L) = \lambda Q(G, L)$ and setting $\lambda = \frac{1}{G}$ we find

$$\frac{\dot{G}}{G} = \frac{sQ(G, L)}{G} = sQ\left(1, \frac{1}{G^{1-n}}\right).$$

Trying $G = G_0 e^{\frac{\sigma}{1-n}t}$, we find:

$$\frac{\sigma}{1-n} = sQ\left(1; \frac{L_0}{G_0^{1-n}}\right).$$

$Q(1, x)$ is monotonic increasing in x. $Q(1, 0) = 0$, since production is impossible without labor input with production function of type I. With infinite labor supply $m = \infty$ and $Q(1, \infty) = F(1, \infty)$. Define $Y = \log G - \frac{\sigma}{1-n} t$. Then

$$\dot{y} = \frac{\dot{G}}{G} - \frac{\sigma}{1-n} = sQ[1, L_0 e^{-(1-n)y}] - \frac{\sigma}{1-n}.$$

Call the function on the right $g(y)$; then $g(y)$ is a monotonic decreasing function of y with $g(\infty) = sQ(1, 0) - \frac{\sigma}{1-n} = -\frac{\sigma}{1-n}$ and $g(-\infty) = sQ(1, \infty) - \frac{\sigma}{1-n} = sF(1, \infty) - \frac{\sigma}{1-n}$.

Using the condition for existence of an exponential path, $sF(1, \infty) - \frac{\sigma}{1-n} > 0$. Thus there is a unique y^* such that $g(y^*) = 0$.

Since $g(y)$ is a decreasing function, $g(y) < 0$ if $y > y^*$ and $g(y) > 0$ if $y < y^*$.

Hence y tends asymptotically to y^*. It is easily seen that $y = \log G_0$ and that $G(t)$ tends asymptotically (in the relative sense) to $G_0 e^{\frac{\sigma}{1-n}t}$.

6. *Production Functions of Type II*

All the results of the previous section can also be proved for the case of production functions with infinite marginal product at $L = 0$. Moreover, since all capital is in use the derivations are easier. The equations describing the system are

$$Q_t = \int_{-\infty}^{t} F[1, H(w_t G_v^{-n})] I_v dv, \qquad \ldots(53)$$

and

$$L_t = \int_{-\infty}^{t} G_v^{-n} H(w_t G_v^{-n}) I_v dv. \qquad \ldots(54)$$

From (54) we get w_t and then we find Q_t from (53). Assuming some savings pattern we observe the behavior of the system over time.

Again we can integrate out and find that Q is a function of G and L, i.e. $Q(G, L)$.

On an exponential path the system is described by a pair of time-independent equations:

$$1 = s\int_{-\infty}^{0} F[1, H(e^{-ngu} w_0 G_0^{-n})] e^{gu} du, \qquad \ldots(55)$$

and

$$L_0 = g^n s^{1-n} Q_0^{1-n} \int_{-\infty}^{0} e^{\sigma u} H(w_0 G_0^{-n} e^{-ngu}) du.[1] \qquad \ldots(56)$$

[1] For the existence (and also for the stability) of the exponential path we need $\frac{s}{g} F(1, 0) < 1$ and $\frac{s}{g} F(1, \infty) > 1$.

(55) is solved for $w_0 G_0^{-n}$ and substituting in (56) we solve for Q_0 (or G_0).

For example, let us prove the golden rule of accumulation. Differentiating (55) and (56) we get

$$0 = \frac{1}{s} + s \int_{-\infty}^{0} e^{gu} \frac{\partial F[1, H(e^{-ngu} w_0 G_0^{-n})]}{\partial H(\ )} \cdot \frac{\partial H(\ )}{\partial w_0} \frac{dw_0}{ds} du, \quad \ldots(57)$$

$$0 = (1-n)\frac{L}{s} + (1-n)L\frac{Q_0'(s)}{Q_0(s)} + g^n s^{1-n} Q_0^{1-n} \frac{dw_0}{ds} \int_{-\infty}^{0} e^{\sigma u} \frac{\partial H(\ )}{\partial w_0} du. \quad \ldots(58)$$

From the definition of $H(\ )$ one easily observes that

$$\frac{\partial F[1, H(w_0 G_0^{-n} e^{-ngu})]}{\partial H(\ )} = w_0 G_0^{-n} e^{-ngu}. \quad \ldots(59)$$

(57) is simplified to

$$0 = \frac{1}{s} + s w_0 G_0^{-n} \frac{dw_0}{ds} \int_{-\infty}^{0} e^{\sigma u} \frac{\partial H(\ )}{\partial w_0} du. \quad \ldots(60)$$

Let $B = \frac{dw_0}{ds} \int_{-\infty}^{0} e^{\sigma u} \frac{\partial H(\ )}{\partial w_0} du$; we then see that $B = -\frac{G_0^n}{s^2 w_0}$.

Using this in (59) and recalling that $G_0^n = \frac{s^n}{g^n} Q_0^n$, we get $(1-n)\frac{L_0}{s} + (1-n)L\frac{Q_0'(s)}{Q_0(s)} - \frac{Q_0}{s w_0} = 0.$

Finally we get

$$\frac{Q_0'(s)}{Q_0(s)} = \frac{1}{s}\left[\frac{Q_0}{(1-n)w_0 L_0} - 1\right]. \quad \ldots(61)$$

For optimum sustainable consumption we again should have $\frac{Q_0'(s)}{Q_0(s)} = \frac{1}{1-s}$ implying that on this path the savings rate equals the profit share or that the marginal productivity of capital is equal to the rate of growth.

7. *A Cobb-Douglas Example*

As an example of our previous discussion we use a Cobb-Douglas production function where we can carry out all the calculations. Let

$$Q_{v,t} = A(G_v^n L_{v,t})^\alpha I_v^{1-\alpha} \quad \ldots(62)$$

or

$$Q_{v,t} = A G_v^{\alpha n} L_{v,t}^\alpha I_v^{1-\alpha}. \quad \ldots(63)$$

The marginal product of labor should be the same for all vintages,

$$\alpha A G_v^{\alpha n} \left(\frac{I_v}{L_{v,t}}\right)^{1-\alpha} = w_t,$$

and

$$L_{v,t} = (\alpha A G_v^{\alpha n})^{\frac{1}{1-\alpha}} w_t^{\frac{-1}{1-\alpha}} I_v. \quad \ldots(64)$$

Using the labor supply equation:

$$L_t = \int_{-\infty}^{t} L_{v,t} dv = \frac{1}{\frac{\alpha n}{1-\alpha} + 1} w_t^{\frac{-1}{1-\alpha}} \alpha A^{\frac{1}{1-\alpha}} G_t^{\frac{\alpha n}{1-\alpha} + 1},$$

we get

$$w_t = \alpha A \left(\frac{1}{\frac{\alpha n}{1-\alpha} + 1} \right)^{1-\alpha} G_t^{\alpha n + (1-\alpha)} L_t^{-(1-\alpha)}. \qquad \ldots(65)$$

Output is $Q_t = \int_{-\infty}^{t} A G_v^{\alpha n} L_{v,t}^{\alpha} I_v^{1-\alpha} dv$, and using (64) and (65) we find

$$Q_t = A \left(\frac{1-\alpha}{\alpha n + 1 - \alpha} \right)^{1-\alpha} G_t^{\alpha n + 1 - \alpha} L_t^{\alpha}. \qquad \ldots(66)$$

Call $B = A \left(\frac{1-\alpha}{\alpha n + 1 - \alpha} \right)^{1-\alpha}$ and the quasi-production function has the form

$$Q_t = B G_t^{\alpha n} G_t^{1-\alpha} L_t^{\alpha}. \qquad \ldots(67)$$

It is easy to see that when labor is multiplied by λ^{1-n} and G_t by λ, output is multiplied by λ. The function is homogeneous of degree $1+\alpha n$. The share of labor, when labor gets its marginal product, is α and the share of capital is $1-\alpha$. If capital is subsidized so as to get its marginal product labor receives $(1-n)\alpha$. With a constant savings rate the behavior of the system over time is according to the differential equation $\dot{G} = sBG_t^{1-\alpha+\alpha n} L_t^{\alpha}$. Solving it, we find

$$G_t = \left[s(1-n)\alpha B \int_0^t L_v^{\alpha} dv + C^* \right]^{\frac{1}{\alpha(1-n)}}, \qquad \ldots(68)$$

and if $L_t = L_0 e^{\sigma t}$ we find:

$$G_t = \left[\frac{sB(1-n)L_0 e^{\alpha \sigma t}}{\alpha} + C^* \right]^{\frac{1}{\alpha(1-n)}}. \qquad \ldots(69)$$

We reach the exponential path asymptotically:

$$G_t = \left[\frac{sB(1-n)L_0}{\alpha} \right]^{\frac{1}{\alpha(1-n)}} e^{\frac{\sigma}{1-n} t} \qquad \ldots(70)$$

and $Q_t = \frac{\sigma}{(1-n)s} G_t$. For the golden rule path we have to maximize $(1-s)Q_0$ with respect to s. That is, we maximize the expression $\frac{s^{\frac{1}{\alpha(1-n)}}(1-s)}{s} = s^{\frac{1}{\alpha(1-n)}-1} - s^{\frac{1}{\alpha(1-n)}}$.

Differentiating with respect to s, $\left[\frac{1}{\alpha(1-n)} - 1 \right] s^{\frac{1}{\alpha(1-n)}-2} - \frac{1}{\alpha(1-n)} s^{\frac{1}{\alpha(1-n)}-1} = 0$, and on the golden rule path the savings rate is

$$s = 1 - \alpha(1-n), \qquad \ldots(71)$$

which is the share of capital if capital gets its marginal product.

If we want to maximize $\int_0^{\infty} e^{-\beta t} C_t dt$, set $\frac{\partial x}{\partial G} = \beta$ (besides some short period when we save or dissave everything, we can determine the nature of the optimal path by using the Pontryagin Maximum Principle). Then

$$\frac{\partial x}{\partial G} = B[\alpha n + (1-\alpha)] G_t^{-\alpha(1-n)} L_t^{\alpha} = \beta,$$

and

$$G_t = \left[\frac{B}{\beta(\alpha n+1-\alpha)}\right]^{\frac{1}{\alpha(1-n)}} L_t^{\frac{1}{1-n}}. \qquad \ldots(72)$$

If $L_t = L_0 e^{\sigma t}$, the path which optimizes $\int_0^\infty e^{-\beta t} C_t dt$ is

$$G_t = \left[\frac{B}{\beta(\alpha n+1-\alpha)}\right]^{\frac{1}{\alpha(1-n)}} L_0^{\frac{1}{1-n}} e^{\frac{\sigma}{1-n}t}. \qquad \ldots(73)$$

As society's rate of time-preference β is increased we choose a lower exponential path with the same growth rate $\frac{\sigma}{1-n}$.

The Hebrew University, Jerusalem. DAVID LEVHARI.

13 A New Model of Economic Growth

N. KALDOR and J. A. MIRRLEES

1. The purpose of this paper is to present a " Keynesian " model of economic growth which is an amended version of previous attempts put forward by one of the authors in three former publications.[1] This new theory differs from earlier theories mainly in the following respects:

(1) it gives more explicit recognition to the fact that technical progress is infused into the economic system through the creation of new equipment, which depends on current (gross) investment expenditure. Hence the " technical progress function " has been re-defined so as to exhibit a relationship between the rate of change of gross (fixed) investment per operative and the rate of increase in labour productivity on *newly installed* equipment;

(2) it takes explicit account of obsolescence, caused by the fact that the profitability of plant and equipment of any particular " vintage " must continually diminish in time owing to the competition of equipment of superior efficiency installed at subsequent dates; and it assumes that this *continuing obsolescence is broadly foreseen by entrepreneurs* who take it into account in framing their investment decision. The model also assumes that, irrespective of whether plant and equipment has a finite physical life-time or not, its *operative* life-time is determined by a complex of economic factors which govern the rate of obsolescence, and not by physical wear and tear;

(3) in accordance with this, the behavioural assumptions concerning the investors' attitudes to uncertainty in connection with investment decisions and which are set out below, differ in important respects from those made in the earlier models;

(4) account is also taken, in the present model, of the fact that some proportion of the existing stock of equipment disappears each year through physical causes—accidents, fire, explosions, etc.—and this gives rise to some " radioactive " physical depreciation in addition to obsolescence;

(5) since, under continuous technical progress and obsolescence, there is no way of measuring the " stock of capital " (measurement in terms of the historical cost of the surviving capital equipment is irrelevant; in terms of historical cost *less* accrued " obsolescence " is question-begging, since the allowance for obsolescence, unlike the charge for physical wear and tear etc., depends on the share of profits, the rate of growth, etc., and cannot therefore be determined independently of all other relations), the model avoids the notion of a quantity of capital, and its corollary, the rate of capital accumulation, as variables of the system; it operates solely with the value of current gross investment (gross (fixed) capital expenditure per unit of time) and its rate of change in time. The macro-economic notions of income, income per head, etc., on the the other hand are retained.

[1] Cf. N. Kaldor, "Alternative Theories of Distribution," *Review of Economic Studies*, 1955-56. (reprinted in *Essays on Value and Distribution*, pp. 228-236). " A Model of Economic Growth," *Economic Journal*, December 1957 (reprinted in *Essays in Economic Stability and Growth*, pp. 256-300) and " Capital Accumulation and Economic Growth " (presented in Corfu, September 1958 and published in *The Theory of Capital*, Macmillan, 1961, pp. 177-220). N. Kaldor's ideas in connection with the present model were worked out during his tenure as Ford Research Professor in Economics in Berkeley, California.

2. The present model is analogous to the earlier models in the following main features:

(1) like all " Keynesian " economic models, it assumes that " savings " are passive—the level of investment is based on the volume of investment decisions made by entrepreneurs, and is independent of the propensities to save; it postulates an economy in which the mechanism of profit and income generation will create sufficient savings (at any rate within certain limits or " boundaries ") to balance the investment which entrepreneurs decide to undertake;

(2) the model relates to an isolated economy with continuous technical progress, and with a steady rate of increase in the working population, determined by exogeneous factors;

(3) the model assumes that investment is primarily *induced* by the growth in production itself, and that the underlying conditions are such that growth-equilibrium necessarily carries with it a state of continuous full employment. This will be the case when the purely ' endogeneous ' growth rate (as determined by the combined operation of the accelerator and the multiplier) which is operative under conditions of an unlimited supply of labour, is appreciably higher than the " natural rate of growth," which is the growth of the " labour potential " (i.e., the *sum* of the rate of growth of the labour force and of (average) labour productivity). In that case, starting from any given state of surplus labour and under-employment, continued growth, as determined by these endogeneous factors, will necessarily lead to full employment sooner or later; and once full employment rules, continued growth involves that the " accelerator-multiplier " mechanism becomes " tethered " (through variations in the share of profits and through the imposition of a quasi-exogeneous growth rate in demand) to the natural rate of growth.

3. In a situation of continuing full employment the volume of investment decisions for the economy as a whole will be governed by the number of workers who become available, per unit period, to " man " new equipment, and by the amount of investment per operative. It may be assumed that each entrepreneur, operating in imperfectly competitive markets, aims at the maximum attainable growth of his own business (subject as we shall explain below, to the maintenance of a satisfactory rate of return on the capital employed) and for that reason prefers to maintain an appreciable amount of excess capacity so as to be able to exploit any chance increase in his selling power either by increasing his share of the market or by invading other markets. However, when gross investment per period is in excess of the number of workers becoming available to " man " new equipment, the degree of excess capacity must steadily rise; hence whatever the desired relationship between capacity and output, sooner or later a point will be reached when the number of workers available for operating new equipment exerts a dominating influence (via the mechanism of the accelerator) on the volume of investment decisions in the economy.[1]

We shall assume that the equipment of any given vintage is in " limitational " relationship to labour—i.e. that it is not possible to increase the productivity of labour by reducing the number of workers employed in connection with already existing equipment (though it is possible that productivity would, on the contrary, be *reduced* by such a reduction, on account of its being associated with a higher ratio of overhead to prime labour). This does not mean that the equipment of any vintage requires a fixed amount of labour to keep it in operation. The latter would assume the case not only of " fixed coefficients " but of complete indivisibility of the plant and equipment as well.

[1] We may assume that for the average, or representative, firm, sales grow at the same rate as production in the economy as a whole. But there will always be of course the exceptional firms who grow at a higher rate, and sub-average firms who grow at a lower rate. Investment in all cases serves the purpose of keeping productive capacity in some desired relationship with expected sales.

Writing n_t for the number of workers available to operate new equipment per unit period and i_t for the amount of investment per operative on machines of vintage t, and I_t for gross investment in fixed capital

$$i_t \equiv \frac{I_t}{n_t} \tag{1}$$

We shall use the symbols Y_t for the gross national product at t, N_t for the working population, and y_t for output per head, so that

$$y_t \equiv \frac{Y_t}{N_t}$$

4. We shall assume that " machines " of each vintage are of constant physical efficiency during their lifetime, so that the growth of productivity in the economy is entirely due to the infusion of new " machines " into the system through (gross) investment.[1] Hence our basic assumption is a technical progress function which makes the annual rate of growth of productivity per worker *operating on new equipment* a function of the rate of growth of investment per worker, i.e., that

$$\dot{p}_t/p_t = f(\dot{i}_t/i_t) \text{ with } f(0) > 0, f' > 0, f'' < 0 \tag{2}$$

This function is illustrated in Figure 1. It is assumed that a constant rate of investment per worker over time will itself increase productivity per worker; but that the rate of growth of productivity will also be an increasing function of the rate of growth of investment per worker, though at a diminishing rate.[2]

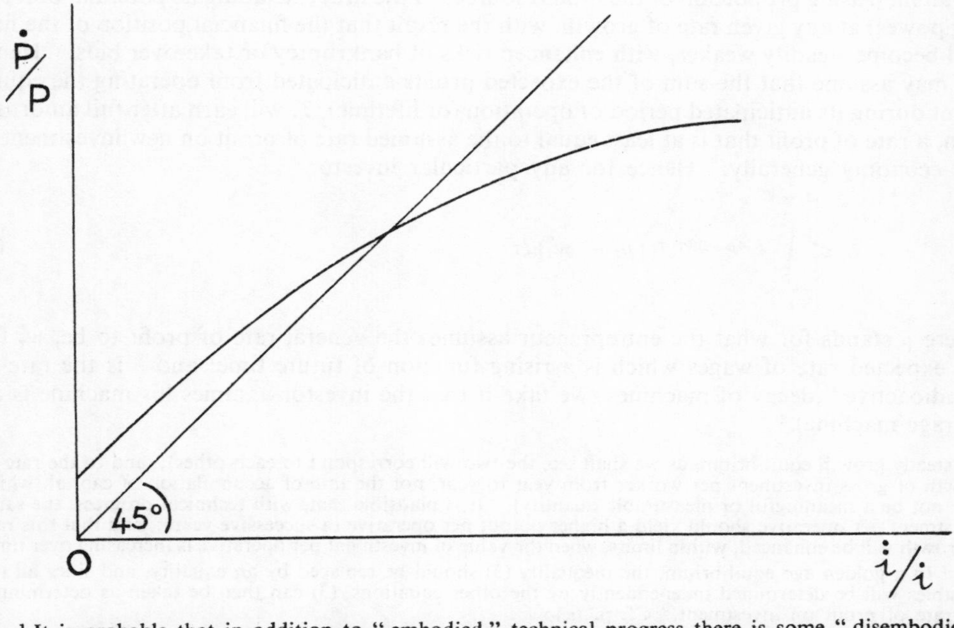

[1] It is probable that in addition to " embodied " technical progress there is some " disembodied " technical progress as well, resulting from increasing know-how in the use of existing machinery. On the other hand it is also probable that the physical efficiency of machinery declines with age (on account of higher repair and maintenance expenditures, etc.); our assumption of constant physical efficiency thus implies that these two factors just balance each other.

[2] It should be noted that the " technical progress function " in this model relates to the rate of growth of output per man-hour of the workers operating newly installed equipment (the equipment resulting from the investment of period t), *not* to the rate of growth of productivity in the economy in general (though in

Both output per operative and investment per operative are measured in terms of money values deflated by an index of the prices of " wage goods " (i.e., consumption goods which enter into the wage-earners' budget). This means that changes in the prices of equipment goods in terms of wage-goods (and also of such consumption goods which only enter into consumption out of profits) will in general cause shifts in the f-function. Provided, however, that there is a reasonably stable trend in the prices of these latter goods in terms of wage goods, we can still conceive of the function as stable in time for any particular value of I_t/Y_t in money terms, and the system may still possess a steady growth equilibrium with a constant (equilibrium) value of I_t/Y_t. A full demonstration of this would require, however, a fully fledged 2-sector model in which the technical progress functions of the consumption goods sector and the capital goods sector, the distribution of employment and of savings between the two sectors, etc., are all treated separately. Since this would go far beyond the scope of this paper, it is better to assume, for the present purposes, that the rate of technical progress, as measured by productivity growth, is the same in all sectors, and hence that relative prices remain constant; bearing in mind, however, that the model could probably be extended to cover a wider range of possibilities.

5. With regard to the manner in which entrepreneurs meet risk and uncertainty, we shall make two important assumptions. In the first place we shall assume that entrepreneurs will only invest in their own business in so far as this is consistent with maintaining the earning power of their fixed assets above a certain minimum, a minimum which, in their view, represents the earning power of fixed assets in the economy in general. This is because, if the earnings of a particular firm are low in relation to the capital employed, or if they increase at a lower rate than the book value of the fixed assets, fixed assets will take up an increasing proportion of the total resources of the firm (including its potential borrowing power) at any given rate of growth, with the result that the financial position of the firm will become steadily weaker, with enhanced risks of bankruptcy or take-over bids. Hence we may assume that the sum of the expected profits anticipated from operating the equipment during its anticipated period of operation (or lifetime), T, will earn after full amortisation, a rate of profit that is at least equal to the assumed rate of profit on new investment in the economy generally. Hence for any particular investor

$$i_t \leqslant \int_t^{t+T} e^{-(\rho+\delta)(\tau-t)}(p_t - w^*_\tau)d\tau \tag{3}$$

where ρ stands for what the entrepreneur assumes the general rate of profit to be, w^*_τ for the expected rate of wages which is a rising function of future time[1] and δ is the rate of " radioactive " decay of machines (we take it that the investor assumes his machine is an average machine).[2]

full steady growth equilibrium, as we shall see, the two will correspond to each other); and to the rate of growth of gross investment per worker from year to year, not the rate of accumulation of capital (which may not be a meaningful or measurable quantity). It is plausible that, with technical progress, the same investment per operative should yield a higher output per operative in successive years; and that this rate of growth will be enhanced, within limits, when the value of investment per operative is increasing over time.

[1] In a golden age equilibrium, the inequality (3) should be replaced by an equality, and since all the variables will be determined independently by the other equations, (3) can then be taken as determining the rate of profit on investment. Cf. p. below.

[2] Our equation (3) thus postulates conditions under which the amount of " finance " available to the firm is considerably greater than its fixed capital expenditure, so that the firm is free to vary its total investment expenditure per unit of time; and that it will adopt projects which pass the tests of adequacy as indicated by (3) even though it could earn a higher *rate* of profit on projects involving a smaller volume of investment and yielding a smaller *total* profit. (In other words we assume that the firm is guided by the motive of maximising the rate of profit on the shareholders' equity, which involves different decisions from the assumption of maximizing the rate of profit on its fixed investment.)

In the second place, under conditions of continuing technical progress, the expectations concerning the more distant future (whether in regard to money wages or in regard to the prices—or demands—of the particular products produced by a firm, both of which are projected in w^*_τ) are regarded as far more hazardous or uncertain than the expectations for the near future, where the incidence of unforeseeable major new inventions or discoveries is less significant. Hence investment projects which qualify for adoption must pass a further test—apart from the test of earning a satisfactory rate of profit—and that is that the cost of the fixed assets must be " recovered " within a certain period—i.e., that the gross profit earned in the first h years of its operation must be sufficient to repay the cost of investment. Hence

$$i_t \leqslant \int_t^{t+h} (p_t - w^*_\tau)\, d\tau \tag{4}$$

We shall assume, for the purposes of this model, that (3) is satisfied whenever (4) is satisfied—hence in (4) the $=$ sign will apply, i.e., the undiscounted sum of profits over h periods must be equal to i_t. There is plenty of empirical evidence that the assumption underlying (4) is a generally recognised method of meeting the uncertainty due to obsolescence in modern business, though the value of h may vary with the rate of technical progress, and also as between different sectors. (In the U.S. manufacturing industry h is normally taken as 3 years; but in other sectors—e.g., public utilities—it is much higher.)[1]

7. It is assumed, as in the earlier Keynesian growth models, that the savings which finance business investment come out of profits, and that a constant proportion, s, of *gross* profits are saved.[2] Hence (dividing income into two categories, profits and wages, which comprise all forms of non-business income) the share of (gross) profits, π_t, in the gross national product will be given by the equation

$$\pi_t = \frac{1}{s}\,\frac{I_t}{Y_t} \tag{5}$$

which, in virtue of equation (1), reduces to

$$\pi_t = \frac{r}{s}\,\frac{i_t}{y_t} \tag{5a}$$

[1] The assumptions represented by these two equations should be contrasted with the assumptions made in " Capital Accumulation and Economic Growth," according to which

$$\frac{P}{K} = r + \rho$$

$$\rho = \xi(v) \quad (\xi' > 0)$$

where P/K the rate of profit, r the money rate of interest, ρ the risk premium, v the capital/output ratio. ρ was assumed to be a rising function of v, because v reflects the ratio of fixed to circulating capital, and investment in the former is considered far more risky or " illiquid " than investment in the latter. The present assumptions are not inconsistent with the former hypothesis concerning the higher returns demanded on fixed investments; but they also take into account that the " riskiness " of the investment in fixed capital will be all the greater the longer the period over which the cost of the investment is ' recovered ' out of the profits—a matter which depends not only on the capital/output ratio (or rather, the investment/output ratio) but also on the share of gross profits in output. " Gross profits " should for this purpose be calculated net of other charges, including a notional interest charge on the ' liquid ' business assets, (i.e., the investment in circulating capital associated with the investment in fixed capital).

[2] Savings out of wages are ignored—i.e., they are assumed to be balanced by non-business (personal) investment (i.e., residential construction). The assumption that business savings are a constant proportion of *gross* profits (after tax) is well supported by data relating to gross corporate savings.

where r is defined by

$$r_t = {}^{n_t}/N_t,$$

where N_t is the total labour force at time t and n_t, as earlier defined, is the number of workers available to operate new equipment per unit period.

We shall assume that once equipment is installed the number of workers operating it will only fall in time by the physical wastage of equipment, caused by accidents, fires, etc. —until the whole of the residual equipment is scrapped on account of obsolescence. Writing δ for the rate of (radioactive) depreciation per unit period, and $T(t)$ for the age of the equipment which is retired at t (i.e., the lifetime of equipment as governed by obsolescence), we have the following relationship for the distribution of the labour force:

$$N_t = \int_{t-T}^{t} n_\tau \, e^{-\delta(t-\tau)} \, d\tau \tag{6}$$

and for total output

$$Y_t = \int_{t-T}^{t} p_\tau \, n_\tau \, e^{-\delta(t-\tau)} \, d\tau \tag{7}$$

Since output Y_t is divided into two categories of income only, wages and profits, the residue left after profits is equal to the total wages bill. Writing w_t for the rate of wages at t, we further have

$$Y_t \, (1 - \pi_t) = N_t \, w_t \tag{8}$$

Finally, since equipment will only be employed so long as its operation more than covers prime costs, the profit on the oldest yet surviving machinery must be zero. Hence

$$p_{t-T} = w_t \tag{9}$$

We shall assume that population grows at the constant rate λ, hence

$$\dot{N}_t = \lambda \, N_t \tag{10}$$

We shall also assume that businessmen anticipate that wages in terms of output units will rise in the foreseeable future at the same rate as they have been rising during the past l periods.

Hence the expected wage rate at a future time T will be

$$w_T^* = w_t \left(\frac{w_t}{w_{t-l}} \right)^{\frac{T-t}{l}} \tag{11}$$

Finally, the model is subject to two constraints (or " boundary conditions ") which are known from earlier models:

$$w_t \geqslant w_{min}$$

$$\pi \geqslant m$$

In other words, the wage rate resulting from the model must be above a certain minimum, (determined by conventional subsistence needs) and at the same time the share of profits resulting from the model must be higher than a certain minimum (the so-called " degree of monopoly " or " degree of imperfect competition ").

8. The above system gives 10 independent equations (regarding (3) only as a boundary condition) which are sufficient to determine the 10 unknowns; I_t, i_t, n_t, p_t, w_t, w^*_t, π_t, T, y_t, N_t, given the parameters, s, h, δ and λ, and the function f.

We shall investigate whether this system yields a solution in terms of a steady growth (or golden age) equilibrium where the rate of growth of output per head is equal to the rate of growth of productivity on new equipment and both are equal to the rate of growth of (fixed) investment per worker, and to the rate of growth of wages; i.e., where

$$\dot{p}/p = \dot{y}/y = \dot{i}/i = \dot{w}/w\ ;$$

and where the share of investment in output I/Y, the share of profits in income π, and the period of obsolescence of equipment, T, remain constant. Finally we shall show that there is a unique rate of profit on investment in a steady growth equilibrium.

The assumptions about the technical progress function imply that there is *some* value $\dot{p}/p$ (let us call it γ) at which

$$\dot{p}/p = \dot{i}/i = \gamma \tag{12}$$

Equilibrium is only possible when this holds.

If we integrate equation (4) using (11), we see that

$$i_t = hp_t - w_t\frac{e^{vh} - 1}{v},$$

where v is the expected rate of growth of w. Hence p could only grow faster than i in the long run if w was growing faster than p: that would imply a continuous reduction in T, which would lead to unemployment and stagnation before T fell to h (at which point the rate of profit would be negative). On the other hand, p cannot grow more slowly than i in the long run, since w cannot fall below w_{min} (and there would in fact be an inflation crisis before that point was reached).

It is clear too that, so long as $\dot{w}/w$ does not diverge too far from $\dot{p}/p$, $\dot{i}/i$ would increase if it were less than $\dot{p}/p$, and decrease if it were greater than $\dot{p}/p$. For if $\dot{p}/p$ were less than γ, it would breed, by equation (4), a rate of growth of investment, $\dot{i}/i$ that would require higher $\dot{p}/p$, and so on, until the equilibrium position is reached. A similar mechanism would be at work if $\dot{p}/p$ were greater than γ. Thus the equilibrium would in general be stable; but instability cannot be excluded, and a movement away from equilibrium would be possible in either of the two ways described above. For example a downward drift of the technical progress function might allow the rate of growth of p to fall off, and remain below the rate of growth of w (which reflects the rate of growth of y over the recent past) sufficiently long until with falling investment, unemployment and stagnation set in.[1] Conversely an upward shift in the technical progress function might lead to an inflationary situation at which investment, by one means or another, would be compressed below that indicated by (4) and (13).

[1] For example, a slowing down of technical progress in the late 1920's may have been responsible for that " sudden collapse of the marginal efficiency of capital " which led to the crisis and stagnation of the 1930's.

Hence, excluding the case where $\dot{p}/p$ is significantly different from $\dot{w}/w$, when

$$\frac{\dot{p}}{p} \gtrless \frac{i}{i}$$

there will be a convergent movement until (12) is obtained.

9. It will be convenient to deduce two further relations from the above equations. The first one relates to n_t, the amount of labour available for new equipment: it is obtained by differentiating (6) with respect to t.

$$n_t = \dot{N}_t + \delta N_t + n_{t-T}\left(1 - \frac{dT}{dt}\right) e^{-\delta T} \tag{13}$$

This equation says that n_t will be composed of three elements: (i) the growth in working population, $\dot{N}_t$; (ii) the labour released by physical wastage of equipment all vintages, which is δN_t; (iii) and finally the labour released by the retirement of obsolete equipment.

Differentiating equation (7) in the same way we obtain

$$\dot{Y}_t = p_t n_t - p_{t-T} n_{t-T}\left(1 - \frac{dT}{dt}\right) e^{-\delta T} - \delta Y_t$$

Substituting w_t for p_{t-T} in accordance with (9) and using (13) this becomes

$$\dot{Y}_t = p_t n_t - w_t (n_t - \dot{N}_t - \delta N_t) - \delta Y_t$$

Dividing both sides by $Y_t = N_t y_t$ we obtain

$$\frac{\dot{Y}_t}{Y_t} = r \frac{p_t}{y_t} - \frac{w_t}{y_t}(r - \lambda - \delta) - \delta$$

Using

$$\frac{\dot{Y}_t}{Y_t} = \frac{\dot{y}_t}{y_t} + \lambda$$

and re-arranging we finally obtain

$$\frac{\dot{y}_t}{y_t} + \lambda + \delta = r \frac{p_t}{y_t} - (r - \lambda - \delta) \frac{w_t}{y_t}. \tag{14}$$

10. In order that entrepreneurial expectations should be fulfilled, it is necessary that wages should grow at constant rate in time, β.

$$\frac{\dot{w}_t}{w_t} = \beta \text{ (constant)} \tag{15}$$

We shall now proceed to demonstrate that when β is constant, T will also be constant, provided that $\gamma < \dfrac{s}{h} - \lambda - \delta$.

It follows from (9) that

$$\frac{\dot{w}_t}{w_t} = \frac{\dot{p}_{t-T}}{p_{t-T}}\left(1 - \frac{dT}{dt}\right)$$

Hence

$$1 - \frac{dT}{dt} = \frac{\beta}{\gamma}, \text{ a constant.}$$

Integrating with respect to t we obtain

$$T = T_o + \left(1 - \frac{\beta}{\gamma}\right)t \tag{16}$$

where T_0 is the lifetime of equipment at some initial date, $t = 0$.

Substituting (16) into (13) and remembering that $r_t = n_t/N_t$, we obtain

$$r_t = \lambda + \delta + r_{t-T}\, e^{-(\lambda+\delta)T}\, \frac{\beta}{\gamma} \tag{17}$$

In order to show that, in a state of steady growth equilibrium $T = T_0$ and $\beta = \gamma$, we shall first consider the cases where $\beta \neq \gamma$.

(i) When $\gamma < \beta$, clearly steady growth cannot continue since entrepreneurs' profits would become negative sooner or later.

(ii) when $\gamma > \beta$, it follows from equation (16) that T becomes indefinitely large with time (and perhaps this is enough to dispose of this case, since for most goods there may be a maximum physical lifetime, quite apart from obsolescence). In any case this implies, in accordance with (17), that r ultimately tends to $\lambda + \delta$; and since w/y must tend to zero, so that the share of profits, π, tends towards unity,

$$i/y \text{ tends to } \frac{s}{\lambda + \delta}. \tag{18}$$

Also from (4);

$$i/p \text{ tends to } h.$$

Hence from (14):

$$\dot{y}/y \text{ tends to } \frac{s}{h} - \lambda - \delta.$$

(18) shows that y ultimately grows at the same rate as i, which grows at the rate γ.

Therefore

$$\gamma = \frac{s}{h} - \lambda - \delta \tag{19}$$

which implies, in Harrod's terms, that the " natural rate " (here, $\gamma + \lambda + \delta$) is equal to what the " warranted rate " would be if wages were zero and profits absorbed the whole output (since then s would equal the proportion of Y saved, and $h = i/p$).

11. It is easy to see that in fact the rate of growth of output per head cannot in the long run be greater than this quantity $\frac{s}{h} - \lambda - \delta$. By (5), i/y can rise no higher, ultimately, than s/r; hence by (4), even if (as might happen ultimately) the wage rate were negligible in relation to output per head, p/y could not be greater than $s/(rh)$. Turning to equation (14), we see that it implies the inequality

$$\dot{y}_t/y_t + \lambda + \delta \leqq r.\ \frac{s}{rh} = \frac{s}{h}.$$

Hence there can be no steady growth equilibrium unless

$$\gamma \leqq \frac{s}{h} - \lambda - \delta.$$

Normally we would not expect to have to worry about this constraint, for the quantity s/h will be large—especially when we remember that h will be small when there is a high rate of growth. If it is asked what would happen if the equilibrium growth rate given by the technical progress function really did fail to satisfy this inequality, the answer must be that the wage rate would be driven down to its minimum level and entrepreneurs would then find themselves unable to invest as much as the prospects would warrant: the equality (4) would become an inequality again. The rest of the discussion will be carried on under the assumption that the equilibrium rate of growth γ does satisfy this inequality.

We can see that, quite apart from the unrealistic value of γ implied by equation (19), equilibrium with $\gamma > \beta$ is a freak case; the slightest shift in γ would either render equilibrium impossible, or make it possible only with $\beta = \gamma$.

12. (iii) It is clear from the above that steady growth equilibrium will involve

$$\beta = \gamma$$

in which case it also involves a constant T.
(17) has now become

$$r_t = \lambda + \delta + r_{t-T}\, e^{-(\lambda+\delta)T},$$

where T is constant, so that r_t will tend to the equilibrium value

$$r = \frac{\lambda + \delta}{1 - e^{-(\lambda+\delta)T}} \tag{20}$$

From equation (5)

$$y_t = w_t + \frac{r}{s}\, i_t,$$

so that, since r is constant in equilibrium, y_t also grows at the equilibrium growth rate γ. It is convenient to write this last equation as

$$\frac{r}{s}\frac{i}{y} + \frac{w}{y} = 1 \tag{21}$$

In equilibrium, expectations are fulfilled, so that $w_t^* = w_t$. Since $w_t = w_0\, e^{\beta t} = w_0\, e^{\gamma t}$ (where w_0 is the wage rate at some initial time), the integral in equation (4) can be evaluated, so that

$$i_t = hp_t - \frac{e^{\gamma h} - 1}{\gamma}\, w_t,$$

which we can write

$$\frac{1}{h}\frac{i}{y} + \frac{e^{\gamma h} - 1}{\gamma h}\frac{w}{y} - \frac{p}{y} = 0 \tag{22}$$

(14) can now be rewritten

$$(r - \lambda - \delta)\,\frac{w}{y} - r\frac{p}{y} = -(\gamma + \lambda + \delta) \tag{23}$$

Equations (21), (22), (23) can be treated as three simultaneous equations for $\frac{i}{y}$, $\frac{w}{y}$, and $\frac{p}{y}$ (which are all constant in a state of steady growth).

Now equation (9) provides an equation for T:

$$e^{\gamma T} = \frac{p}{w} = \frac{p/y}{w/y}. \tag{24}$$

Using the values of r, $\frac{p}{y}$, $\frac{w}{y}$ found by solving (21), (22) and (23), we obtain:

$$e^{\gamma T} = \frac{1 - \dfrac{h(\gamma + \lambda + \delta)}{s}\,\dfrac{e^{\gamma h} - 1}{\gamma h} + \dfrac{\gamma}{r}}{s} \tag{25}$$

And from (20), since $e^{\gamma T} = [e^{-(\lambda+\delta)T}]^{-\gamma/(\lambda+\delta)}$

$$e^{\gamma T} = \left[1 - \frac{\lambda + \delta}{r}\right]^{-\frac{\gamma}{\lambda+\delta}} \tag{26}$$

(25) and (26) determine T and r simultaneously in terms of the parameters λ, δ, h, s, and the steady growth rate γ (which was determined by the technical progress function). Equation (20) is not valid when $\lambda + \delta = 0$. In that case we go back to equation (6); integration gives

$$r\,T = 1, \tag{27}$$

which replaces (26) in this particular case.

13. Although (25) and (26) are rather cumbersome equations, numerical solution for particular values of the parameters presents no particular difficulty. Once T and r are calculated, simultaneous solution of (23) and (24) yields the values of $\frac{p}{y}$ and $\frac{w}{y}$ (the share of wages). Then $\frac{i}{y}$ is found from (22). A demonstration of the existence of a unique meaningful solution to the equations is given in the Appendix.

If capital stock were valued at historic cost, without any allowance for reduction in value through obsolescence, we should have

$$K = \int_{t-T}^{t} i_\tau\, n_\tau\, e^{-\delta(t-\tau)}\, d\tau,$$

and

$$Y = \int_{t-T}^{t} p_\tau\, n_\tau\, e^{-\delta(t-\tau)}\, d\tau, \tag{28}$$

so that the aggregate capital-output ratio,

$$\frac{K}{Y} = \frac{i}{p},$$

since this latter is constant.

However, when obsolescence is *foreseen* the knowledge of the share of profits, π, and of the historical cost of invested capital as shown by (28), does not enable us to calculate either net profits or the rate of profit on capital. The value of capital at any one time will be lower than K_t by the accrued provision made for obsolescence, and the appropriate obsolescence provision — which must take into account the annual reduction in the profits earned on equipment of a given vintage, as well as the retirement of equipment when it becomes T years old—cannot be calculated without knowing the capital on which the profit is earned, which in turn cannot be known without knowing the rate of profit.

14. In a state of fully-fledged golden age equilibrium, where (1) expectations are (in general) fulfilled and the expected profit on new investments is therefore the same as the realised profit, and (2) the rate of profit earned on all investment will be the same, the inequality (3) above can be replaced by an equality and regarded as an additional equation determining ρ (since i_t, p_t, w_t and T are all determined by the other equations of the system.)

$$i_t = \int_O^T e^{-(\rho+\delta)\tau} (p_t - w_{t+\tau}) \, . \, d\tau \tag{3a}$$

ρ is constant, so the familiar relation

$$\gamma + \lambda = \rho\, \sigma, \tag{29}$$

where σ is the proportion of *net* profits saved, holds; for it is easy to check that the value of capital—in terms of output to come—grows at the equilibrium growth rate $\gamma + \lambda$, and that ρ defined by (3*a*) is equal to the ratio of net profit to the stock of capital. In general, of course, σ depends on ρ, and is best calculated from the relation (29). But when $s = 1$, *i.e.*, when all (gross) profits are invested, σ must also be equal to unity, so that the rate of profit is equal to the rate of growth of output: $\rho = \gamma + \lambda$. On the face of it, it is not clear that this value of ρ satisfies (29): yet it must do. To show that it does, we use the fact that total output,

$$Y_t = \int_O^T p_{t-\tau}\, n_{t-\tau}\, e^{-\delta\tau}\, d\tau,$$

$$= p_t\, n_t \int_O^T e^{-(\gamma+\lambda+\delta)\tau}\, d\tau.$$

Thus, when we put $\rho = \gamma + \lambda$ in the right hand side of (3*a*), we get:

$$\frac{y_t}{r_t} - w_t \int_O^T e^{-(\lambda+\delta)\tau} d\tau.$$

This last integral $= \dfrac{1 - e^{-(\lambda+\delta)T}}{\lambda + \delta} = \dfrac{1}{r}$, by equation (20). Hence the right hand side of equation (3*a*) is equal to $(y_t - w_t)/r$, which is equal to i_t when $s = 1$ (by equation (21).)

If $s \neq 1$, we must find ρ from equation (3*a*). If we perform the integration (which we can do, since *p* and *w* are growing exponentially), we get the following relation, which can be solved numerically for $\rho + \delta$:

$$\frac{i}{y} = \frac{1 - e^{-(\rho+\delta)T}}{\rho + \delta} \frac{p}{y} - \frac{1 - e^{-(\rho+\delta-\gamma)T}}{\rho + \delta - \gamma} \frac{w}{y}. \tag{30}$$

Outside a golden age equilibrium a rate of profit on investment does not exist except in the sense of an *assumed* rate of profit, based on a mixture of convention and belief, which enables entrepreneurs to decide whether any particular project passes the test of adequate profitability.

15. *Some Numerical Results*

The following are the solution of the equations for various arbitrarily selected values of the parameters.[1]

For $s = 0.66$:

h years	$\lambda + \delta$%	γ %	T years	r	π %	I/Y%	i/p	$\rho+\delta$%
3	2	2	8·03	·135	8·0	5·3	·367	21·7
		2·5	8·15	·133	10·1	6·7	·459	22·1
		3	8·27	·131	12·2	8·1	·551	22·4
	4	2	8·68	·136	8·9	5·9	·401	23·0
		2·5	8·82	·135	11·2	7·5	·501	23·4
		3	8·97	·133	13·5	9·0	·601	23·7
4	2	2	11·20	·100	11·2	7·5	·672	17·0
		2·5	11·44	·098	14·1	9·6	·839	17·3
		3	11·68	·096	17·1	11·4	1·006	17·6
	4	2	12·54	·101	12·9	8·6	·759	18·2
		2·5	12·84	·100	16·3	10·9	·948	18·6
		3	13·15	·098	19·8	13·2	1·136	18·9
5	2	2	14·69	·078	14·6	9·7	1·080	14·1
		2·5	15·10	·077	18·5	12·3	1·348	14·4
		3	15·53	·075	22·4	14·9	1·615	14·7
	4	2	17·13	·081	17·8	11·9	1·267	15·4
		2·5	17·71	·079	22·5	15·0	1·579	15·7
		3	18·34	·077	27·4	16·4	1·888	16·0

[1] We are indebted to Mr. D. G. Champernowne for programming these calculations, and to the Director of the Mathematical Laboratory of Cambridge University for making the computer available.

Some representative values for different s:

s	h	$\lambda+\delta\%$	$\gamma\%$	T	r	$\pi\%$	$I/Y\%$	i/p	$\rho+\delta\%$
·33	3	2	2	20·66	·059	20·4	6·8	·955	30·6
			2·5	21·26	·058	25·6	8·5	1·169	30·8
·50	4	4	2	19·98	·073	20·7	10·3	1·207	21·7
			2·5	20·66	·071	26·2	13·1	1·490	22·0
			3	21·42	·070	31·8	15·9	1·765	22·3
	5	2	2	22·61	·055	22·2	11·1	1·655	17·0
			2·5	23·47	·053	28·1	14·0	2·038	17·3
			3	24·41	·052	34·1	17·0	2·407	17·6
1·00	4	4	2·5	6·08	·185	7·7	7·7	·387	6·5
			3	6·22	·182	9·4	9·4	·474	7·0
	5	2	2·5	7·28	·148	9·0	9·0	·561	4·5
			3	7·49	·144	11·1	11·1	·691	5·0
		4	2·5	8·20	·143	10·4	10·4	·662	6·5
			3	8·44	·140	12·7	12·7	·812	7·0

For the U.S. in the 1950's, reasonable values of the parameters are $\gamma = 2$ to $2\frac{1}{2}\%$, $\lambda + \delta = 2 - 4\%$, $s =$ ·66, $h = 4$ to 5 years. The average lifetime of equipment in manufacturing industry has been estimated at 17 years. π as indicated by the ratio of gross corporate profit after tax to the gross income originating in corporations after corporation tax has been 21%, and the ratio of business fixed capital to business gross product around 1·5. These, as the table shows, are close to the results of the model when $s =$ ·66, $h = 5$, $\lambda + \delta = 4\%$, and when γ is 2 — 2·5%.[1]

The rate of profit on investment, on the other hand, appears rather high. However it must be remembered that our equation (3) derives the rate of (net) profit from the stream of gross profit *after* tax, and not (as is usually done) from the gross profit before tax. This involves a smaller provision for obsolescence, and consequently a higher net profit, than in the usual method of calculation. It also implies that in " grossing up " for tax, the relevant rate is the effective tax charge on profits before depreciation, and not the rate of tax on profits net of depreciation. Hence, if the tax on corporation profits is one third of gross profits before tax, a rate of net profit (net of tax) of 12·5 per cent (assuming $\lambda = 1\%$, $\delta = 3\%$) corresponds to a rate of net profit *before* tax of 18·5 per cent.[2]

It can be seen from the figures, too, that π and i/p are quite sensitive to changes in the technical progress function (i.e. in γ), and highly sensitive to changes in s and h, but stable

[1] It should be borne in mind, of course, that no allowance was made in the model for net investment in working capital (inventory accumulation) which would affect the values of T, π, I/Y and i/p, but the effect of which can be subsumed in h. Equally, the model assumes that government savings and investment are equal—i.e., that there is no financial surplus or deficit arising out of government operations, and that personal savings and personal investments (mainly in housing) are equal.

[2] U.S. estimates put the average rate of profit on (business) investment 16 per cent before tax and 8 per cent after tax.

for changes in λ and δ. T is only sensitive to changes in s and h, but *not* to γ. These results may sound surprising at first. One would expect T to be inversely related to γ, and one would also expect r ($= n_t/N_t$) to be positively correlated with ($\lambda + \delta$). However, a rise in γ leads to a rise in i/p, and hence of π, which more than compensates for the rise in γ in determining the associated change in T; a rise in ($\lambda + \delta$) reduces (as between one steady growth equilibrium and another) the amount of labour released through obsolescence in relation to the current labour force (since the labour force T years ago was that much smaller, when λ is larger; and of the equipment built T years ago so much less survives to be scrapped when δ is larger) so that it compensates for the increase in ($\lambda + \delta$), leaving the value of r pretty much the same.

16. *General Conclusions*

The model shows technical progress—in the specific form of the rate of improvement of the design, etc., of newly produced capital equipment—as the main engine of economic growth, determining not only the rate of growth of productivity but—together with other parameters—also the rate of obsolescence, the average lifetime of equipment, the share of investment in income, the share of profits, and the relationship between investment and potential output (*i.e.*, the " capital/output ratio " on new capital).

The model is Keynesian in its mode of operation (entrepreneurial expenditure decisions are primary; incomes, etc., are secondary) and severely *non*-neo-classical in that technological factors (marginal productivities or marginal substitution ratios) play no role in the determination of wages and profits. A " production function " in the sense of a single-valued relationship between *some* measure of capital, K_t, the labour force N_t and of output Y_t (all at time t) clearly does not exist. Everything depends on past history, on how the collection of equipment goods which comprises K_t has been built up. Thus Y_t will be greater for a given K_t (as measured by historical cost) if a greater part of the existing capital stock is of more recent creation; this would be the case, for example, if the rate of growth of population has been accelerating.

Whilst " machines " earn quasi-rents which are all the smaller the older they are (so that, for the oldest surviving machine, the quasi-rents are zero) it would be wrong to say that the position of the marginal " machine " determines the share of quasi-rents (or gross profits) in total income. For the total profit is determined quite independently of the structure of these " quasi-rents " by equation (5), i.e., by the factors determining the share of investment in output and the proportion of profits saved and therefore the position of the " marginal " machine is itself fully determined by the other equations of the system. It is the macro-economic condition specified in (5), and not the age-and-productivity structure of machinery, which will determine what the (aggregate) share of quasi-rents will be.

This technical progress function is quite consistent with a technological " investment function ", i.e., a functional relationship (shifting in time) between investment per worker and output per worker.[1] However, owing to anticipated obsolescence and to uncertainty, it would not be correct to say that the " marginal product " of investment, dp_t/di_t, plays

[1] On the relationship of a technical progress function and a production function c.f. John Black, " The Technical Progress Function and The Production Function," *Economica*, May 1962. Whilst it is possible to make assumptions under which a technical progress function is merely one way of representing an (ex-ante) production function of constant elasticity which shifts at some pre-determined rate in time, the postulate of a technical progress function is also consistent with situations in which the rate of technical progress does not proceed at some pre-determined rate (where the shift of the " curve " is bound up with the movement *along* the " curve ") and where therefore one cannot associate a unique production function with a given " state " of knowledge.

a role in determining the amount per man. Since the profitability of operating the equipment is expected to diminish in time, the marginal addition to the stream of profits (which we may call the " marginal value productivity ") will be something quite different from the marginal product in the technological sense, and unlike the latter, it will not be a derivative of a technological function alone but will depend on the whole system of relationships. Further, owing to the prevailing attitude to uncertainty, it would not even be correct to say that " profit-maximising " will involve adding to investment per man until the marginal increment in anticipated profits, discounted at the ruling rate of interest or at some " assumed " rate of profit becomes equal to the marginal addition to investment. Whenever the desire to recover the cost of investment within a certain number of years—owing to the greater uncertainty of the more distant future—becomes the operative restriction (as is assumed in equation (4)), investment per man will be cut short before this marginal condition is satisfied.

The inequality (3) together with equation (4) enables us to specify an investment function in terms of the parameters of the system which determine both n_t and i_t without regard to the relationship between the expected rate of profit on investment and the rate of interest. In previous " Keynesian " models the existence of an independent investment function was closely tied to the postulate of some relationship between the " marginal efficiency " of investment and—an independently determined—rate of interest. This was a source of difficulty, since it either caused such models to be " over-determined "[1] or else it required the postulate that the capital/output ratio (or the amount of investment per worker) itself varied with the excess of the rate of profit over the money rate of interest[2]. The weakness of this latter approach has been that it assigned too much importance to the rate of interest. So long as one could assume that the rate of interest was a constant, determined by some psychological minimum (the " pure " liquidity preference of Keynesian theory), this did not matter very much. But it was unsatisfactory to rely on the *excess* of the rate of profit over the rate of interest as an important element—determining the chosen capital/output ratio and through that, the other variables—considering that this excess is under the control of the monetary authorities; if the authorities were to follow a policy of keeping the money rate of interest in some constant relationship to the rate of profit—which they may be easily tempted to do—this would have endowed them with an importance in the general scheme of things which is quite contrary to common experience.

The present model, by contrast, allows the money rate of interest to move up and down, without the slightest effect on investment decisions, provided such movements do not violate certain constraints.[3] This is in much better accord with the oft-repeated assertions of business men (both in the U.K. and the U.S.) that the rate of interest has *no* influence on their investment decisions at least as far as investment in fixed capital is concerned.

Finally there is the question how far the postulate of a " technical progress function " as specified in (2) implies some restraint on the *nature* of technological change. Every change in the rate of investment per worker implies a change in the extent to which new ideas (" innovations ") are actually exploited. Since the " capital saving " innovations—which increase the output/capital ratio as well as the output/labour ratio—are much more profitable to the entrepreneur than the " labour-saving " ones that yield the same rate of

[1] Cf. R. C. O. Matthews, " The Rate of Interest in Growth Models," *Oxford Economic Papers*, October 1960, pp. 249-268.

[2] Cf. Kaldor, " Capital Accumulation and Economic Growth," *op. cit.*, pp. 217.

[3] For it must still remain true, of course, that the expected rate of profit on (fixed) investment must exceed the rate of interest by more than some minimum compensation for the " illiquidity " or other risks.

increase in labour productivity, clearly the former are exploited first and the balance of technological change will appear more "capital-using" (all the less "capital-saving") the greater the rate of increase in investment per man. There is therefore always *some* rate of increase in investment per worker which allows output per man to grow at the same rate as investment per man and in that sense takes on the appearance of "neutral" technical progress; to assume that this rate of increase in investment per man remains unchanged over time implies also assuming that the relative importance of "capital saving" and "capital using" innovations in the total flow of innovations remains unchanged. To assume this is really implied in the assumption that the rate of technical progress is *constant*; since a growing incidence of "capital saving" innovations is the same thing as an upward drift in the technical progress function, and *vice versa*. Therefore the only sense in which the technical progress function postulates some "neutral" technical progress is the sense in which "unneutral" technical progress necessarily involves either a continuous acceleration or deceleration in the rate of increase in productivity for any given value of $\dot{i}/i$.

The main "practical" conclusion for economic policy that emerges from this model is that any scheme leading to the accelerated retirement of old equipment (such as a tax on the use of obsolete plant and equipment) is bound to accelerate for a temporary period the rate of increase in output per head $\dot{y}/y$, since it will increase n_t (the number of workers "available" for new machines) and hence I_t; and will thus involve a reduction in p_t/y_t. A more permanent cure, however, requires stimulating the technical dynamism of the economy (*raising* the technical progress function) which is not only (or perhaps mainly) a matter of more scientific education and more expenditure on research, but of higher quality business management which is more alert in searching for technical improvements and less resistant to their introduction.

Cambridge.

NICHOLAS KALDOR.

JAMES A. MIRRLEES.

APPENDIX

We must enquire whether the solution of the equations for a state of steady growth is unique. Equation (25) is a linear equation for $e^{\gamma T}$ in terms of $\frac{1}{r}$; it can be represented on a diagram, with $\frac{1}{r}$ measured along one axis and $e^{\gamma T}$ along the other, by a straight line.

Equation (26), on the other hand, represents a curve of increasing slope (as shown in the diagram). The curve representing equation (26), BB', passes through the point $e^{\gamma T} = 1$, $\frac{1}{r} = 0$; AA', which represents equation (25), has $e^{\gamma T} < 1$ when $\frac{1}{r} = 0$.

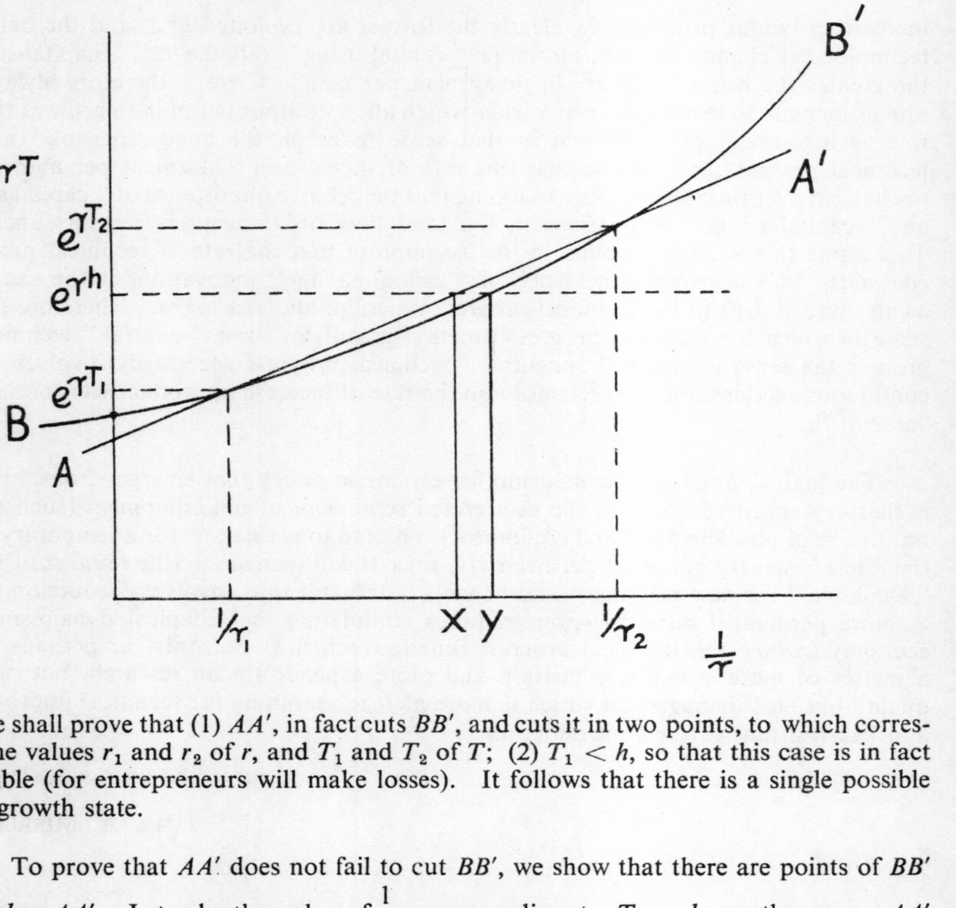

We shall prove that (1) AA', in fact cuts BB', and cuts it in two points, to which correspond the values r_1 and r_2 of r, and T_1 and T_2 of T; (2) $T_1 < h$, so that this case is in fact impossible (for entrepreneurs will make losses). It follows that there is a single possible steady growth state.

(1) To prove that AA' does not fail to cut BB', we show that there are points of BB' lying *below* AA'. Let x be the value of $\frac{1}{r}$ corresponding to $T = h$ on the curve AA' (*i.e.*, found by solving equation (25)); and let y be the value of $\frac{1}{r}$ corresponding to $T = h$ on the curve BB' (i.e., found by solving equation (26)).

Then

$$\gamma\, x = e^{\gamma h}\left[1 - \frac{h(\gamma + \lambda + \delta)}{s}\right] + \frac{h(\gamma + \lambda + \delta)}{s}\;\frac{e^{\gamma h} - 1}{\gamma^{h}} - 1$$

$$= e^{\gamma h} - 1 - \frac{(\gamma + \lambda + \delta)}{\gamma\, s}\,[\gamma h \,.\, e^{\gamma h} - e^{\gamma h} + 1]$$

$$= \gamma\, h + \tfrac{1}{2}(\gamma h)^2 + \tfrac{1}{6}(\gamma\, h)^3 + \ldots$$

$$- \frac{\gamma + \lambda + \delta}{\gamma s}\,[\tfrac{1}{2}(\gamma\, h)^2 + \tfrac{1}{3}(\gamma\, h)^3 + \tfrac{1}{8}(\gamma\, h)^4 + \;\ldots]$$

$$= \gamma\, h + \tfrac{1}{2}(\gamma\, h)^2\left[1 - \frac{\gamma + \lambda + \delta}{\gamma\, s}\right] + \tfrac{1}{6}(\gamma\, h)^3\left[1 - 2\,\frac{\gamma + \lambda + \delta}{\gamma\, s}\right]$$

$$+ \tfrac{1}{24} (\gamma h)^4 \left[1 - 3 \frac{\gamma + \lambda + \delta}{\gamma s} \right] + \dots$$

Clearly $\gamma + \lambda + \delta > \gamma s$, so that all the terms in square brackets are negative. Hence:

$$\gamma x < \gamma h - \tfrac{1}{2}(\gamma h)^2 \left[\frac{\gamma + \lambda + \delta}{\gamma s} - 1 \right],$$

so that $\quad \gamma x < \gamma h - \tfrac{1}{2} \gamma h^2 \,.\, (\lambda + \delta),$ (28)

since $s \leqq 1$

$$\text{Also, } \gamma y = \frac{\gamma}{\lambda + \delta} (\lambda + \delta)\, y = \frac{\gamma}{\lambda + \delta} \left[1 - e^{-(\lambda + \delta)h}\right]$$

$$> \frac{\gamma}{\lambda + \delta} \left[(\lambda + \delta)h - \tfrac{1}{2} (\lambda + \delta)^2 h^2\right]$$

$$= \gamma h - \tfrac{1}{2} \gamma h^2 (\lambda + \delta),$$

which, as we have just shown, $> \gamma x$.

Hence $y > x$;

which is to say, that when $T = h$, the curve BB' lies to the right of AA'. Hence AA' meets BB'; for AA' cuts the $e^{\gamma T}$-axis below BB', and BB' eventually rises above AA'.

(2) It also follows from the fact that BB' lies to the right of AA' when $T = h$ that one of the points at which AA' and BB' cut has $t < h$; i.e., $T_1 < h$. Thus only T_2 (which is $> h$) is a possible value for T.

What we have shown is that there exists a single possible solution to our equations for the state of steady growth at rate γ. [The case $\lambda + \delta = 0$ follows in the same way; from (28), $\gamma x < \gamma h$; and $h = y$ in this case.]

14 Rate of Profit and Income Distribution in Relation to the Rate of Economic Growth[1]

L. L. PASINETTI

One of the most exciting results of the macro-economic theories which have recently been elaborated in Cambridge is a very simple relation connecting the rate of profit and the distribution of income to the rate of economic growth, through the inter-action of the different propensities to save. The interesting aspect of this relation is that—by utilizing the Keynesian concepts of income determination by effective demand and of investment as a variable independent of consumption and savings—it gives a neat and modern content to the deep-rooted old Classical idea of a certain connection between distribution of income and capital accumulation. In this sense, it represents a break with the hundred-year-old tradition of marginal theory, and it is no wonder that it has immediately become the target of attacks and eulogies of such strongly emotional character. Approval and rejection have almost invariably coincided with the commentators' marginalistic or non-marginalistic view.

The purpose of this paper is to present a more logical reconsideration of the whole theoretical framework, regarded as a system of necessary relations to achieve full employment. A proof will be given that the model, as originally formulated, cannot be maintained. However, once the necessary modifications are introduced, the conclusions which emerge appear much more general and—it seems to me—much more interesting than the authors themselves thought them to be.

1. A Post-Keynesian Theory of Income Distribution and of the Rate of Profit

The profit and distribution theory which is common to a number of macro-dynamic models recently elaborated in Cambridge[2] has emerged as a development of the Harrod-

[1] I have received helpful comments and criticism on a first draft of this paper from almost all my colleagues in Cambridge. I should like to thank them all.

[2] The theory of distribution is due to Nicholas Kaldor, who put it forward in "Alternative Theories of Distribution," *The Review of Economic Studies*, 1955-56. The relation of the rate of profit to the rate of growth has a longer story. In the thirties, J. von Neumann and also N. Kaldor, while still accepting a marginal productivity theory of the rate of interest, analysed the case of a slave economy, showing that the rate of growth is maximum when it is equal to the rate of interest. (J. von Neumann, " A Model of General Economic Equilibrium," *The Review of Economic Studies* 1945-46, a paper first presented at a seminar of Princeton University in 1932; N. Kaldor, "The Controversy on the Theory of Capital," *Econometrica* 1937, p. 228 and ff.). It was, however, only with the recent macro-dynamic models that the causal link has been reversed. A relation of *dependence* of the rate of profit on the rate of growth appeared first, in the form of verbal statements supplemented with an arithmetical example, in Joan Robinson, *The Accumulation of Capital*, London 1956, p. 255, and then, in the shape of a formal equation, in Nicholas Kaldor, " A Model of Economic Growth," *The Economic Journal*, 1957. The same formal relations have been adopted by D. G. Champernowne, " Capital Accumulation and the Maintenance of Full Employment," *The Economic Journal*, 1958, and by Richard F. Kahn, " Exercises in the Analysis of Growth," *Oxford Economic Papers*, 1959.

Domar model of economic growth.[1] As is well known, all these models are theories of *long-run equilibrium*. They consider full employment systems where the possibilities of economic growth are externally given by population increase and technical progress. Therefore, the amount of investment—in physical terms — necessary in order to keep full employment through time, is also externally given. The interesting device which has made the analytical formulation of these models so simple and manageable consists in assuming that the externally given possibilities of growth increase at a *steady proportional rate* through time, i.e., according to an exponential function. When this happens, and the corresponding investments are actually carried out, all economic quantities grow in time at the same proportional rate of growth, so that all the ratios among them (investment to income, savings to income, rate of profits, etc.) remain constant. The system expands though keeping all proportions constant.

Now, for any given rate of population growth and of (neutral) technical progress[2]—i.e. for any given *natural rate of growth*, in Harrod's terminology—there is only one saving ratio which keeps the system in equilibrium growth. This sounds an awkwardly rigid conclusion. But the Cambridge economists have gone on to show that an externally given *aggregate* saving ratio is not incompatible with independently given individual propensities to save, because the aggregate ratio is simply a weighted average of individual ratios, where the weights represent individual shares in national income. Therefore, within certain limits, there is always a distribution of income at which the system produces the required amount of savings.

On this problem it is useful to follow the neat and simple formulation given by Mr. Kaldor.[3] Consider total net income (Y) as divided into two broad categories, wages and profits (W and P); and total net savings as also divided into two categories, workers' savings (S_w) and capitalists' savings (S_c), so that

$$Y \equiv W + P, \tag{1}$$

$$S \equiv S_w + S_c. \tag{2}$$

Suppose now simple proportional savings functions $S_w = s_w W$ and $S_c = s_c P$ (where s_w and s_c, both being no less than zero and no more than unity, and $s_w \neq s_c$, represent the propensities to save of the workers and of the capitalists respectively). Suppose, moreover, that the amount of investment necessary to cope with population growth and technical progress—which we may call I —is actually carried out. (This assumption is taken to mean that in the long run—provided that the rate of profit stays above a certain minimum level, below which capitalists would refuse to invest—decisions concerning

[1] Roy F. Harrod, *Towards a Dynamic Economics*, London 1948; E. D. Domar, " Capital Expansion, Rate of Growth and Employment," *in Econometrica* 1946.

[2] The concept of " neutral " technical progress—defined as such that, at the same rate of interest, the capital-output ratio remains unchanged—is another concept introduced by Harrod (*op. cit.* pp. 22-23). Jointly with the hypothesis of an exponential growth of productivity and of population, it makes the formulation of all these model extremely simple.

[3] N. Kaldor, " Alternative Theories of Distribution "*op. cit.*

investment are governed by the possibilities of expansion of the markets.) The condition under which the system will remain in a dynamic equilibrium, namely

$$I = S, \tag{3}$$

has straightforward implications. Substituting from the saving functions:

$$I = s_w W + s_c P = s_w Y + (s_c - s_w)P,$$

whence

$$\frac{P}{Y} = \frac{1}{s_c - s_w} \frac{I}{Y} - \frac{s_w}{s_c - s_w}, \tag{4}$$

and

$$\frac{P}{K} = \frac{1}{s_c - s_w} \frac{I}{K} - \frac{s_w}{s_c - s_w} \frac{Y}{K}, \tag{5}$$

which means that there is a distribution of income between wages and profits—equation (4) —and a corresponding rate of profit—equation (5)—at which the equilibrium condition (3) remains satisfied through time. Two particular cases of special interest arise when $s_w = 0$, so that (5) becomes

$$\frac{P}{K} = \frac{1}{s_c} \frac{I}{K},$$

and when $s_c = 1$ (besides $s_w = 0$) in which case, (5) simply reduces to

$$\frac{P}{K} = \frac{I}{K}.$$

It is the two more general equations (4) and (5) which have been considered so far as expressing what we may call the post-Keynesian theory of income distribution and of the rate of profit. To them we must add two restrictions, in order to limit the validity of the mathematical formulations to the range in which they have an economic meaning:

$$s_w < \frac{I}{Y}, \tag{6}$$

and

$$s_c > \frac{I}{Y}. \tag{7}$$

Restriction (6) excludes the case of a dynamic equilibrium with a null or negative share of profit, and restriction (7) excludes the case of a dynamic equilibrium with a null or negative share of wages. In practice, if (6) were not satisfied, the system would enter a situation of chronic Keynesian underemployment. Similarly, if (7) were not satisfied the system would enter a situation of chronic inflation. (As a matter of fact the latter limit becomes operative much before s_c even approaches $\frac{I}{Y}$, because there is a minimum level below which the wage-rate cannot be compressed). It is within these limits that the above model is meant to apply, and that equations (4) and (5) show the existence of a distribution of income and a rate of profit which, through time, will keep the system in equilibrium.

But Mr. Kaldor has gone further. He has pointed out that, if there is in the system a price mechanism by which the level of prices with respect to the money wages (i.e. profit margins) is determined by demand; and if $s_c > s_w$—which after all is implied by (6)-(7)—then income distribution (4) and rate of profit (5) will not only exist but also will be the ones that the system actually tends to produce.

2. A Correction

There is a logical slip, in the theory reported above, which has so far passed unnoticed. The authors have neglected the important fact that, in any type of society, when any individual saves a part of his income, he must also be allowed to own it, otherwise he would not save at all. This means that the stock of capital which exists in the system is owned by those people (capitalists or workers) who in the past made the corresponding savings. And since ownership of capital entitles the owner to a rate of interest, if workers have saved—and thus own a part of the stock of capital (directly or through loans to the capitalists)—then they will also receive a share of the total profits. Therefore total profits themselves must be divided into two categories: profits which accrue to the capitalists and profits which accrue to the workers.

It is this distinction that is missing in the theory just considered. By attributing all profits to the capitalists it has inadvertently but necessarily implied that workers' savings are always totally transferred as a gift to the capitalists. Clearly this is an absurdity. To eliminate it, we must reformulate the model from the beginning and clear up the confusion which has been made of two different concepts of distribution of income: distribution of income between profits and wages, and distribution of income between capitalists and workers. The two concepts only coincide in the particular case in which there is no saving out of wages.

3. Reformulating the Model

For a correct reformulation of the model, we must resume equations (1), (2), (3) and add a further identity:

$$P \equiv P_c + P_w,$$

where P_c and P_w stand for profits which accrue to the capitalists and profits which accrue to the workers. The saving functions now become $S_w = s_w(W + P_w)$ and $S_c = s_c P_c$; and the equilibrium condition becomes

$$I = s_w(W + P_w) + s_c P_c = s_w Y + (s_c - s_w)P_c,$$

from which—by following exactly the same steps which led to equations (4) and (5)—we obtain

$$\frac{P_c}{Y} = \frac{1}{s_c - s_w}\,\frac{I}{Y} - \frac{s_w}{s_c - s_w}, \tag{8}$$

and

$$\frac{P_c}{K} = \frac{1}{s_c - s_w}\,\frac{I}{K} - \frac{s_w}{s_c - s_w}\,\frac{Y}{K}. \tag{9}$$

As the reader can see, the right hand sides of (8) and (9) exactly coincide with the right hand sides of (4) and (5), but the left hand sides do not. This means that the expressions used so far *do not refer to total profits*. They only refer to that part of profits which accrue to the capitalists. Let us examine the implications.

As far as the distribution theory is concerned, equation (8) still retains a definite, but restricted, meaning. It now only expresses the distribution of income between capitalists and workers. The distribution of income between profits and wages is something different, and to obtain it, one must add the share of workers' profit into income $\left(\frac{P_w}{Y}\right)$ to both sides of equation (8). As to the theory of the rate of profit, the consequences of our reformulation are even more serious. Expression (9) simply represents the ratio of a *part* of profits (P_c) to *total* capital, but this concept has no useful or interesting meaning. The expression which is really needed is one for the ratio of total profits to total capital (rate of profit), and to obtain it, we must again add a ratio $\left(\frac{P_w}{K}\right)$ to both sides of equation (9). In other words, we have to find suitable expressions for

$$\frac{P}{Y} = \frac{P_c}{Y} + \frac{P_w}{Y}, \tag{10}$$

and

$$\frac{P}{K} = \frac{P_c}{K} + \frac{P_w}{K}.$$

Let us start with the latter equation. We know $\frac{P_c}{K}$ already from (9). Thus, writing K_w for the amount of capital that the workers own indirectly—through loans to the capitalists—and r for the rate of interest on these loans, we obtain

$$\frac{P}{K} = \frac{1}{s_c - s_w}\frac{I}{K} - \frac{s_w}{s_c - s_w}\frac{Y}{K} + \frac{rK_w}{K}.$$

An expression for $\frac{K_w}{K}$ can easily be found. In dynamic equilibrium:

$$\frac{K_w}{K} = \frac{S_w}{S} = \frac{s_w(Y - P_c)}{I} = \frac{s_w s_c}{s_c - s_w}\frac{Y}{I} - \frac{s_w}{s_c - s_w},$$

which, after substitution into the previous expression, finally gives us:

$$\frac{P}{K} = \frac{1}{s_c - s_w}\frac{I}{K} - \frac{s_w}{s_c - s_w}\frac{Y}{K} + r\left(\frac{s_w s_c}{s_c - s_w}\frac{Y}{I} - \frac{s_w}{s_c - s_w}\right). \tag{11}$$

By exactly following the same procedure, the expression for equation (10) comes out as

$$\frac{P}{Y} = \frac{1}{s_c - s_w}\frac{I}{Y} - \frac{s_w}{s_c - s_w} + r\left(\frac{s_w s_c}{s_c - s_w}\frac{K}{I} - \frac{s_w}{s_c - s_w}\frac{K}{Y}\right). \tag{12}$$

These are the two general equations we were looking for. By now, we have all the elements which are necessary to correct the post-Keynesian theory of income distribution and of the rate of profit. Equation (5) of section 1, expressing the rate of profit, must be replaced by equation (11); and equation (4) must be replaced by two distinct equations: equation (8) for the distribution of income between workers and capitalists, and equation (12) for the distribution of income between wages and profits.

4. Rate and Share of Profits in Relation to the Rate of Growth

The most immediate consequence of the reformulation which has just been carried out is that, in order to say anything about share and rate of profits, one needs first *a theory of the rate of interest*. In a long run equilibrium model, the obvious hypothesis to make is that of a rate of interest equal to the rate of profit. If we do make such a hypothesis, equations (11) and (12) become very simple indeed. By substituting $\frac{P}{K}$ for r, in equation (11), we get

$$\frac{P}{K}\left(1-\frac{s_w s_c}{s_c-s_w}\,\frac{Y}{I}+\frac{s_w}{s_c-s_w}\right)=\frac{1}{s_c-s_w}\,\frac{I}{K}-\frac{s_w}{s_c-s_w}\,\frac{Y}{K},$$

$$\frac{P}{K}\,\frac{s_c(I-s_wY)}{I}=\frac{I-s_wY}{K}.$$

Whence, provided that

$$I-s_wY\neq 0, \tag{13}$$

(otherwise the ratio $\frac{P}{K}$ would be indeterminate) the whole expression simply becomes

$$\frac{P}{K}=\frac{1}{s_c}\,\frac{I}{K}. \tag{14}$$

And by an analogous process, equation (12) reduces to

$$\frac{P}{Y}=\frac{1}{s_c}\,\frac{I}{Y}. \tag{15}$$

The reader will notice that these results are formally similar to those which have been shown in section 1 as particular cases. But now they have been reached without making any assumption whatsoever on the propensities to save of the workers. This is the most striking result of our analysis. It means that, in the long run, workers' propensity to save, though influencing the distribution of income between capitalists and workers—equation (8)—does not influence the distribution of income between profits and wages—equation (15). Nor does it have any influence whatsoever on the rate of profit—equation (14) !

5. A Fundamental Relation Between Profits and Savings

The novelty of the conclusion reached in the previous section makes it perhaps worth our while trying to investigate a little more closely the logic behind it.

Let me point out immediately that the model has been built on the institutional principle, inherent in any production system, that wages are distributed among the members of society in proportion to the amount of labour they contribute and profits are distributed in proportion to the amount of capital they own. The latter proposition implies something which has passed unnoticed so far, namely that, in the long run, profits will turn out to be distributed in proportion to the amount of savings which are contributed. In other words, no matter how many categories of individuals we may consider, in a long run exponential growth, the ratio of the profits that each category receives to the savings that it provides will always be the same for all categories. In our model:

$$\frac{P_w}{S_w}=\frac{P_c}{S_c}. \tag{16}$$

This indeed sets a proportionality relation between profits and savings which is fundamental to the whole problem of profits and distribution. It means that, for each category, *profits are in the long run proportional to savings.* Let me stress that this relation does not depend on any behavioural assumption whatsoever; it simply and logically follows from the institutional principle that profits are distributed in proportion to ownership of capital.

This principle, however, still leaves the actual value of ratio (16) indeterminate, as it only requires that this ratio be the same for all categories. It is at this point that the particular types of income out of which savings are made become relevant. If there is in the system a category of individuals who—owing to the position they occupy in the production process—derive all their incomes, and therefore savings, exclusively from profits, the saving behaviour of just this group of individuals will set up, independently of (16), another and more definite relation between savings and profits. The only way in which this new behavioural relation can be compatible with (16) is for it to determine the actual value of the ratio of profits to savings for the whole system. We can see this immediately by substituting our saving functions into (16). We obtain

$$\frac{P_w}{s_w(W + P_w)} = \frac{P_c}{s_c P_c},$$

which may also be written in either of the two following ways:

$$s_w (W + P_w) = s_c P_w, \tag{17}$$

or

$$s_w W = [(1 - s_w) - (1 - s_c)]P_w. \tag{18}$$

These expressions now allow us some insight into the reason why workers' propensity to save does not, and capitalists' propensity to save does, play a role in determining *total* profits. Expression (17) says that, in the long run, when workers save, they receive an amount of profits (P_w) such as to make their total savings exactly equal to the amount that the capitalists would have saved out of workers' profits (P_w) if these profits remained to them. Expression (18) is even more explicit. Savings out of wages always turn out to be equal to workers' extra consumption out of profits (extra consumption meaning consumption in excess of what the capitalists would have consumed if those profits remained to them). Another way of interpreting these results is to say that whatever workers' propensity to save (s_w) may be, there is always a distribution of income and a distribution of profits which makes the ratio $\frac{P_w}{s_w(W + P_w)}$ equal to any pre-determined ratio $\frac{P_w}{S_w}$. Or, to look at the problem the other way round, for any given s_w, there are infinite proportions between profits and savings which can be used in (16) and which at the same time can make $\frac{P_w}{s_w(W + P_w)}$ equal to $\frac{P_w}{S_w}$. All this is, after all, a complicated way of saying that, on the part of the workers, the rate of profit is indeterminate. They will always receive, in the long run, an amount of profits proportional to their savings, whatever the rate of profit may be.

The situation is entirely different when we consider the capitalists. The fact that all capitalists' savings come out of profits sets a straight relation between savings and profits. No other variable enters into it, in contrast with the previous case where the wage share was also in the picture. It follows that, for any given s_c, there is only one proportionality relation between profits and savings—this relation being required by (16)—which can also make the ratio $\frac{P_c}{s_c P_c}$ equal to $\frac{P_c}{S_c}$. This proportionality relation can be nothing but s_c, which will therefore determine the ratio of profits to savings for all the saving groups, and consequently also the income distribution between profits and wages and the rate of interest for the whole system. The reader may complete his view of the problem by thinking for a moment of the practically irrelevant but interesting case, in which capitalists' profits are nil (i.e. $P_c = 0$). In this case, the behavioural relation ($s_c P_c$) determining the rate of profit drops out of the picture altogether and the rate of profit becomes indeterminate. (The parameter s_w, which remains, cannot determine the rate of profit!) We have met this case already in the process of finding $\frac{P}{K}$, in section 4, where non-fulfilment of (13) would exactly imply $P_c = 0$ and an indeterminate rate of profit.

6. Implications

We may now synthesize the implications of the foregoing analysis in two conclusions. First of all, the irrelevance of workers' propensity to save gives the model a much wider generality than was hitherto believed. Since the rate of profit and the income distribution between profits and wages are determined independently of s_w, there is no need for any hypothesis whatever on the *aggregate* savings behaviour of the workers. The non-capitalists might well be divided into any number of sub-categories one likes; the subdivision might even be carried as far as to consider single individuals; yet equations (14)-(15) would not change. Of course the particular behaviour of the sub-categories or single individuals would influence the distribution of income among the various workers, and between the workers and the capitalists, as equation (8) shows. But the distribution of income between total wages and total profits, and the rate of profit would remain exactly the same.

Secondly, the relevance of the capitalists' propensity to save, which is the only one to appear in the final formulae (14) and (15), uncovers the absolutely strategic importance for the whole system of the decisions to save of just one group of individuals: the capitalists. The particular saving function of this group transforms the open proportionality relation (16) into a definite function in which the proportion that profits must bear to savings *in the whole system*, is given by the saving propensity of one single category of individuals.[1] The similar decisions to save of all the other individuals, the workers, do not count in this respect. Whatever the workers may do, they can only share in an amount of total profits which for them is predetermined; they have no power to influence it at all.

These conclusions, as the reader may clearly realise, now suddenly shed new light on the old Classical idea, hinted at already at the beginning, of a relation between the savings of that group of individuals who are in the position to carry on the process of production and the process of capital accumulation. This idea has always persisted in economic literature but in a vague and muddled form. Economists have never been able to bring it out clearly. In particular they have always thought—and the post-Keynesian theories

[1] It may be useful to remind the reader that the whole analysis refers to states of long-run equilibrium. The relevant behavioural process must not necessarily be looked for in association with particular physical persons, but rather in association with specific kinds of decisions: those concerning savings out of profits as such. It must, moreover, be noticed that in a modern economic system, where large corporations have a certain autonomous power to retain profits, the profit retention ratios of the corporations and the individuals' propensities to save out of (distributed) profits add up.

examined in section 1 seemed to confirm—that the relation between capitalists' savings and capital accumulation depended on particularly simplifying and drastic assumptions about negligible savings by the workers. The novelty of the present analysis has been to show that the relation is valid independently of any of those assumptions. It is valid whatever the saving behaviour of the workers may be.

7. The Conditions of Stability

Our analysis would be incomplete if, after showing that there exists a distribution of income between profits and wages which keeps the system in long run equilibrium, we did not also specify the limits within which such distribution has economic meaning and the conditions under which it is stable.

On this problem we may recall the discussion that Mr. Kaldor has carried out already. The limits (6) and (7) of section 1 must here be confirmed. Moreover, we must confirm that if there is in the system a price mechanism by which the level of prices with respect to the level of wages (profit margins) rises or falls according as to whether demand exceeds or falls short of supply, and if equilibrium investments are actually carried out, then the system is stable. For it will tend to get back to its dynamic equilibrium path whenever displaced from it.

But we are now in a position to examine these problems in a much better way. The propositions stated above may be expressed as follows:

$$\frac{d}{dt}\left(\frac{P}{Y}\right) = f\left(\frac{I}{Y} - \frac{S}{Y}\right), \tag{19}$$

with the properties

$$f(0) = 0,$$
$$f' > 0,$$

which simply means that, as time (t) goes on, the profit margins, and therefore the share of total profits, remain constant, increase or decrease according as to whether total savings produced by the system turn out to be equal, smaller, or greater than total investments.

Equation (19) is a simple differential equation. By solving it with respect to deviations from the equilibrium share of profits,[1] the only requirement for stability emerges as

[1] Call $\left(\frac{P}{Y}\right)^*$ the equilibrium value of $\frac{P}{Y}$ at which $\frac{I}{Y} - \frac{S}{Y} = 0$. By expanding (19) in Taylor series around this equilibrium value, and neglecting the terms of higher order than the first, we obtain

$$\frac{d}{dt}\left[\frac{P}{Y} - \left(\frac{P}{Y}\right)^*\right] = f(0) + \\ + f'(0)\left[\frac{d}{d\left(\frac{P}{Y}\right)}\left(\frac{I}{Y}\right) - \frac{d}{d\left(\frac{P}{Y}\right)}\left(\frac{S}{Y}\right)\right]_{\left(\frac{P}{Y}\right)^*}\left[\frac{P}{Y} - \left(\frac{P}{Y}\right)^*\right],$$

where the last but one square brackets contain derivatives taken at the particular point $\left(\frac{P}{Y}\right)^*$, so that the whole term is constant. Calling now

$$\left[\frac{d}{d\left(\frac{P}{Y}\right)}\left(\frac{I}{Y}\right) - \frac{d}{d\left(\frac{P}{Y}\right)}\left(\frac{S}{Y}\right)\right]_{\left(\frac{P}{Y}\right)^*} = m,$$

and integrating, we obtain

$$\left[\frac{P}{Y} - \left(\frac{P}{Y}\right)^*\right]_t = \left[\frac{P}{Y} - \left(\frac{P}{Y}\right)^*\right]_0 e^{f'mt}.$$

Since $f' > 0$, the only condition for this expression to tend to zero as time goes on (i.e. for the system to be stable) is $m < 0$.

$$\frac{d}{d\left(\frac{P}{Y}\right)}\left(\frac{I}{Y}\right) < \frac{d}{d\left(\frac{P}{Y}\right)}\left(\frac{S}{Y}\right), \tag{20}$$

which means that the response of $\frac{I}{Y}$ to deviations of $\frac{P}{Y}$ from its equilibrium value must be smaller than the response of $\frac{S}{Y}$. But, in our model, there can be no response of $\frac{I}{Y}$ to $\frac{P}{Y}$ because I has been defined as that amount of investments which has to be undertaken in order to keep full employment over time. This amount of investments, as a proportion of total income, is uniquely determined from outside the economic system, by technology and population growth[1]; and the share of profits can in no way alter it. Therefore $\frac{d}{d\left(\frac{P}{Y}\right)}\left(\frac{I}{Y}\right) = 0$. We are thus left with the right hand side of (20) required to be greater than zero. After substituting from the savings functions,

$$\frac{d}{d\left(\frac{P}{Y}\right)}\left(\frac{S}{Y}\right) = \frac{d}{d\left(\frac{P}{Y}\right)}\left(s_w\frac{W}{Y} + s_w\frac{P_w}{Y} + s_c\frac{P - P_w}{Y}\right) > 0. \tag{21}$$

[1] Those readers who have been brought up in the neo-classical tradition might think that I am implicitly assuming the existence of only one technique of production. Since I am not, it may be useful to clarify the issue by making explicit the implications of the foregoing analysis for what has been called the *neo-classical* theory of economic growth (as expounded, for example, by Professor Solow in a " Contribution to the Theory of Economic Growth, " *The Quarterly Journal of Economics* 1956, or by Professor Meade in *A Neo-Classical Theory of Economic Growth*, London 1961). Suppose there exists an infinite number of possible techniques expressed by a traditional production function

$$Y = F(K, L), \tag{1'}$$

assumed to be homogeneous of the first degree and invariant to time; and suppose that labour (L) is increasing at an externally given rate of growth n, so that $L(t) = L(0)e^{nt}$. The whole previous analysis remains unaltered. We may now read $F(K, L)$ whenever we have written Y, and we may write, if we like, the final expression (14) as

$$s_c[F(K, L) - W] = I. \tag{2'}$$

However, as we have assumed more information about technology, we can now inquire further into the composition of I. By defining $k = \frac{K}{L}$, so that $K = kL$, we may write

$$I = \frac{dK}{dt} = k\frac{dL}{dt} + L\frac{dk}{dt} = knL + L\frac{dk}{dt}.$$

Substituting into (2′), we obtain

$$s_c[F(K, L) - W] = knL + L\frac{dk}{dt}.$$

But on the steady growth path $\frac{dk}{dt} = 0$, so that the equilibrium relation is

$$s_c[F(K, L) - W] = \frac{K}{L}nL,$$

whence

$$\frac{P}{K} = \frac{n}{s_c}. \tag{3'}$$

" The equilibrium rate of profit is determined by the natural rate of growth divided by the capitalists' propensity to save; independently of anything else in the model. This basic relation is confirmed. Therefore, the link between (14) and (15) that the extra technical equation (1′) has introduced, can only go one way. Since it cannot influence the rate of profit, it can only contribute to determining the investment-income ratio. In this way the equilibrium amount of investment is uniquely and exogenously determined. All this means that the foregoing analysis has singled out one of those asymmetrical chains of relations to which in science the concept of causality is associated. This causality chain may here be expressed as follows. The externally given rate of population growth and the capitalists' propensity to save determine first of all the rate of profit. At this rate of profit, the optimum technique is chosen (in such a way as to satisfy the marginal productivity conditions). Then, the optimum technique, together with the rate of population growth, uniquely determine the equilibrium investment-income ratio. In this system, therefore, technical relation (1′) simply comes to determine one more variable—the equilibrium quantity of capital."

We may first consider an intermediate step. In the short run, the share of profits which accrue to the workers is fixed, as it takes time for the rate of interest to adapt itself to the rate of profit (even if the two coincide in the long run). And since $\dfrac{d}{d\left(\dfrac{P}{Y}\right)}\left(\dfrac{W}{Y}\right) = -1$, condition (21) becomes

$$s_c - s_w > 0.$$

This is exactly the stability condition given by Mr. Kaldor. The above analysis proves that it is only a short-run condition.

But let us consider the long run, when the share of workers' profits is no longer fixed and P_w adapts itself to a proportion of K_w equal to the proportion that P_c bears to K_c. By substitution from (18), condition (21) simply becomes

$$s_c > 0.$$

This is all that is required. We may conclude that, in a system where full employment investments are actually carried out, and prices are flexible with respect to wages, the only condition for stability is $s_c > 0$, a condition which is certainly and abundantly satisfied even outside the limits in which the mathematical model has an economic meaning.

8. The Case of a Socialist System

Going back now to our basic model, the reader will notice how few, after all, are the assumptions which have been used. These assumptions become even fewer if we consider the case of a socialist system.

In a socialist society, all the members of the community belong to the category of workers. There is no place for capitalists; the responsibility for carrying on the production process and the direct ownership of all means of production are taken over by the State. However, the State, as such, cannot consume: consumption can be carried out only by individuals. Therefore, if any amount of the national product is not distributed to the members of the community, either as wages or as interest on their loans to the State, that amount is *ipso facto* saved. This means that the parameter s_c becomes unity ($s_c = 1$), as an inherent property of the system; so that even the one behavioural parameter that still remained in our final formulae, disappears.

Equations (14) and (15) become:

$$\frac{P}{Y} = \frac{I}{Y}, \tag{22}$$

and

$$\frac{P}{K} = \frac{I}{K}, \tag{23}$$

with the evident meaning that, in equilibrium, total profits are equal to total investments, and the rate of profit (and of interest) is equal to the ratio of investment to capital, i.e. equal to the *natural* rate of growth. It follows that total wages always turn out to be equal to total consumption and total profits always turn out to be equal to total savings. However, this does not mean that all wages are consumed and all profits are saved! The (22)-(23), have been reached without any assumption whatsoever on individual decisions to save. Each individual may be left completely free to decide the proportion of his income (wages plus interest) that he likes to save, without in the least affecting the (22)-(23). This result is simply the counterpart, for a socialist system, of what has been pointed out in section 4 as the most striking outcome of our analysis.

An explanation can be given by following the same procedure used in section 5, which here becomes even simpler. By putting $s_c = 1$ in (18), the interesting property immediately emerges that, in a dynamic equilibrium, individual savings out of wages are exactly equal to individual consumption out of interest; so that total consumption (out of wages and out of interests) turns out to be equal to total wages.

The important corollary that follows is that there is no need for a socialist State to exert any interference whatsoever in individual decisions to consume and to save. Only one limit must be respected, a limit which is the same encountered in the case of a capitalist system and expressed by inequality (6). The community, as a whole, cannot remain in equilibrium if it insists in saving more than what is required by the *natural* rate of growth; if it did, the system would fall into a situation of chronic under-employment due to lack of effective demand.[1] Provided that this limit is not overcome, no restriction need be put on individual savings. The only effect of these savings is to require from the State the issuing of a national debt for a part of the stock of capital, and the consequent distribution of a part of profits, which will however come back under the form of lent savings.

To conclude, we may put these results in the following way. In a full employment economic system in which all net revenues that accrue to the organizers of the process of production are saved, there exists one particular rate of interest, which we may indeed call the *natural rate of interest*—since it turns out to be equal to the natural rate of growth—which has the following property. If it is applied both in the process of pricing and in the payment of interest on loans, it causes the system, *whatever the individual decisions to save may be*, to produce a total amount of savings which is exactly equal to the amount of investment needed to cope with technical progress and population growth.

9. Models and Reality

At this point, the reader may have become a little impatient and may begin to wonder: But what is after all the practical relevance of the whole macro-economic exercise?

There are two different problems raised by this question. The first one concerns aggregation. It must be noticed that the foregoing investigation is not " macro-economic " in the sense of representing a first simplified rough step towards a more detailed and disaggregated analysis. It is macro-economic because it could not be otherwise. Only problems have been discussed which are of a macro-economic nature; an accurate investigation of them has nothing to do with disaggregation. They would remain the same—i.e. they would still arise at a macro-economic level—even if we were to break down the model into a disaggregated analysis, and therefore introduce the necessary additional information (or assumptions) about consumers' choice of goods and producers' choice of techniques. I might add that in fact, the present paper has originated from a *multi-sector* growth model, on which I have been working for some time, and whose results have turned out to be incompatible with the post-Keynesian theories examined in section 1.

A second and separate problem concerns the interpretative value of the model. When

[1] We are considering, of course, a closed system. In an open system, in which the State might lend abroad, full employment might be kept even if total savings go beyond required total investments.

Mr. Kaldor presented his theory of income distribution, he pointed out that the interpretative value of the theory depends on the Keynesian hypotheses on which it is built. In particular it depends on the crucial hypothesis (post-Keynesian rather than Keynesian) that investment can be treated as an independent variable governed by technical progress and population growth.

But this is not the approach that I should like to take here. Whether we are or whether we are not prepared to accept the model in this behavioural sense, there are important practical implications which are valid in any case. I should look, therefore, at the previous analysis simply and more generally as a logical framework to answer interesting questions about what *ought* to happen if full employment is to be kept over time, more than as a behavioural theory expressing what actually happens.

The case of a socialist system, which came last in our analysis, is the most straightforward on this respect. The amount of investments that must be undertaken in order to maintain full employment—once this has been reached—is indeed that which is required by technical progress and population growth. And if these investments are carried out, the rate of profit (when uniformly applied) must be equal to the natural rate of growth, if total demand is to be such as to allow the full utilization of the productive capacity and of the labour force. These results do not depend on any behavioural assumption whatsoever. They are true whatever individual behaviour may be; as a simple matter of logical necessity.

In the case of a capitalist system, the additional problem arises of whether the capitalists will or will not spontaneously undertake the amount of investments necessary to cope with the natural possibilities of growth. We may of course discuss at length in this case the circumstances under which equilibrium will or will not be automatically reached. But again we should not let these discussions obscure the conclusions, which are valid in any case, about the relations that must be satisfied if full employment is to be kept. If full employment is to be maintained, *that* amount of investment *must* be undertaken. And if it is undertaken; there is—for any given proportion of capitalists' income which tends to be saved[1]—only one rate of profit, i.e. one distribution of income between profits and wages, that keeps the system on the dynamic path of full employment.

This, it seems to me, is the relevant way to look at the model which has been elaborated above. The whole analysis has been carried out with constant reference to a situation of full employment because full employment is the situation that matters, and that indeed, now-a-days, forms one of the agreed goals of any economic system. The conclusions, therefore, acquire an important practical relevance whether the system is automatically able to reach full employment or whether it is not. In the latter case, I should say that they become even more important, because it is then that practical measures have to be taken and it becomes essential to have clear ideas about the direction in which to move.

Cambridge. LUIGI L. PASINETTI

[1] Let me point out that, in this context, the objection so commonly advanced against the theory formulated in section 1—namely, that to classify the members of a modern society in only two groups is an arbitrary and crude simplification—entirely loses its ground. The central outcome of the previous analysis has just been to show that, as far as the determination of the rate of profit is concerned, the distinction between individuals who save exclusively out of profits and individuals who save out of wages is the only one that matters.

15 The Neoclassical Theorem and Distribution of Income and Wealth [1]

K. SATO

1. The neoclassical theorem, provided by Mrs Robinson and others, states that *per capita* consumption is maximized in the state of balanced growth (or the *Golden Age*) if the rate of profit is equal to the rate of growth. In such a state, the average saving ratio should be equal to the relative profit share. Except for this condition, " it does not matter at all who does the saving so long as the rate of profit is equal to the rate of growth," in Mrs Robinson's words ([1], p. 226). Commenting on this theorem, Samuelson states that " it has nothing essential to do with saving propensities " in the sense that " it is really a theorem about technology and production " ([1], p. 251). An identical comment is also given by Solow ([1], p. 257).

These statements are true but yet misleading in some important respects. In a private-enterprise economy, savings by capitalists and workers lead to wealth accumulation in their hands and affect further income distribution. Therefore, the neoclassical theorem must have particular implications about individual propensities to save and income and wealth distributions. Consider a case where capitalists remain capitalists and workers remain workers, no matter how much wealth they accumulate. (We shall call this the case of no capital transfer.) The present paper will show that the situation envisaged by the neo-classical theorem requires that the capitalists' propensity to save should be unity or that the workers' propensity to save should be equal to the relative profit share. In this sense, the neoclassical theorem is not entirely independent of the distribution and spending sides of the economy.

2. Following neoclassical tradition, assume that there is an aggregate production function, continuous and differentiable, subject to constant returns to scale

$$Y = F(K, L) \qquad \text{...(1)}$$

where Y, K and L are output (net of depreciation), capital and labour. (Time subscripts are omitted.) For the sake of simplicity, assume that technology remains unchanged over time. Labour grows at a constant exponential rate, n, i.e.

$$L = L_0 e^{nt}. \qquad \text{...(2)}$$

(1) can be rewritten as

$$y = f(k) \qquad \text{...(1a)}$$

where y is output per man (Y/L), k capital per man (K/L), and $f(k) = F(k, 1)$.

The neoclassical theorem can be derived very simply as follows: in balanced growth, capital grows at the same rate as labour. Hence, net investment is represented by nK along the balanced growth path. Then, per capita consumption is given by

$$c = y - nk. \qquad \text{...(3)}$$

Clearly, c is maximized at $k = k^*$ which satisfies

$$f'(k^*) = n. \qquad \text{...(4)}$$

[1] The views expressed in this paper are the author's private views and do not necessarily reflect the views of the United Nations. I would like to make acknowledgement to the referee, whose comments contributed to expository improvements.

Thus, when the neoclassical theorem holds, the equilibrium profit rate, i.e. the marginal product of capital, is equal to the growth rate. At the same time, net investment is equal to net profits.

3. In the proof given above, nothing has been said about individual propensities to save or distribution of income and wealth. Thus, Mrs Robinson and others are justified in considering the neoclassical theorem to be of a purely technological character. However, this independence of the neoclassical theorem from propensities to save is only superficial. We may examine this neglected aspect of the theorem by explicitly considering income and wealth distributions.

On the assumption of perfect competition, the wage rate (w) and the profit rate (r) are determined by the marginal products of labour and capital. Hence,

$$w = f(k) - kf'(k) \qquad \text{...(5)}$$

and

$$r = f'(k). \qquad \text{...(6)}$$

Output is distributed between wages and profits, i.e.

$$Y = wL + rK.$$

We denote by π the relative profit share, i.e.

$$\pi = \frac{rK}{Y}.$$

As both capitalists and workers do save, profits are further distributed between them as property income.[1] For the sake of simplicity, assume that such distribution is made at the current profit rate to all equity holders. Denote by K_p and K_w the equities held by capitalists and workers, i.e.

$$K = K_p + K_w.$$

We define the capitalists' wealth share by

$$z = K_p/K. \qquad \text{...(7)}$$

The workers' total income is now given by $(wL + rK_w)$ and the capitalists' total income by rK_p. Now assume that capitalists save $100s_p$ per cent and workers $100s_w$ per cent of their respective income. On *a priori* grounds, we assume that the capitalists' propensity to save is larger than the workers' propensity to save,[2] i.e.

$$1 \geqq s_p > s_w \geqq 0. \qquad \text{...(8)}$$

Assume that there is no capital transfer between the workers and the capitalists.[3] Then, we have

$$\dot{K}_p = s_p r K_p \quad \text{and}$$
$$\dot{K}_w = s_w(wL + rK_w). \qquad \text{...(9)}$$

The equations given above determine the time paths of all variables concerned. As is well known, these time paths converge toward those of balanced growth, which are of immediate interest for the neoclassical theorem.[4] In order to get the balanced growth solution, we shall first reduce these equations to two differential equations in k and z only.

[1] See Pasinetti [2]. In this respect, capitalists are treated as rentiers receiving dividends.
[2] Note that this is the short-run stability condition in the Kaldorian theory of income distribution.
[3] This assumption is implicit in Pasinetti [2].
[4] The stability conditions of the balanced growth path in a two-sector model with this type of saving behaviour and income and wealth distributions are discussed in detail in [3].

From (8) and (9), we have

$$\frac{\dot{K}}{K} = [s_p z + s_w(1-z)]r + s_w \frac{w}{k}.$$

Hence,

$$\frac{\dot{k}}{k} = (s_p - s_w)zf'(k) + s_w \frac{f(k)}{k} - n, \qquad \text{...(10)}$$

which determines the time path of the capital-labour ratio. The relative wealth share z is also subject to change over time. By differentiating (7), we have

$$\frac{\dot{z}}{z} = \frac{\dot{K}_p}{K_p} - \frac{\dot{K}}{K},$$

which is transformed into

$$\frac{\dot{z}}{z} = (s_p - s_w)(1-z)f'(k) - s_w\left(\frac{f(k)}{k} - f'(k)\right). \qquad \text{...(11)}$$

4. The balanced growth solution of (10) and (11) are given by the stationary values of k and z satisfying the two equations. There are two such solutions. The first one is obtained by putting $\dot{k} = 0$ in (10) and $\dot{z}/z = 0$ in (11). We may call it Case A and denote the solution by subscript A. Adding the resulting equations together, we readily find

$$f'(k_A) = \frac{n}{s_p}. \qquad \text{...(12)}$$

Substituting (12) into (11), we get

$$1 - z_A = \frac{s_w}{s_p - s_w}\left(\frac{1}{\pi_A} - 1\right). \qquad \text{...(13)}$$

(12) states that the equilibrium profit rate is equal to the ratio of the growth rate to the capitalists' propensity to save. Therefore, the profit rate is independent of the workers' propensity to save in balanced growth.[1] This interesting property was originally discovered by Pasinetti. Comparing (12) with (4), we readily find that per capita consumption is maximized when $s_p = 1$. Thus, quite contrary to the generally accepted view, for the neoclassical theorem to hold in this case, it is necessary that the capitalists' propensity to save should be unity, while the workers' propensity to save is not relevant.[2] Note, however, that the solution is economically meaningful only if the relative wealth share lies between zero and one. From (13), we see that this condition is satisfied if and only if [3]

$$s_w \leqq s_p \pi_A, \qquad \text{...(14)}$$

i.e. if s_w is not more than the long-run equilibrium aggregate saving ratio. For $s_p = 1$, a meaningful solution exists if s_w does not exceed π^*.

5. When the workers' propensity to save violates (14), the workers' equity holding increases faster than the capitalists' equity holding. The capitalists' wealth share eventually converges to zero. This solution is obtained by putting $\dot{k} = 0$ and $z = 0$ in (10). We may call it Case B and denote the solution by subscript B.[4] We have

$$\frac{f(k_B)}{k_B} = \frac{n}{s_w} \qquad \text{...(15)}$$

1 The aggregate saving ratio is equal to $s_p \pi_A$ as if all savings were made from profits. Dividend payments to workers result in a loss of saving because of their lower propensity to save. However, this loss is exactly compensated by their saving from wages.

2 This proviso is true only in so far as we are concerned with long-run maximization.

3 Pasinetti was not aware of this side condition.

4 It can easily be verified that the Case A solution is stable if it is economically meaningful. The Case B solution is stable otherwise.

and $$z_B = 0. \qquad \text{...(16)}$$

The aggregate propensity to save is equal to s_w. Hence, corresponding to (4), we find that per capita consumption is maximized at $s_w = \pi^*$. Combining these two cases and considering the short-run stability condition, we obtain the combinations of s_p and s_w which maximize the long-run level of per capita consumption, as shown by lines *ABC* in Fig. 1.

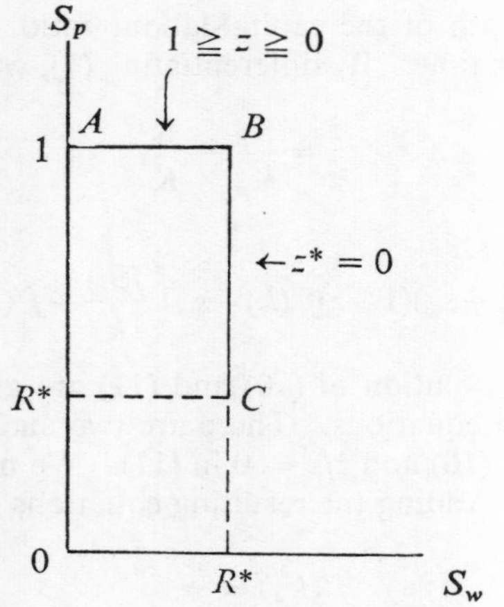

FIGURE 1

6. The extremely simple and elegant relationships obtained in the preceding sections are due to the assumption of no capital transfer, i.e. rigid segmentation between capitalists and workers. It may be that as the workers accumulate wealth, some workers would move into the capitalist class and thus capital would flow from workers to capitalists. Then, the equilibrium relationships must be modified. For instance, such capital transfer may be proportional to the workers' current equity holding. It is easy to see that this continual capital flow into the capitalist class would make the capitalists' wealth share converge to a positive fraction irrespective of the workers' propensity to save. In other words, the Case *B* solution vanishes. Similarly, in equilibrium growth, the capital-labour ratio would be larger and the profit rate lower than before. *Per capita* consumption is maximized in balanced growth for a value of s_p less than unity unless s_w is zero. Such values of s_p would be inversely related to s_w.[1] However, this modification does not alter in any essential way the point that I have made above concerning the distributional implications of the neoclassical theorem.

United Nations, New York. K. SATO.

REFERENCES

[1] " Symposium on Production Functions and Economic Growth ", *Review of Economic Studies*, **29** (June 1962).

[1] There are two cases in which the capital transfer does not play any explicit role. One is the case where workers consume all their income. z, of course, converges to one if it was originally less than one. The situation envisaged by the neoclassical theorem holds if capitalists save all their income. This is a familiar case, corresponding to point A in Fig. 1.

The second is the case where every individual saves the same proportion of his income. In this case, though the wealth share depends on the degree of capital transfer, the wealth distribution itself has no influence on the aggregate saving ratio. Hence, it is not necessary to make the wealth distribution an explicit variable. This factor may justify the use of this simple assumption in such a macroeconomic model as that of Harrod. In terms of the neoclassical theorem, this case corresponds to point C in Fig. 1.

[2] Pasinetti, L. L. " Rate of Profit and Income Distribution in Relation to the Rate of Economic Growth ", *Review of Economic Studies*, **29** (October 1962), pp. 267-279.

[3] Sato, K. " Neo-classical Economic Growth and Saving: An Extension of Uzawa's Two-sector Model ", *Economic Studies Quarterly*, **14** (February and June 1964).

16 The Adjustment of Savings to Investment in a Growing Economy

J. E. MEADE

I

A major issue underlying the differences between what have come to be known as the Neo-Keynesian and the Neo-Classical theories of economic growth is the extent to which, and the mechanisms by which, savings and investment are brought into balance in a growing economy with full employment. To what extent for equilibrium growth must the level of investment be, somehow or another, adjusted to the level of the savings which the community is prepared to make in 'equilibrium' conditions? Or may the level of investment be determined independently (by government policy or the animal spirits of the entrepreneurs) with the level of savings adjusting itself to that level of investment? And, given these mechanisms, what will be the effect upon employment, output, growth, and price inflation of a policy which stimulates investment without affecting the citizens' propensities to save?

It is not the purpose of this paper to examine this central question in all its possible aspects. Our present objective is a very limited one. We shall assume that the level of money expenditure on investment is kept strictly equal to a given fixed proportion (S_i) of the money national income. There is no time lag and there are no mistakes. We shall not enquire how this occurs.[2] We are frankly not building a complete model of the economic system which would certainly require the inclusion of a more plausible investment function than this. Our purpose is merely to examine the way in which the proportion of the national income which is saved may be adjusted to this given investment proportion.

Even here our objective is a very limited one. We shall concern ourselves with only two out of the almost infinite number of possible forms of behaviour which would help to adjust the savings proportion to the investment proportion. We assume that a fixed proportion (S_w) of wages and a fixed proportion (S_v) of other incomes are saved.[3] Let us suppose that if the labour market were in equilibrium (we will explain below more

[1] Mr. F. H. Hahn has discussed with me many of the problems involved in the preparation of this paper and I would like to acknowledge the great help which he has given me.

[2] Those who like to have some institutional model in mind are advised to imagine a supremely efficient and well-informed Government which is able by various devices (fiscal and monetary measures and planned socialised investment) to keep the level of investment expenditure in a planned ratio (S_i) to the actual national income with negligibly short time-lags and errors of judgement.

[3] Mr. Pasinetti ("Rate of Profit and Income Distribution in Relation to the Rate of Economic Growth." *The Review of Economic Studies*, Vol. XXIX, No. 4) has shown the great importance of distinguishing this assumption from the assumption that wage-earners save a proportion S_w of their total incomes while non-wage-earners save a proportion S_v of their incomes. For, if wage-earners save, they will receive profits on their accumulated savings, so that the proportion S_w would have to refer to wages plus profits accruing to wage-earners. I have maintained the pre-Pasinetti Kaldorian assumption because it is a main purpose of this article to reconcile the clash between the 'neo-Keynesian' and the 'neo-classical' theories of distribution. I make no apology, therefore, for illustrating this clash by maintaining the 'neo-Keynesian' savings propensities in their most familiar Kaldorian form and by using later in this article the familiar Cobb-Douglas production function to represent the 'neo-classical' forces of marginal productivity. An institutional set-up which would lead to the Kaldorian savings propensities would exist if all individuals saved the same proportion (S_w) of their incomes, while all non-wage incomes were in the first place earned by companies which placed to reserve a proportion $\left(\frac{S_v - S_w}{1 - S_w}\right)$ of their earnings before distributing the remainder in dividends to individual shareholders.

precisely what is meant by this) the proportion of the national product which would go to wages would be EQ (we will explain below the reason for this apparently clumsy notation) so that the proportion going to non-wage incomes would be $1 - EQ$. It follows that the proportion of the national income which recipients of income would plan to save if there were an equilibrium distribution of income between wage incomes and non-wage incomes would be $EQ\ S_w + (1 - EQ)\ S_v$, which we will call S_s.

We assume that S_i is set above S_s. Actual investment is greater than planned equilibrium savings. There is an inflation of total demand. This inflation of total demand has a two-fold effect in reconciling the proportion of income actually saved to the proportion actually invested. (1) In so far as recipients of income plan their consumption expenditures in terms of money, the inflation of their money incomes will tend to cause the actual proportion of income saved to rise above the planned proportion. (2) In so far as an inflation of total demand will in the first instance cause profits to rise, there will be an inflationary shift from wage incomes to non-wage incomes. If recipients of income plan to save a smaller proportion of wages than of other incomes ($S_w < S_v$), this shift to profit will cause the proportion of income saved to rise above the equilibrium planned proportion.

Section II of this paper examines the possible interrelationships between these two mechanisms of adjustment.

II

The following four equations[1] show the basic relationships in our models:—

$$I = S_i\ Y \quad . \ . \ . \ . \ (1)$$

Y measures the national income in money terms and S_i is the proportion of this national income which is invested.

$$C = \frac{\mu}{D + \mu}\left\{(1 - S_w)\ W + (1 - S_v)\ (Y - W)\right\} \quad . \ . \ . \ . \ . \ (2)$$

W measures total money wage income, so that $(1 - S_w)\ W$ is desired consumption expenditure out of wages and $(1 - S_v)\ (Y - W)$ is desired consumption expenditure out of other incomes. But actual consumption expenditures (C) may differ from these desired levels. Equation (2) is based on the very simple behavioural assumption that recipients of income never foresee a rise in their money incomes but simply adjust their expenditure on consumption with a time lag to their actual incomes. In fact they are assumed to raise their expenditure on consumption at a proportionate rate which is equal to μ times the proportionate excess of desired consumption over actual consumption at any one time.

$$W = \frac{\theta}{D + \theta}\ EQY \quad . \ (3)$$

Let Q = the proportional marginal product of labour (i.e. $\dfrac{L}{X}\dfrac{\partial X}{\partial L}$ where L is the amount of labour in employment and X is physical output) so that Q would be equal to the proportion of the national income which would go to wages if labour were paid a

[1] In these and the following equations D stands for the differential operator $\dfrac{d\,(-)}{dt}$. For the use of this operator see Appendix A of R. G. D. Allen's " Mathematical Economics ".

wage rate equal to the value of its marginal product. We assume Q to be constant.[1] But because of elements of monopoly and monopsony in the markets for the sale of the product of labour and for the hire of labour itself (i.e. because of the absence of perfect competition), the micro-economic conditions in our economy may be such that the markets are in equilibrium when labour is paid less than its marginal product. Let E be a fraction expressing the proportion of its marginal product which labour will be paid when micro-markets are in equilibrium.[2] We will at first assume E to be a constant given by unchanging conditions of monopoly and monopsony in the individual markets, though later we will allow E itself to be affected by the degree of inflationary pressure. Equation (3) assumes on the part of the employers the same sort of simple-minded behaviour as equation (2) assumed for consumers. Employers do not foresee future increases in their sales proceeds and profits; but with a time lag they adjust their expenditure on labour to what it would be profitable for them to spend on labour in present conditions. They will be raising their expenditure on labour at a proportionate rate equal to θ times the proportionate excess of the equilibrium wage bill ($EQ\ Y$) over the actual wage bill (W) at any one time.

$$Y = I + C \qquad \ldots\ldots\ldots\ldots \qquad (4)$$

Equation (4) states the identity that at any one time the actual level of money income must be equal to the actual level of money expenditures on investment and consumption.

From equations (1), (2), (3) and (4) we can eliminate I, C and W and obtain

$$Y(1 - S_i) = \frac{\mu}{D + \mu} \left\{ (1 - S_v)\,Y + (S_v - S_w) \frac{\theta}{D + \theta}\, EQY \right\}$$

Multiplying both sides by $(D + \mu)(D + \theta)$ and writing S_s for $EQS_w + (1 - EQ)\,S_v$ we obtain:—

$$D^2Y + \left(\theta + \mu \frac{S_v - S_i}{1 - S_i}\right) DY - \mu\,\theta\, \frac{S_i - S_s}{1 - S_i}\, Y = 0 \qquad \ldots\ldots \qquad (5)$$

The roots of this equation are:—

$$\tfrac{1}{2} \left\{ -\theta - \mu \frac{S_v - S_i}{1 - S_i} \pm \sqrt{\left(\theta + \mu \frac{S_v - S_i}{1 - S_i}\right)^2 + 4\mu\theta \frac{S_i - S_s}{1 - S_i}} \right\}$$

[1] This implies (i) a production function with unitary elasticities of substitution between the factors and (ii) neutral technical progress. See J. E. Meade " A Neo-Classical Theory of Economic Growth ", 2nd edition. Chapter 4 and Appendix I.

[2] If $-\varepsilon$ is the elasticity of demand facing the individual seller of the product and η is the elasticity of supply facing the individual hirer of labour, then the marginal labour cost is $\left(1 + \frac{1}{\eta}\right)$ times the wage rate and the marginal revenue is $\left(1 - \frac{1}{\varepsilon}\right)$ times the price of the product. Profit will be maximised when $\overline{W}\left(1 + \frac{1}{\eta}\right) = \left(1 - \frac{1}{\varepsilon}\right) P \frac{\partial X}{\partial L}$ where $\overline{W}$ is the money wage rate, and P is the money price of the product, i.e. when $\overline{W}L = \frac{1 - \frac{1}{\varepsilon}}{1 + \frac{1}{\eta}} PX \frac{L}{X} \frac{\partial X}{\partial L} = \frac{1 - \frac{1}{\varepsilon}}{1 + \frac{1}{\eta}} QY$. In other words $E = \frac{1 - \frac{1}{\varepsilon}}{1 + \frac{1}{\eta}}$.

These roots are both real,[1] one positive and—provided that $S_i < S_v + \frac{\mu}{\mu + \theta}(1 - S_v)$—one negative. The larger of these two roots will measure the growth rate of the national income which will become the dominant rate of growth, which we will call π. If, as a numerical example, we assume $S_i = \frac{1}{3}$, $S_v = \frac{1}{2}$, $S_w = 0$, $EQ = \frac{1}{2}$ (so that $S_s = \frac{1}{4}$), $\mu = 1$, and $\theta = 1$, then this dominant rate of growth (π) will be $9\frac{3}{8}$ per cent per annum.

From equation (3) we can see that the proportion of income going to wages will approach $\frac{\theta}{\pi + \theta} EQ$ which, with our numerical example will be equal to $\frac{1}{1{\cdot}09375} \times \frac{1}{2} =$ ·457, so that as a result of the inflation only 45·7% of the national income in the state of steady inflation will be going to wages instead of 50%. Thus we can say that, with our numerical example,

(i) the planned equilibrium proportion of savings is $S_w EQ + S_v (1 - EQ) = 0{\cdot}25$

(ii) the planned proportion of savings is

$$S_w \frac{\theta}{\pi + \theta} EQ + S_v \left(1 - \frac{\theta}{\pi + \theta} EQ\right) = 0{\cdot}2715$$

and (iii) the actual proportion of savings is $S_i = 0{\cdot}\dot{3}$.

The difference between (i) and (ii) marks the influence of the θ-mechanism or of the shift to profit in raising savings and the difference between (ii) and (iii) marks the influence of the μ-mechanism or of the lag of consumption on incomes in raising actual savings.

This general case when both the θ-mechanism and the μ-mechanism are operating simultaneously we will call Case I. Let us now consider two special cases, Case II where only the μ-mechanism is at work and Case III where only the θ-mechanism is operative.

Case II rests on the assumption that there is an instantaneous adjustment of actual wage payments to the equilibrium level i.e. that $\theta \to \infty$. In this case equation (5) becomes

$$DY = \mu \frac{S_i - S_s}{1 - S_i} Y \quad \ldots \ldots \ldots \ldots \quad (6)$$

so that there is a single real positive rate of growth of $\pi = \mu \frac{S_i - S_s}{1 - S_i}$. With our same numerical example (except that $\theta = \infty$ instead of $= 1$) π is raised from $9\frac{3}{8}$ to $12\frac{1}{2}$ per cent per annum. The inflationary pressure is this much raised by the absence of any shift to profits. The proportion of income going to wages is, of course, equal to its equilibrium value of EQ or $\frac{1}{2}$. Planned equilibrium savings are equal to $\frac{1}{4}$. The whole difference

[1] If one writes $S_s = S_v - EQ (S_v - S_w)$ in the expression given for these roots we obtain

$$\frac{1}{2}\left\{ -\theta - \mu \frac{S_v - S_i}{1 - S_i} \pm \sqrt{\left(\theta - \mu \frac{S_v - S_i}{1 - S_i}\right)^2 + 4\mu\theta EQ \frac{S_v - S_w}{1 - S_i}} \right\}$$

From this it is clear that the roots are real except in the very peculiar case in which S_w *exceeds* S_v by more than $\frac{1 - S_i}{4\mu\theta EQ}\left(\theta - \mu \frac{S_v - S_i}{1 - S_i}\right)^2$. If we rule out all cases in which $S_w > S_v$, the roots of equation (5) are real whether (as in the text) we confine our attention to situations in which the national income in money terms will be rising ($S_i > S_s$ and the dominant root is > 0) or whether we also consider cases in which the money income will be falling ($S_i < S_s$ and the dominant root < 0).

between this and the actual proportion of income saved ($S_i = \frac{1}{3}$) is closed by the higher rate of inflation ($12\frac{1}{2}$ per cent per annum) operating on the lag between income and expenditure on consumption.

It is of interest to note that if in Case I (equation 5) one writes $S_v = S_w$ so that $S_v = S_s$, the roots of the equation become $-\theta$ and $\mu \frac{S_i - S_s}{1 - S_i}$. The dominant root in Case I is then the same as the single root in Case II. This is what one would expect. If the proportion of non-wage income saved were the same as the proportion of wage income saved (Case I with $S_v = S_w$), this would have essentially the same effect as the absence of the θ-mechanism (Case II), since the distribution of income between wages and non-wage income would have no effect on planned consumption.[1]

Case III rests on the assumption that there is an instantaneous adjustment of actual consumption to planned consumption. Only the shift to profits caused by inflation maintains the balance between savings and investment by raising the proportion of income planned to be saved. In this case (with $\mu \to \infty$) equation (5) becomes

$$D\,Y = \theta \frac{S_i - S_s}{S_v - S_i} Y \quad . \; . \; . \; . \; . \; . \; . \; . \; . \; . \; . \; . \; . \quad (7)$$

so that there is a single real root of $\pi = \theta \frac{S_i - S_s}{S_v - S_i}$. With our same numerical example π is now raised to a growth rate of no less than 50% per annum. From equation (3) we can see once more that the proportion of income going to wages will be equal to $\frac{\theta}{\pi + \theta} EQ^2$ which with our present numerical example is $\frac{1}{1{\cdot}5} \times \frac{1}{2} = \frac{1}{3}$. The rate of inflation (of 50 per cent per annum) is sufficient to reduce the proportion of income going to wages from $\frac{1}{2}$ to $\frac{1}{3}$, and this is sufficient to raise the planned proportion of savings to income from $\frac{1}{4}$ to $\frac{1}{3}$.

If we compare equations (7) and (6), it can be seen that the difference in effectiveness between the consumption adjustment lag (μ) and the wage adjustment lag (θ) depends upon two things: first, the relative sizes of μ and θ and, secondly, the difference of S_v from unity. In so far as θ were less than μ, i.e. in so far as wage adjustments were less quick than consumption adjustments, the θ-mechanism would be more effective in checking inflation than the μ-mechanism. But if these rates of adjustment were the same, the θ-mechanism would be as effective as the μ-mechanism only if the whole of profits were saved [$S_v = 1$]. The μ-mechanism works by the whole of an increase in income being

[1] The only difference is the presence of a damped element in Y associated with the root $-\theta$ in case I with $S_v = S_w$. In case II the initial growth rate of Y cannot diverge from the root $\mu \frac{S_i - S_s}{1 - S_i}$. In case I with $S_v = S_w$, the initial growth rate of Y can diverge from $\mu \frac{S_i - S_s}{1 - S_i}$. But any such initial divergence will be removed by the damping factor $-\theta$.

[2] If one substitutes the value of $\pi = \theta \frac{S_i - S_s}{S_v - S_i}$ into this expression for the ratio of actual wages to income one obtains the result $\frac{W}{Y} = \frac{S_v - S_i}{S_v - S_w}$ which is precisely Mr. Kaldor's expression for the distribution of income.

temporarily added to savings, until actual consumption is adjusted to the higher incomes. The θ-mechanism works by the whole of an increase in incomes being added to profits, until actual wages are adjusted to the higher national expenditure, but it is only if the whole of profits are saved that this causes an equivalent temporary increase in savings.

The following points about the θ-mechanism of Case III are worth noting:—

1. The mechanism will work only if $S_i < S_v$. From equation 7 it can be seen that as S_i rises towards S_v, so the rate of inflation approaches infinity. It is only if the proportion of profits saved is higher than the planned proportion of income to be invested, that a shift to profit of a sufficient magnitude can bring actual savings up to this planned investment proportion. This condition that $S_v > S_i$ is not necessary for the working of the μ-mechanism.

2. We are assuming that $S_i > S_s$. If $S_i < S_v$ then $S_v > S_s$. In other words, the mechanism will work only if a higher proportion of profits than wages is saved; for S_s can be $< S_v$ only if $S_w < S_v$. Thus we must have $S_v > S_i > S_w$. The condition $S_v > S_w$ is not necessary for the working of the μ-mechanism.

3. With the numerical example which we have taken (i.e. with $\mu = \theta$ and $S_v = \frac{1}{2}$) the θ-mechanism is much less effective than the μ-mechanism in restraining inflation.

III

The model which we have built has so far been entirely in terms of flows of money income and expenditure on consumption (C), on investment (I), on all goods and services (Y), and on labour (W). We shall proceed in this and the next section to split these money flows up into real quantities multiplied by their prices. In this section we shall deal with the labour market and split the total wage bill (W) into the volume of employment (L) and the wage per worker ($\overline{W}$), where

$$W = L\overline{W}$$

so that

$$l = w - \bar{w} \qquad (8)$$

where $l = \frac{1}{L}\frac{dL}{dt}$, $w = \frac{1}{W}\frac{dW}{dt}$, and $\bar{w} = \frac{1}{\overline{W}}\frac{d\overline{W}}{dt}$.

In all the three cases which we are considering there will, as we have seen, emerge a dominant rate of growth of the national income which we call π. Moreover, as this dominant rate of growth asserts itself the total wage bill will also grow at the same dominant rate, π, so that eventually w will also equal π. The basic simplifying assumption about the labour market which we are making is that the employers raise their wage bills at a proportionate rate equal to θ times the proportionate excess of the equilibrium wage they would be willing to pay in current market conditions over the actual wage which they are paying. We are assuming that this rate of increase in their total money outlay on labour is the same whether in fact it results in an equivalent rate of rise in the volume of labour which they can employ at current wage rates or an equivalent rate of rise in the wage rate which they have to pay for an unchanged volume of labour or partly in the one and partly in the other. This assumption permits very great simplification of the analysis without necessarily being very unrealistic. We can write equation (8) as

$$l = \pi - \bar{w} \qquad (9)$$

We shall assume that the rate of rise of the money wage rate, $\bar{w}$, depends upon the proportion of the labour force which is unemployed, J. We assume (i) that the lower is the unemployment percentage the higher will be the rate at which the money wage rate is being raised through the competition of employers and employed, (ii) that there is a finite limit to the rate at which the money wage rate can be lowered as the unemployment proportion rises towards unity, but (iii) that there is no limit to the rate at which the money wage rate can be raised as the unemployment proportion falls towards zero.

One function which would satisfy these conditions is

$$\bar{w} = -\bar{w}_x \left\{ \left(\frac{J_x}{J}\right)^{\gamma} - 1 \right\} \quad . \quad . \quad . \quad . \quad . \quad . \quad . \quad . \quad . \quad . \quad . \quad (10)$$

where $-\bar{w}_x$ (>0) is the maximum rate of fall of the wage rate as $J \rightarrow \infty$, J_x is the unemployment percentage at which the money wage rate is constant, and γ is a positive parameter which measures the extent to which a fall in the unemployment proportion causes an increase in the rate of inflation of money wage rates.[1]

If we write L for the total demand for labour and $\bar{L}$ for the total supply of labour and if we assume that the available working population is growing at a constant proportionate rate, λ, so that $\bar{L} = \bar{L}_0 e^{\lambda t}$, we have $J = 1 - \frac{L}{\bar{L}_0 e^{\lambda t}}$. We have then from (9) and (10)

$$l = \pi + (-\bar{w}_x) \left\{ 1 - \left(\frac{J_x}{1 - \frac{L}{\bar{L}_0 e^{\lambda t}}} \right)^{\gamma} \right\} \quad . \quad . \quad . \quad . \quad . \quad (11)$$

Since $l = \frac{1}{L}\frac{dL}{dt}$, this gives us a differential equation in L and t, the general solution of which would determine the behaviour of employment over time, starting from any given initial position.

The general solution of (11) is, however, not necessary for our purpose. We are concerned only with (i) what will be the rates of growth in a state of steady growth and (ii) whether the system, starting from any initial conditions, will always move towards this state of steady growth. In the case of equation (11) we wish, therefore, to know (i) whether there is a particular solution of (11) which gives a steady rate of growth of L and (ii) whether the system is stable in the sense that it will always converge onto this rate of growth for L.

The first question is easily answered. The LHS of (11) is the rate of growth of L and this will be constant only if the RHS of (11) is constant. But the RHS of (11) will be constant only if $\frac{L}{\bar{L}_0 e^{\lambda t}}$ is constant, i.e. only if $l = \lambda$. If we write $l = \lambda$ in (11) we obtain

$$\bar{J} = \left(\frac{-\bar{w}_x J_x^{\gamma}}{\pi + [-\bar{w}_x] - \lambda} \right)^{\frac{1}{\gamma}} \quad . \quad . \quad . \quad . \quad . \quad . \quad . \quad . \quad . \quad . \quad . \quad (12)$$

where $\bar{J}$ is the equilibrium level of the unemployment proportion, $1 - \frac{L}{\bar{L}_0 e^{\lambda t}}$. This equi-

[1] For a discussion of this function see Appendix at the end of this paper.

librium unemployment proportion is the value of J at which the rate of change of the money wage rate ($\bar{w}$) would be such that, taken together with the rate of rise in the total wage-bill (π), the volume of employment would rise at a rate equal to the rise in the supply of labour ($l = \lambda$), so that the unemployment proportion (J) would in fact stay unchanged.

Now we shall assume that $\pi > \lambda - (-\bar{w}_x)(1 - J_x^\gamma)$. It will be seen from (10) that $\bar{w}_x(1 - J_x^\gamma)$ is the value of $\bar{w}$ when $J = 1$. Our assumption therefore, implies only that the investment proportion is sufficient to raise π (the dominant rate of growth of the money national income and so of the total money wage bill) to a sufficient degree to absorb the growing working population (λ) at least when the unemployment proportion is very high and the money wage rate is itself already falling at nearly its maximum rate $(-\bar{w}_x)(l - J_x^\gamma)$. If this were not so the unemployment percentage would rise continuously since the volume of employment would be growing less rapidly than the supply of labour.

Since $0 < J_x < 1$ and $\gamma > 0$, it follows that $0 < 1 - J_x^\gamma < 1$. Hence with $\pi > \lambda - (-\bar{w}_x)(1 - J_x^\gamma)$ we have $\pi > \lambda - (-\bar{w}_x)$. From this it follows that the equilibrium value of J given in (12) lies between 0 and 1. In other words, there is an economically possible equilibrium value of J which leads to a steady rate of growth of L equal to λ.

From (12) it can be seen that this equilibrium unemployment proportion ($\bar{J}$) will be greater (or less) than the unemployment proportion required to keep the money wage rate constant (J_x) according as the rate of growth of the money national income is less (or greater) that the rate of growth of the working population which has to be absorbed at the current wage rate (i.e. as $\pi \lesseqgtr \lambda$).

From 12 it can also be seen that $\frac{\partial \bar{J}}{\partial \pi} < 0$. In other words the more inflationary is the investment policy the lower will be the equilibrium unemployment proportion because a higher rate of inflation of the money wage rate is compatible with the absorption into employment of the given growth in the working population.

We have shown that there is an equilibrium unemployment proportion ($\bar{J}$) and have considered some of its features. But will our system always approach this equilibrium level of J if it started initially at some other level? It would appear intuitively probable that it would do so. Suppose by accident that one started with a value of J far above the equilibrium level $\bar{J}$. Money wage rates would be falling; the money wage bill would be rising at its given rate π and this, combined with the fall in the money wage rate, would cause the amount of employment to be rising at a higher proportionate rate than the supply of labour; J would be falling towards its equilibrium level. Conversely, if J were below $\bar{J}$, there would be forces at work tending to raise J.

This argument can be expressed rigorously in the following way. We know that $0 < J < 1$ or, what is the same thing, $0 < 1 - J < 1$.[1] We can, therefore, treat both J and $1 - J$ as positive quantities.

[1] $1 - J = \frac{L}{L_0 e^{\lambda t}}$. Since $L_0 > 0$ and $e^{\lambda t} > 0$, $1 - J > 0$ if $L > 0$. We assume $L_0 > 0$. Moreover we assume $\pi > 0$. It follows *a fortiori* that $\pi + (-\bar{w}_x) > 0$ and, therefore, that before L falls to zero it will start to grow, since $l = \pi - \bar{w}$. Therefore, L cannot fall below zero. Therefore, $1 - J > 0$. We can also show that $J > 0$. We assume that $J_0 > 0$. Given any finite value of π, there will always be a low enough positive value of J to cause $\bar{w} > \pi - \lambda$ since $\bar{w} \to \infty$ as $J \to 0$. But if $\pi - \bar{w} < \lambda$, we have $l > \lambda$, since $\pi - \bar{w} = l$; and therefore J will be rising. It follows that J, being initially > 0, must remain > 0.

Now $1 - J = \frac{L}{L_0 e^{\lambda t}}$, so that

$$\frac{dJ}{dt} = -(1 - J)(l - \lambda)$$

or from equation (11)

$$\frac{dJ}{dt} = -(1 - J)(\pi + [-\bar{w}_x] - \lambda - [-\bar{w}_x] J_x^{\gamma} J^{-\gamma})$$

Given $1 - J > 0$, it follows that $\frac{dJ}{dt} \lesseqgtr 0$, as

$$\pi + (-\bar{w}_x) - \lambda \gtreqless (-\bar{w}_x) J_x^{\lambda} J^{-\lambda}.$$

Since, as we have explained above, we may assume $\pi + (-\bar{w}_x) - \lambda > 0$, $(-\bar{w}_x) J_x^{\gamma} > 0$, and $J > 0$, it follows that $\frac{dJ}{dt} \lesseqgtr 0$ according as $J \gtreqless \bar{J}$, where $\bar{J}$ has the value given in equation (12). Moreover, $\frac{dJ}{dt} = 0$ only when $J = \bar{J}$. It follows that if J starts above $\bar{J}$, J will fall continuously so long as $J > \bar{J}$ but will never fall below $\bar{J}$. Similarly, if J starts below $\bar{J}$, J will rise continuously towards but never above $\bar{J}$. J moves to its steady-growth level, $\bar{J}$.

IV

Let us turn next to the market for goods and to the general level of money prices. Let us assume that the technical conditions of production are such as to enable a state of steady growth of real output to be reached when the proportion of income actually saved and invested is constant. A production function of the kind

$$X = R\, N^Z\, K^U\, L^Q\, e^{rt} \qquad (13)$$

will have this effect, where X is real output, N, K, and L are the amounts of Land, Capital, and Labour in employment, r is the rate of technical progress, Z, U, and Q are the proportional marginal products of Land, Capital, and Labour respectively, and R is the amount of output that could be produced by one unit each of Land, Capital, and Labour in the state of technical knowledge at time o. R, N, Z, U, Q, and r are assumed constant. Then if a constant proportion S_i of real income X is invested and added to the capital stock and if there is a constant rate of growth of the volume of employment, the economy, whatever its starting point, will in time reach a steady rate of growth equal to $\frac{Ql + r}{1 - U}$ where l is the constant growth rate of employment.[1]

Now we know from the previous Section of this paper that in our present model in time there will be a constant rate of growth of employment equal to the growth rate of the population, λ. It follows that the growth rate in real output will eventually be equal to $\frac{Q\lambda + r}{1 - U}$.

[1] See J. E. Meade, *A Neo-Classical Theory of Economic Growth*, 2nd edition, pages 108 and 109.

Now $Y = X P$ where P is the money price of real output, so that $p = y - x$, where $y = \frac{1}{Y}\frac{dY}{dt}$, $x = \frac{1}{X}\frac{dX}{dt}$ and $p = \frac{1}{P}\frac{dP}{dt}$. We also know from Section II of this paper that the growth rate of total money expenditure (y) will eventually be at a constant rate π. It follows that

$$p = \pi - \frac{Q\lambda + r}{1 - U} \qquad (14)$$

where p is the rate of inflation of the general level of prices. Since Q, λ, r, and U are all constant, it is clear that $\frac{\partial p}{\partial \pi} > 0$. In other words a more inflationary investment policy will eventually raise the rate of inflation of money prices.[1]

We have now shown the connection between investment policy and price inflation. To illustrate the connection let us suppose that the object of policy is to stabilise the price level and that we have to rely exclusively either on the μ-mechanism (Case II) or on the θ-mechanism (Case III) to keep actual savings in balance with actual investment. Setting $p = 0$ we have from equation (14)

$$\text{(case II)} \qquad \frac{Q\lambda + r}{1 - U} = \mu \frac{S_i - S_s}{1 - S_i}$$

$$\text{and (case III)} \qquad \frac{Q\lambda + r}{1 - U} = \theta \frac{S_i - S_s}{S_v - S_i}$$

[1] The immediate effect of an increase in the investment proportion would necessarily be to raise the absolute level of prices but it might also *temporarily* reduce the subsequent rate of rise of prices. The *temporary* effect of an increase in the investment proportion is to raise the rate of growth; but *ultimately* its effect is to raise the ratio of capital to output $\left(\frac{K}{X}\right)$ with the restoration of the original rate of growth (See J. E. Meade, *A Neo-Classical Theory of Economic Growth*, Chapter 4.) During the temporary phase while the rate of growth of output is higher than normal, it is possible that the increase in the investment proportion raises x (the rate of growth of output) more than it raises π (the rate of growth of total money expenditure.) Consider Case II by way of example. We have then $\pi = \mu \frac{S_i - S_s}{1 - S_i}$ and (see J. E. Meade, *op. cit.*) $x = U\frac{S_i X}{K} + Ql + r$ so that $p = \mu \frac{S_i - S_s}{1 - S_i} - U\frac{S_i X}{K} - Q\lambda - l$. In this case a rise in S_i causes an immediate adjustment of the rate of growth of total money demand to the new value of $\pi = \mu \frac{S_i - S_s}{1 - S_i}$. Suppose that the adjustment in the labour market, examined in the last Section is also rapid so that l is quickly restored to λ. The output-capital ratio $\left(\frac{X}{K}\right)$ will, however, change only gradually as the higher proportion of income saved causes capital to be accumulated more abundantly. Before $\frac{X}{K}$ has time to change significantly

$$\frac{\partial p}{\partial S_i} = \mu \frac{1 - S_s}{(1 - S_i)^2} - \frac{UX}{K}$$

This might be < 0. But as time passes the rate of growth of X would fall again to $\frac{Q\lambda + r}{1 - U}$ and ultimately, comparing one steady-growth state with another, $\frac{\partial p}{\partial S_i} = \mu \frac{1 - S_s}{(1 - S_i)^2}$ which is necessarily > 0.

From these equations we can derive

$$\text{(case II)} \qquad S_i - S_s = \cfrac{1 - S_s}{1 + \mu \cfrac{(1 - U)}{Q\lambda + r}}$$

$$\text{and (case III)} \qquad S_i - S_s = \cfrac{E\, Q\, (S_v - S_w)}{1 + \theta \cfrac{(1 - U)}{Q\lambda + r}}$$

These show the extents to which in the two cases the planned level of investment can be raised above the equilibrium planned level of savings while preserving a stable money price level.

We showed in the last Section that a more inflationary investment policy (a rise in S_i), while it would raise the rate of rise in money wage rates, would also have the effect of raising the employment percentage. Similarly, we can now show that a rise in S_i, while—as we have already seen—it will raise the rate of inflation of the money prices of goods, will also cause the real capital stock in equilibrium steady growth to be higher than it would otherwise be. In the state of steady real growth we know that[1]

$$\frac{S_i\, X}{K} = \frac{Q\lambda + r}{1 - U} \qquad \text{or } K = \frac{1 - U}{Q\lambda + r} S_i X \qquad \ldots \ldots \quad (15)$$

Since $L = (1 - \bar{J})\, \bar{L}_0 e^{\lambda t}$ it follows from (13) and (15) that

$$K = \left\{ \frac{1 - U}{Q\lambda + r} S_i\, R\, N^z\, (1 - \bar{J})^{\,Q} \bar{L}_0^{Q} \right\}^{\frac{1}{1 - U}} e^{\frac{Q\lambda + r}{1 - U} t} \qquad \ldots \ldots \quad (16)$$

It follows that a once-for-all permanent increase in S_i will cause K to be larger than it would otherwise have been at any point of time in the subsequent ultimate state of steady growth because on the RHS of (16) both S_i and $1 - \bar{J}$ will be higher. In other words, at any one time the capital stock will be higher because in the past a greater proportion (S_i higher) of a larger output ($\bar{J}$ lower) will have been invested. At the same time current output (though not necessarily consumption[2]) will be greater both because the capital stock will be greater for the two reasons just given and also because the fall in $\bar{J}$ will mean that a larger amount of employment is associated with this larger stock of capital.

V

So far we have assumed that the degrees of monopoly and monopsony in the micro-markets for labour and for output are constant. But it is possible that the higher is the level of pressure of demand upon resources, the greater the degrees of monopsony in labour markets and/or of monopoly in product markets.[3] The smaller the general volume of unemployed labour, the more fearful will the individual employer become that attempts

[1] See J. E. Meade, *A Neo-Classical Theory of Economic Growth*, Chapter 4.

[2] See J. E. Meade, *A Neo-Classical Theory of Economic Growth*, 2nd Edition, pp. 110-113.

[3] Mr. Kaldor has stressed the former possibility and Sir Roy Harrod the latter in his book, *The Trade Cycle*.

on his part to build up his labour force will involve driving up the wage rate against himself. The greater the shortage of products relatively to final demand, the less will the individual producer fear that he will lose his market if he raises the price of his product. In our system E, which we have so far regarded as a given constant, is better regarded as itself a variable depending upon J, the unemployment percentage.

In this Section we will briefly indicate the lines on which the preceding analysis might be modified in order to take account of this possibility. We will carry out this analysis only for our two special cases—Case II which relies solely on the μ-mechanism to achieve equality between actual savings and investment and Case III which relies solely on the θ-mechanism. Moreover, we will carry out the analysis solely for the purpose of examining the effect of an increase in S_i on y, the rate of growth of total money national income, confining this analysis to steady-state equilibrium rates of growth.

In other words, we assume a steady-state rate of growth of national income. The actual investment proportion (S_i) is then raised. As we have already seen in the previous Sections, this raises the rate of inflation of the national income until a new and higher steady-state rate of growth of money national income is achieved. In the labour market there is a higher level of demand and a lower unemployment percentage. This causes a higher rate of rise of the money wage rate, until the higher rate of rise of the money wage rate combined with the unchanged rate of growth of the total working population enables the lower unemployment percentage to be maintained with a rate of rise of the total wage bill equal to the new and higher rate of inflation of the total money national income.

The modification which we are now making in this analysis is to add the fact that the lower unemployment percentage will cause a reduction in EQ, the equilibrium proportion of the national income which goes to wages. If $S_v > S_w$, this will cause a rise in S_s, the planned equilibrium proportion of the national income which is saved. The rise in S_i will thus indirectly cause a rise in S_s; the rise in S_i will, therefore, cause a smaller inflationary pressure in this case in which we allow E to fall as J falls; the effect of the increase in S_i will therefore be to cause (i) a smaller increase in the rate of inflation of the national income and (ii) a smaller decrease in J than would have been the case if E were constant.

Let us apply this analysis more rigorously to the situation of Case II. An examination of equations (1) to (4) will show that, if we allow θ to approach ∞, we have

$$y = \mu \frac{S_i - S_s}{1 - S_i} \quad \ldots \ldots \ldots \ldots \quad (17)$$

even though we no longer assume that E, and thus S_s are constant. Since $S_s = S_v - (S_v - S_w)\, EQ$, it is no longer certain that S_s is constant even though S_v, S_w and Q are all constant. E may be changing. Consequently it is no longer certain that y is constant even though μ and S_i are constant, since S_s may be changing as a result of changes in E.

But perhaps y will in fact always reach a constant level given the values of S_i, S_v, S_w, Q, and μ, because E will always reach a constant level appropriate to those given values of S_i, S_v, S_w, Q and μ. Without giving a formal mathematical proof[1] we shall

[1] A formal proof would require the re-writing of Section III on the following lines. From equation 3 with $\theta = \infty$ we have $w = y + \frac{1}{E(J)} \frac{dE(J)}{dt}$ where $J = 1 - \frac{L}{L_0 e^{\lambda t}}$. Using the value of y from (18), taking a suitable function $E(J)$, and substituting the above value of w and the value of $\bar{w}$ from (10) into (8), we should obtain a differential equation, the solution of which would give the path of L over time. Our proof would require that as $t \to \infty$ $\frac{L}{L_0 e^{\lambda t}} \to$ some constant value between 0 and 1.

assume that this is in fact the case. The plausibility of this assumption can be seen in the following way. E decreases as J, the unemployment percentage decreases. If J finds a constant level, E finds a constant level and in consequence S_s and y find constant levels. Assume then certain values for S_i, S_v, S_w, Q and μ. Suppose J to be very high. Then E is very high. S_s is very low. $S_i - S_s$ is very high and y is very high. Now if J were constant at this exceptionally high level, E would also be constant. EQ would, therefore, be constant. Since in our present case $\theta = \infty$, EQ measures the proportion of income actually going to wages. This would be constant, if J were constant, so that the total wage would be rising at the same exceptionally high rate as y. But with a very high J, the rate of rise of the wage rate will be exceptionally low. The high rate of rise in the total demand for labour will, therefore, result in an exceptionally high rate of rise in the volume of employment. If this is higher than the rate of rise of the total supply of labour, J will in fact be falling. Thus we may assume that if J is ' too ' high, it will fall, and—by a similar process of reasoning—that if it is too low it will rise. We assume that J will remain at the steady-state level at which E, S_s, and y will be constant. In this position y will be equal to the sum of the growth rate in the total supply of labour plus the growth rate in the money wage rate which is itself associated with this equilibrium level of J.

Let us write both E and $\bar{w}$ (the growth rate of the money wage rate) as functions of J, namely $E(J)$ and $\bar{w}(J)$, $\frac{\partial E}{\partial J}$ being > 0 and $\frac{\partial \bar{w}}{\partial J} < 0$. We have in case II by writing $S_s = S_v - (S_v - S_w)\, EQ$ in equation (17):—

$$y = \mu \frac{S_i - S_v}{1 - S_i} + \mu\, Q \frac{S_v - S_w}{1 - S_i} E(J) \qquad (18)$$

In a steady-growth state we know that the growth rate of total national income must equal the growth rate of the wage bill, this latter growth rate being itself the sum of the growth rate of the supply of labour (λ) and the growth rate of the money wage rate ($\bar{w}[J]$). We have, therefore,

$$\mu \frac{S_i - S_v}{1 - S_i} + \mu\, Q \frac{S_v - S_w}{1 - S_i} E(J) = \lambda + \bar{w}(J) \qquad (19)$$

If we knew the form of the functions $E(J)$ and $\bar{w}(J)$, equation (19) would determine the unemployment percentage, J, ruling in the steady-growth state.

Let us now consider the effect of a small increase in S_i on J and on y, on the assumption that μ, S_v, S_w, Q, and λ remain constant. By partial differentiation of equation (19) we obtain:—

$$\frac{\partial J}{\partial S_i} = - \frac{\mu \dfrac{1 - S_s}{1 - S_i}}{\mu\, Q\, (S_v - S_w) \dfrac{\partial E}{\partial J} + (1 - S_i) \left(- \dfrac{\partial \bar{w}}{\partial J}\right)} \qquad (20)$$

We can see from (20) that if either $\frac{\partial E}{\partial J} = 0$ or else $S_v = S_w$ (in which case a shift to profit has no effect in stimulating savings and mitigating inflationary pressures), then

$$\frac{\partial J}{\delta S_i} = - \mu \frac{1 - S_s}{(1 - S_i)^2 \left(- \dfrac{\partial \bar{w}}{\partial J}\right)} \qquad (21)$$

In both cases a rise in S_i causes a fall in the employment percentage; but this fall is less in equation 20 than in equation 21.[1]

By partial differentiation of (18), keeping μ, S_v, S_w, and Q constant we obtain

$$\frac{\partial y}{\partial S_i} = \mu \frac{1 - S_s}{(1 - S_i)^2} + \mu\, Q \frac{S_v - S_w}{1 - S_i} \frac{\partial E}{\delta J} \frac{\partial J}{\delta S_i}$$

Making use of the value of $\frac{\partial J}{\partial S_i}$ from (20) we obtain

$$\frac{\partial y}{\partial S_i} = \mu \frac{1 - S_s}{(1 - S_i)^2} \frac{1}{1 + \dfrac{\mu\, Q\, (S_v - S_w) \left(\dfrac{\partial E}{\partial J}\right)}{(1 - S_i) \left(-\dfrac{\partial \bar{w}}{\partial J}\right)}} \quad . \; . \; . \; . \; . \; . \; . \; . \; . \quad (22)$$

If either $\frac{\partial E}{\partial J} = 0$ or $S_v = S_w$, then

$$\frac{\partial y}{\partial S_i} = \frac{1 - S_s}{(1 - S_i)^2}.^{2}$$

The value of $\frac{\partial y}{\partial S_i}$ in (22) is less than this. The fact that an increased inflationary pressure due to a rise in S_i causes a shift to profit through the reduction in E is itself a factor mitigating the inflationary pressure.

A similar process of analysis can be applied to the situation of Case III when we assume that $\mu = \infty$ and rely solely on the θ-mechanism. Once again an examination of equations (1) to (4) shows that $y = 0 \frac{S_i - S_s}{S_v - S_i}$, even though we no longer assume E and so S_s to be constant, so that instead of equation (18) we have:—

$$y = -\theta + \theta\, Q \frac{S_v - S_w}{S_v - S_i} E(J) \quad . \; . \; . \; . \; . \; . \; . \; . \; . \; . \quad (23)$$

If we consider only steady-growth states we have instead of equation (19):—

$$-\theta + \theta\, Q \frac{S_v - S_w}{S_v - S_i} E(J) = \lambda + \bar{w}(J) \quad . \; . \; . \; . \; . \quad (24)$$

[1] That is to say, on the assumption that $-\frac{\partial \bar{w}}{\partial J}$ is the same in the two cases. But the two cases may refer to very different market situations; and it is very questionable whether the relationship between pressure in the labour market and the rate of rise of wage rates would be the same.

[2] This corresponds with the result already obtained at the end of footnote 1 on page

From (24) by partial differentiation we can obtain instead of equation (21):—

$$\frac{\partial J}{\partial S_i} = -\frac{\theta \dfrac{S_v - S_s}{S_v - S_i}}{\theta\, Q\, (S_v - S_w) \left(\dfrac{\partial E}{\partial J}\right) + (S_v - S_i) \left(-\dfrac{\partial \bar{w}}{\partial J}\right)} \quad . \quad . \quad . \quad . \quad (25)$$

Finally, by partial differentiation of (23) and use of (25) we have instead of equation (22):—

$$\frac{\partial y}{\partial S_i} = \theta\, \frac{S_v - S_s}{(S_v - S_i)^2} \frac{1}{1 + \dfrac{\theta\, Q\, (S_v - S_w) \dfrac{\partial E}{\partial J}}{(S_v - S_i)\left(-\dfrac{\partial \bar{w}}{\partial J}\right)}} \quad . \quad . \quad . \quad . \quad . \quad . \quad . \quad . \quad . \quad . \quad (26)$$

In this case we must assume $S_v > S_i > S_w$. The θ-mechanism depends upon this assumption. But the assumption that $\frac{\partial E}{\partial J} > 0$ instead of $= 0$ is seen once again to reduce the (numerical) values of $\frac{\partial J}{\partial S_i}$ and $\frac{\partial y}{\partial S_i}$.

Cambridge. J. E. MEADE.

APPENDIX

The function given in equation (9) of the main text is the same function as that used by Professor A. W. Phillips in his " The Relation between Unemployment and the Rate of Change of Money Wage Rates " in *Economica*, November 1958, page 290. His equation is $y = -a + bx^c$ where y is the percentage rate of rise of the money wage rate and x is the unemployment percentage and where a and $b > 0$ and $c < 0$. His equation can therefore be written

$$\bar{w} = -\frac{a}{100} + \frac{b}{100^{1-c}} \left(\frac{1}{J}\right)^{-c}$$

As $J \to \infty$, $\bar{w} \to -\frac{a}{100}$, and we write $\bar{w}_x = -\frac{a}{100}$. We also have $O = -\frac{a}{100} + \frac{b}{100^{1-c}}\left(\frac{1}{J_x}\right)^{-c}$ where J_x is the value of J which makes $\bar{w} = 0$, so that $\frac{b}{100^{1-c}} = -\bar{w}_x J_x^{-c}$. If in addition we write $\gamma = -c$ we have our equation (9)

$$\bar{w} = -\bar{w}_x \left\{ \left(\frac{J_x}{J}\right)^{\gamma} - 1 \right\}$$

The interpretation of the parameter γ can best be understood from the following diagram:—

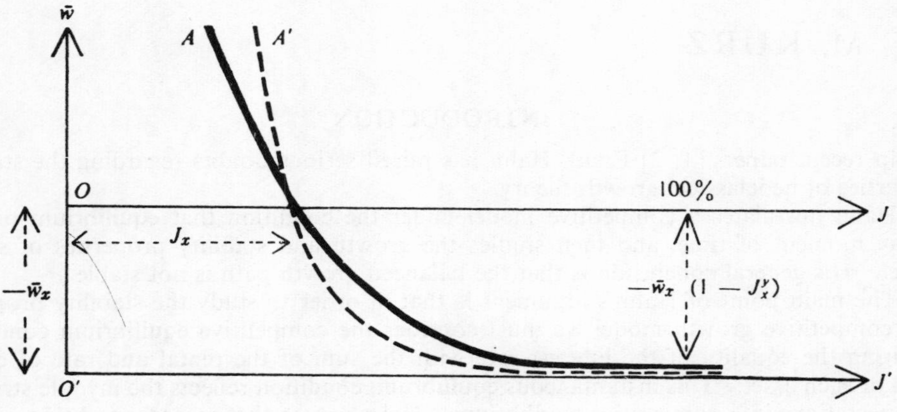

Measure along the OJ axis the unemployment percentage and up the $O\bar{w}$ axis the rate of rise of the money wage rate. The curve A showing this relationship falls as J increases. It crosses the axis OJ at $J = J_x$. At $J = 100\%$ it is $(-\bar{w}_x)\ (1 - J_x^{\gamma})$ below the OJ axis. But as $J \rightarrow \infty$ it approaches asymptotically a level $-\ \bar{w}_x$ below the OJ axis. Now

$$\gamma = -\frac{J}{\bar{w} + (-\bar{w}_x)} \cdot \frac{d\,[\bar{w} + (-\bar{w}_x)]}{dJ}.$$

In other words, it is the arithmetical value of the negative elasticity of the curve A if we measure its base not from the axis OJ but from the axis $O'J'$. The curve A' has the same values for $\bar{w}_x$ and J_x but a higher value of γ than curve A. Professor Phillips's calculations make $\bar{w}_x = -\cdot 009$ per annum, $J_x = \cdot 054$, and $\gamma = 1\cdot 394$.

17 The General Instability of a Class of Competitive Growth Processes[1]

M. KURZ

INTRODUCTION

In recent papers [1, 2] Frank Hahn has raised serious doubts regarding the stability properties of neoclassical growth theory.

Hahn postulates a competitive model under the condition that equilibrium prevails at any moment of time, and then studies the growth and stability properties of such a model. His general conclusion is that the balanced growth path is not stable.

The main point of Hahn's argument is that in order to study the stability properties of a competitive growth model we must consider the competitive equilibrium conditions requiring the equality of the interest rate with the sum of the rental and rate of capital gains of each asset. This instantaneous equilibrium condition reflects the myopic structure of expectations in a competitive equilibrium. Hahn argues that in order to bring out this point one must consider models with heterogeneous capital structure so that the multitude of assets can give rise to different rates of capital gains. We shall argue below that Hahn's argument does not require the existence of more than one capital good.

In his exposition Hahn uses Cobb-Douglas production functions, while his stability argument is presented for the case of two capital goods only.

The purpose of this paper is to generalize Hahn's results. We shall not use his method of analysis, but rather attempt to establish an interesting link between the theory of optimal growth and the theory of competitive deterministic growth. As it turns out, our approach raises a whole spectrum of new questions regarding the " inverse optimal " problem.

The paper is divided into three parts. In the first part we discuss the general conceptual questions involved, utilizing the example of a one-sector growth model. The second part presents the basic instability theorem, and the third part discusses the interpretation of the stability properties of the Solow [6] model in the light of the instability theorem.

I. CONCEPTUAL BACKGROUND

Consider the following growth process:

$$\dot{k} = f(k) - nk - c, \qquad \ldots(1)$$

where

k = capital labour ratio,
n = the constant growth rate of the labour force, and
c = consumption *per capita*..

Now suppose we maximize a utility functional:

$$\int_0^\infty e^{-\delta t} U(c)dt, \quad \delta \geqq 0, \qquad \ldots(2)$$

[1] This work was supported by Office of Naval Research Contract 225(50) at Stanford University. Reproduction in whole or in part is permitted for any purpose of the United States Government.

The author is deeply indebted to R. E. Kalman and T. N. Srinivasan for many valuable suggestions which led to the final version of this paper. He is also indebted to K. J. Arrow, Frank Hahn, and David Starrett, with whom he had many stimulating discussions on the subject.

subject to the constraint (1). From the theory of optimal growth we know that the optimal path is characterized by the existence of a price function $P(t)$ such that

$$\dot{P}(t) = P(t)[\rho - f'(k)], \text{ where } \rho = \delta + n, \qquad \text{...(3a)}$$

and

$$U_c = P. \qquad \text{...(3b)}$$

However, we do have an additional critical result: The optimal path $(P^*(t), k^*(t))$ is a saddle point in the class of all pairs of functions, $(P(t), k(t))$, which satisfy the first-order conditions. Thus, the optimal path is characterized by a function, $P^*(k)$, such that if $k(0)$ is the given initial condition, then $P^*(k(0))$ is the initial condition for P and together $k(0)$ and $P^*(k(0))$ constitute a set of initial conditions for the system (1) and (3). The saddle point property, which is an instability property, implies in this case that for any other set of initial conditions the resulting path becomes either infeasible (in finite time or asymptotically) or infinitely " inferior ".

Now there are two types of optimal paths which can be encountered:

Type 1: " *Stationary-point directed* " *optimal path.* This is the path which asymptotically converges to a stationary point (P^*, k^*). An example of such a path is depicted in Fig. 1.

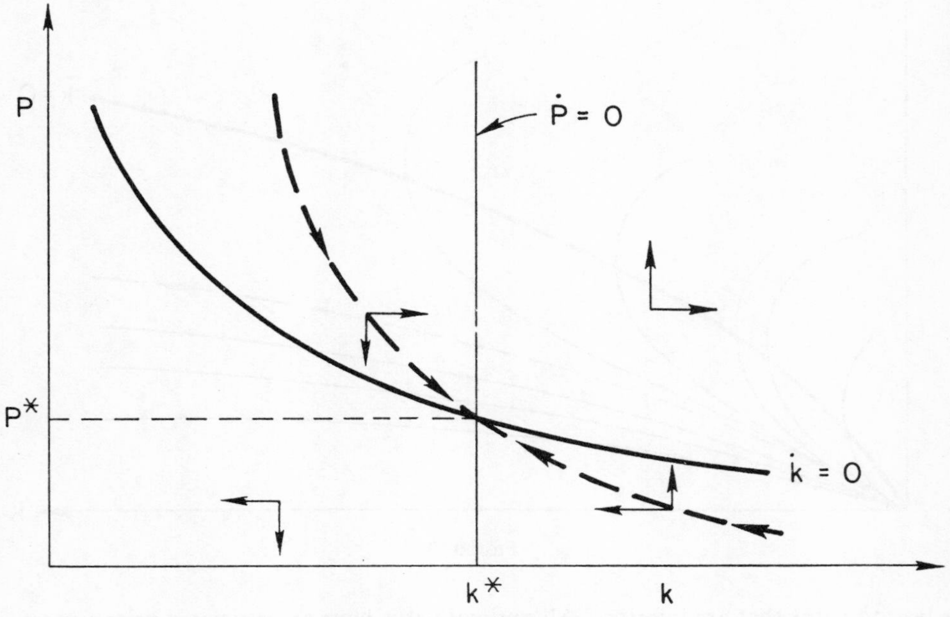

FIGURE 1

Type 2: " *Sustained-growth directed* " *optimal path.* This is the path which may arise as a result of the fact that the marginal product of capital is bounded away from the discount factor; thus, no stationary point can exist. For example, consider $f(k) = k^{\alpha} + bk$ and $U(c) = c^{1-\sigma}$. If there exists an optimal path it will have no stationary point when $b > \rho$; however, an optimal path can exist. To see this, consider all paths which satisfy the Euler equations and along which $k \to \infty$. Then $\frac{\dot{k}}{k} \to b - n - \lim_{k \to \infty} \left(\frac{c}{k}\right)$. For the path to be efficient we must have $b - n \geqq \lim_{k \to \infty} \left(\frac{c}{k}\right) > 0$. Thus, $\lim_{k \to \infty} \left(\frac{c}{k}\right) = \lambda$, and hence $\frac{\dot{c}}{c} \to \frac{1}{\sigma}(b - \rho)$.

But for $0<\lambda \leqq b-n$ we must have $(b-n)-\frac{1}{\sigma}(b-\rho)>0$. This will be satisfied if $\rho>\sigma n+(1-\sigma)b$, and this can be satisfied since we have $n<\rho<b$. Finally, considering such converging paths we note that $\lim_{t\to\infty}\left(\frac{\dot{U}}{U}-\delta\right)=\frac{1-\sigma}{\sigma}(b-p)-\delta$. Hence, if $\frac{1-\sigma}{\sigma}<\frac{\delta}{b-\rho}$, then the integral $\int_0^\infty e^{-\delta t}U(c)dt$ converges. A simple check shows that all these conditions can be satisfied simultaneously. Now, since along this path consumption is rising at the maximal rate and since $\lambda=\frac{1}{\sigma}[\rho-\sigma n-(1-\sigma)b]$ is uniquely defined, all other paths which satisfy the Euler equations must be inferior to the asymptotic path which we have demonstrated.

This kind of path is described in Fig. 2. The figure indicates that for all initial $c(0)$ above the dotted line, the system becomes infeasible, while all initial $c(0)$ below the dotted

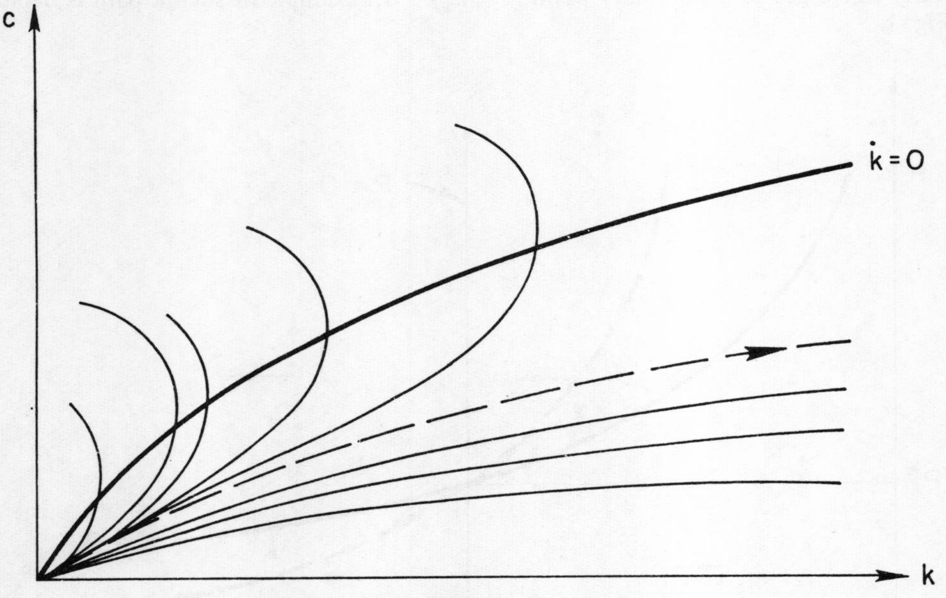

FIGURE 2

line lead to paths that are inferior. All optimal paths have an associated price system such that

$$f'(k)+\frac{\dot{P}}{P}=\rho. \qquad \ldots(4)$$

ρ can be viewed as an " own rate of interest ", where the " commodity " in question is utility, and ρ is indeed the marginal rate of transformation between utility today and tomorrow. Thus, this own rate of interest is equal to the rate of return on capital $f'(k)$, plus the rate of capital gains $\frac{\dot{P}(t)}{P(t)}$. The fact that we are dealing with a one-sector model does not obscure the point that there is a second good in this economy which is called " utility ", and this commodity serves as numeraire.

In terms of Hahn's expectation scheme we see that along any path which satisfies the first-order conditions, expectations are indeed myopic and self-realizing. This is the basic connection between competitive growth processes and the theory of optimal growth: If we require the competitive model to possess a structure of expectations which are myopic and self-realizing, then indeed we end up with paths identical to those described above. Now suppose the converse: We start with any one-sector deterministic model; suppose *we can prove* that the deterministic model can be viewed as resulting from some implicit optimization of a functional of the family $\int_0^\infty e^{-\delta t}U(c)dt$. *Then we have actually proved that this competitive growth path is unstable*! This follows from the fact that this dynamic path will be described by a system of differential equations identical to (1) and (3*a*) above. From the theory of optimal growth we know that this system is unstable, thus leading to the conclusion that the corresponding competitive process is unstable. This is the basic idea of this paper.

The natural question arises: Is this result restricted to a one-sector model, or will it be generally true for any n capital goods and m consumption goods (thus, we have $m+n$ sectors)? The purpose of the next section is to prove this instability property for n capital and m consumption goods.

II. A GENERAL GROWTH MODEL

II.1. *Formulation.* We start with notation. Let

K_i = the amount of capital type $i = 1, \ldots, n$,
C_j = the amount of consumption type j, $j = n+1, \ldots, m$.

We then have the system:

$$\begin{aligned} \dot{K}_1 &= F^1(K_{11}, K_{21}, \ldots, K_{n1}, L_1) \\ &\vdots \\ \dot{K}_n &= F^n(K_{1n}, K_{2n}, \ldots, K_{nn}, L_n) \\ C_{n+1} &= F^{n+1}(K_{1,n+1}, K_{2,n+1}, \ldots, K_{n,\ n+1}, L_{n+1}) \\ &\vdots \\ C_m &= F^m(L_{1m}, K_{2m}, \ldots, K_{nm}, L_m), \end{aligned} \qquad \ldots(5)$$

where all F^j are concave, constant returns to scale production functions and

$$K_i = \sum_{j=1}^{m} K_{ij}, \qquad \ldots(5a)$$

$$L = \sum_{i=1}^{m} L_i = e^{nt} \text{ (by assumption).} \qquad \ldots(5b)$$

This model is basically inconvenient to work with since it lacks the symmetric treatment of the variables. We can simplify its structure by observing that for any set of capital stocks $(K_1, K_2, \ldots, K_n)$, consumption levels $(C_{n+1}, \ldots, C_m)$, labour supply L and the efficiency conditions (assuming the existence of interior solution)

$$\frac{F_j^k}{F_i^k} = \frac{F_j^m}{F_i^m}, \qquad \ldots(6)$$

we have $n(m-1)$ equations from the efficiency conditions, and $m+1$ constraints from the capital, consumption, and labour constraints. Together we have $mn+m-(n-1)$ constraints with $mn+m$ unknown coefficients K_{ij} and L_i. This means that we have $n-1$

free rates K_i. This is why Samuelson [5] elected to formulate his frontier in the special form:

$$\dot{K}_1 = S_1(\dot{K}_2, \ldots, \dot{K}_n, K_1, \ldots, K_n, C_{n+1}, \ldots, C_m, L). \qquad \ldots(7)$$

This frontier can also be described by the following system:

$$\begin{aligned} \dot{K}_1 &= G^1(V_2, V_3, \ldots, V_n, K_1, \ldots, K_n, C_{n+1}, \ldots, C_m, L) \\ \dot{K}_2 &= V_2 \\ &\vdots \\ \dot{K}_n &= V_n. \end{aligned} \qquad \ldots(8)$$

This, however, is a special way of defining the frontier. It is possible to specify any $(n-1)$ coefficients K_{ij} or L_j as decision (control) variables, and then obtain the reduced form of (5), (5*a*, *b*) and (6) in the general form:

$$\begin{aligned} \dot{K}_1 &= G^1(V_2, V_3, \ldots, V_n, K_1, \ldots, K_n, C_{n+1}, \ldots, C_m) \\ &\vdots \\ \dot{K}_n &= G^n(V_2, V_3, \ldots, V_n, K_1, \ldots, K_n, C_{n+1}, \ldots, C_m) \end{aligned} \qquad \ldots(8a)$$

where the system (8*a*) inherits the constant returns to scale of the original system. Thus, we can write

$$\begin{aligned} \dot{k}_1 &= g^1(v_2, v_3, \ldots, v_n, k_1, \ldots, k_n, c_{n+1}, \ldots, c_m) - nk_1, \\ &\vdots \\ \dot{k}_n &= g^n(v_2, v_3, \ldots, v_n, k_1, \ldots, k_n, c_{n+1}, \ldots, c_m) - nk_n, \end{aligned} \qquad \ldots(9)$$

where $v_i = \dfrac{V_i}{L}$, $k_i = \dfrac{K_i}{L}$.

Now, given the system (9), we want to maximize the functional

$$\int_0^\infty U(t, c_{n+1}, c_{n+2}, \ldots, c_m)dt, \qquad \ldots(10)$$

subject to (9), and $k_i(0)$ given. Writing it in vector notation, we have

$$\text{Maximize} \int_0^\infty U(t, c)dt \qquad \ldots(11)$$

subject to

$$\frac{dk}{dt} = g(v, k, c) - nk, \ k(0) \text{ given.} \qquad \ldots(12)$$

To solve this system, introduce the Hamiltonian function

$$H(t, k, P, v, c) = U(t, c) + (P, g(v, k, c) - nk), \qquad \ldots(13)$$

and if the optimal programme (v^*, c^*) leading to $(P^*(t), k^*(t))$ exists, then the conditions of the Maximum Principle must be satisfied.

Throughout this discussion we shall assume (1) that an optimal programme exists, (2) that for any given P and k, the Hamiltonian function (13) has a unique maximum with respect to v and c which we shall denote by

$$\max_{(v, c)} H(t, k, P, v, c) = \hat{H}(t, k, P).$$

By the Maximum Principle, we have

$$\frac{dk}{dt} = \frac{\partial \hat{H}}{\partial P} \qquad \ldots(14a)$$

$$\frac{dP}{dt} = -\frac{\partial \hat{H}}{\partial k}. \qquad \ldots(14b)$$

II.2. *The Dynamic Behaviour of a Perturbation.* Assume that an optimal strategy, (v^*, c^*), exists and is uniquely determined. Then the optimal path, $(P^*(t), k^*(t))$, is well defined. We shall argue now that this path has the instability property that if $P^*(0)$ is the optimal initial value for P, and if the system starts off from any $P(0) \neq P^*(0)$, then it will diverge from the optimal path. Let us remark that in the literature of the calculus of variations this result is not new. Our purpose here is to present this result in the context of the theory of optimal growth and show that it has some implications for the analysis of competitive growth theory.

Case 1. *No discounting.* Let us first consider the case in which the objective function $U(t, c)$ depends on c only so that $U(c)$ is to replace $U(t, c)$ in (11). In this case the system (14*a*)-(14*b*) is autonomous.

To examine the stability property of the optimal path we start off from some $P(0) \neq P^*(0)$. Expanding the differential equation system and the Hamiltonian by the Taylor expansion, we have

$$k(t)-k^*(t) = \xi(t)+o(\| P(0)-P^*(0)\|) \qquad \text{...(15}a\text{)}$$

$$P(t)-P^*(t) = \eta(t)+o(\| P(0)-P^*(0)\|) \qquad \text{...(15}b\text{)}$$

where $\xi(t)$ and $\eta(t)$ satisfy

$$\frac{d\eta}{dt} = -\hat{H}_{kk}(t)\xi-\hat{H}_{kP}(t)\eta \qquad \text{...(16}a\text{)}$$

$$\frac{d\xi}{dt} = \hat{H}_{Pk}(t)\xi+\hat{H}_{PP}(t)\eta \qquad \text{...(16}b\text{)}$$

where

$$\hat{H}_{kk} = \frac{\partial^2\hat{H}}{\partial k^2}, \quad \hat{H}_{kP} = \frac{\partial^2\hat{H}}{\partial k\partial P},$$

$$\hat{H}_{Pk} = \frac{\partial^2\hat{H}}{\partial P\partial k}, \quad \hat{H}_{PP} = \frac{\partial^2 H}{\partial P^2}.$$

$\eta(t)$ has the initial conditions $\eta(0) = P(0)-P^*(0)$. Note that

ξ is an n vector
η is an n vector

and $\hat{H}_{Pk}$, $\hat{H}_{PP}$, $\hat{H}_{kk}$, and $\hat{H}_{kP}$ are $n\times n$ matrices.

Define now the following function:

$$\overline{H}(\xi, \eta) = \tfrac{1}{2}[\xi'\hat{H}_{kk}\xi+2(\eta'\overline{H}_{Pk}\xi)+\eta' H_{PP}\eta]. \qquad \text{...(17)}$$

This is a quadratic form in the variables ξ and η. Note, however, that

$$\frac{\partial\overline{H}}{\partial\xi} = \overline{H}_{kk}\xi+\hat{H}_{kP}\eta, \qquad \text{...(18}a\text{)}$$

$$\frac{\partial\overline{H}}{\partial\eta} = \hat{H}_{Pk}\xi+\hat{H}_{PP}\eta. \qquad \text{...(18}b\text{)}$$

Comparing (18*a*)-(18*b*) with (16*a*)-(16*b*), we observe that

$$\frac{d\xi}{dt} = \frac{\partial\overline{H}}{\partial\eta},$$

$$\frac{d\eta}{dt} = -\frac{\partial\overline{H}}{\partial\xi}.$$

Thus, $\xi(t)$ and $\eta(t)$ follow a system of differential equations which act as if they result from the optimization of the quadratic Hamiltonian function (17).[1] Hence, the variations $(\xi(t), \eta(t))$ behave like a Hamiltonian system of differential equations as follows.

Let

$$z(t) = \begin{pmatrix} \xi(t) \\ \eta(t) \end{pmatrix},$$

$$B(t) = \begin{bmatrix} \hat{H}_{Pk}(t) & \hat{H}_{PP}(t) \\ -\hat{H}_{kk}(t) & -\hat{H}_{kP}(t) \end{bmatrix};$$

then the differential equation system is

$$\frac{dz}{dt} = B(t)z,$$

and we have the following

Theorem 1. *Let λ be an eigenvalue of the matrix $B(t)$. Then $-\lambda$ is also an eigenvalue.*

Proof. Consider the matrix of blocks

$$J = \begin{bmatrix} 0 & -I_n \\ I_n & 0 \end{bmatrix}$$

where I_n is an $n \times n$ identity matrix. Note that $J' = -J$. Also,

$$JB = \begin{bmatrix} 0 & -I_n \\ I_n & 0 \end{bmatrix} \begin{bmatrix} \hat{H}_{Pk} & \hat{H}_{PP} \\ -\hat{H}_{kk} & -\hat{H}_{kP} \end{bmatrix} = \begin{bmatrix} \hat{H}_{kk} & \hat{H}_{kP} \\ \hat{H}_{Pk} & \hat{H}_{PP} \end{bmatrix} = M$$

and since $\hat{H}_{Pk} = \hat{H}'_{kP}$, M is symmetric. Now let λ be an eigenvalue of B. Then there exist $z \neq 0$ such that $Bz = \lambda z$. Since $JB = B'J'$, it follows that

$$J(\lambda z) = J(Bz) = B'J'z.$$

Since $J' = -J$, we have

$$J(\lambda z) = B'(-J)z;$$

hence,

$$-\lambda(Jz) = B'(Jz).$$

Let $Jz = y$. Then

$$B'y = -\lambda y;$$

hence, y is an eigenvector and $-\lambda$ is the corresponding eigenvalue of B'. Therefore, $-\lambda$ is an eigenvalue of B.

Case 2. *Constant discount factor.* In this case we assume

$$U(t, c) = e^{-\delta t} U(c),$$

and $\delta \geqq 0$ is a constant.

The system (14*a*)-(14*b*) is not autonomous in this case; however, with a simple transformation we can analyze the stability properties of (14*a*)-(14*b*) with the aid of an autonomous system. To do this we rewrite the Hamiltonian (13) as

$$H = e^{-\delta t} U(c) + (e^{-\delta t} \tilde{P},\ g(v, k, c) - nk),$$

where

$$P = e^{-\delta t} \tilde{P}.$$

Thus,

$$H = e^{-\delta t} [U(c) + (\tilde{P},\ g(v, k, c) - nk)].$$

[1] We present this fact although we make no use of it later on. The reader may note, however, that this indicates that the study of the stability properties of optimization problems with quadratic Hamiltonian is equivalent to the study of local stability of any nonlinear system.

Maximization of H with respect to v and c is equivalent to the maximization of the expression in brackets. Thus,

$$\max_{(v,c)} H(t, k, \tilde{P}, v, c) = \hat{H}(t, k, \tilde{P}) = e^{-\delta t}\overline{H}(k, \tilde{P}).$$

By the maximum principle,

$$\frac{dk}{dt} = \frac{\partial \hat{H}}{\partial(e^{-\delta t}\tilde{P})} = \frac{\partial \overline{H}}{\partial \tilde{P}},$$

$$\frac{d(\tilde{P}e^{-\delta t})}{dt} = -\frac{\partial \hat{H}}{\partial k}.$$

But

$$\frac{\partial \hat{H}}{\partial k} = e^{-\delta t}\frac{\partial \overline{H}}{\partial k}$$

and

$$\frac{d(\tilde{P}e^{-\delta t})}{dt} = -\delta\tilde{P}e^{-\delta t} + e^{-\delta t}\frac{d\tilde{P}}{dt}.$$

Thus, we have

$$\frac{dk}{dt} = \frac{\partial \overline{H}}{\partial \tilde{P}}, \qquad \text{...(14}a'\text{)}$$

$$\frac{d\tilde{P}}{dt} = -\frac{\partial \overline{H}}{\partial k} + \delta\tilde{P}. \qquad \text{...(14}b'\text{)}$$

This new system is autonomous. If we now perform the same Taylor expansion as before we find that the local stability of this system depends on the properties of the matrix:

$$\overline{B} = \begin{bmatrix} \overline{H}_{\tilde{p}k} & \overline{H}_{\tilde{p}\tilde{p}} \\ -\overline{H}_{kk} & -\overline{H}_{k\tilde{p}} + \delta I_n \end{bmatrix},$$

where I_n is the $n \times n$ identity matrix. Now let

$$F\left(\frac{\delta}{2}\right) = \begin{bmatrix} \overline{H}_{\tilde{p}k} - \frac{\delta}{2}I_n & \overline{H}_{\tilde{p}\tilde{p}} \\ -\overline{H}_{kk} & -\overline{H}_{k\tilde{p}} + \frac{\delta}{2}I_n \end{bmatrix}.$$

We have then

Theorem 2. *Let λ_1 be an eigenvalue of the matrix $\overline{B}$. Then there exists a corresponding eigenvalue λ^1 such that $\lambda_1 = \frac{\delta}{2} + \mu$ and $\lambda^1 = \frac{\delta}{2} - \mu$,* and the pair *$\pm\mu$ is a pair of eigenvalues of the matrix $F\left(\frac{\delta}{2}\right)$.*

Proof. The matrix $\overline{B}$ can be decomposed into

$$\overline{B} = \begin{bmatrix} \overline{H}_{\tilde{p}k} & H_{\tilde{p}\tilde{p}} \\ -\overline{H}_{kk} & -\overline{H}_{k\tilde{p}} \end{bmatrix} + \begin{bmatrix} 0 & 0 \\ 0 & \delta I_n \end{bmatrix}$$

$$= \frac{\delta}{2}I + \begin{bmatrix} \overline{H}_{\tilde{p}k} & \overline{H}_{\tilde{p}\tilde{p}} \\ -\overline{H}_{kk} & -\overline{H}_{k\tilde{p}} \end{bmatrix} + \begin{bmatrix} -\frac{\delta}{2}I_n & 0 \\ 0 & \frac{\delta}{2}I_n \end{bmatrix}$$

$$= \frac{\delta}{2}I + F\left(\frac{\delta}{2}\right).$$

Thus, let λ_1 be an eigenvalue of $\bar{B}$ with the corresponding eigenvector $z \neq 0$. $\bar{B}z = \lambda_1 z$ can be written as

$$\bar{B}z = \frac{\delta}{2} z + F\left(\frac{\delta}{2}\right) z = \lambda_1 z.$$

Thus,

$$F\left(\frac{\delta}{2}\right) z = \left(\lambda_1 - \frac{\delta}{2}\right) z.$$

This shows that z is an eigenvector of the matrix $F\left(\frac{\delta}{2}\right)$ with an eigenvalue $\mu = \lambda_1 - \frac{\delta}{2}$, and hence $\lambda_1 = \frac{\delta}{2} + \mu$ is the eigenvalue of the matrix $\bar{B}$. However, the matrix $F\left(\frac{\delta}{2}\right)$ satisfies all the condition of the matrix B in Theorem 1. Thus, $-\mu$ is also an eigenvalue of the matrix $F\left(\frac{\delta}{2}\right)$; this in turn means that $-\mu = \lambda^1 - \frac{\delta}{2}$; hence, $\lambda^1 = \frac{\delta}{2} - \mu$ is the second eigenvalue of $\bar{B}$.

Theorem 3. *Suppose* $\delta > 0$. *Then the system* (14a')-(14b') *is either totally unstable or has the instability characterized by the saddle point property.*

Proof. Denote by $\operatorname{Re} u$ the real part of a complex number u. Suppose first that $|\operatorname{Re} \mu| < \frac{\delta}{2}$. Then it is clear that

$$\operatorname{Re} \lambda_1 = \frac{\delta}{2} + \operatorname{Re} \mu > 0$$

$$\operatorname{Re} \lambda^1 = \frac{\delta}{2} - \operatorname{Re} \mu > 0.$$

If, however, $|\operatorname{Re} \mu| > \frac{\delta}{2}$, then suppose that $\operatorname{Re} \mu > 0$. Then

$$\operatorname{Re} \lambda_1 = \frac{\delta}{2} + \operatorname{Re} \mu > \delta$$

$$\operatorname{Re} \lambda^1 = \frac{\delta}{2} - \operatorname{Re} \mu < 0.$$

If, however, $\operatorname{Re} \mu < 0$, then

$$\operatorname{Re} \lambda_1 = \frac{\delta}{2} + \operatorname{Re} \mu < 0$$

$$\operatorname{Re} \lambda^1 = \frac{\delta}{2} - \operatorname{Re} \mu > \delta.$$

Thus, in the above two cases either both $\operatorname{Re} \lambda_1 > 0$ and $\operatorname{Re} \lambda^1 > 0$, or $(\operatorname{Re} \lambda_1)(\operatorname{Re} \lambda^1) < 0$. In the first instance we have total instability, and in the second the saddle point property.

To complete the proof we have to show that it is not possible to have all eigenvalues of the matrix $\bar{B}$ purely imaginary. To see this, let $\mu = a + ib$ be an eigenvalue of $F\left(\frac{\delta}{2}\right)$. Then

$$\lambda_1 = \frac{\delta}{2} + a + ib$$

$$\lambda^1 = \frac{\delta}{2} - a - ib.$$

For λ_1 and λ^1 to be purely imaginary numbers it is necessary that $\frac{\delta}{2}+a = \frac{\delta}{2}-a = 0$. But this is impossible as long as $\delta > 0$.

Corollary. Suppose $\delta = 0$. Then if the matrix B has at least one eigenvalue which is not a purely imaginary number, the corresponding system of differential equations is either totally unstable or has the saddle point property.

Remarks

(1) It is conceivable that for $\delta = 0$ the matrix B will have only purely imaginary eigenvalues. In such a case the system can have undamped oscillatory behaviour.

(2) It is interesting to note that it is possible that a stationary point of the optimal programme will *not* have the saddle point property. An example of such a case was presented by Kurz [3], where multiplicity of stationary points resulted from the introduction of wealth effects. In that case the stationary points appear in an alternating sequence along the capital axis: one having the totally unstable feature followed by a saddle point. However, one can construct simpler examples. Consider the following, due to K. J. Arrow:

Let the utility function be

$$U(c) = -\tfrac{1}{2}(\bar{c}-c)^2 \ (c \geqq 0)$$

and the production function

$$F(K) = \alpha K.$$

The maximization problem is as follows: Maximize

$$\int_0^\infty -e^{-\delta t}\tfrac{1}{2}(\bar{c}-c)^2 dt$$

subject to

$$\dot{K} = I$$

$$c \geqq 0$$

$$c+I \leqq \alpha K.$$

Assume $\delta > \alpha$. The maximum can be described as follows: Let $P(t)$ be the associated price; then

$$\dot{P}(t) = (\delta-\alpha)P$$

and

$$c = \begin{cases} \bar{c}-P & \text{if } P \leqq \bar{c} \\ 0 & \text{if } P > \bar{c}. \end{cases}$$

The only finite stationary point is $\left(K = \frac{\bar{c}}{\alpha}, P = 0\right)$ with $c = \bar{c}$. As is seen in the phase diagram (Fig. 3), the curve $\dot{K} = 0$ is described by $P+\alpha K-\bar{c} = 0$ while $\dot{P} = 0$ is represented by the entire K-axis. Since $\delta > \alpha$, $\dot{P} = (\delta-\alpha)P \geqq 0$ for $P(0) \geqq 0$. Thus, the stationary point $\left(K = \frac{\bar{c}}{\alpha}, P = 0\right)$ is totally unstable. However, the optimal path is described by the dotted line. Along this line $P \leqq \bar{c}$; thus the equality $P = \bar{c}-c$ holds. Note that for $K(0) = \frac{\bar{c}}{\alpha}$, the economy stays at the point $\left(K = \frac{\bar{c}}{\alpha}, P = 0\right)$; for $K(0) > \frac{\bar{c}}{\alpha}$ the optimal programme calls for $c = \bar{c}$ and K growing indefinitely. For $K(0) < \frac{\bar{c}}{\alpha}$, the economy moves first to the point ($K = 0$, $P = $ c) but then proceeds along the P-axis where $K = 0$ and

$\lim_{t \to \infty} P(t) = \infty$. Thus, the two abstract points ($K = \infty$, $P = 0$) and ($K = 0$, $P = \infty$) are, in a sense, saddle points. With this interpretation the optimal programme here, under the condition $\delta > \alpha$, is formally similar to the one analyzed in [3].

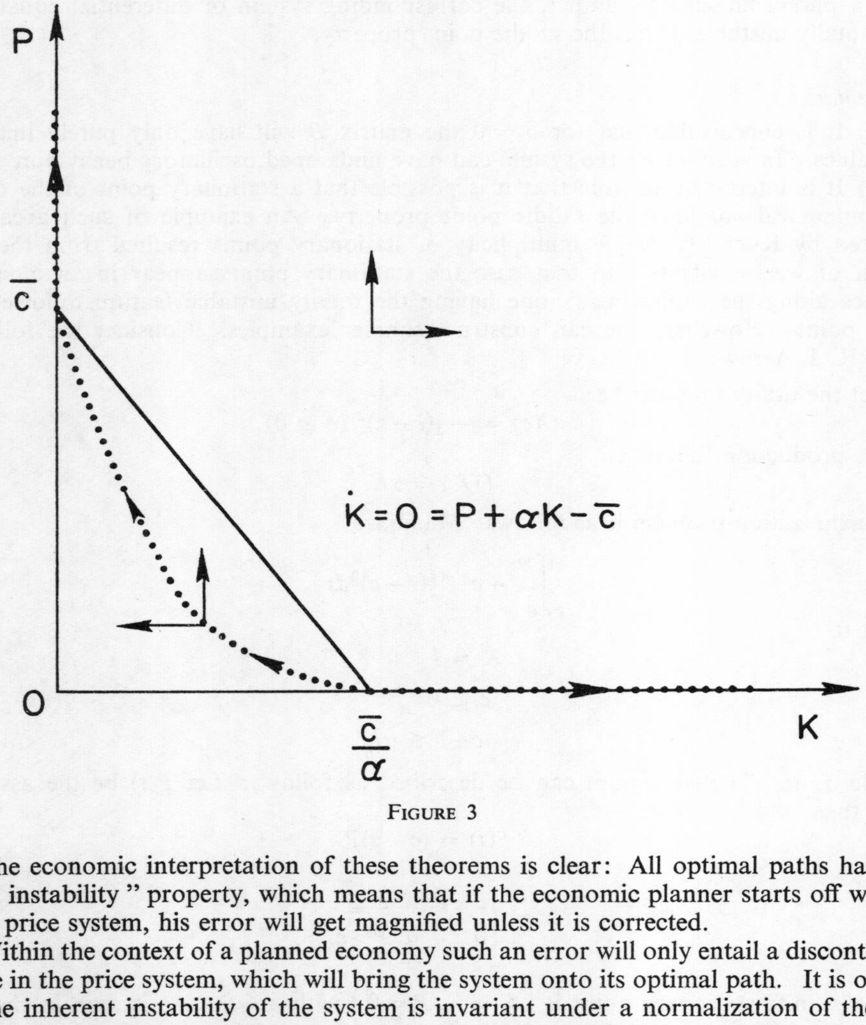

FIGURE 3

The economic interpretation of these theorems is clear: All optimal paths have this " local instability " property, which means that if the economic planner starts off with the wrong price system, his error will get magnified unless it is corrected.

Within the context of a planned economy such an error will only entail a discontinuous change in the price system, which will bring the system onto its optimal path. It is obvious that the inherent instability of the system is invariant under a normalization of the price system. In a planning situation, the price system reflects the planner's utility. If he then normalizes these accounting prices by his marginal utility, he does not change the unstable character of the system.

It is very important to note that the matrix $B(t)$ is changing over time so that the eigenvalues must be viewed as changing over time. Thus, the interpretation of the theorems should be that the system tends to diverge at any moment of time. However, if we add the condition that the system has a stationary solution, then at that point the matrix B is constant, and we obtain the result that the balanced growth path is unstable.

The application of these results to competitive, deterministic systems with myopic self-realizing expectations is now clear: Suppose we observe any competitive economy which is always in a competitive equilibrium. Suppose further that we can prove that this system behaves as if it is the result of optimization of some implicit functional of the type $\int_0^\infty e^{-\delta t}U(c)dt$; then we can assert that it is locally unstable. Thus, we have the following

Instability Proposition: *All competitive growth processes which are always in equilibrium (thus, follow the myopic, self-realizing expectation system), and which could be constructed from an optimization over an intertemporally independent utility functional with a constant discount factor, are locally unstable.*

One can define the notions of weak and strong local instability in order to distinguish between systems with a balanced growth and without it. Systems having no balanced growth path would then be defined as weakly locally unstable, and those having a balanced growth path would be defined as strongly locally stable. This distinction was motivated earlier by the behaviour of the matrix $B(t)$ over time.

The above results are of a local nature. It is not possible, with the tools at hand and at this level of generality, to say anything significant about the global behaviour of the economy. It may be conjectured that the deviation from the optimal path is very rapid at the earlier phases, but this slows down over time. Actual infeasibilities in finite time could result in highly specialized cases.

Note, finally, that our approach to the question of competitive stability raises a whole spectrum of new problems that could be called the " inverse optimal " problems of constructing the class of objective functions which could give rise to given specified consumption-investment functions. Apart from the significance of this question to the analysis of stability, the solution of the inverse optimal problem can remove some of the objections to the cardinal nature of the theory of optimal growth. To see its significance, we note that in general economists have no objections to postulating various types of savings functions. Now if we could establish some interesting correspondence between savings and utility functions, and if it could further be proved that most " reasonable " savings functions could be constructed from an optimization of a utility function coming from some well-defined class, then the objections to the use of cardinal utility functions in the theory of optimal growth could be removed. It is obvious that the notion of " reasonable savings functions " requires a definition we are not ready to make here. This will be the subject of another paper. However, we can point out that such a research strategy will surely face grave difficulties when a given savings function depends critically on income distribution. The difficulties are even greater when we consider the class of savings functions which are functions of intergenerational income distribution. In such cases we can't hope to obtain these savings functions as the optimal solutions of problems involving utility functionals which are intertemporally independent.

In the following, we shall solve the inverse optimal problem for the Solow growth model, and present our interpretation of its peculiar properties.

III. THE SOLOW MODEL: AN INTERPRETATION

The Solow growth model,

$$\begin{cases} \dot{K} = sF(K, L), & 0<s<1 \text{ constant} \\ L = e^{nt} \end{cases} \qquad \text{...(19)}$$

is supposed to be a description of a deterministic competitive economy. This model can be written as

$$\dot{k} = f(k) - nk - c(t), \qquad \text{...(20a)}$$

$$c(t) = (1-s)f(k), \quad 0<s<1 \text{ constant.} \qquad \text{...(20b)}$$

We know that this model demonstrates strong stability properties. Frank Hahn [1, 2] attributed this stability to the fact that this is a unique result of the one-commodity assumption. If we take our alternative point of view and assume that the Solow model has a solution for the inverse optimal problem, then the function $\hat{c}(r) = (1-s)f(\hat{k})$ should be viewed as the optimal solution of some optimization problem. Now we have seen in Section A of this paper that the optimal path resulting from a functional of the form $\int_0^{\infty} e^{-\delta t}U(c)dt$ must be

$$U_c = P, \qquad \text{...(21}a\text{)}$$

$$\dot{P} = P[\rho - f'(k)], \quad \rho = n+\delta. \qquad \text{...(21}b\text{)}$$

So in general $c(t)$ should be a function of P written as $c(P)$. However, it is also possible to synthesize the solution in the following manner: From (21a) we have

$$\left(\frac{U_{cc}}{U_c}c\right)\frac{\dot{c}}{c} = \frac{\dot{P}}{P}. \qquad \text{...(22)}$$

Now define

$$\sigma(c) = -\frac{U_{cc}}{U_c}c. \qquad \text{...(23)}$$

Thus, from (23), (22), and (21b) we have

$$\frac{\dot{c}}{c} = \frac{1}{\sigma(c)}[f'(k)-\rho]. \qquad \text{...(24)}$$

Now adding (20a) we have the system:

$$\dot{c} = \frac{c}{\sigma(c)}[f'(k)-\rho] \qquad \text{...(25}a\text{)}$$

$$\dot{k} = f(k) - nk - c, \quad k(0) \text{ given.} \qquad \text{...(25}b\text{)}$$

This system of differential equations has a solution for every given $c(0)$. We know that the optimal path is the unique path in the (c, k) plane, such that $\hat{c}(0)$ satisfies $\hat{P}(0) = U_c(\hat{c}(0))$. This means that the optimal path $\hat{c}(t)$ can be reconstructed from (25a) and (25b) as a function

$$c(k) = \phi(k). \qquad \text{...(26)}$$

The unique feature of this synthesis [1] is that *it is* the optimal path and converges to a stationary point. This stability is nothing but a reflection of the fact that for different $k(0)$ we choose different $\hat{P}(k(0))$, and hence different $\hat{c}(\hat{P})$ reflected in the value $\phi(\hat{k})$. Thus, in the special case of the Solow model, where

$$\phi(k) = (1-s)f(k), \qquad \text{...(27)}$$

the stability of the model is the result of the fact that any changes in $k(0)$ lead to changes in the corresponding $\hat{P}(k(0))$ and $\hat{c}(k(0))$ so as to keep the economy on the optimal path. The stability is nothing but a reflection of the movement along the optimal path, which has the usual convergence properties to its stationary point.

The question to which we must now turn is the characterization of the solution of the inverse optimal problem for the Solow model.

It follows from (20b) that

$$\frac{\dot{c}}{c} = \varepsilon_f \frac{\dot{k}}{k}, \qquad \text{...(28}a\text{)}$$

[1] For additional discussion of the synthesis problem in the theory of optimal control, see [4, pp. 22-45].

where

$$\varepsilon_f = \frac{f'(k)k}{f(k)} = \text{the elasticity of the production function.} \qquad \ldots(28b)$$

Since $\dot{k} = sf(k) - nk$, it follows that

$$\frac{\dot{k}}{k} = s\frac{f(k)}{k} - n. \qquad \ldots(29)$$

In order to characterize the class of utility functions which will give rise to a constant savings ratio as an optimal solution, we shall assume (21*a*) and (21*b*) to hold for an unknown function U_c. Thus, we have

$$\frac{\dot{c}}{c} = \frac{1}{\sigma(c)}[f'(k) - \rho], \qquad \ldots(30)$$

and combining (30) with (28*b*) and (29) we have

$$\sigma(c) = \frac{f'(k) - \rho}{\varepsilon_f \left[s\dfrac{f(k)}{k} - n \right]}. \qquad \ldots(31)$$

Equation (31) can now be viewed as a differential equation in c where $k = f^{-1}\left(\dfrac{c}{1-s}\right)$. We rewrite (31) as

$$\sigma(c) = -\frac{U_{cc}}{U_c}c = \frac{f'(k) - \rho}{\varepsilon_f \left[s\dfrac{f(k)}{k} - n \right]} = \frac{f'(k) - \rho}{s\dfrac{f(k)}{k} \cdot \dfrac{f'(k)k}{f(k)} - n\dfrac{f'(k)k}{f(k)}}, \quad k = f^{-1}\left(\frac{c}{1-s}\right); \qquad \ldots(32)$$

hence,

$$-\frac{U_{cc}}{U_c}c = \left(\frac{1}{s}\right)\frac{1 - \dfrac{\rho}{f'(k)}}{1 - \dfrac{n}{s}\dfrac{k}{f(k)}}, \quad k = f^{-1}\left(\frac{c}{1-s}\right). \qquad \ldots(33)$$

Now since $c = (1-s)f(k)$ and $dc = (1-s)f'(k)dk$, we have

$$-\frac{U_{cc}}{U_c} = \left(\frac{1}{s}\right)\frac{1 - \rho(1-s)\dfrac{dk}{dc}}{c - \dfrac{n}{s}(1-s)k(c)}. \qquad \ldots(34)$$

The solution of the inverse optimal problem for the Solow model is equivalent to integrating the differential equation (34). The general solution can be written as

$$U_c = M\exp\left\{\frac{1}{s}\int \frac{1 - (1-s)\dfrac{dk}{dc}}{c - \dfrac{n}{s}(1-s)k(c)}\,dc\right\}. \qquad \ldots(34a)$$

Before proceeding to the analysis of (34*a*), we present the following

Proposition: *Assume that* (34*a*) *has a solution. Suppose the Solow model possesses a stationary point at* k^*, *then* $\lim_{t\to\infty} \sigma(c) = \dfrac{1}{s\sigma_f^*}$, *where* $\sigma_f^* = -\dfrac{f'(k^*)(f(k^*) - k^*f'(k^*))}{f''(k^*)f(k^*)k^*}$ *(the elasticity of substitution).*

Proof. Since at k^* we have

$$s\frac{f(k^*)}{k^*} = n,$$

$$f'(k^*) = \rho,$$

it follows that

$$\rho = \left(\frac{n}{s}\right)\left(\frac{f'(k^*)k^*}{f(k^*)}\right).$$

From (32) we have

$$\sigma(c) = \left(\frac{1}{s}\right)\frac{f'(k)-\rho}{f'(k)-\left(\frac{n}{s}\right)\left(\frac{f'(k)k}{f(k)}\right)};$$

hence,

$$\sigma(c) = \left(\frac{1}{s}\right)\frac{f'(k)-\left(\frac{n}{s}\right)\frac{f'(k^*)k^*}{f(k^*)}}{f'(k)-\left(\frac{n}{s}\right)\left(\frac{f'(k)k}{f(k)}\right)}.$$

Thus, we have

$$\lim_{k\to k^*}\sigma(c) = \left(\frac{1}{s}\right)\frac{f''(k^*)}{f''(k^*)-\frac{n}{s}\left[\frac{f''(k^*)k^*f(k^*)+f'(k^*)f(k^*)-f'(k^*)f'(k^*)k^*}{f(k^*)^2}\right]}$$

$$= \left(\frac{1}{s}\right)\frac{1}{1-\frac{n}{s}\left[\frac{k^*}{f(k^*)}+\frac{f'(k^*)(f(k^*)-k^*f'(k^*))}{f''(k^*)f(k^*)k^*}\left(\frac{k^*}{f(k^*)}\right)\right]}$$

$$= \left(\frac{1}{s}\right)\frac{-f''(k^*)f(k^*)k^*}{f'(k^*)(f(k^*)-k^*f'(k^*))} = \frac{1}{s\sigma_f^*}.$$

Let us consider now two special cases which are of some interest.

Case 1. *Cobb-Douglas production function.* In this case we have

$$f'(k)-\rho = \alpha A k^{\alpha-1}-\rho, \qquad \text{...(35a)}$$

$$\varepsilon_f\left[s\frac{f(k)}{k}-n\right] = \alpha[sAk^{\alpha-1}-n]. \qquad \text{...(35b)}$$

Note, however, that since $f(k) = Ak^\alpha$, the Solow model has a stationary point k^* such that

$$s\frac{f(k^*)}{k^*} = n,$$

and

$$f'(k^*) = \rho.$$

Thus,

$$\frac{sf(k^*)}{f'(k^*)k^*} = \frac{n}{\rho}$$

or

$$n = \frac{1}{\alpha}(s\rho).$$

Inserting this value of s into (32) with $\varepsilon_f = \alpha$, we have, since $\rho = n+\delta \geqq 0$,

$$s = \alpha \frac{n}{\rho} \leqq \alpha,$$

and

$$\sigma(c) = -\frac{U_{cc}}{U_c} c = \frac{\alpha A k^{\alpha-1} - \rho}{s[\alpha A k^{\alpha-1} - \rho]} = \frac{1}{s}. \qquad \text{...(36)}$$

It follows that

$$\frac{U_{cc}}{U_c} = \left(-\frac{1}{s}\right)\left(\frac{1}{c}\right), \quad s \leqq \alpha.$$

Thus, we have

$$U_c(c) = Bc^{-1/s},\ B>0,\ s \leqq \alpha,\ \rho = n\frac{\alpha}{s}, \qquad \text{...(37)}$$

and

$$U(c) = Mc^{-\left(\frac{1-s}{s}\right)} + N,\ M<0,\ s \leqq \alpha,\ \rho = n\frac{\alpha}{s}. \qquad \text{...(38)}$$

Hence, a Cobb-Douglas production function implies that the solution of the inverse optimal problem for the constant savings ratio with $s \leqq \alpha$ must be the family of all constant elasticity utility functions.

Case 2. *Divergent sustained growth.* In the Solow model it is possible to have a situation like the one in Fig. 4. In such a case it is still possible for the system to converge

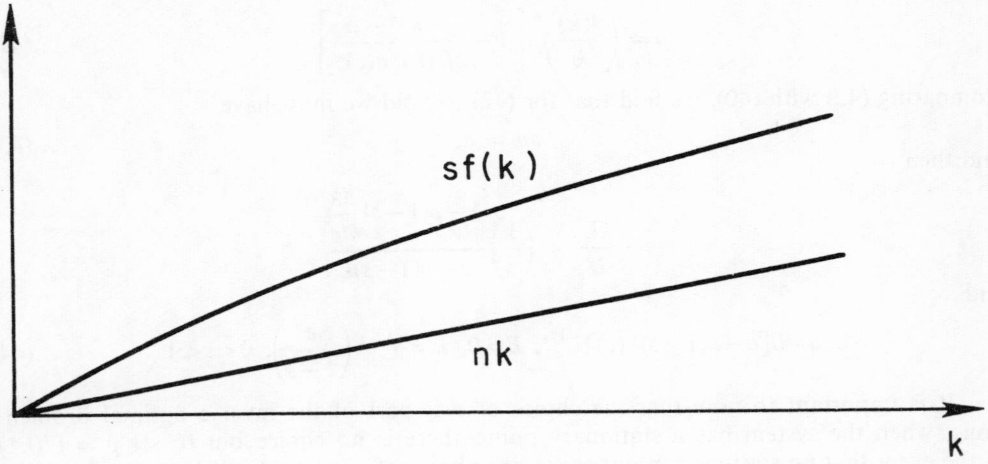

FIGURE 4

to a growth rate $\lim_{t\to\infty} \frac{\dot{k}}{k} = \lambda > 0$. Note that in this case $f'(k)$ is bounded away from n, the growth rate of population; it follows that $k(t) \to \infty$, and we shall assume that the elasticity, ε_f converges so that $\lim_{t\to\infty} \varepsilon_f = \varepsilon_f^*$. In this case,

$$\frac{\dot{k}}{k} \to \lambda = \lim_{k\to\infty} s\frac{f(k)}{k} - n = s\left(\frac{f(k)}{k}\right)^* - n,$$

and thus

$$\lim_{t\to\infty} \frac{\dot{c}}{c} = \left(\lim_{k\to\infty} \varepsilon_f\right)\lambda = \varepsilon_f^* \lambda = \left(\frac{f'(k)-\rho}{\sigma(c)}\right)^*.$$

Thus,

$$\lambda + n = s\left(\frac{f(k)}{k}\right)^*.$$

Since $f(k)$ is concave, $f'(k)$ must converge. Thus, $\lim_{k\to\infty} f'(k) = (f'(k))^* =$ a constant. It follows that $\sigma(c)$ must also converge to $(\sigma(c))^*$. We have then

$$\lambda = \frac{1}{\varepsilon_f^*}\frac{f'(k)^* - \rho}{\sigma(c)^*}; \qquad \text{...(39)}$$

hence,

$$\frac{1}{\varepsilon_f^*}\frac{f'(k)^* - \rho}{\sigma(c)^*} + n = s\left(\frac{f(k)}{k}\right)^*,$$

or

$$n = s\left(\frac{f(k)}{k}\right)^* - \frac{1}{f'(k)^*}\left(\frac{f(k)}{k}\right)^*\frac{f'(k)^* - \rho}{\sigma(c)^*}. \qquad \text{...(40)}$$

Thus, from (34) we have

$$-\frac{U_{cc}}{U_c} = \left(\frac{1}{s}\right)\frac{f'(k) - \rho}{c - \left(\frac{f(k)}{k}\right)^*\left[1 - \frac{f'(k) - \rho}{sf'(k)^*\sigma(c)^*}\right](1-s)k}. \qquad \text{...(41)}$$

Since ρ is an unrestricted parameter, (41) can be exactly integrated if

$$\rho = \left(\frac{f(k)}{k}\right)^*\left[1 - \frac{f'(k)^* - \rho}{sf'(k)^*\sigma(c)^*}\right]. \qquad \text{...(42)}$$

Comparing (42) with (40), we find that for (42) to hold we must have

$$s\rho = n, \qquad \text{...(43)}$$

and then

$$-\frac{U_{cc}}{U_c} = \left(\frac{1}{s}\right)\frac{1 - \rho(1-s)\frac{dk}{dc}}{c - \rho(1-s)k}$$

and

$$U_c = B[c - \rho(1-s)k(c)]^{-1/s},\ B>0,\ k = f^{-1}\left(\frac{c}{1-s}\right),\ 0<s<1. \qquad \text{...(44)}$$

It is important to note that the choice of ρ is part of the inverse optimal problem. Thus, when the system has a stationary point, there is no choice but to set $\rho = f'(k^*)$. In the event that no stationary point exists, the choice of ρ is free, leading to the simplification of (34*a*) and the resulting solution (44).

Case 3. *The general solution* (34*a*) *with a stationary point*. The general solution of the inverse optimal problem for the Solow model was given by (34*a*). Here we shall make a few additional comments concerning this integral.

If we assume that the Solow model has a unique stationary point, k^* (and thus $c^* = (1-s)f(k^*)$), then the differential equation (34) can be written:

$$-\frac{U_{cc}}{U_c} = \left(\frac{1}{s}\right)\frac{f'(k) - \frac{n}{s}\varepsilon_f^*}{cf'(k) - \frac{n}{s}(1-s)f'(k)k}, \qquad \text{...(45)}$$

and since $\frac{dk}{dc} = \frac{1}{(1-s)f(k)}$, we have

$$-\frac{U_{cc}}{U_c} = \left(\frac{1}{s}\right)\frac{1-\frac{n}{s}(1-s)\varepsilon_f^*\frac{dk}{dc}}{c-\frac{n}{s}(1-s)k}. \quad \ldots(46)$$

Note that at $k = k^*$, both the numerator and the denominator of the right-hand side of (46) vanish. But the expression on the right is always positive: When $k>k^*$, both the numerator and denominator are negative, and when $k<k^*$, both are positive. To carry out the integration, we can consider $k>k^*$ and $k<k^*$ separately.

Now rewrite (46) as

$$-\frac{U_{cc}}{U_c} = \frac{\varepsilon_f^*}{s}\left[\frac{1-\frac{n}{s}(1-s)\frac{dk}{dc}}{c-\frac{n}{s}(1-s)k(c)} - \frac{1-\frac{1}{\varepsilon_f^*}}{c-\frac{n}{s}(1-s)k(c)}\right].$$

Hence,

$$\int\frac{U_{cc}}{U_c}\,dc = -\left(\frac{\varepsilon_f}{s}\right)\int\frac{1-\frac{n}{s}(1-s)\frac{dk}{dc}}{c-\frac{n}{s}(1-s)k(c)}\,dc - \left(\frac{\varepsilon_f^*}{s}\right)\left(\frac{1}{\varepsilon_f^*}-1\right)\int\frac{dc}{c-\frac{n}{s}(1-s)k(c)}. \quad \ldots(47)$$

It follows that

$$U_c = \begin{cases} A\left[c-\frac{n}{s}(1-s)k(c)\right]^{-\varepsilon_f^*/s}\exp\left\{-\frac{1-\varepsilon_f^*}{s}\int\frac{dc}{c-\frac{n}{s}(1-s)k(c)}\right\} & \text{for } k<k^*, \\ A\left[\frac{n}{s}(1-s)k(c)-c\right]^{-\varepsilon_f^*/s}\exp\left\{\frac{1-\varepsilon_f^*}{s}\int\frac{dc}{\frac{n}{s}(1-s)k(c)-c}\right\} & \text{for } k>k^*, \end{cases} \quad \ldots(48)$$

and from (47), we have

$$U_c = A\left|c-\frac{n}{s}(1-s)k(c)\right|^{-\varepsilon_f^*/s}\exp\left\{-\frac{1}{s}(1-\varepsilon_f^*)\int\frac{dc}{c-\frac{n}{s}(1-s)k(c)}\right\}, \quad k \neq k^*, \quad \ldots(49)$$

while the value of U_c at k^* would naturally be taken to be the limit of (49) as $k \to k^*$. This limit will exist if there exists a solution to the inverse optimal problem.

It is clear from (49) that the general solution for U_c is a combination of power functions. First we have the power function of c and $k(c)$, which is $\left|c-\frac{n}{s}(1-s)k(c)\right|^{-\varepsilon_f^*/s}$, and the second integral can also be viewed as an integral of the sum of power functions involving $\frac{k^n}{c^{n+1}}$. This is so since if, for example, $k<k^*$, then

$$\int\frac{dc}{c-\frac{n}{s}(1-s)k(c)} = \int\left(\frac{1}{c}\right)\frac{dc}{1-\frac{n}{s}(1-s)\frac{k(c)}{c}}$$

$$= \int \left(\frac{1}{c}\right)\left[1+\frac{n}{s}(1-s)\frac{k(c)}{c}+\left(\frac{n}{s}(1-s)\frac{k(c)}{c}\right)^2+\ldots\right]dc$$

$$= \int \left[\sum_{n=0}^{\infty}\left(\frac{n}{s}(1-s)\right)^n\frac{k(c)^n}{c^{n+1}}\right]dc,$$

and similarly for $k<k^*$.

Behaviour of U_c for large k (and c). If the marginal product function, $f'(k)$, tends to 0 for large k, then $\frac{k(c)}{c}$ tends to $+\infty$. Examination of the two terms in (47) shows that for large k, U_c behaves as

$$U_c \sim A\left(\frac{n}{s}(1-s)k(c)\right)^{-\varepsilon_f^*/s}.$$

Behaviour of U_c for small k (and c) depends on $\lim_{k\to 0} f'(k)$. If $\lim_{k\to 0} f'(k) \to +\infty$, then

$$\int \frac{dc}{c-\frac{n}{s}(1-s)k} \sim \log c,$$

and thus

$$U_c \sim A[c]^{-\frac{\varepsilon_f^*}{s}}[c]^{-\frac{1}{s}(1-\varepsilon_f^*)};$$

hence,

$$U_c \sim A[c]^{-1/s}, \qquad \ldots(50)$$

and thus, for small k, U_c behaves similarly to the uniform behaviour of U_c when f is a Cobb-Douglas production function.

Finally, we must consider the restriction $\delta+n = \rho = f'(k^*) \geqq n$ (or $\delta \geqq 0$). This will put some limits on the values of s for which there is a solution to the inverse optimal problem in the Solow model. To see this, note that $f'(k^*) \geqq n$ means

$$\varepsilon_f^* = \frac{f'(k^*)k^*}{f(k^*)} \geqq \frac{nk^*}{f(k^*)}. \qquad \ldots(51)$$

But from the differential equation $\dot{k} = sf(k)-nk$, it follows that at k^*,

$$sf(k^*) = nk^*. \qquad \ldots(52)$$

Thus, (51) and (52) together imply the natural condition

$$s \leqq \varepsilon_f^* \qquad \ldots(53)$$

and hence

$$\delta = f'(k^*)\left[\frac{\varepsilon_f^*-s}{\varepsilon_f^*}\right] \geqq 0. \qquad \ldots(54)$$

IV. A FINAL NOTE

Our starting point in this paper was the analysis of the dynamic evolution of economies where the myopic, self-realizing system of expectations prevails at all times. These economies are described by a system of differential equations arising from the equation of all rates of return of capital goods (including capital gains). Hahn observed that such economies may be unstable, and he proved this conjecture for a special case; our purpose was to generalize Hahn's results.

There is one critical step which has been overlooked so far: the claim that economies of the type described above should be called " competitive ". This claim is subject to serious questioning since it is true that in short-term competitive equilibrium the so-called " myopic rule " will be followed. However, it is clear that in general such paths will be inefficient; thus, the claim becomes one which argues that competitive economies are in general inefficient.

One would expect a competitive economy to possess some adjustment mechanism which will result from an interaction between spot and futures markets. Shell and Stiglitz [7] take a first step in this direction.

It seems that further work on the analysis of stability should examine alternative adjustment mechanisms of spot prices in response to futures prices. Thus, the interaction between them should be incorporated into a dynamic analysis which will then result in two dynamic forces operating on the system at all times: the myopic rule as analyzed here, and the adjustment mechanism resulting from the interaction of spot and futures prices.

Stanford University M. Kurz.

REFERENCES

[1] Hahn, F. H. " On the Stability of Growth Equilibrium ", Memorandum, Institute of Economics, University of Oslo (April 19, 1966).

[2] Hahn, F. H. " Equilibrium Dynamics with Heterogeneous Capital Goods ", *Quarterly Journal of Economics* (forthcoming).

[3] Kurz, M. " Optimal Economic Growth and Wealth Effects ", to appear in the *International Economic Review* (1968).

[4] Pontryagin, L. S. and Associates. *The Mathematical Theory of Optimal Processes* (Translation from the Russian, Interscience Publishers, New York, 1962).

[5] Samuelson, P. A. " Efficient Paths of Capital Accumulation in Terms of the Calculus of Variations ", in Arrow, Karlin and Suppes (eds.), *Mathematical Methods in the Social Sciences*, 1959 (Stanford: Stanford University Press, 1960).

[6] Solow, R. M. " A Contribution to the Theory of Economic Growth ", *Quarterly Journal of Economics* (February 1956).

[7] Shell, K., and Stiglitz, J. E. " Notes on Heterogeneous Capital Accumulation ", Mimeographed, Department of Economics, Massachusetts Institute of Technology, Cambridge, Mass.

18 On Warranted Growth Paths

F. H. HAHN

Recently I showed [2] that the steady state path of an economy with more than one capital good was not the asymptotic state of all equilibrium paths. For some special cases I demonstrated that indeed all equilibrium paths diverged. This is in marked contrast to the well known result of Solow for the one-sector world and to the equally familiar two-sector propositions. Partly through discussions with Mirrlees, I had become aware that my analysis bore a family resemblance to the " local turnpike theorems " of Dosso, Samuelson and McKenzie [4, 6], which exploit the fact that the Neumann ray is a saddle point[1] in the phase space of all inter-temporally efficient paths. However I could not make a firm connection since my construction allowed for a separate consumption sector, a descriptive consumption function and for an exogenously given labour force. The " turnpike " results had none of these features. But further study of the problem has enabled me to clarify the connection between the descriptive and the " planning " model and it is the first purpose of this paper to report on this.

It has been shown by Kurz and Goldman [3, 1] that in the case of one capital good a descriptive model of a neo-classical economy can be converted into one where the equilibrium path taken by the economy is the same it would take if its rate of change of consumption were governed by the Euler equations for an appropriately chosen Ramsey objective function. If that conclusion were to hold for any number of capital goods, then since for many cases the Ramsey paths have a unique singular point which is also a saddle point, it would follow that the same is true for a large class of descriptive economies. The second purpose of this paper is to examine this question.

Lastly I should like to take the opportunity to offer some rather general remarks on the economics of the problem discussed. These should be taken as supplementing the excellent recent analysis of Shell and Stiglitz [7].

I. THE MODEL

Consider a world of one consumption good, (indexed " 0 ") and m capital goods, (indexed $1 \ldots m$). Let $Y_i(t)$,$(i = 0 \ldots m)$ be the output *per man* at time t and $K_i(t)$ $(i = 1 \ldots m)$, the stock *per man* of the ith capital good at time t. Time arguments will be omitted when the context makes this safe.

*Assumption A.*1. There exists a twice differentiable, concave efficiency frontier:

$$Y_1(t) = F(Y_0(t),\ Y_2(t) \ldots Y_m(t),\ K_1(t) \ldots K_m(t)). \qquad \ldots(1)$$

The choice of the output (per man) of the first capital good as the dependent variable is of course arbitrary.[2] Note that constant returns have been stipulated. We shall write F_i as the partial differential coefficient of F with respect to its ith argument and F_{ij} as the partial differential coefficient of F_i with respect to its jth argument.

[1] This is inexact terminology for the case where the differential equations in the vicinity of the steady state have roots which come in pairs $(+\lambda, -\lambda)$. These need not be real, which is *the* saddle point case. We shall sometimes just call these motions catenary.

[2] For many purposes the analysis which follows could have been simplified by writing:

$$Y_0 = F(Y_1(t) \ldots Y_m(t),\ K_1(t) \ldots K_m(t)).$$

The reason I have not done so is that (1) makes comparison with the literature easier. I also felt there to be an expositional advantage in having the own rate of return of one capital good independent of price expectations.

Assumption A.2. (*a*) capital goods last forever, (*b*) the labour force force grows at a given rate " n ", (*c*) there is no technical change.

Part (*a*) of this assumption is introduced for tidiness' sake only. Part (*c*) could be replaced by the supposition of a given and identical rate of Harrod-neutral technical change in all sectors.

In view of *A.2.*(*b*) we may write:

$$Y_i = \dot{K}_i + nK_i \qquad i = 1...m \qquad ...(2)$$

and substitute this into (1). (A dot over a symbol denotes the operation d/dt.)

Assumption A.3. Let $P_i(t)$ be the price of the ith good, in terms of the first, at t and $\dot{P}_i^e(t)$ the rate at which, at t, this price is expected to change. Then (*a*) for all $i = 1...m$, $\dot{P}_i(t) = \dot{P}_i^e(t)$ and (*b*) for all $i = 1...m$, the own rates of return (including expected changes in capital values), in terms of good one, are the same. This assumption is made because we are interested in the behaviour of warranted paths. It has nothing to recommend it on the grounds of realism and I return to it below (see V.).

Assumption A.4. At every t the economy is in competitive equilibrium.

This assumption is made for the same reasons as is *A.3.* It implies that for all t:

$$P_i(t) = -F_i(t) \qquad i = 0...m$$

(where $F_i(t)$ is the shorthand notation for $F_i(Y_o(t), Y_2(t)... Y_m(t), K_1(t)...K_m(t))$).

From *A.3.* (*a*) and (*b*) we then have:[1]

$$F_i(t)F_{m+1}(t) + F_{m+i}(t) = \dot{F}_i(t) \qquad i = 2...m \qquad ...(3)$$

which is a well known [6], necessary condition for the intertemporal efficiency of an accumulation path.

Assumption A.5. There is no saving out of wages and no consumption out of profit.

I make this assumption because the " proportional " savings case has already been investigated by Samuelson [7], because it is the case in which the " inverse optimum " approach would encounter the greatest difficulties and because I used it in my earlier paper. In view of *A.4*, this assumption implies[2]:

$$F - F_{m+1}K_1 - \sum_{i=2} (nF_i + F_{m+i})K_i - \sum_{i=2} F_i\dot{K}_i = 0 \qquad ...(4a)$$

which it will be more convenient to write, using (1), as:

$$(F_{m+1} - n)K_1 + \Sigma(nF_i + F_{m+i})K_i + \sum_{i=2} F_i\dot{K}_i - \dot{K}_1 = 0. \qquad ...(4)$$

Now, from (3) we have

$$F_{m+1} = \dot{F}_i - F_iF_{m+1} \qquad i = 2...m.$$

So on substituting in (4) we have:

$$(F_{m+1} - n)[K_1 - \sum_{i=2} F_iK_i] + (\Sigma\dot{F}_iK_i + \Sigma F_i\dot{K}_i - \dot{K}_1) = 0. \qquad ...(4')$$

1 Suppose I own one unit of good one and use it in production to gain $\frac{\partial Y_1}{\partial K_1} = F_{m+1}$ units of good one. I could also have bought $-\frac{1}{F_i}$ units of good i and gained $-F_i\left(-\frac{1}{F_i}\frac{\partial Y_i}{\partial K_i}\right) = -\frac{F_{m+t}}{F_i}$ units of good one by producing good i as well as the capital gain (loss) of $\dot{F}_i/F_i$. To be indifferent between these two courses of action we must have

$$F_{m+1} = -\frac{F_{m+i}}{F_i} + \frac{\dot{F}_i}{F_i},$$

which gives (3) of the text.

2 Let L be labour. Then since $-F_0$ is the price of consumption good in numeraire we have from A.5: $-F_0Y_0 = \frac{\partial(LY_1)}{\partial L}$. But using (2) in (1) we find

$$\frac{\partial(LY_1)}{\partial L} = F - F_{m+1}K_1 - \sum_{i=2} (nF_i + F_{m+i})K_i - \sum_{i=2} F_i\dot{K}_i - F_0Y_0,$$

and so (4) follows.

We note that the term in square brackets is the value of capital in terms of capital good one and that the term in the last bracket is the rate of change in that value. However, for reasons which will become clear, we shall be interested in the behaviour of " wealth " measured in terms of the consumption good. Let w represent this. Then on revaluation, (4′) may be written[1]

$$\left(F_{m+1}-n-\frac{\dot{F}_0}{F_0}\right)=\frac{\dot{w}}{w}. \qquad \ldots(5)$$

I shall have more to say concerning this version of (4′) below.

Consider the systems (1), (3) and (4) with $K_i(0)$ $(i=1\ldots m)$ given, (i.e. " momentary " equilibrium. The unknowns are: $\dot{K}_i(i=1\ldots m)$, $\ddot{K}_i(i=2\ldots m)$, Y_0 and $\dot{Y}_0$. There are $(m+1)$ equations and $2m+1$ unknowns; this gives m degrees of freedom. However, we are only interested in paths along which expectations can be fulfilled and so we require that 4(*a*) should hold at all t. Differentiating 4(*a*) with respect to t yields one further equation and no additional unknowns. Taking this into account we have $(m-1)$ degrees of freedom. Their significance was discussed in [2]. In a descriptive model such as this they can be made good by stipulating the price expectations: $\dot{P}_i(0)/P_i(0)$, $i=2\ldots m$. In a finite planning model the transversality conditions provide the missing information.

II. THE STEADY STATE

The system (1), (3) and (4) is said to be in steady state when

$$Y_i(t)=nK_i(t) \qquad i=1\ldots m \qquad t\geqq 0.$$

Clearly the " endowment ", $K_i(0)$, $(i=1\ldots m)$ must be treated as an unknown in solving for the steady state of the economy. The equations in (4) provide the necessary extra information. Since we have $\ddot{K}_i=0$ $(i=2\ldots m)$, we lose all degrees of freedom.

Assumption A.6. The system (1), (3) and (4) has a unique steady state solution

$$K_i^*(i=1\ldots m),\ Y_0^*, \text{ with } K_i^*>0 \text{ all } i.$$

This assumption implies a certain connectedness property of the production set but it is sufficiently familiar to require no elaboration here.

In a steady state, (4) becomes:

$$(n-F_{m+1})K_1^*-\sum_{i=2}(nF_i+F_{m+i})K_i^*=0, \qquad \ldots(4'')$$

which will certainly be satisfied if all the terms in brackets are zero. By *A*.6 this must be the only steady state solution i.e.

$$\frac{\partial Y_i}{\partial K_i}=n \qquad i=1\ldots m.$$

It is painfully obvious that this is also the " golden rule " path of the system, i.e.,

$$\frac{\partial Y_0}{\partial K_i}=0 \text{ all } i.$$

III. STABILITY

The question which now concerns us is this: consider the system (1), (3) and (4) with given endowments $K_i^*(0)$ and given expectations $\dot{P}_i(0)/P_i(0)$. We can trace its subsequent

[1] Let W be the value of capital in terms of the first capital good. Then (4′) gives: $(F_{m+1}-n)=\dot{W}/W$. But $-\dfrac{1}{F_0}$ is the price of good one in terms of assumption good, and so $\dfrac{\dot{w}}{w}=\dfrac{\dot{W}}{W}-\dfrac{\dot{F}_0}{F_0}$.

development on the assumption (A.3), that all expectations are fulfilled. Will this development tend to the steady state?

In answering the question we shall consider an economy in the vicinity of a steady state, which as it turns out, will mean that no complete answer can be provided. If it is true that for all " starting points " in this neighbourhood, the economy does not approach the steady state then we can certainly assert that this state will not be approached from any starting point (since to do so it would have to pass through this small neighbourhood). Unfortunately so strong a result is not generally available.

It will be convenient to adopt the following further notation and conventions:

$$R_i \equiv F_{m+1}F_i + F_{m+i} \qquad i = 2 \ldots m$$

where of course R_i depends on the arguments of F. I shall write

$$R_{im+j} = \frac{\partial R_i}{\partial K_j} + n\frac{\partial R_i}{\partial Y_j} \text{ and } R_{ij} = \frac{\partial R_i}{\partial Y_j}.$$

We also chose units in which to measure goods such that in steady state:

$$F_0 = F_2 = \ldots = F_m = -1.$$

I define Z to be the value of capital per man at steady state prices, i.e. in view of the convention just adopted:

$$Z = \sum_{i=1} K_i.$$

Lastly, I shall write small letters to denote deviations from steady state values thus:

$$z = Z - Z^* = \Sigma k_i;\ y_0 = Y_0 - Y_0^*, \quad i = 1 \ldots m.$$

I start the story with a special case the significance of which is discussed below (III). That is, I consider all paths starting from $(K_1(0) \ldots K_m(0))$, such that there exists a function $g(Y_o)$ such that

$$\frac{\dot{w}}{w} + g(Y_0)(\dot{Y}_0/Y_0) = 0. \qquad \ldots(6)$$

The question of the existence of such paths is also postponed for later consideration. At the moment I am interested in the linear part of the Taylor expansion of (1), (3) and (5) subject to (6).

The expansion of (1) yields[1]:

$$y_o + \dot{z} = 0 \qquad \ldots(1^*)$$

The expansion of $R_i - \dot{F}_i = 0$, making use of (1*) gives[2]:

$$R_{im+1}z - (F_{im+1} + R_{i0})\dot{z} + F_{i0}\ddot{z} + \sum_{j=2} a_{ij}k_j + \sum_{j=2} b_{ij}k_j - \sum_{j=2} F_{ij}\ddot{k}_j = 0 \qquad \ldots(3^*)$$

where

$$a_{ij} = R_{im+j} - R_{im+1},\ b_{ij} = R_{ij} - R_{ji}$$

1 From (1):

$$\dot{k}_1 + nk_1 = F_0 y_0 + \sum_{i=2}(nF_i + F_{m+i})k_i + F_{m+1}k_1 + \sum_{i=2} F_i\dot{k}_i.$$

In steady state all terms in brackets under the summation sign are zero. Also $F_{m+1} = n$. We use the normalization of goods giving $F_i = -1$ to obtain (1*).

2 Expansion of $R_i - \dot{F}_i = 0$ gives

$$R_{im+1}k_1 + \sum_{j=2} R_{im+j}k_j + R_{i0}y_0 + \sum_{j=2} R_{ij}\dot{k}_j - \sum_{j=2}(nF_{ij} + F_{im+j})k_j - F_{im+1}\dot{k}_1 - F_{i0}\dot{y}_0 - \sum_{j=2} F_{ij}\ddot{k}_j.$$

Let $k_1 = z - \sum_{j=2} k_j$, $\dot{k}_1 = z - \sum_{j=2} \dot{k}_j$ and note from (1*): $y_0 = -\dot{z}$, $\dot{y}_0 = -\ddot{z}$. Substituting gives (3*) since

$$(nF_{ij} + F_{im+j} - F_{im+1}) = R_{ji}.$$

From this we easily verify[1]:

$$a_{ij} = a_{ji},\ b_{ij} = -b_{ji}, \qquad i, j = 2\ldots m \qquad \ldots(7)$$

Next consider the expansion of (5) in the form:

$$-\frac{1}{F_0}[-F_0(F_{m+1}-n)+\dot{F}_0)]+g(Y_0)\frac{\dot{Y}_0}{Y_0} = 0, \qquad \ldots(8)$$

which gives[2]

$$F_{m+1m+1}z-(F_{00}+g(Y_0^*))\ddot{z}+\sum_{j=2} R_{jm+1}k_j+\sum_{j=2}(R_{j0}+F_{m+1j})\dot{k}_j+\sum_{j=2} F_{0j}\ddot{k}_j = 0 \quad \ldots(5^*)$$

$$\left(\hat{g}(Y_0^*) = \frac{g(Y_0)}{Y_0} \text{ for steady state } Y_0\right).$$

Let

$$a_{11} = F_{m+1m+1}, a_{i1} = R_{im+1} \text{ for } i>1;\ b_{i1} = -(F_{im+1}+R_{i0}), (i>1),$$

and let $a_{i1} = a_{1i}, b_{i1} = -b_{1i}$. Then if A and B are the $m \times m$ matrices with elements a_{ij}, b_{ij}, $(i, j = 1\ldots m)$, respectively, certainly from (7): $A = A'$, $B = -B'$. Lastly let C be the $m \times m$ matrix defined as:

$$C = \begin{bmatrix} F_{00}+g(Y_0^*)-\{F_{20}\ldots F_{m0}\} & \\ -\begin{Bmatrix} F_{20} \\ \vdots \\ F_{m0} \end{Bmatrix} & F_{ij} \end{bmatrix}$$

so that $C = C'$. Then we may write (3*) and (5*) compactly as:

$$A\begin{pmatrix} z \\ k \end{pmatrix} + B\begin{pmatrix} \dot{z} \\ \dot{k} \end{pmatrix} - C\begin{pmatrix} \ddot{z} \\ \ddot{k} \end{pmatrix} = 0,$$

where (z, k) is the m-vector: $\{z, k_2\ldots k_m\}$. We thus seek the roots of

$$|\, A+\lambda B-\lambda^2 C \,| = 0.$$

But these are the same as those of $|\, A'+\lambda B'-\lambda^2 C' \,| = 0$, that is, of

$$|\, A-\lambda B-\lambda^2 C \,| = 0.$$

We thus conclude that for this special case if λ is a root then so is $-\lambda$. The motions are thus what Samuelson calls catenary. Indeed the argument here is quite close to that found in the " Turnpike " discussions [6]. Since in the local expansion $g'(Y_0)$ does not appear we obtain the same result if for all neighbouring paths (6) holds with $g(Y_0)$ replaced by a constant. However the economic interpretation of this condition is obscure while that of (6) is not (see below).

[1] $R_{im+j} = n[nF_{ij}+F_{im+j}]+[nF_{m+ij}+F_{m+im+j}]-[nF_{+1j}+F_{m+1m+j}]$
$R_{im+1} = nF_{im+1}+F_{m+im+1}-F_{m+1m+1}$,

whence

$R_{im+j}-R_{im+1} = n^2F_{ij}+n(F_{im+j}+F_{m+ij})+F_{m+im+j}-n(F_{m+1j}+F_{im+1})-(F_{m+im+1}+F_{m+1m+j})+F_{m+1m+1}$
$= R_{jm+i}-R_{jm+1}$.

[2] The expansion of $-F_0(F_{m+1}-n)$ is given by:

$$\sum_{j=2}(nF_{m+1j}+F_{m+1m+j})k_j+F_{m+1m+1}k_1+\sum_{j=2}F_{m+1j}\dot{k}_j+F_{m+10}y_0.$$

Substituting z for k, as before and $-\dot{z}$ for y_0 then gives

$$\sum_{j=2}R_{jm+1}k_j+F_{m+1m+1}z-F_{m+10}\dot{z}+\sum_{j=2}F_{m+1j}\dot{k}_j. \qquad \text{(i)}$$

The expansion of $\dot{F}_0$ is:

$$\sum_{j=2}(nF_{0j}+F_{0m+j})\dot{k}_j+F_{0m+1}\dot{k}_1+F_{00}\dot{y}_0+\sum_{k=2}F_{0j}\ddot{k}_j,$$

which on the usual substitution, becomes:

$$\sum R_{j0}\dot{k}_j+F_{0m+1}\dot{z}-F_{00}\ddot{z}+\sum_{j=2}F_{0j}\ddot{k}_j. \qquad \text{(ii)}$$

For the general case, when (6) does not hold, the answer is not quite so definite. We know that (4) is equal to: $\frac{\partial(LY_1)}{\partial L}+F_0Y_0$, which expression I shall now write as X_0 and this is evidently the value of the excess demand for consumption goods per man (zero throughout the story). I again write

$$X_{0m+j}=\frac{\partial X_0}{\partial K_j}+n\frac{\partial X_0}{\partial Y_j};\ X_{0j}=\frac{\partial X_0}{\partial Y_j}.$$

The expansion of (4) is now given by:

$$X_{0m+1}z-X_{00}\dot{z}+\sum_{j=2}(X_{0m+j}-X_{0m+1})k_j+\sum_{j=2}X_{0j}\dot{k}_k=0, \qquad \text{...(4*)}$$

and one is now interested in the differential equation system (3*) and (4*).

Let $\hat{A}$, $\hat{B}$ and $\hat{C}$ be the matrices: A, B and C with their first rows and columns deleted. Let $\alpha(\lambda)$ be an $(m-1)$ row vector with components: $(X_{0m+j}-X_{0m+1})+\lambda X_{0j}$, $(j=2...m)$ and let $\beta(\lambda)$ be an $(m-1)$ column vector with components: $R_{im+1}-\lambda(F_{im+1}+R_{i0})+\lambda^2F_{i0}$, $(i=2...m)$. Then we are looking for the roots of $\Delta(\lambda)=0$, where:

$$\Delta(\lambda)=\begin{vmatrix} X_{0m+1}-\lambda X_{00} & \alpha(\lambda) \\ \beta(\lambda) & \hat{A}+\lambda\hat{B}-\lambda^2\hat{C} \end{vmatrix}$$

Let $\Delta(\lambda,\theta)$ be the determinant $\Delta(\lambda)$ when $\alpha(\lambda)$ is multiplied by $0\leqq\theta\leqq 1$. Then

$$\Delta(\lambda,0)=(X_{0m+1}-\lambda X_{00})\,|\,\hat{A}+\lambda\hat{B}-\lambda^2\hat{C}\,|.$$

Since A and C are symmetric and $B=-B'$, we conclude that for "almost all" roots, if $\lambda(0)$ is a root of $\Delta(\lambda,0)$, then so is $-\lambda(0)$. $\left(\text{The exception is the root } \lambda^*(0)=\frac{X_{0m+1}}{X_{00}}.\right)$

Let us generally write $\lambda(\theta)$ as a root of $\Delta(\lambda,\theta)=0$. Assume: (i) for all θ, $\Delta(0,\theta)\neq 0$, so that there are no zero real roots for any value of θ in the range; (ii) for all (θ) there are no pure imaginary roots; and (iii) that for all θ all roots are distinct. Then, since $\lambda(\theta)$ is certainly continuous in θ, we may conclude that the real part of no root can change sign as θ goes from zero to unity. For if it did we would either have some θ^* for which some $\lambda(\theta^*)$ were pure imaginary or some real root vanished. Also, since no multiple roots are possible it cannot be that a real root for some value of θ became complex for some other value. For in order for this to happen there would have to be some θ^* for which there are two roots which can be written $a(\theta^*)\mp ib(\theta^*)$ with $b(\theta^*)=0$, contradicting the supposition that there are no multiple roots.

Hence if these assumptions are made, then $\Delta(\lambda,1)\equiv\Delta(\lambda)$, has as many roots with positive real parts as does $\Delta(\lambda,0)$; but we know that there must be roots of $\Delta(\lambda,0)$ which have positive real parts. Therefore the steady state does not satisfy the necessary conditions for local stability.[1] But for the special cases (i.e., assumptions (6)), where the roots were in pairs $(+\lambda,-\lambda)$, there will for any $(K_1(0)...K_m(0)$, be in general only one possible value of $(\dot{K}_2(0)...\dot{K}_m(0))$ for which the system would approach the steady state. This need now no longer be the case and it may be that there are a number of accumulation paths which converge. However, not all such paths, staying in the small neighbourhood of the steady state, can converge to it.

[1] It will be obvious that the assumptions just made in the text are a good deal stronger than is required to show that the necessary conditions for local stability do not hold. For the postulates ensure that $\Delta(\lambda,1)=0$ has as many roots with positive real parts as does $\Delta(\lambda,0)=0$. Even so they allow the construction of a wide class of examples since the one parameter variation of θ leaves parts of every coefficient in the polynomial unchanged and we have, in the context of the postulate of strict concavity of F a wide choice of possible values to assign to these. This consideration is *a fortiori* stronger if we only seek to establish the existence of one unstable root in $\Delta(\lambda,1)$.

I conclude from this that in the general case no completely general propositions can be deduced. Certainly examples can be given, as I did in [2], for which for a wide class of initial conditions the accumulation paths diverged and the demonstration of this possibility is really all that is required to make the point that the single capital good results are very special. But it does not seem possible for the very general production assumptions here made, to deduce more than that the steady state will not, in general, satisfy the necessary conditions of local stability. This is *a fortiori* even more the case, when one considers constructions with several consumption goods.

IV. THE INVERSE OPTIMUM

We are now in a position to consider the view that the descriptive model, ((1), (3) and (4)), can be " mimicked " by a suitable model of optimum accumulation.

Consider a valuation function $u(Y_0(t))$ and the Ramsey integral:

$$V = \int_0^\infty u(Y_0(t))dt.$$

We are given the problem of maximizing V subject to (1). Routine calculations give the Euler equations, which here are the equations in (3) and:

$$F_{m+1} - n - (\dot{F}_0/F_0) + \left(\frac{u''}{u'} Y_0\right)(\dot{Y}_0/Y_0) = 0. \qquad \ldots(10)$$

If we put $g(Y_0) = \left(\frac{u''}{u'} Y_0\right)$, then we see that (10) is condition (8), so that this restriction will be satisfied for any accumulation path which behaves according to the Euler equations of the present maximization problem and we know that these paths in the vicinity of the steady state will have the " catenary " property. If it could be shown that my descriptive model is such that, for a proper choice of $u(\cdot)$, it behaves like a maximizing one,[1] then (8) would cease to be a restriction of this model but instead be an implication.

Now it seems pretty plain that this view must, in general, be false: it will not be possible to transform the descriptive, into the normative case.

Consider the model at $t = 0$ and write, $K(0) = \{K_1(0)\ldots K_m(0)\}$ $Y(0) = \{Y_2(0)\ldots Y_m(0)\}$, $\dot{\mu}(0) = \frac{d \log w}{dt} \Big/ \frac{d \log Y_0}{dt}$. With $K(0)$ given, we have, as we know, $(m-1)$ degrees of freedom, and we therefore consider various choices of the vector $Y(0)$. All unknowns at $t = 0$ may be written as functions of $(K(0), Y(0))$. In particular $Y_0(0)$ depends on these $2m-1$ " initial conditions ". Let $H(K(0), \overline{Y}_0(0)) = \{Y(0) \mid Y_0(0) = \text{constant}, K(0) \text{ given}\}$. In general $H(K(0), \overline{Y}_0(0))$ will have many members. Then (8) demands that if $L(K(0), \dot{\mu}(0)) = \{Y(0) \mid \dot{\mu}(0) = \text{constant}.\ K(0) \text{ given}\}$, that $L(K(0), \dot{\mu}(0)) = H(K(0), \overline{Y}_0(0))$.

Now suppose that $H(K(0), Y_0(0))$ has two components: $Y(0)$, $Y'(0)$, and that (8) is indeed satisfied so that $L(K(0), \dot{\mu}(0))$ has the same two components. Certainly the set $L(.)$ depends on the second order properties[2] of F, while the set $H(.)$, derived from (1) and (4)[3], does not at $Y(0)$ or $Y'(0)$, depend on those second order properties. But then we are at liberty to distort F slightly say at $Y'(0)$ without in any way affecting $H(K(0))$ at $Y(0)$

1 Note that since in steady state $F_{m+1} = n$, we cannot " mimick " the descriptive model by a Ramsey model with discounting.

2 Given $Y_0(0)$, we may regard $\mu(0)$ on $K(0)$ and $\dot{Y}(0)$. For any $K(0)$, $Y(0)$, we may use expansions like (3*), at this point, to find $\dot{Y}(0)$ in terms of $K(0)$ and $Y(0)$. Doing this involves the inverse Jacobian $(F_{ij})^{-1}$ evaluated at $Y(0)$, $K(0)$.

3 Equation (4) may be written

$$Y_1 = \sum_{i=2} (\alpha_i - \beta_i Y_i) Y_i + \sum_{i=1} (a_i - b_i K_i) K_i.$$

Subtract this from the equation in the text for the production surface.

or $Y'(0)$. But then we have a way of constructing any number of counterexamples to the claim that the two sets must coincide.

Although this seems, as I say, quite plain, a simple example may help to make it plainer.

Consider F given by:

$$Y_1 = \alpha_0 Y_0 + \sum_{i=2} \left(\alpha_i Y_i - \frac{\beta_i}{2} Y_i^2 \right) + \sum_{i=1} \left(a_i K_i - \frac{b_i}{2} K_i^2 \right)$$

where we take $\alpha_i < 0$, $i = 0 \ldots m$, $\beta_i > 0$, $i = 2 \ldots m$, $a_i > 0$, $b_i > 0$, $i = 1 \ldots m$, and confine our attention to that part of the frontier where all goods are produced and all marginal products positive.

From (1) and (4) we now have

$$-\alpha_0 Y_0 = \tfrac{1}{2}\Big[\sum_{i=2} \beta_i Y_i^2 + \sum_{i=1} b_i K_i^2 \Big]$$

(where time notation is omitted). Fix $\bar{Y}_0 = -1/\alpha_o$ so that

$$H(K, 1) = \{ Y(0) \mid \Sigma \beta_i Y_i^2 + \Sigma b_i K_i^2 = 1 \}.$$

Equations (3) are now

$$(\alpha_i - \beta_i Y_i)(a_1 - b_1 K_1) + a_i - b_i K_i = -\beta_i \dot{Y}_i, \; i = 2 \ldots m. \qquad \ldots(3')$$

We note that $\dot{F}_0 / F_0 = 0$ in this example so that, since $F_{m+1} - n = a_1 - b_1 K_1 - n$. We may write

$$a_1 - b_1 K_1 - n = \frac{\dot{w}}{w} = g(Y_0)(\dot{Y}_0 / Y_0) \qquad \ldots(8')$$

for condition (8).

If we evaluate $\dot{Y}_0 / Y_0$, using (3′), we find

$$\dot{Y}_0 / Y_0 = -\frac{1}{\alpha_0} \Big[\sum_{i=2} \beta_i Y_i^2 (a_1 - b_1 K_1) - (a_1 - b_1 K_1) \sum_{i=2} \alpha_i Y_i + \sum_{i=1} (a_i + b_i K_i) + \sum_{i=1} b_i K_i Y_i - n \sum_{i=1} b_i K_i^2 \Big]. \qquad \ldots(11)$$

Now consider Y and $Y' \in H(K, 1)$. Evidently $\dot{w}/w$ is the same for both these choices. If $\dot{Y}_0 / Y_0$ is to be the same, (so that Y and $Y' \in L(\dot{K}, 1)$), we must have

$$\frac{1}{\alpha_0} \Big[(a_1 - b_1 K_1) \sum_{i=2} a_i (Y_i - Y'_i) - \sum_{i=1} b_i K_i (Y_i - Y'_i) \Big] = 0. \qquad \ldots(12)$$

By an appropriate choice of a_1 and $(\alpha_2 \ldots \alpha_m)$ we can always falsify (12) without in any way affecting $H(K, 1)$.

One may look at the matter in yet another way. If the inverse optimum exists, then knowledge of Y_0 and of $\dot{Y}_0 / Y_0$ suffices to determine the common value, in terms of consumption good, of all the own rates of return. But as the example shows, this cannot generally be done. For using all the information we have i.e. the production relation, the consumption function and the condition that all rates should be the same does not allow us to infer, from knowledge of Y_0 and $\dot{Y}_0 / Y_0$, what $K_1 \ldots K_m$ and $Y_2 \ldots Y_m$ must be uniquely, and so does not allow us to determine what the own rate will be.

This becomes perhaps even clearer if we consider the special case considered by Kurz when only one single good is produced and there is only one kind of capital. From the production relation $Y_1 = F(Y_0, K_1)$ and the consumption function it is clear that Y_0 is uniquely determined by K_1 or (since everything is " well behaved "), that K_1 is uniquely determined by Y_0. But then since the consumption good is identical with the investment good, knowledge of Y_0 uniquely determines $\dot{K}_1$ and so $\dot{Y}_0 / Y_0$ and one is home.

V. CONCLUDING REMARKS

In an a-temporal world of a certain class it is easy to show that every equilibrium is efficient. In situations where the future extends indefinitely, this is not always the case [9]. In particular it is important to distinguish between two views of competitive equilibrium: there is the situation where producers are in equilibrium from moment to moment—this is the case of the present paper. However if we trace the economy forward far enough this equilibrium may cease to be possible or efficient, although there may be no way of discovering this in finite time. On the other hand we could think of producers as being in equilibrium also in the sense that at each t the present value of their assets is maximized (if such a maximum exists). The economy then behaves as one which had infinitely many future markets. In such a world the actual path chosen by the economy will be Pareto-efficient, and it will be quite different from the economy investigated here.

Now it is certainly possible for the paths generated by the present construction to be Pareto-inefficient for a long enough horizon [8]. I conclude from this that if the world behaves in this manner, the way for the economy to be made to behave efficiently is for someone to " aim " it at a target. Thus there may be, given $K(0)$, a unique choice of $Y(0)$, which if now made, will lead the economy along its expectation fulfilling path to the steady state. [If indeed the motion were always " catenary " we could assert that there will be one such choice of $Y(0)$—as it is, there may be several.] In that case, if a planning board announced the appropriate rate of change in relative capital goods prices, producers ought to expect at $t = 0$, the economy thereafter will seek the steady state. In any case what our idealization shows is, that even if we assume all the frictions, which stop say, the equalization of own rates, at all t away, the invisible hand will generally need a visible one to guide it. To say that this is due to the absence of an infinity of futures markets, is correct but not consoling.

The paradoxical fact is that if we do not make such very strong demands on the invisible hand at all moments of time it may perform in some sense " better " in the long run. Thus for instance if we suppose producers to expect current prices to persist forever even when the steady state has been perturbed, but retain all our other assumptions, then Morishima has shown [5] that the economy will seek the steady state. Thus while at all moments the economy is making mistakes they are never the big ones it is capable of in the " correct expectation " case. This suggests that it may well be that by idealizing as much as we have done, we have not only created some artificial problems, but we are prevented from analyzing the rôle of one of the most important features of a decentralized and unguided economy, namely that at most times economic agents find that their decisions with consequences for the future, were not the appropriate ones. There is also the plain fact that not all agents have the same expectations as to the future values of the same variable, and of course that these expectations are uncertain. It may well be that it is precisely such " frictional aspects " of the world we live in which prevent it going disastrously " off the rails ", but no one really knows.

London School of Economics. F. H. HAHN.

REFERENCES

[1] Goldman, S. " Optimal Growth and Continual Planning Revision ", *Review of Economic Studies*, **35** (April 1968).

[2] Hahn, F. H. " Equilibrium Growth with Heterogeneous Capital Goods ", *Quarterly Journal of Economics*, 1966.

[3] Kurz, M. " The General Instability of a Class of Competitive Growth Processes ", *Review of Economic Studies*, **35** (April 1968).

[4] McKenzie, L. " The Dorfman-Samuelson-Solow Turnpike Theorem ", *International Economic Review*, **4** (January 1963).

[5] Morishima, M. *Equilibrium, Stability and Growth*, Oxford 1964.

[6] Samuelson, P. A. " Efficient Paths of Capital Accumulation in Terms of the Calculus of Variations ", *Mathematical Methods in the Social Sciences*, 1959.

[7] Shell K. Editor. *Essays on the Theory of Optimum Growth* (1967).

[8] Shell, K. and Stiglitz, J. " The Allocation of Investment in a Dynamic Economy ", *Quarterly Journal of Economics* (forthcoming).

[9] " Symposium on Optimal Infinite Programmes ", *Review of Economic Studies*, **34** (January 1967).

Comment by F. H. HAHN

In his book *Equilibrium, Stability and Growth*, Morishima shows that if agents hold stationary price expectations and if they expect a constant rate of profit at all times, then convergence of prices to their steady-state values occurs. This, then, is an example in which non-equilibrium paths, and that is plainly what the Morishima paths must be, behave " better " than do equilibrium paths. The requirement that myopic expectations be correct at all times in my paper is therefore responsible for the misbehaviour of the economy. What I now wish to add is this: when agents are allowed to entertain false expectations such as stationary prices, but if none the less at every moment the rate of profit with these stationary expectations is equalized, the Morishima result will not in general hold. It is therefore not the case that stationary price expectations are enough to " cure " the problems discussed in my paper. All expectations must be stationary and that seems a rather strong requirement.

19 The Timescale of Economic Models: How Long is the Long Run?[1]

A. B. ATKINSON

Although models of economic growth have been intensively studied in recent years, relatively little attention has been given to the underlying timescale of these models.[2] While in many cases we know how the major variables of the models change over time, in very few cases do we know how *quickly* they will change. Yet the speed of change is a prediction of the model, and by examining this we have a further test of the model's properties. For example, in many cases it is shown that all paths converge to a long-run equilibrium, but we also want to know how soon the paths will reach the vicinity of this equilibrium. The speed of convergence makes a great deal of difference to the way in which we think about the model. Alternatively, where a model gives rise to oscillations, we need to have some idea as to their probable period. If we throw away information about the time dimension, we are reducing still further our limited understanding of the relationship between these models and the real world.

In an attempt to show how an analysis of the timescale may provide valuable additional information, I have examined three very different models of economic growth. The first is that of a one-sector economy where there is non-neutral technical progress (in the Harrod sense). In such an economy, one of the factor shares tends asymptotically to zero, and the aim of section 1 is to examine how quickly this will happen. In section 2, I analyze a model with heterogeneous capital, and attempt to throw further light on some of the problems discussed in the recent literature. Finally, section 3 is concerned with a model of cyclical growth recently suggested by Dr Goodwin, and examines the period of the growth cycles generated by this model.

1. FACTOR SHARES AND TECHNICAL PROGRESS

This section is concerned with a simple one-sector economy where there are constant exponential rates of capital- and labour-augmenting technical progress and savings are a constant proportion of income. As is well known, in such a model a non-zero rate of capital-augmentation means that one of the factor shares tends asymptotically to zero. This has led several writers (notably Drandakis and Phelps [3]) to conclude that this model is inconsistent with the " stylized reality " of constant factor shares (Bowley's Law). They then go on to argue that there must, therefore, be some endogenous mechanism which ensures that technical progress is purely labour-augmenting. But although one of the factor shares falls to zero, we have little idea as to how quickly this happens. It is quite possible that the period required, say, for the capital share to fall from 35 to 15 per cent is much longer than that for which we have time series. Further, while no one would suggest that there have been dramatic changes in the observed factor shares, Bowley's Law has not been accepted without question; and a model that predicts a slow decline in one factor share may still be a reasonable approximation to reality. The purpose of

1 I should like to thank F. H. Hahn, R. E. Hall, G. de Menil, D. M. G. Newbery, M. Rothschild, K. Shell, J. E. Stiglitz, and J. H. Williamson for helpful comments on an earlier version of this paper. They bear no responsibility for any remaining errors. The calculations in the paper were carried out at the Massachusetts Institute of Technology Computation Center.

2 References to the limited literature on this subject are given below. This has largely been confined to one-sector Cobb-Douglas models (see [2], [14], and [15]). One exception is Morishima and Kaneko [12], which discusses a matrix multiplier model.

this section is to give some idea as to the speed with which factor shares are predicted to change by this model.

The Model

The assumption that all technical progress is factor-augmenting means that the production function may be written

$$Y = F(e^{bt}K, e^{at}L) \qquad \text{...(1.1)}$$

where a denotes the rate of labour-augmentation, and b the rate of capital-augmentation. On the further assumption of constant returns to scale, this may be written in intensive form

$$y = e^{at}f(e^{(b-a)t}k) \qquad \text{...(1.2)}$$

where y is output per head, and k is capital per head. The gross competitive share of capital is given by

$$\phi = e^{(b-a)t}kf'/f,$$

so that its proportionate rate of change is [1]

$$\dot{\phi}/\phi = (1-\phi)\frac{(1-\sigma)}{\sigma}[a+n-(b+G)] \qquad \text{...(1.3)}$$

where σ denotes the elasticity of substitution, n the rate of population growth, and $G = \dot{K}/K$. Suppose that σ is 0·6, and that effective capital is growing relative to effective labour at the rate of 1·5 per cent per year. Then from (1.3) it can be seen that when the capital share is 40 per cent, it will be falling at a rate of 0·24 percentage points per year; and at this rate it would take over 40 years for the capital share to fall by ten percentage points. But this " back of an envelope " calculation takes no account of the fact that the rate of capital accumulation (G) and the capital share itself will be changing over time. The rest of this section aims to provide a more precise estimate of the speed with which factor shares change in the context of a complete model of the economy.

It is assumed that savings are a constant proportion of income; depreciation, however, introduces an element of ambiguity. If gross savings are a constant proportion of gross income (referred to below as the " gross savings case "), then

$$G = \frac{sY}{K} - d \qquad \text{...(1.4}a\text{)}$$

where d is the exponential rate of decay. But if net savings are a constant proportion of net income (the " net savings case ")

$$G = \frac{sY}{K} - ds. \qquad \text{...(1.4}b\text{)}$$

Differentiating, we derive the rate of change of G

$$\dot{G} = (G+d\gamma)(1-\phi)\left(a+n-G+\frac{\phi}{(1-\phi)}b\right) \qquad \text{...(1.5)}$$

where $\gamma = 1$ for gross saving and $\gamma = s$ for net saving.

The qualitative form of the solution to these equations for arbitrary constant a and b can be seen from phase diagrams such as those shown in Figs. 1.1 and 1.2.[2] Where there is positive capital-augmentation, $\sigma<1$ implies that the capital share tends to zero, while $\sigma>1$ means that the same happens to the labour share. But these phase diagrams

1 For details of the derivation of equation (1.3), see [3].
2 It is assumed that the elasticity of substitution is bounded away from unity.

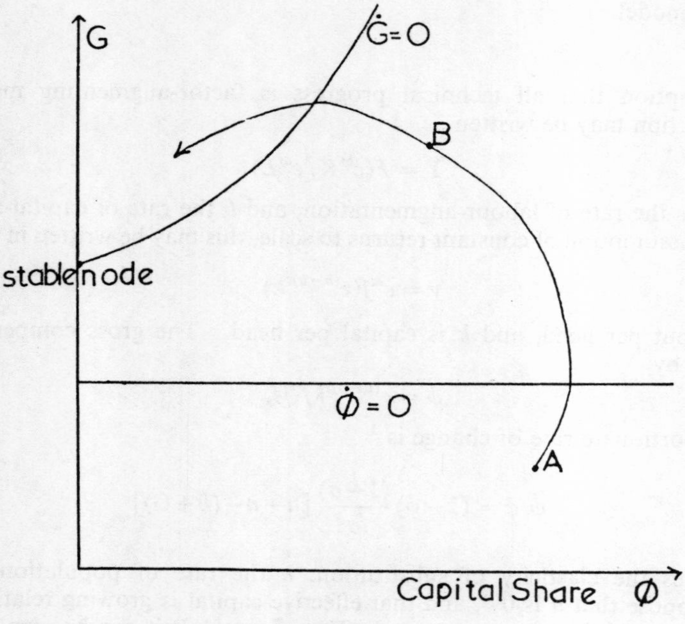

FIGURE 1.1
$\sigma<1,\ b>0$

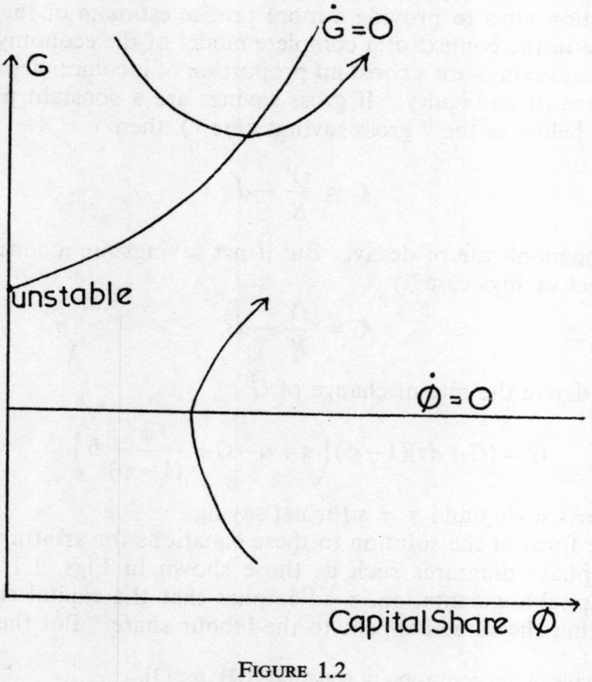

FIGURE 1.2
$\sigma>1,\ b>0$

do not tell us anything about the timescale. We have no indication whether (with reasonable values of the parameters) it takes the economy two months or two decades to travel a distance such as *AB* in Fig. 1.1.

Numerical Solution of the Equations

Since the equations do not lend themselves to analytic solution, I have adopted the method of numerical integration.[1] In Table 1.1 I give the results for a typical run for 120 years. The situation shown in this table corresponds to Fig. 1.1. The values of the parameters used are given below the table.

TABLE 1.1

Behaviour of the capital share

Year	Gross share of capital per cent	Net share per cent	Capital/Output ratio	Gross rate of profit per cent
1	42·8	35·0	3·00	14·3
10	43·1	36·1	2·72	15·9
20	42·4	36·0	2·52	16·9
30	41·0	34·8	2·39	17·1
40	39·2	32·9	2·32	16·9
50	37·1	30·8	2·28	16·3
60	34·9	28·4	2·26	15·4
70	32·7	26·0	2·26	15·4
80	30·5	23·6	2·26	13·5
90	28·5	21·4	2·26	12·6
100	26·6	19·3	2·27	11·7
110	24·8	17·3	2·28	10·9
120	23·2	15·4	2·29	10·1

Parameters: $a = 0{\cdot}02$, $b = 0{\cdot}01$, $d = 0{\cdot}04$, $\sigma = 0{\cdot}6$, $n = 0{\cdot}015$, $\gamma = 1$, initial $G = 0{\cdot}02$.

The gross share of capital first rises then falls (as on path *AB* in Fig. 1.1), but as can be seen it changes relatively slowly. In fact it takes 132 years to reach half its initial value. Since most empirical studies refer to the net rather than the gross share, this is also given.[2] The net share will fall more slowly than the gross share when the capital-output ratio is falling (up to year 71), thereafter it falls more rapidly. Even so it takes 109 years to fall to half its initial value.

These results suggest a relatively slow rate of change for the capital share. One possible way of assessing the importance of this change is to see what happens if one mistakenly tries to fit a Cobb-Douglas production function to the data generated by this model. The resulting equation estimated over a 50 year period and with the conventional statistical measures (standard errors of coefficients are given in brackets) is

$$\dot{y}/y = 0{\cdot}0102 + 0{\cdot}3920\ G. \quad \bar{R}^2 = 0{\cdot}9951.$$
$$(0{\cdot}0001)\ (0{\cdot}0039)$$

The fit is apparently quite good. If we had used the estimated equation to predict the rate of growth of output per head ten years beyond the period, the error would have been only 0·06 percentage points.

Sensitivity Analysis

This kind of analysis has little meaning, however, without some discussion of the extent to which the results depend on the particular values chosen for the parameters

1 A fourth-order Runge-Kutta method was used. This has a truncation error of the order of h^5, where h is the step length—see [7]. The step length used was 0·05 years, but check calculations were also made with different step lengths.

2 The net share is given by $(\phi_G - dv)/(1 - dv)$ where d is the capital-(gross) output ratio and ϕ_G denotes the gross share.

and on the initial conditions. In the present case, the absence of exponential terms in the basic differential equations provides some *a priori* grounds for thinking that the results may not be greatly affected by changes in the parameters (with the obvious exception of σ).

(a) *Initial Conditions.* The first question is how far the results depend on the initial value of the capital share. Studies of Cobb-Douglas models have found that the results were very sensitive to the value of the capital exponent.[1] If this were true in our case, then it would appear in the form of the results depending critically on the starting value of ϕ. Table 1.2 suggests, however, that the results are very similar for a wide range of initial values for the net share.

TABLE 1.2

Sensitivity to Initial Capital Share

Initial net share per cent	Index of net share in year						
	1′	20	40	60	80	100	120
25	100·0	104·8	94·8	80·0	65·2	51·6	39·6
35	100·0	102·9	94·7	81·1	67·4	55·1	44·0
45	100·0	101·1	94·2	82·2	69·6	57·6	46·9

(Same parameters as Table 1.1).

Experimentation shows that raising the initial value of the capital-output ratio raises the speed of adjustment of the nèt share, but not by a great deal: with initial $v = 4{\cdot}0$ rather than 3·0, it takes 4 years less to fall by a half from 35 per cent. Finally, it might be thought that it is the choice of initial G such that the capital share is initially rising that is responsible for the long adjustment times. But in fact the net share rises for only 13 years, and the gross share for only 8.

(b) *Savings Assumption and the Rate of Depreciation.* The results so far have been based on a gross savings assumption. If we replace this by a net savings assumption (s = 15 per cent), then this slows down the rate of change of the capital share, as shown in Fig. 1.3. But the effect is smaller than might be expected. For example, in 120 years the gross share falls by 14·9 percentage points instead of 19·6 with the gross savings assumption. In the same figure is shown the effect of a higher rate of depreciation ($d = 0{\cdot}07$). This leads to a faster decline in the share, but as can be seen its effect is much smaller than that resulting from a change in the savings assumption.

It may also be interesting to see the effect of replacing the proportional savings assumption by a classical savings function, with G depending on the share of capital. If we make the extreme assumption that there is no saving out of wages, then

$$G = s_p \phi Y/K - d$$

where s_p denotes the proportion of profits saved and savings are assumed to be gross. From this,

$$\dot{G} = (G+d)\left[(1-\phi)\left(a+n-G+\frac{\phi}{(1-\phi)}b\right)+\dot{\phi}/\phi\right].$$

When ϕ is falling, this reduces the rate of increase in G, and from equation (1.3) we can see that this will in turn slow down the fall in ϕ; so that with classical savings we should expect an even lower speed of adjustment. This is borne out by the results shown in

[1] See, for example, [2].

Table 1.3. With classical savings, the gross share falls by only 11 percentage points in 100 years, as compared with 16 percentage points in 100 years with proportional savings.

(c) *Rates of Technical Progress.* The effect of varying the rates of technical progress is shown in Table 1.4, which gives the value reached by the gross share after 100 years starting from 42·8 per cent. As we should expect, variation in the rate of capital-augmenting

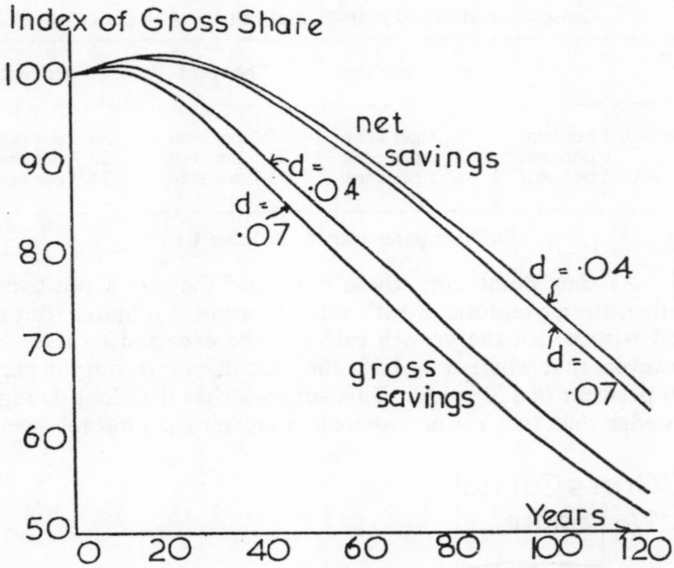

FIGURE 1.3
Alternative saving and depreciation assumptions

TABLE 1.3
Behaviour of gross share—proportional and classical savings

Year	Proportional saving	Classical saving
1	42·8	42·8
20	42·4	42·4
40	39·2	39·9
60	34·9	36·9
80	30·5	34·0
100	26·6	31·4
120	23·2	28·9

(Parameters as in Table 1.1.)

technical progress (b) has a significant effect on the speed of adjustment. The results are not greatly affected by variation in the rate of labour-augmentation (a).

(d) *Elasticity of Substitution.* The value of 0·6 used in the results above is representative of the estimates that have been made based on the CES function (see [13]). As is to be expected, the speed of adjustment depends sensitively on the value taken by this parameter—see Fig. 1.4. All the same, even where $\sigma = 0{\cdot}45$, the speed of change is fairly slow: it takes 84 years for the gross share to fall by a half. As this shows, we have to go a long way from Cobb-Douglas for the factor shares to change dramatically.

So far we have confined our attention to the case where $\sigma<1$. Table 1.5 shows the results of a run where $\sigma = 1{\cdot}25$ and there is a net savings assumption. Since b is positive, the capital share rises, but as the figures suggest, the rate of increase may be quite slow.

These results are also relevant to a recent article by Akerlof and Nordhaus discussing

TABLE 1.4

Effect of varying the rates of technical progress

Gross share after 100 years (initial value = 42·8 per cent)

	a = 1 per cent	2 per cent	3 per cent
b = 0·5 per cent	33·3 per cent	36·6 per cent	39·8 per cent
1 per cent	24·2 per cent	26·6 per cent	28·9 per cent
2 per cent	12·5 per cent	13·7 per cent	14·9 per cent

(Other parameters as in Table 1.1.)

this model [1]. As they point out, where $\sigma>1$ and there is a positive rate of capital-augmentation, then the asymptotic growth rate of output is infinite. But they say nothing about the speed with which the growth rate may be expected ro rise. From Table 1.5 we can see, however, that where $\sigma = 1{\cdot}25$, the growth rate of output per head rises only from 1·8 to 3·0 per cent in 120 years. This suggests that the Cobb-Douglas case may be less of a razor's edge than they claim: where σ is greater than but relatively close to unity,

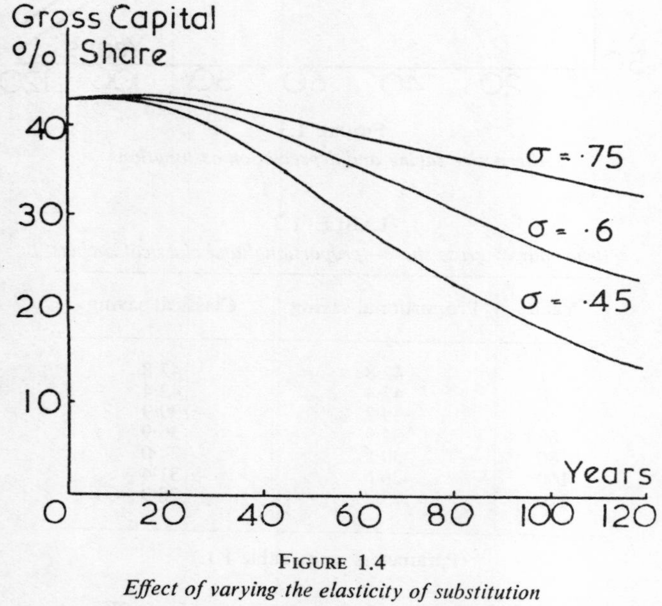

FIGURE 1.4

Effect of varying the elasticity of substitution

the growth rate explodes, but the time required for any appreciable rise to show may be very large.

An Evaluation

The tentative conclusion that can be drawn from the results of this section is that with quite reasonable values of the parameters the approach to a long-run equilibrium with one factor share zero may take a relatively long time. For example, in the case of a net savings hypothesis, it can take 108 years for the net share to fall from 35 to 25 per cent.

This suggests that the fall in the net capital share of 5·8 percentage points over 41 years observed by Kendrick and Sato [8] for the private US economy would be quite consistent with a positive rate of capital-augmentation.[1] I should emphasise, however, that I hold no brief for this particular model, which has many unsatisfactory aspects. The assumption that all technical progress is purely factor-augmenting is highly restrictive. But the results of this section do suggest that it cannot be rejected solely on the grounds that the predicted

TABLE 1.5

Elasticity of substitution greater than unity

Year	Gross share per cent	Net share per cent	Gross profit rate per cent	Growth rate of output per head per cent
1	48·7	35·0	16·2	1·8
20	48·5	37·9	20·0	2·1
40	49·0	40·2	23·3	2·4
60	50·0	42·3	26·2	2·6
80	51·4	44·4	28·7	2·8
100	53·0	46·6	30·9	2·9
120	54·9	48·9	33·0	3·0

(Other parameters as Table 1.1.)

outcome of one factor share tending to zero is inconsistent with " stylised reality ". Particularly where the elasticity of substititution is between 0·6 and 1, the time required for the capital share to fall by a half may be considerably longer than that for which we have time series.

2. A HETEROGENEOUS CAPITAL MODEL

The model discussed in section 1 followed much of modern growth theory in assuming that there was only one type of capital good in the economy. In this section, I analyze the timescale of a model which allows for heterogeneous capital. As has been demonstrated by Hahn,[2] the existence of more than one type of capital good casts serious doubt on the stability of steady state growth. In the case of one particular model, he shows that for any given initial capital stocks, there is only one set of initial prices which would allow the economy to approach balanced growth and for all other initial prices the economy will diverge.

In a further examination of this problem, Shell and Stiglitz [16] have analyzed the very simplest heterogeneous capital model—a one sector economy with two types of capital. In the context of this model, they show that, although there is only one set of initial prices which allows the economy to approach steady growth, on all diverging paths the price of one of the capital goods falls to zero in a finite period of time. If capital is freely disposable, then the market for capital goods will not clear with a zero price for one good (since there is then an infinite rate of return to holding the capital good with zero price). As Shell and Stiglitz then argue, this means that where there are futures markets for all periods in the future, or investors exercise long-run perfect foresight, a path on which one price goes to zero will not be observed and convergence to balanced growth is guaranteed. Where, however, there are only incomplete futures markets, or foresight is less than perfect, the economy may follow a diverging path for a considerable period. Moreover, since such a diverging path will involve a period when investment is being specialised to the capital good with the lower marginal product, divergence entails

1 These figures should, of course, be interpreted cautiously: one must, for example, make proper allowance for factors such as the return to investment in education.

2 [5]. See also Hahn [6] and Kurz [10].

a definite welfare loss.[1] It is therefore of interest to know for how long the economy could follow such a path—to know whether it is a matter of a few years before the fact that it is diverging from steady growth is revealed or whether it may take considerably longer. Now it is clear that the time at which one price reaches zero provides an upper bound to this time (assuming free disposability), and the main purpose of this section is to give some idea as to how long this may be.

The assumptions of the Shell-Stiglitz model may be set out very briefly. The production function is assumed to be Cobb-Douglas with constant returns to scale:

$$y = Ak_1^{a_1}k_2^{a_2} \qquad \text{...(2.1)}$$

where y denotes output per head and k_i the quantity of the ith capital good per head. Current output can be used for consumption or for investment in either of the two types of capital, but once capital of one type has been installed, it cannot be transformed into the other type or into consumption—it is " bolted down ". All wages are consumed and all profits saved, so that consumption and investment are always positive. Shell and Stiglitz take the consumption good as numéraire and denote by p_i the price of the ith capital good. Since the goods are interchangeable on the supply side, the price of the capital good in current production must be unity: i.e. $\max(p_1, p_2) = 1$. Further, the condition for equilibrium in the market for already existing capital requires that the return (rental plus capital gain) for holding each type should be equal;

$$[a_1y/(k_1p_1)]+[\dot{p}_1/p_1] = [a_2y/(k_2p_2)]+[\dot{p}_2/p_2] \qquad \text{...(2.2)}$$

Let us consider what happens if the economy follows a diverging path. Suppose that $p_2<1$, so that all investment is devoted to the first capital good (Shell and Stiglitz refer to this as Regime I). Then

$$\dot{k}_1 = (a_1+a_2)y-nk_1, \qquad \text{...(2.3)}$$

$$\dot{k}_2 = -nk_2 \text{ or } k_2 = k_{20}e^{-nt}, \qquad \text{...(2.4)}$$

where n denotes the sum of depreciation and population growth, and x_0 denotes the value of variable x at time 0. The price of the first capital good remains at 1, but the capital goods market clearing equation requires

$$\dot{p}_2 = y[(p_2a_1/k_1)-(a_2/k_2)] = y[(p_2a_1/z)-a_2]/k_2, \qquad \text{...(2.5)}$$

where $z = k_1/k_2$. From the first two equations,

$$\dot{z} = (a_1+a_2)yz/k_1 = Be^{nbt}z^{a_1}, \qquad \text{...(2.6)}$$

where $b = 1-a_1-a_2$ and $B = A(a_1+a_2)k_{20}^{-b}$.

With this information we can illustrate the behaviour of the economy in (z, p_2) space—see the bottom half of Fig. 2.1 (Regime I).[2] The point A is where the capital stocks are balanced (in the sense that the marginal products of the two capital goods are equal) and where the price of both capital goods is unity. From equation (2.5) we can see that p_2 is rising where $p_2>(a_2z/a_1)$—or to the left of the line OA. From (2.6), z is rising everywhere in Regime I. For initial $z_0<(a_1/a_2)$, there is only one path BA that leads to A, and hence allows the economy to approach steady growth. For initial $z_0>(a_1/a_2)$, there is no such path, and the economy can only approach the balanced growth path via Regime II (defined by $p_2 = 1$, $p_1<1$). On all paths other than BA, p_2 either falls to zero (e.g. CE) or rises to unity (e.g. DF). In the latter case, the economy enters Regime II with $z<(a_1/a_2)$, and the price of the first capital good goes to zero. The behaviour of the economy in Regime II is shown in the upper half of Fig. 2.1.

1 See [16], page 602.

2 This is not a phase diagram in the usual sense, since the equations are non-autonomous. However, I find this diagram more illuminating than that given by Shell and Stiglitz.

Although Shell and Stiglitz do not do so, equations (2.5) and (2.6) can in fact be integrated analytically. This will then allow us to calculate the time which it takes for the price of the second capital good to fall to zero. Integrating (2.6), we have

$$z^{1-a_1} = z_0^{1-a_1} + B(1-a_1)(e^{nbt}-1)/nb.$$

Turning to the price equation,

$$\dot{p}_2 - p_2 A z^{a_1-1} k_2^{-b} a_1 = -a_2 A z^{a_1} k_2^{-b},$$

$$\dot{p}_2 - p_2 a_1(\dot{z}/z)/(a_1+a_2) = -a_2 \dot{z}/(a_1+a_2),$$

or

$$d/dt[z^{-a_1/(a_1+a_2)} p_2] = -a_2 z^{-a_1/(a_1+a_2)} \dot{z}/(a_1+a_2)$$

which gives

$$p_2 z^{-a_1/(a_1+a_2)} = z_0^{-a_1/(a_1+a_2)}[z_0+p_{20}] - z^{a_2/(a_1+a_2)}.$$

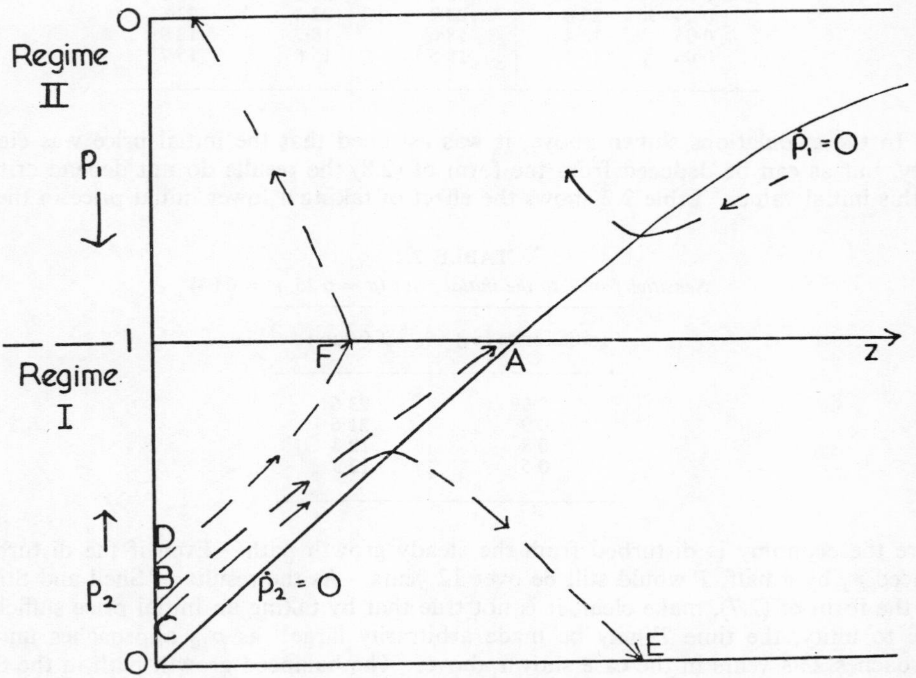

FIGURE 2.1

To determine the time at which p_2 reaches zero (for paths such as CE), we set the right hand side to zero, which after re-arrangement gives the time (denoted by T) as

$$T = \frac{1}{nb}\log_e\left[1+\frac{nbk_{10}\{[1+(p_{20}/z_0)]^{(1-a_1)(a_1+a_2)/a_2}-1\}}{y_0(1-a_1)(a_1+a_2)}\right]. \qquad \ldots(2.7)$$

We may begin by considering the case where the economy is initially in balanced growth, from which it is disturbed at time zero so that $p_{20} = 0{\cdot}99$ instead of $1{\cdot}0$. In that case T is given by (where it is also assumed for simplicity that $a_1 = a_2 = a$)

κ*

$$T = \frac{1}{nb}\log_e\left[1+\frac{b\{(1+p_{20})^{2(1-a)}-1\}}{2(1-a)}\right]. \qquad \ldots(2.8)$$

Table 2.1 shows the result of evaluating T for a range of values of a and n. As the form of (2.8) indicates, the value of T depends sensitively on the rates of population growth and depreciation—the higher are these, the lower is T. It would, however, require n to be as high as 9·2 per cent per annum for T to fall below 10 years. As the Table shows, T rises with a but only very slightly over the likely range of values. Similarly if we drop the simplifying assumption that $a_1 = a_2$, this does not make a great deal of difference to the value of T: for example, with $n = 0{\cdot}04$, $a_1 = 0{\cdot}1$, $a_2 = 0{\cdot}3$ implies $T = 22{\cdot}3$ and $a_1 = 0{\cdot}3$, $a_2 = 0{\cdot}1$ implies $T = 24{\cdot}2$.

TABLE 2.1

Time required for price to fall to zero (years)

$a =$	0·1	0·15	0·2	0·25
$n =$ 0·03	30·7	30·9	31·2	31·5
0·04	23·0	23·2	23·4	23·6
0·05	18·4	18·6	18·7	18·9
0·06	15·4	15·5	15·6	15·7

In the calculations shown above, it was assumed that the initial price was close to unity, but as can be deduced from the form of (2.8) the results do not depend critically on this initial value. Table 2.2 shows the effect of taking a lower initial price in the case

TABLE 2.2

Sensitivity of T to the initial price ($a = 0{\cdot}25$, $n = 0{\cdot}04$)

Initial price (p_2)	T (years)
0·99	23·6
0·9	21·6
0·8	19·3
0·5	12·3

where the economy is disturbed from the steady growth path. Even if the disturbance reduced p_2 by a half, T would still be over 12 years. As the results of Shell and Stiglitz, and the form of (2.7), make clear, it is not true that by taking an initial price sufficiently close to unity, the time T may be made arbitrarily large: as p_{20} approaches unity, T approaches 23·8 years in the case shown above. The balanced growth path in the Shell-Stiglitz model is not a saddlepoint in the usual sense, even though it has some saddlepoint properties. Since the production possibility frontier has no curvature, the differential equations $\dot{k}_i$ are not continuous in the prices p_i in a neighbourhood of the balanced growth path. This brings out the special nature of the model discussed by Shell and Stiglitz. In a more general model, where there is curvature to the production possibility frontier and the balanced growth path is a true saddlepoint, the time required for the price of one capital good to fall to zero can be made arbitrarily large by taking initial prices sufficiently close to the " correct " ones.

We may now consider what happens if the economy is not initially in the steady state. Suppose first that the initial capital stocks are balanced (i.e. in the steady growth ratio) but that they are above or below their steady state level. If in this case we measure the " distance " from the steady growth path by the ratio (denoted by x) of the initial capital-output ratio (k_{10}/y_0) to the steady growth capital-output ratio, then it can be shown that T rises with x—see Table 2.3. For an economy where the initial capital stocks are only a quarter of their steady state levels T is only 7 years, whereas for an economy with capital stocks 50 per cent higher than the steady state levels T is 32 years. In other words, the " capital-rich " economy is more likely to have problems.

In terms of Fig. 2.1, the assumption that the initial capital stocks are balanced means that the economy begins with $z = (a_1/a_2)$ or on a vertical line through A. This Figure suggests, however, that on paths such as CE, it may take considerably longer for p_2 to reach zero than where the capital stocks are initially balanced. Consider a path that begins with $z = (0{\cdot}1)(a_1/a_2)$ and where p_2 rises to just short of 1 and then falls to zero. In this case it would take some 35-40 years for p_2 to reach zero.

Conclusion

Any conclusions drawn from the results of this section must be even more tentative than those from the previous one. As we have seen, the time taken for one price to reach zero reacts sensitively to changes in the initial conditions and in particular parameters. In broad terms, however, the results show that while it may take only a few years for the

TABLE 2.3

Time T for different x

x	T
0·25	7·2
0·5	13·4
0·75	18·7
1·00	23·4
1·25	28·6
1·50	31·5
2·00	38·3

($a_1 = a_2 = 0{\cdot}2$, $n = 0{\cdot}04$.)

price of one capital good to go to zero, there are circumstances in which this will not happen for over 35 years. This means in turn that under certain market structures and behavioural assumptions, the economy may follow an errant path for a considerable period. Finally, to illustrate the kind of cost that following an errant path may impose on the economy, I have calculated the reduction in output entailed by a divergence from the steady growth path. For $a_1 = a_2 = 0{\cdot}2$, $n = 0{\cdot}04$, output (and hence consumption) at time T is 9·8 per cent below the steady state level. The total cumulative loss over the 23 years was 0·95 times steady state output—or an average loss of something over 4 per cent per year.

3. CYCLES AND GROWTH

While much of modern growth theory has been concerned with long-run growth at a steady rate, there has at the same time been a growing recognition of the need for a theory that explains both a long-run upward trend in output and cyclical fluctuations about this trend. One interesting attempt to fill this gap is the model of growth and cycles recently presented by Goodwin [4]. The main elements of this model are the dependence of the rate of capital formation on the distribution of income between wages and profits, and the existence of an inverse relationship between the rate of increase of real wages and the level of unemployment (a real " Phillips " curve). With the further assumptions of fixed coefficients and Harrod-neutral technical progress, Goodwin shows that the model will generate a path characterised by cyclical fluctuations in the level of employment and the rate of growth of output.

While the existence of such a real "Phillips" curve is open to question, the model promises to provide a more accurate description of recent economic history than either steady state growth or the trendless trade cycle theories. But the relevance of Goodwin's model as an explanation of this phenomenon depends very much on the period of the cycles that the model is likely to generate. This question is not dealt with in his paper, and the purpose of this section is to estimate the period of the cycles generated for reasonable values of the parameters.

The Model

The model may be set out formally using the following notation: [1]

ϕ share of profits in output,

u unemployment rate (unemployment/labour supply),

n rate of population growth,

a rate of Harrod-neutral technical progress,

$\mu = n+a$,

v capital-output ratio (K/Y),

s_p proportion of profits saved.

The share of profits in output will be falling at any moment if real wages are increasing more rapidly than productivity:

$$\dot{\phi} = (1-\phi)(a-P(u)) \qquad \text{...(3.1)}$$

where $P(u)$ is the real "Phillips" curve and $P'(u)<0$. Since there are fixed coefficients, the generation of employment depends on the rate of capital formation;

$$\dot{u} = (1-u)[\mu-(\dot{K}/K)] = (1-u)[(\mu-(s_p\phi/v)] \qquad \text{...(3.2)}$$

This gives a pair of differential equations in ϕ and u of the Volterra type,[2] with an equilibrium given by

$$P(u^*) = a, \quad \phi^* = v\mu/s_p. \qquad \text{...(3.3)}$$

As Goodwin shows, this equilibrium is a centre, so that the economy will follow a closed path about this equilibrium whatever its starting position. On this path, the rate of growth and the level of unemployment will show regular oscillations.

The Period of the Growth Cycles

As a first approach we may take a linear expansion about the equilibrium and use this to approximate the period for small disturbances. This is given by the roots λ of the characteristic equation for (3.1) and (3.2)

$$\begin{vmatrix} -\lambda & (1-\phi^*)(-P') \\ -s_p(1-u^*)/v & -\lambda \end{vmatrix} = 0,$$

which gives

$$\lambda^2 = -(1-\phi^*)(1-u^*)s_p(-P')/v = -(1-u^*)(-P')[(s_p/v)-\mu].$$

This implies a period of

$$\theta = 2\pi[(1-u^*)(-P')[(s_p/v)-\mu]]^{-\frac{1}{2}} \qquad \text{...(3.4)}$$

[1] I have adopted a somewhat different notation from that used by Goodwin in order to maintain conformity with Sections 1 and 2.

[2] Cf. Minorsky [11], pp. 65-70.

If we take the capital-output ratio as 3·2 (where time is measured in years), and the proportion of profits saved as 40 per cent, then a combined rate of growth of population and productivity of 4 per cent implies an equilibrium labour share of 68 per cent. If the equilibrium level of unemployment is 3 per cent, then this gives

$$\theta = 2\pi[0{\cdot}08(-P')]^{-\frac{1}{2}}.$$

The value of P' presents some problems, since most empirical work has dealt with money rather than real wage rates. It would seem reasonable, however, to assume that the rise in the rate of increase of real wages resulting from a fall of 1 per cent in the unemployment rate would lie in the range 0-5 per cent,[1] and the table below gives the value of θ for this

TABLE 3.1

Period for different slopes of the real "Phillips" curve

$-P'(u^*)$	Period (years)
1	21·9
2	15·5
3	12·7
4	10·9
5	9·8

range. The period clearly depends sensitively on the value of $(-P')$. Moreover, for the range given, the period is considerably longer than that usually suggested for the postwar trade cycle. If $(-P')$ were 9, then θ is still over 7 years, and in order to reduce θ to 5 years, $(-P')$ must be raised to the ridiculously high value of 19·0.

These results refer only to one particular, although quite reasonable, set of parameter values. From equation (3.4), it is clear that θ is a declining function of (s_p/v). If we set s_p at its maximum of 1 (as indeed Goodwin assumes it to be) and set $v = 2{\cdot}0$ (at the lower end of the reasonable range), then we can form some idea as to how short the period could be[2] —see Table 3.2. Even with extreme values for s_p and v, it still needs $(-P')$ to be greater than 3 to reduce the period below 5 years.

TABLE 3.2

Period with extreme values for s_p and v

$(-P')$	Period (years)
1	9·5
2	6·7
3	5·5
4	4·7
5	4·2

In fact it seems very unlikely that these extreme values of the parameters would be observed. Moreover, there are two factors which we have not yet taken into account and which lend further support to the view that values for θ as low as those shown in Table 3.2 are unlikely to be found, The first is that we have not allowed for any possible saving out of wages. Denoting by s_w the propensity to save out of wages, the rate of capital formation becomes

$$\dot{K}/K = [s_w + \phi(s_p - s_w)]/v$$

1 It is not clear whether one should deflate by the cost of living index or by an index of product price. Kuh's data for the latter in the U.S. shows no systematic relationship between the rate of growth of real wages and the level of unemployment [9].

2 Clearly any variation in u^* within its expected range will have very little effect on θ.

so that in equation (3.4) s_p is replaced by $(s_p - s_w)$ and hence θ will be higher. Secondly, we have taken no account of depreciation. It can easily be shown that this leads to a constant term $(-d)$ [1] on the right hand side of equation (3.2), so that its effect is equivalent to raising the rate of population growth. But from (3.3), raising the rate of population growth will raise the equilibrium share of profits and hence raise θ. If $(a+n+d)$ were 6 per cent instead of 4 per cent, the values of θ in Table 3.1 would be raised by 16 per cent and $(-P') = 1{\cdot}0$ would imply $\theta = 25{\cdot}3$.

These results were based on a linear expansion about the equilibrium; this approximation is only valid, however, for small deviations. As a check on the accuracy of these estimates, we can apply to equations (3.1) and (3.2) the technique of numerical integration used in section 1. This gives values for the period very similar to those based on a linear expansion about the equilibrium. As we move further away from the equilibrium, there is a tendency for θ to rise, but within the likely range of unemployment levels this makes very little difference to the results.

Conclusion

In this section I have used two alternative methods to estimate the period of the cycles likely to be generated by Goodwin's model of cyclical growth. Both methods show that with reasonable values of the parameters, the period is considerably longer than the 4 or 5 years of the typical recent trade cycle. A cycle with this period is only likely to be generated if all profits are saved, if the capital-output ratio is very low (less than 2), and real wages respond very strongly to a fall in unemployment. In fact the model as it stands may be better suited to explaining the 16-22 year " Kuznets " cycle than the postwar trade cycle.

4. CONCLUDING COMMENTS

In this paper I have discussed three quite different models of economic growth and tried to show that in each case examination of the timescale provides useful information about their behaviour. This is not altogether surprising, since some kind of time dimension is implicit or explicit in our thinking about any real economy; and we should expect the timescale of these models to be important for understanding their relationship to the real world.

In the course of the paper I have made considerable use of numerical methods of analysis, and in particular of numerical methods to solve differential equations which could not be solved analytically. This technique seems to have been relatively little used in recent economic literature, although similar methods were used in the 1950's to analyze the behaviour of trade cycle models. While such numerical methods cannot yield results of the strength which economists have come to expect, I hope that the present paper has demonstrated that this capital-intensive approach can have considerable value.

St John's College, Cambridge A. B. ATKINSON.

First version received 29.11.67; *final version received* 21.10.68

REFERENCES

[1] Akerlof, G. and Nordhaus, W. D. " Balanced Growth—A Razor's Edge? " *International Economic Review* (October 1967).

[2] Conlisk, J. " Unemployment in a Neo-Classical Growth Model ", *Economic Journal* (September 1966).

[1] Where d is the rate of depreciation and savings are assumed to be gross.

[3] Drandakis, E. and Phelps, E. S. " A Model of Induced Invention, Growth and Distribution ", *Economic Journal* (December 1966).

[4] Goodwin, R. M. " A Growth Cycle ", in *Socialism, Capitalism and Economic Growth—Essays Presented to Maurice Dobb*, edited by C. H. Feinstein (Cambridge University Press, 1967).

[5] Hahn, F. H. " Equilibrium Dynamics with Heterogeneous Capital Goods ", *Quarterly Journal of Economics* (November 1966).

[6] Hahn, F. H. " On Warranted Growth Paths ", *Review of Economic Studies* (April 1968).

[7] Hildebrand, F. B. *Introduction to Numerical Analysis* (McGraw-Hill, 1956).

[8] Kendrick, J. W. and Sato, R. " Factor Prices, Productivity and Economic Growth ", *American Economic Review* (December 1963).

[9] Kuh, E. " Unemployment, Production Functions and Effective Demand ", *Journal of Political Economy* (June 1966).

[10] Kurz, M. " The General Instability of a Class of Competitive Growth Processes ", *Review of Economic Studies* (April 1968).

[11] Minorsky, N. *Nonlinear Oscillations* (Van Nostrand, 1962).

[12] Morishima, M., and Kaneko, Y. " On the Speed of Establishing Multi-Sectoral Equilibrium ", *Econometrica* (October 1962).

[13] Nerlove, M. " Notes on Recent Empirical Studies of the CES and Related Production Functions ", in *The Theory and Empirical Analysis of Production*, edited by M. Brown (National Bureau of Economic Research, 1967).

[14] Sato, K. " On the Adjustment Time in Neo-Classical Growth Models ", *Review of Economic Studies* (July 1966).

[15] Sato, R. " Fiscal Policy in a Neo-Classical Growth Model: An Analysis of the Time Required for Equilibrating Adjustment ", *Review of Economic Studies* (February 1963).

[16] Shell, K. and Stiglitz, J. E. " The Allocation of Investment in a Dynamic Economy ", *Quarterly Journal of Economics* (November 1967).

20 Stability of a Dynamic Input-Output System

D. W. JORGENSON

Cumulative processes of inflation and changes in relative prices have been almost entirely neglected in discussions of the theory of economic growth. The neglect of relative prices may be attributed to the restriction of theoretical analysis to models involving only a single commodity, national output. The neglect of inflation and deflation is a consequence of confining analysis to equilibrium situations such as Harrod-Domar[1] steady growth equilibrium or the Cassell-vonNeumann evenly progressing economy.[2] While a study of the behavior of an economic system in equilibrium must be part of any complete theory of economic growth, the analysis of the inter-relationship of inflation and growth requires in addition a theory of disequilibrium describing the cumulative processes of expansion and contraction, inflation and deflation, which characterize the behavior of decentralized economic systems.

The purpose of this paper is to develop a theory of growth and inflation based on a multi-sector generalization of the familiar Harrod-Domar growth model, namely, Leontief's dynamic input-output system.[3] There is an interesting dual or price system corresponding to the model for output determination as Solow has demonstrated.[4] Unfortunately, there are serious obstacles in the way of any application of the dynamic input-output model and the corresponding price system to the analysis of inflation and economic growth. The first obstacle is that both the price system and the model of output determination are models for the determination of price and output levels in equilibrium. Specifically, it is assumed that profits are zero in each industry, or that all profits have reached some kind of long-run equality among industries. Changes in relative prices reflect changes in relative costs. In the theory of output determination, output levels are equal to the rates at which output is utilized. Changes in the level of output reflect changes in the level of demand. A second obstacle to application of this theory is a certain difficulty in maintaining the non-negativity of output levels and prices required for economic interpretation of the time-paths of price and output levels determined by the model. This difficulty is summarized in the dual stability theorem: If output levels can be guaranteed to remain

[1] Harrod, R., "An Essay in Dynamic Theory," *Economic Journal*, Vol. 49, No. 193, March, 1939, pp. 14-33.

———, *Towards a Dynamic Economics*, London, Macmillan, 1948.

Domar, E., "Capital Expansion, Rate of Growth, and Employment," *Econometrica*, Vol. 14, No. 2, April, 1946, pp. 137-47.

[2] Cassell, G., *The Theory of Social Economy*, New York, Harcourt Brace, 1924.

vonNeumann, J., "A Model of General Economic Equilibrium," *Review of Economic Studies*, Vol. 13, No. 1, 1945-6, pp. 1-9.

[3] Leontief, W., "Dynamic Analysis," *Studies in the Structure of the American Economy*, ed. W. Leontief, New York, Oxford, 1953, pp. 53-92.

[4] Solow, R., "Competitive Valuation in a Dynamic Input-Output System," *Econometrica*, Vol. 27, No. 1, January, 1959, pp. 30-53; see the references listed there for previous discussion of a dual or price system corresponding to the dynamic input-output system.

[5] Jorgenson, D., "On a Dual Stability Theorem," *Econometrica*, Vol. 28 No. 4, October 1960, pp. 892-2

non-negative for any—meaningful—initial output levels (that is, output levels whicl themselves non-negative), then prices must become negative for some meaningful initial price levels, and conversely.

To avoid dual instability, a number of re-interpretations of the basic model have been proposed. The basic idea underlying each of the attempts to re-interpret the dynamic input-output system and its dual is the same: the requirement that outputs must be equal to total utilization of the corresponding commodity and that prices must be equal to the corresponding costs must be relaxed. This alteration of the model is essential if the economic interpretation of the results is to be retained. However, while the system for which equalities between output and utilization and prices and cost hold exactly provides a determinate time-path of prices and quantities, the behavior of the system when inequalities are introduced can be determined only by adding further behavioral conditions to the system. One proposal is that the additional relations be obtained by invoking some explicit principle of maximization. The resulting theory may be interpreted as a model of optimal capital accumulation along the lines suggested by Dorfman, Samuelson, and Solow.[1] While this interpretation is appealing for applications of the dynamic input-output system to problems of planning, there is little evidence to suggest that such a theory of capital accumulation will be useful in descriptive studies. A second proposal is that the dynamic input-output system be supplemented by requiring that capital accumulation be irreversible.[2] This interpretation presents serious difficulties; the effect of irreversibility of capital accumulation on the formation of prices has nowhere been explored. Nevertheless, this approach provides descriptive realism and is not without promise.

In this paper a third re-interpretation of the model is suggested. Inequalities between output and utilization or prices and cost are held to define disequilibrium variables, each of which has a natural economic interpretation. For example, the difference between output and utilization of a given commodity may be interpreted as an excess supply of that commodity; similarly, the difference between price and cost for a commodity may be interpreted as profit per unit of the commodity sold. Classical theories of the business cycle have been based largely on the reactions of economic decision-makers to disequilibrium, that is, to excess demands and supplies on the one hand and profits and losses on the other.[3] When the classical reaction patterns are combined with technological relationships determining the character of equilibrium price and output levels, a complete and determinate theory of inflation and economic growth results. More specifically, disequilibrium analysis will be based on the theory of speculative stocks[4]: Entrepreneurs react to disequilibrium primarily through alteration of levels of investment in inventories and fixed capital equipment. Investment policies are determined by capital requirements dictated by three separate motives for the holding of stocks: For use in production or for transactions purposes, in anticipation of an increase in prices or for speculative purposes, and

[1] Dorfman, R., P. Samuelson, and R. Solow, *Linear Programming and Economic Analysis*, New York, McGraw-Hill, 1958.

[2] McManus, M., " Self-contradiction in Leontief's Dynamic Model," *Yorkshire Bulletin of Economic and Social Research*, Vol. 6, No. 9, May, 1957, pp. 1-21.
Leontief, *op. cit*.

[3] " Classical " is used here in the sense of " pre-Keynesian." The typical " classical " mechanism is Wicksell's cumulative process of inflation. For detailed references, see below, footnote 1, page .

[4] The theory of speculative stocks considered here is based on that of N. Kaldor, "Speculation and Economic Stability," *Review of Economic Studies*, Vol. 7, No. 1, October, 1939, pp. 1-27. Kaldor discusses in detail the microeconomic basis of the theory of speculative stocks and applies the theory to the stability of commodity markets and of aggregate income.

to avoid risk or for precautionary purposes.[1] In the discussion that follows, the analysis is confined to investment policy as determined by holding of stocks for transactions and speculative purposes. As a consequence of the level of stocks held in the economy, prices for a commodity may rise or fall. In general the higher the level of stocks the less the price of a commodity will rise or the more its price will fall. This theory supplements the equilibrium relations in two important respects: First, the behavior of the system depends not only on the technological characteristics of the system, but also on the behavior of economic decision-makers in each of the sectors of the economy. Secondly, the complete system surmounts the difficulties associated with dual instability; by suitable restrictions on the initial values of the disequilibrium variables, the non-negativity of all economic variables is preserved.

To begin the analysis it is necessary to review the main facts about the dynamic input-output system and its dual. This review is followed by a discussion of the interaction of output and price determination through the adjustment of speculative stocks. Close attention is paid throughout to the non-negativity of output levels and prices and to the economic interpretation of disequilibrium.

The closed form of the dynamic input-output system with time continuous is given by the following set of simultaneous, first-order, differential equations:

$$x = Ax + B\dot{x},$$

where x is a vector of output levels; the ith component of x, x_i, is the level of output of the ith sector. The vector $\dot{x}$ is the set of rates of change of the output levels; the ith component, $\dot{x}_i = \frac{dx_i}{dt}$, is the rate of change of the level of output in the ith sector. The matrices A and B are input-output and stock-flow matrices, respectively. The typical element of A, say a_{ij}, is the amount of the ith output required by the jth industry as input for production of one unit of its own output. The typical element of B, say b_{ij}, is the amount of the ith output required as a stock by the jth industry for each unit of its own output. For the case in which there is a single output, the dynamic input-output system reduces to the familiar Harrod-Domar growth model. The input-output matrix, A, corresponds to the marginal propensity to consume and the stock-flow matrix, B, corresponds to the accelerator coefficient or " relation ". In the closed version of the dynamic input-output model, households are treated as one of the sectors of the model; households have labor and property services as output and consumer goods as input. For a more detailed interpretation of the model of output determination, the classic work of Leontief may be consulted.[2]

To begin the discussion of the dual or price system, let us denote by p_i the price of the ith output and by ρ the rate of interest; let $\dot{p}_i = \frac{dp_i}{dt}$ be the rate of change of the price of the ith input. Suppose first that prices are constant and equal to the cost of

[1] The classification of motives for holding of stocks follows K. Arrow, " Historical Background," *Studies in the Mathematical Theory of Inventory and Production*, ed. K. Arrow, S. Karlin, and H. Scarf, Stanford, Stanford University Press, 1958, pp. 3-15. Arrow follows Keynes' classification of the motives for holding money stocks in the *General Theory*, pp. 170-1, 195-6.

[2] Leontief, *op. cit.*

production, including the price of variable inputs *and* interest on capital. Then p_i, the price of the ith output, is given by:

$$p_i = \sum_j a_{ji}\, p_j + \rho \sum_j b_{ji}\, p_j, \qquad (i = 1, 2 \ldots n).$$

The first of the two sums is the current cost of production; a typical element of this sum, $a_{ki}\, p_k$, is the price of the kth commodity multiplied by the amount of that commodity required for production of one unit of the ith commodity. The second sum is total interest charges on stocks; to compute these charges, the sum of all stock values is multiplied by the rate of interest. A typical element of the sum of stock values, say $b_{ki}\, p_k$, is the price of the kth commodity multiplied by the amount of that commodity held by the ith sector for production of one unit of the ith commodity. Using matrix notation, this version of the dual may be written in the form:

$$p = A'\, p + \rho\, B'\, p,$$

where p is a vector with elements p_i, ρ is a scalar, and A', B' are the transposed matrices corresponding to A, B. Now suppose that prices are permitted to change; if prices rise, holders of stocks benefit from appreciation in the value of stocks held; if prices fall, holders of stocks suffer losses on depreciation in the value of stocks. If each price is equal to cost of production, including variable costs, interest charges, and depreciation on the value of stocks held, p_i, the price of the ith commodity, is given by:

$$p_i = \sum_j a_{ji}\, p_j + \rho \sum_j b_{ji} p_j - \sum_j b_{ji}\, \dot{p}_j.$$

The first two sums correspond to current costs of production and interest charges, as before. The third sum represents the return to the holder of stocks on the appreciation of stocks. If prices are rising, the change in value is added to revenue (or subtracted from cost). If prices are falling the change in value is added to cost (subtracted from revenue). A typical element of this sum, $b_{ki}\, \dot{p}_k$, is the time-rate of change of the value of the ith stock due to appreciation of the price of the corresponding commodity. An alternative interpretation of this term is perhaps more familar: Suppose r_i is the own-rate of interest on the ith commodity:[1]

$$r_i = \frac{dp_i}{dt} \Big/ p_i, \qquad (i = 1, 2 \ldots n).$$

Then the typical element may be written:

$$b_{ki}\, \dot{p}_i = \frac{\dot{p}_i}{p_i}\, b_{ki}\, p_i = r_i\, b_{ki}\, p_i.$$

Employing matrix notation two alternative versions of the dual to the dynamic input-output system are as follows:

$$\begin{aligned} p &= A'p + \rho B'p - B'\dot{p}, \\ &= A'p + \rho B'p - B'Rp, \end{aligned}$$

where $\dot{p}$ is a vector with elements $\dot{p}_i$, R is a diagonal matrix with elements r_i, and the remaining terms are defined as before.

[1] Own-rates were introduced into economic literature by P. Sraffa, " Dr. Hayek on Money and Capital," *Economic Journal*, Vol. 42, No. 165, March, 1932, pp. 42-53.

The dynamic input-output system and its dual may be solved by putting each in normal form:

$$\dot{x} = B^{-1} (I-A) x,$$
$$\dot{p} = [-(B')^{-1} (I-A') + \rho I] p.$$

At the outset of the discussion of the solutions to this set of simultaneous differential equations, it is convenient to assume that the rank of the matrices B and $I-A$ is equal to the order of the output and price systems. In this case B^{-1} exists and $B^{-1} (I-A)$, $(B')^{-1} (I-A')$ are non-singular. If this condition is not satisfied initially, the order of the system can be reduced until the condition is satisfied by eliminating variables and equations. In effect, it is assumed that such a reduction has already taken place. Secondly, it is convenient to assume that the matrix $(I-A)^{-1}B$ is indecomposable in the sense of Debreu and Herstein.[1] It is a simple matter, of little economic interest, to generalize the results given below to the decomposable case. Under the conditions stated, there is a unique positive set of output proportions and a unique positive set of relative prices which satisfy the dynamic input-output system and its dual. Existence of such solutions is implied by the non-negativity of $(I-A)^{-1}B$ and $B'(I-A')^{-1}$ provided that A is an input-output matrix. Uniqueness of such solutions is a consequence of the indecomposability of these two matrices. Secondly, since the two matrices have the same characteristic values, the characteristic value of the dynamic input-output system associated with the unique positive set of output proportions, that is, the rate of growth of the system in long-run equilibrium, corresponds to a characteristic value of the price system associated with the equilibrium relative prices. The latter may be interpreted as the equilibrium commodity own-rate of interest for all commodities. The equilibrium commodity own-rate is equal to the money rate of interest less the rate of growth of the system.

The unique equilibrium output proportions are globally stable if and only if the initial output levels lie in the subspace spanned by characteristic vectors of $B^{-1}(I-A)$ less than the long-run equilibrium rate of growth in real part. Similarly, the equilibrium relative prices are globally stable if and only if the initial price levels lie in the subspace spanned by characteristic vectors of $[-(B')^{-1}(I-A] + \rho I]$ associated with characteristic values less than the long-run equilibrium commodity own-rate of interest in real part. These facts are an immediate consequence of the following theorem on relative stability:

A characteristic solution to a system of linear differential equations with constant coefficients is relatively stable in the large if and only if all characteristic roots of the system have real parts less than the real part of the characteristic root associated with the solution in question.[2] By the dual stability theorem, these conditions cannot be satisfied for both the dynamic input-output system and its dual for any non-negative initial price and output levels. To retain the economic interpretation of price and output variables, it is necessary to relax the assumption that outputs are strictly equal to requirements for current production and desired capital accumulation and that prices are strictly equal to the costs of production.

If the requirements of strict equality of output to utilization and price to cost are relaxed, we may introduce disequilibrium variables, corresponding to the excess (or deficiency)

[1] Debreu, G. and I. Herstein, " Non-negative Square Matrices," *Econometrica*, Vol. 21, No. 4, October, 1953, pp. 597-607. This terminology is not standard. In the theory of Markov chains, " irreducible " is used in place of Debreu and Herstein's " indecomposable."

[2] For proof, see D. Jorgenson, *op. cit.*

of output over utilization and price over cost of production. Where ξ_i is the excess of the ith output over current utilization of the ith commodity, we have:

$$\xi_i = x_i - \sum_j a_{ij} x_j - \sum_j b_{ij} \dot{x}_j, \qquad (i = 1, 2 \ldots n),$$

or where ξ is a vector with components ξ_i:

$$\xi = x - Ax - B\dot{x}.$$

Similarly, where π_i is the excess of the ith price over cost of production, we have:

$$\pi_i = p_i - \sum_j a_{ji} p_j - \rho \sum_j b_{ji} p_j + \sum_j b_{ji} \dot{p}_j, \qquad (i = 1, 2 \ldots n),$$

or where π is a vector with components π_i:

$$\pi = p - A'p - \rho B'p + B' \dot{p}.$$

The disequilibrium variables for output are flow variables; since excess supply results in the accumulation of inventories and excess demand in decumulation of inventories and excess demand in decumulation, it is useful to introduce disequilibrium variables corresponding to excessive or deficient stocks. Where s is a vector of stocks of each commodity held through the economy, stocks are equal to ordinary technical requirements when

$$s = Bx.$$

Let ψ be a vector of excess stocks; then:

$$\psi = s - Bx.$$

But, by definition, output is current utilization plus accumulation of stocks:

$$x = Ax + \dot{s},$$

so that:

$$x = Ax + B\dot{x} + \dot{\psi},$$

and we have the fundamental stock-flow identity of the disequilibrium system:

$$\dot{\psi} = \xi,$$

the rate of change in excess stocks is equal to the excess supply of the corresponding commodity.

The problem for disequilibrium theory is this: What governs the time-path of the disequilibrium variables? A hypothesis based on the investment decisions of participants in the market for each commodity will be discussed. The hypothesis combines investment for speculative and transactions purposes with a market mechanism by which stocks in excess of required levels result in a decline in prices. The interaction of market price formation and decisions to hold stocks generates a cumulative process of disequilibrium, similar in form to the cumulative processes of accumulation and decumulation or inflation and deflation of classical theories of the business cycle.

To begin the discussion of disequilibrium theory for the dynamic input-output system we recall first that the output in any industry is equal to current utilization of the corresponding commodity plus increments to stock holdings. Using the notation introduced in the previous section, we have for each sector:

$$x_i = \sum_j a_{ij} x_j + \dot{s}_i, \qquad (i = 1, 2 \ldots n).$$

If the accumulation of stocks is for transactions purposes (inventories) or for productive investment (fixed capital), change in holdings of stock may be divided into two parts: the accumulation required for expansion of output plus (or minus) an amount related to the excess of current stocks over equilibrium stocks. It is simplest to assume that the adjustment of accumulation for excessive or deficient stocks already in hand is proportional to the excess or deficiency. If stocks held are in excess of desired stocks, investment will be reduced; if stocks are held less than technical requirements investment will be increased. Under these assumptions the rate of change of stocks of the ith commodity held throughout the economy is given by:

$$\dot{s}_i = \sum_j b_{ij} x_j + h_i (s_i - s_i^+), \qquad (i = 1, 2 \ldots n),$$

where s_i^+ is the desired stock and s_i is the actual stock held of the ith commodity.[1] The constant of proportionality between investment and excess stocks, h_i, must be negative. Using matrix notation, the system of equations governing investment behavior is given by

$$x = Ax + B\dot{x} + H(s - s^+),$$

where H is a diagonal matrix with negative elements h_i along the main diagonal.

This disequilibrium adjustment mechanism is closely related to the flexible accelerator of Goodwin.[2] The second component of the rate of change of stocks held is proportional to the difference between actual and desired levels of stock. A similar disequilibrium mechanism for inventory investment has been discussed by Mills.[3] A good deal of empirical evidence for the validity of the flexible accelerator mechanism as a theory of fixed investment has been assembled by Chenery and Koyck.[4] The validity of the mechanism as a theory of inventory investment has been substantiated empirically by the recent study of Darling.[5] In the flexible accelerator theory of investment, desired stocks are usually determined by requirements for transactions or productive purposes alone. If holding of stocks for speculative purposes is significant, the stocks which entrepreneurs desire to hold are no longer equal to technical requirements alone. Desired stocks may be separated into two parts: Those required for transactions and productive purposes and those held in anticipation of an increase in the price level. Investment is equal to technical requirements plus (or minus) an amount which is proportional to the difference between actual and desired stocks. In addition to this theory of investment, the complete model includes a disequilibrium mechanism which describes the adjustment of price levels to costs and to stocks held in excess of technical requirements.

[1] A similar but not identical mechanism is discussed by H. Rose, " The Possibility of Warranted Growth," *Economic Journal*, Vol. 69, No. 274, June, 1959, pp. 313-33. Further discussion of the flexible accelerator is contained in: D. Jorgenson, " Growth and Fluctuations, a Causal Interpretation," *Quarterly Journal of Economics*, Vol. 74, No. 3, August, 1960, pp. 416-36. For discussion of some alternative mechanisms, see J. D. Sargan, " The Instability of the Leontief Dynamic Model," *Econometrica*, Vol. 26, No. 3, July, 1958, pp. 381-92.

[2] Goodwin, R., " Secular and Cyclical Aspects of the Multiplier and Accelerator," *Income, Employment and Public Policy*, essays in honour of A. H. Hansen, New York, Norton, 1948, pp. 108-32.

[3] Mills, E., " Expectations, Uncertainty, and Inventory Fluctuations," *Review of Economic Studies*, Vol. 22, No. 1, 1954-5, pp. 15-22.

[4] Chenery, H., " Overcapacity and the Acceleration Principle," *Econometrica*, Vol. 20, No. 1, January, 1953, pp. 1-28.

Koyck, L., *Distributed Lags and the Theory of Investment*, Amsterdam, North-Holland, 1954.

[5] Darling, P., " Manufacturer's Inventory Investment, 1947-58," *American Economic Review*, Vol. 49. No. 5, December, 1959, pp. 950-62.

To begin the discussion let us denote the desired stock of the ith commodity by s_i^+. As before technical requirements are given by the stock-flow coefficients; it is simplest to assume that speculative holdings of a commodity are proportional to the difference between current price and expected or long-run normal price for the commodity. Then if desired stock is equal to technical requirements plus speculative holdings we have:

$$s_i^+ = \sum_j b_{ij} x_j + n_i (p_i - p_i^+), \qquad (i = 1, 2 \ldots n),$$

where p_i^+ is the long-run equilibrium price level and is equal to the cost of production, that is:

$$p_i^+ = \sum_j a_{ji} p_j + \rho \sum_j b_{ji} p_j - \sum_j b_{ji} \dot{p}_j, \qquad (i = 1, 2 \ldots n),$$

and n_i is a negative constant of proportionality. This constant may be referred to as the *coefficient of speculative stocks* by analogy with Kaldor's elasticity of speculative stocks.[1] The coefficient of speculative stocks may be defined as the rate of change in the desired level of stocks with respect to a change in the difference between current and long-run equilibrium prices. This coefficient is negative since holdings of stocks decrease as the margin of current price over long-run equilibrium price increases. The flexible accelerator mechanism for determination of the level of investment in the ith commodity discussed above, is given by:

$$\dot{s}_i = \sum_j b_{ij} \dot{x}_j + h_i (s_i - s_i^+), \qquad (i = 1, 2 \ldots n),$$

where h_i is a negative constant; if desired stock is determined solely by technical requirements the constants h_i may be interpreted as rates of growth in stocks held in excess of technical requirements; this interpretation is not valid if desired stocks include stocks held for speculative purposes.

Combining the flexible accelerator theory of investment with the theory of speculative stocks, where stocks are held for both transactions and speculative purposes, we have for each commodity:

$$\dot{s}_i = \sum_j b_{ij} \dot{x}_j + h_i [s_i - \sum_j b_{ij} x_j - n_i (p_i - p_i^+)],$$

or, using matrix notation throughout:

$$\dot{s} = B\dot{x} + H[s - Bx - N(p - p^+)],$$

where N is a diagonal matrix with elements n_i along the main diagonal. Combined with the original dynamic input-output model given by:

$$x = Ax + \dot{s},$$

this gives the following theory for determination of the level of output:

$$x = Ax + B\dot{x} + H[s - Bx - N(p - p^+)].$$

In addition to the relationship between investment and opportunity for speculative gain, the complete system must include a description of the market mechanism by which changes in the gap between current and long-run normal prices are related to the level of stocks held in excess of requirements for transactions and productive purposes. If

[1] Kaldor, *op. cit.*, p. 7.

holdings of stocks are in excess of ordinary technical requirements, the gap between prices and costs will decline; if such stocks are negative the gap between prices and costs will increase. If it is assumed that the price-cost gap will decline in proportion to the quantity of speculative stocks held, this relationship may be given the following form:

$$\dot{p}_i = \dot{p}_i^+ + m_i \left(s_i - \sum_j b_{ij} x_j\right).$$

The rate of change of prices is equal to the rate of change of costs (long-run normal prices) less an amount which is proportional to the speculative stock holdings. The constant of proportionality, m_i, must be negative. These constants will be referred to as *coefficients of speculative profits*. The coefficient of speculative profits for a given commodity may be defined as the rate of change of changes in profits with respect to changes in the level of stocks in excess of technical requirements. In matrix notation this mechanism is given by:

$$\dot{p} = \dot{p}^+ + M(s - Bx).$$

The complete system is composed of the market mechanism for price formation, the theory of investment given by the flexible accelerator and the theory of speculative stocks, and by the dynamic input-output system and its dual. The complete system consists of the following sets of differential equations:

$$\begin{aligned} x &= Ax + B\dot{x} + \psi, \\ p &= A'p + \rho B'p + B'\dot{p} + \pi, \\ \psi &= H[s - Bx - N(p - p^+)], \\ \dot{p} &= \dot{p}^+ + M(s - Bx). \end{aligned}$$

Substituting ψ for $s - Bx$ and π for $p - p^+$, the system may be written in normal form as follows:

$$\begin{bmatrix} \dot{x} \\ \dot{p} \\ \dot{\psi} \\ \dot{\pi} \end{bmatrix} = \begin{bmatrix} B^{-1}(I-A) & 0 & B^{-1}H & -B^{-1}HN \\ 0 & (-B')^{-1}(I-A' - \rho B') & 0 & (B')^{-1} \\ 0 & 0 & H & -HN \\ 0 & 0 & M & 0 \end{bmatrix} \begin{bmatrix} x \\ p \\ \psi \\ \pi \end{bmatrix}$$

This system is decomposable and possesses a causal interpretation in the sense of Orcutt, Simon, and Wold.[1] Price and output levels are influenced by the level of stock holdings in excess of technical requirements and by the level of profit and stock holdings in excess of desired stocks, respectively. However, the rate of change of excess stocks and profits is not affected by current output and price levels. If prices are equal to costs and stocks are equal to technical requirements the complete system reduces the dynamic input-output system and its dual:

[1] Orcutt, G., " Actions, Consequences and Causal Relations," *Review of Economics and Statistics*, Vol. 34, No. 4, November, 1952, pp. 305-13.

Simon, H., " Causal Ordering and Identifiability," *Studies in Econometric Method*, ed. W. Hood and T. Koopmans, New York, Wiley, 1953, pp. 49-74.

Wold, H., " A Generalization of Causal Chain Models," *Econometrica*, Vol. 28, No. 2, April, 1960, pp. 443-63, and the references listed there.

Strictly speaking, the model discussed is causal only in the " vector sense " of Simon.

$$\dot{x} = B^{-1}(I-A)\,x,$$

$$\dot{p} = (-B')^{-1}(I-A' - \rho B')\,p.$$

When speculative profits and losses are just balanced by corresponding losses and profits in operation, price movements are governed by technological considerations alone. Speculative stocks are zero and all investment is in accord with the increase in technical requirements. Output levels are also determined by purely technological considerations. So long as there are no speculative stock holdings and speculative profits and losses are just balanced by losses and profits in operations, prices follow a course which is independent of the movement of output levels and vice-versa. In the following discussion the dynamic input-output system and its dual will be referred to as the *equilibrium part* of the complete system. It should be observed that a second type of reduction of the system is possible. If the coefficient of speculative stocks for each commodity is set equal to zero the output system and the associated disequilibrium mechanism together reduce to the simple version of the flexible accelerator discussed by Goodwin.

To characterize the behavior of the complete dynamic input-output system, it is necessary to discuss two separate, and essentially unrelated, questions of stability. First, to retain the economic interpretation of the output variables it is required that they be non-negative for any non-negative initial levels of output; similarly, prices must be non-negative for any non-negative initial price levels. A necessary condition for non-negativity is that the unique positive equilibrium output proportions and relative prices be stable among the solutions of the equilibrium system. An immediate consequence of the causal interpretation of the complete system is that the stability of the system depends on the relative stability of the equilibrium part and the disequilibrium part of the system, where the disequilibrium part consists of the relations governing the development of excess stocks and profits together. This is easily verified by observing that characteristic values of the complete system are simply the characteristic values of the equilibrium and disequilibrium parts, separately. From this observation it is immediately clear that if macro-economic stability is assured, stability of the equilibrium part of the system is equivalent to the condition that all characteristic values of the disequilibrium part are less than the smaller of the two numbers: the equilibrium rate of growth and the equilibrium own-rate of interest. This result on relative stability is an immediate consequence of the theorem on relative stability given above.

The *disequilibrium part* of the system generates cumulative processes of inflation (or deflation) of profit levels and accumulation (or decumulation) of stocks in excess of technical requirements. The form of the disequilibrium part reveals that the cumulative process is self-sustaining: Deficient stocks raise profits. Profits depress desired stock-holding levels and thereby generate investment decisions which result in changes in the level of stocks held. These changes affect the level of profits and the chain of causation is renewed. Such cumulative processes are familiar from classical theories of the business cycle, perhaps best exemplified by the cumulative process of inflation discussed by Wicksell.[1] To analyze the cumulative process generated by holdings of speculative stocks and market price reactions to such holdings, we differentiate the flexible accelerator to obtain:

$$\ddot{\psi} = H\,\dot{\psi} - HN\,\dot{\pi}.$$

But $\dot{\pi}$ is determined by the market mechanism as follows:

$$\dot{\pi} = M\,\dot{\psi}.$$

[1] Wicksell, K., *Interest and Prices*, London, Macmillan, 1936.
———, *Lectures on Political Economy*, Vol. II, London, Routledge, 1935.

Combining these two disequilibrium mechanisms we obtain the relation:

$$\dot{\psi} = H\,\psi - HNM\,\psi.$$

The characteristic values of the system have the form:

$$\frac{h_i \pm \sqrt{h_i^2 - 4h_i\, m_i\, n_i}}{2},$$

where h_i, m_i, and n_i are diagonal elements of the matrices H, M, and N. Since h_i, m_i are negative numbers and n_i is a positive number, all characteristic values of the disequilibrium part are negative and all complex characteristic values have a negative real part, equal to the corresponding value of h_i.

The cumulative process generated by disequilibrium will exhibit two characteristic modes of behavior. Each disequilibrium variable will either decline exponentially or oscillate with steadily diminishing amplitude. The rate of diminution of the amplitude of fluctuations will increase with any increase in the constants h_i, the proportion between stocks in excess of desired stocks and investment. Similarly, the rate of decline in exponentially declining excess stocks will increase with any increase in these parameters. Where the disequilibrium path involves oscillations the rate of decline in amplitude will be unaffected by the size of the coefficients of speculative stocks and speculative profits. However, the rate of decline of exponentially decreasing components of excess stocks and profits will be reduced by any increase in these coefficients. In general, the effect of speculation is either to reduce the rate at which the system would approach equilibrium if no speculation were to take place or to give rise to oscillations which are damped at the same rate as the disequilibrium variables decrease when no speculation takes place. If the system is macro-economically stable, the equilibrium system is stable relative to the disequilibrium system if the money rate of interest is at least as great as the rate of growth. Provided that this condition is satisfied, the presence of speculation will not make a system unstable if the system is stable with no speculation.

To assure macro-economic stability, it is required that initial profits and excess stocks be consistent with the requirement that long-run equilibrium output proportions and relative prices be relatively stable within the output and price systems, respectively. Beginning with the equilibrium part of the complete system alone, let the matrix of characteristic vectors of this system be represented by:

$$\begin{bmatrix} X_1 & X_2 & 0 \\ 0 & P_1 & P_2 \end{bmatrix}$$

where X_1, P_1 are associated with characteristic values of $B^{-1}(I-A)$ and $(-B'^{-1}(I-A' - \rho B')$ less than the long-run equilibrium rate of growth and smaller than the money rate of interest less the equilibrium rate of growth in real part, respectively, together with the long-run equilibrium output proportions and the equilibrium relative prices, respectively. Then X_2, P_2 are associated with characteristic values greater than these quantities in real part together with complex roots with real part equal to these quantities in real part. Then we have:

$$\begin{bmatrix} X_1 & X_2 & 0 \\ 0 & P_1 & P_2 \end{bmatrix} \begin{bmatrix} a_1 \\ a_2 \\ b_1 \\ b_2 \end{bmatrix} = \begin{bmatrix} x(0) \\ p(0) \end{bmatrix}$$

where a_2 and b_2 are vectors of zeros, by macro-economic stability. But then, for the complete system, let the matrix of characteristic vectors be represented by:

$$\left[\begin{array}{ccc:cc} X_1 & X_2 & 0 & Y_{11} & Y_{12} \\ 0 & P_1 & P_2 & Y_{21} & Y_{22} \\ \hdashline 0 & 0 & & Z_{11} & Z_{12} \\ 0 & 0 & & Z_{21} & Z_{22} \end{array}\right] \left[\begin{array}{c} a_1 \\ 0 \\ \hdashline b_1 \\ 0 \\ \hdashline c \\ \hdashline d \end{array}\right] = \left[\begin{array}{c} x(0) \\ \hdashline p(0) \\ \hdashline \psi(0) \\ \hdashline \pi(0) \end{array}\right]$$

so that c and d may be calculated from the equations:

$$Y_{11}c + Y_{12}d = x(0) - X_1a_1,$$

$$Y_{21}c + Y_{22}d = p(0) - P_1b_1,$$

The constants c and d may be used to compute the initial values of ψ (0) and π (0) and these initial values, together with the initial values of prices and outputs, determine the behavior of the complete system.

In this paper we have constructed a model of inflation and economic growth based on the dynamic input-output system and its dual and the theory of speculative stocks. The theory has a causal interpretation as follows: The complete model may be decomposed into two parts, an equilibrium part composed of the dynamic input-output system and its dual, and a disequilibrium part composed of a model of cumulative inflation or deflation and expansion or contraction based on the theory of speculative stocks. Changes in prices and outputs are affected by the level of profits and excess stocks; but changes in excess stocks and profits are not determined by price and output levels but comprise a self-generating cumulative process of the type familiar from the classical theory of the business cycle. The casual interpretation of the complete system reduces the problem of stability to that of the relative stability of equilibrium and disequilibrium parts.

There are many directions in which this theory could be generalized. First, stocks desired for precautionary motives were omitted from the analysis. In order to combine speculation with trading in futures contracts, it would be necessary to analyze precautionary holdings as well as transactions and speculative holdings of stocks. Secondly, alternative assumptions about the formation of expectations of future prices could be adopted rather than the hypothesis examined here, that expected price is equal to the long-run normal price, which is equal to the cost of production. Finally, it would be of interest to deal explicitly with the problem of the irreversibility of accumulation of fixed capital equipment.

The main conclusions of this study are as follows. First, the investment is determined by capital requirements, steady growth output proportions and equilibrium relative prices are stable within the complete system, provided that the money rate of interest is at least equal to the equilibrium rate of growth. This conclusion may be verified when capital requirements are determined by transactions motives alone and remains true when capital requirements are determined by both transactions and speculative motives. The chief consequence of speculative activity is to generate damped oscillations in speculative stocks and profits or to slow the approach to equilibrium which would take place if no speculative investment were undertaken.

Berkeley, California. DALE W. JORGENSON.